The Gospel after
Christendom

The Gospel after Christendom

New Voices, New Cultures,
New Expressions

Edited by
Ryan K. Bolger

Baker Academic

a division of Baker Publishing Group
Grand Rapids, Michigan

Published by Baker Academic
a division of Baker Publishing Group
P.O. Box 6287, Grand Rapids, MI 49516-6287
www.bakeracademic.com

Printed in the United States of America

Library of Congress Cataloging-in-Publication Data
    The Gospel after Christendom : new voices, new cultures, new expressions / edited by
Ryan K. Bolger.
        p.   cm.
    Includes bibliographical references and index.
    ISBN 978-0-8010-3943-0 (pbk.)
    1. Christianity—21st century. 2. Postmodernism—Religious aspects—Christianity.
I. Bolger, Ryan K., 1963–
BR121.3.G67 2012
270.8′3—dc23   2012025763

12   13   14   15   16   17   18   7   6   5   4   3   2   1

To Eddie Gibbs,
My teacher, role model, and advocate.
You are the wisest one I know about all things church.
You inspire leaders to overcome inertia and embrace innovation.
Careful with words, you tell the truth in ways that invite the other to transform.
You celebrate those who overcome barriers to pursue God's call.
You appeal to the church to follow God into the world.
You readily laugh at life's absurdities.
With all gratitude.

Contents

Acknowledgments

I want to thank my dean, Doug McConnell, for trusting me with this project and for his support and encouragement throughout.

I am thankful to Bob Hosack and Baker Academic for the support, patience, and flexibility they have given to the project as a whole. I am grateful to Georgia Grimes Shaw for her huge gift of copyediting this project. What a labor of love!

I feel so fortunate to have people like Kurt Fredrickson, Mark Lau Branson, Wilbert Shenk, Barry Taylor, and Charles Van Engen in my life. They served as helpful conversation partners at turning points in the life of the project. It is so useful to get a quick and helpful answer to "What do I do now?"

I am indebted to Peter Brierley, Chan Kim-Kwong, Dae-Hyoun Lee, R. Daniel Reeves, and Barry Taylor for their contributions to an early version of this project. Their efforts are deeply appreciated.

I was so pleased with my Church Planting class from fall 2010. They read these chapters and offered helpful feedback. They jumped into class discussions of early versions of many of the chapters in the volume. These students are Daniel Ban, Jonathan Barker, Graham Bates, Barbara Beboua, Rebekah Bolin, Heather Engel, Alicia Grey, Calvin Ho, Christoffer Hojlund, Duck Young Hwang, Poul Kristensen, Laura Johnson, Kristian Kappel, Khup Ngaihte, Kyu Suk "Joshua" Rho, Tiffany Robison, Sergio Ruiz, Gilbert Sim, Byungsun So, Peter Thise, Kate Wentland, Austin Willard, and Michael Woosley.

I was surprised to see how many of my heroes were willing to submit ideas for this book. I could not be happier with the 272 ideas that these 76 authors shared. These experts provided the direction for the work that followed, and I am in their debt: Peter Aschoff, Jonny Baker, Kelly Bean, Jim Belcher, David Bjork, Luke Bretherton, Kester Brewin, Peter Brierley, Troy Bronsink, Eric Bryant, Bill Burrows, Soong-Chan Rah, Jason Clark, Graham Cray, Darren

Cronshaw, John Drane, Ben Edson, Daniel Ehniss, Doug Estes, Tobias Faix, Jonathan Finley, David Fitch, John Franke, Kurt Fredrickson, Dwight Friesen, Michael Frost, Oscar García-Johnson, Doug Gay, Matthew Glock, Colin Greene, Simon Hall, Hugh Halter, Barry Harvey, Graham Hill, Steve Hollinghurst, Bob and Mary Hopkins, George Hunter III, Todd Hunter, Todd Johnson, Tony Jones, Tim Keller, Mark Lau Branson, Mark MacDonald, Frederick Marais, Gerardo Marti, Juan Martinez, Gary McIntosh, Ian Mobsby, Sally Morgenthaler, MaryKate Morse, Jeppe Bach Nikolajsen, Stefan Paas, Andrew Perriman, Carl Raschke, Paul Roberts, Martin Robinson, Alan Roxburgh, Mark Scandrette, Wilbert Shenk, Tom Sine, Howard Snyder, Bryan Stone, Richard Sudworth, Barry Taylor, Steve Taylor, Phyllis Tickle, Knut Tvetereid, Charles Van Engen, Craig Van Gelder, Nico-Dirk van Loo, Blayne Waltrip, Pete Ward, Ralph Watkins, Markus Weimer, Bob Whitesel, and Eric Zander.

I am thankful for others who participated in the sidebars and read over specific chapters, particularly Matthias Radloff and Joannah Saxton.

I am deeply grateful to the twenty-eight authors who joined me on this trek. Not only were they willing to write and rewrite in order to bring their essays more in line with the vision of the book, as well as with the other authors, but they were also willing to sidebar others' essays and to respond to those sidebars in their own chapter. They did not initially sign up for all the back-and-forth, and so, for all their efforts, I am extremely pleased. Their labors make the book what it is. They remain my teachers.

I coveted the prayers of my friends at First Presbyterian Church, Altadena. I could not have made it without their support.

I want to thank my family for their support when nights and weekends were given over to this project. As always, they are the ones who keep me sane and in touch with the everyday, the ones who bring me never-ending joy.

I give all thanks and honor to God the Father, Son, and Holy Spirit for this project and the many graces bestowed along the way. I give you all praise.

Abbreviations

Works of Eddie Gibbs frequently quoted in the text in sidebars are denoted by the following abbreviations, arranged in order of publication date:

IBCG   *I Believe in Church Growth*. Grand Rapids: Eerdmans, 1982.

INO   *In Name Only: Tackling the Problem of Nominal Christianity*. Wheaton: BridgePoint Books, 1994.

CN   *ChurchNext: Quantum Changes in How We Do Ministry*. Downers Grove, IL: InterVarsity, 2000.

LN   *LeadershipNext: Changing Leaders in a Changing Culture*. Downers Grove, IL: InterVarsity, 2005.

CM   *ChurchMorph: How Megatrends Are Reshaping Christian Communities*. Grand Rapids: Baker Academic, 2009.

Contributors

Peter Aschoff teaches a course in church history at IGW International in Zurich. He wrote *Kaum zu fassen*, an introduction to the Christian faith, as well as books on Celtic Christianity and faith in the workplace. He was also contributor to and coeditor of *Zeitgeist* and *Zeitgeist 2*. Peter is part of ELIA, a new community within the Lutheran church. He labels himself as "contemplactive," "charismystic," and "ecotholic." He likes books and good coffee, and if you can put up with occasional irony, you can read his blog at http://www .elia-erlangen.de/wordpress. He lives in Erlangen, Germany.

Kelly Bean is cultivator of Third Saturday organic community, which has gathered in her living room for twenty-four years. She is coplanter of Urban Abbey, an egalitarian intergenerational intentional community in North Portland. A pastor, speaker, writer, mentor, contemplative, activist, and artist, Kelly is passionate about creating environments that seed deep community with diverse groups. Kelly has been creating and leading strategic networks for women in ministry for the past ten years. She is the author of the forthcoming *How to Be a Christian without Going to Church*.

Ryan K. Bolger is associate professor of church in contemporary culture in the School of Intercultural Studies at Fuller Theological Seminary. He is the coauthor of *Emerging Churches: Creating Christian Community in Postmodern Cultures*. He has served on several church planting teams in the southern California area. He and his wife, children, cats, and chickens make their home near Pasadena.

Nadia Bolz-Weber is the mission developer for a Lutheran emerging church called House for All Sinners and Saints in Denver, Colorado. She is a contributing writer for Jim Wallis's *God's Politics* blog and is the author of *Salvation on the Small Screen? 24 Hours of Christian Television*—a theological and social commentary based on her experience of having watched twenty-four consecutive hours of Trinity Broadcasting Network and survived. She blogs at http://www.sarcasticlutheran.com.

Troy Bronsink is a musician and author helping shape the worship practices of the future church. An ordained Presbyterian minister and consultant with over twenty years of experience in parachurch, emerging church, pastoral, and worship ministry, Troy has spoken to and made music with camps, conferences, schools, and congregations large and small. The Neighbors Abbey congregation that Troy helped form closed in the fall of 2011. He and his wife and two children currently live in Cincinnati.

Graham Cray is the missioner for the archbishops of Canterbury and York, and leader of the ecumenical Fresh Expressions Team in the UK. Previously he was bishop of Maidstone, principal of Ridley Hall Cambridge, and vicar of St. Michael le Belfrey in York. He is a former chairman of the Greenbelt Festival and current chairman of the Soul Survivor Trust. He is married to Jackie, a parish priest, and they have two adult children.

Darren Cronshaw trains leaders through the Baptist Union of Victoria, is the pastor of Auburn Baptist Church, and serves as an honorary research associate at Whitley College (Melbourne College of Divinity). He recently published *The Shaping of Things Now: Emerging Church Mission and Innovation in 21st Century Melbourne*. Darren is a husband to Jenni, proud dad to three children, lover of good books and movies, and eager learner from missional churches.

Tobias Faix teaches theology and missiology at the Marburg Bildungs-und Studienzentrum (Centre for Education) and is academic dean for the postgraduate degree program Transformational Studies. He is the founder and head of the research institute Empirica for youth culture and religion and has published over twenty books about church and society. He lives with his family in Marburg, Germany.

Dwight J. Friesen teaches practical missional theology at The Seattle School of Theology and Psychology. He planted and pastored a network of simple churches before transitioning into missional leadership training. He has published a number of books, including *Thy Kingdom Connected* and *Routes and Radishes*. Dwight is active locally and internationally with missional and place-based church movements. He lives on Seattle's Eastside with his partner, Lynette, and son, Pascal.

Oscar García-Johnson is assistant professor of systematic theology at Fuller Theological Seminary. He is a church planter, pastoral and lay leadership developer, practical theologian, and ordained minister with the American Baptist Churches USA. He is the author of *The Mestizo/a Community of the Spirit: A Latino/a Postmodern Ecclesiology*, among other writings. He is married to Karla and lives in Sylmar, California.

Eddie Gibbs is the Donald McGavran professor emeritus of church growth in the School of Intercultural Studies at Fuller Theological Seminary and director of the Institute for the Study of Emerging Churches at the Brehm Center for Worship, Theology, and the Arts. He is the former associate rector for discipleship at All Saints' Episcopal Church in Beverly Hills, California. Eddie is the author of numerous books, including *ChurchMorph*, *LeadershipNext*, and *ChurchNext*, and coauthor of *Emerging Churches*. He is the cohost of the Church Then and Now website, http://www.churchthenandnow.com.

Steve Hollinghurst is researcher in evangelism to post-Christian culture at the Church Army Sheffield Centre in the UK, a member of the Lausanne Issue Group on New Religious Movements, and is a speaker in the UK and abroad on mission and culture. He helps run Elemental, a venue offering Christian spirituality at the Glastonbury Festival and Christian stalls at Mind/Body/Spirit fairs. He is author of *Mission-Shaped Evangelism*.

Mark MacDonald is the national indigenous Anglican bishop of Canada and the former bishop of Alaska and pastoral bishop of Navajoland. He coedited *The Chant of Life: Inculturation and the People of the Land*. He is a frequent contributor to *First Peoples Theology Journal* and wrote "Finding Communion with Creation," in *Holy Ground: A Gathering of Voices on Caring for Creation*. After spending a good part of their lives in remote places, he and his wife, Virginia, and children, Rose May Li, Brenna, and Blake, live in Toronto.

Ian Mobsby is an Anglican ordained missioner and a founding member of the Moot Community (http://www.moot.uk.net). Ian is an associate missioner of the archbishops of Canterbury and York Fresh Expressions Team and a member of the Church of England's College of Evangelists. Ian has written and edited a number of books, including: *Emerging and Fresh Expressions of Church*, *The Becoming of G-d*, *New Monasticism as Fresh Expression of Church*, and

Ancient Faith Future Mission: Fresh Expressions in the Sacramental Traditions. Ian blogs at http://www.moot.uk.net and http://www.ianmobsby.net.

MaryKate Morse is professor of leadership and spiritual formation at George Fox Evangelical Seminary. She did her doctorate at Gonzaga University where she studied the characteristics of renewal leadership as modeled by Jesus. She is an ordained Quaker pastor, church planter, spiritual director, conference and retreat speaker, writer, and author of *Making Room for Leadership*. MaryKate is married to Randy and has three adult children and three grandchildren. She enjoys being with family, hiking, reading, exploring Oregon, and playing with her puppy, Tess.

Andreas Østerlund Nielsen is a PhD student at the Faculty of Theology at Aarhus University. He constituted half of the founding team of the Danish missional church plant Bykirken and served as pastor for seven years. Andreas is coeditor of *Walk Humbly with the Lord: Church and Mission Engaging Plurality*. He is married to Trine, and they have two young boys.

Stefan Paas is a professor of church planting and church renewal at the Free University in Amsterdam and a lecturer in missiology at the Free Reformed Theological University in Kampen (the Netherlands). He has spent most of his life in evangelism or thinking and writing about evangelism. He has been involved in two church plants in the Netherlands. Stefan is married to Dorret, and they live in Amsterdam with their three children.

Matthias Radloff is professor at the Institute Biblique et Missionaire, St-Legier, Switzerland. For nineteen years, he pastored a church and worked in publishing. He has hosted a French blog on the subject of church growth and new ventures since 2006.

Paul Roberts is tutor in worship at Trinity College, Bristol. He was one of the pioneers of alternative worship in Britain in the early 1990s and has continued to work in the area of emerging forms of church and creative worship since that time. He has served on the Liturgical Commission and General Synod of the Church of England, has pastored two Anglican parishes, and has helped initiate two alternative worship communities over the past twenty years. He cohosts, with Steve Collins, the website http://www.alternativeworship.org.

Mark Scandrette is the cofounder of ReIMAGINE: A Center of Life Integration in San Francisco. He is the author of *Practicing the Way of Jesus* and

Soul Graffiti: Making a Life in the Way of Jesus. He lives with his wife and three teenage children in an old Victorian in San Francisco's Mission District.

Osías Segura-Guzmán is affiliate assistant professor at Fuller Theological Seminary in Pasadena, California. He received his doctor of missiology degree from Asbury Theological Seminary's ESJ School of World Mission and Evangelism. He is Costa Rican and married to Desiree Segura-April, assistant professor of children-at-risk at Fuller Theological Seminary.

Ruth Skree works with developing, emerging, and existing communities of faith and churches through Normisjon in Norway. Her long-term focus has been the missiological challenge for the Scandinavian and northern European church as it tries to find its place in post-Christendom cultures. She holds master's degrees in cross-cultural studies and theology from Fuller Theological Seminary.

Richard Sudworth has been a Church Mission Society mission partner in North Africa and Birmingham, England, for over ten years. He is now a pioneer curate in the Church of England in a Muslim-majority parish in Birmingham. Richard is a PhD candidate at Heythrop College, University of London, researching the political theology of the Church of England in relation to Islam. He is author of *Distinctly Welcoming: Christian Presence in a Multifaith Society.*

Eileen Suico is cofounder and pastor of With in Seattle, Washington. Eileen received her master of arts in global leadership in 2009 and is currently a doctoral student at Fuller Theological Seminary. Eileen's current project includes work in cultivating community living in a highly individualistic culture by promoting reciprocity, generosity, compassion, kindness, social justice, and appreciation of diversity as characterized by our trinitarian God. She is a wife and a mother of three children.

Steve Taylor is director of missiology at Uniting College of Leadership and Theology and a senior lecturer at Flinders University. He is author of *The Out of Bounds Church? Learning to Create a Community of Faith in a Culture of Change* and has had chapters published in *The Bible in/and Popular Culture* and *Exploring U2*, among others. He speaks widely on areas of mission and church in today's world and blogs at http://www.emergentkiwi.org.nz.

Nico-Dirk van Loo with Martijn Vellekoop wrote *Ploeteren en Pionieren*, a book on emerging churches in the Netherlands. He works as a project manager for the Dutch government. Together with his wife, Diana, he initiated an open space arts collective: http://www.ruisfabriek.nl (also on Twitter at @ruisfabriek). They have three kids and two Russian wolfhounds. He blogs at http://www.nicodirkvanloo.nl and tweets at @nicodirkvanloo.

Blayne Waltrip is director of extensions for SEMISUD (Seminario Sudamericano) throughout Latin America and teaches adjunct at academic institutions around the world. He taught intercultural studies and Christian education as a full-time faculty member at the European Theological Seminary (ETS) in Kniebis, Germany, from 2005 to 2009. Blayne is an international trainer and conference speaker on church and culture, church planting, evangelism, and missional church. He is married to Dr. Angela McCain-Waltrip, and they have one daughter, Noëlle.

Ralph Watkins is associate professor for church growth and evangelism at Columbia Seminary in Decatur, Georgia. His work has focused on listening to the hip-hop generation and putting them in dialogue with their elders. He considers himself an old hip-hop head who was called to preach. Ralph continues to find ways to connect hip-hop culture with Christ to make a difference in the world. His latest book is *Hip-Hop Redemption: Finding God in the Rhythm and the Rhyme*.

Markus Weimer is vicar of the Protestant Church in Baden. He served as curate near Freiburg and as vicar in Stockach for four years before he was appointed as teacher for practical theology at Albrecht-Bengel-Haus in Tübingen. He is currently working on PhD research that examines the missional transition process within the Church of England. He is leader of the network Church-Convention, member of the milieu-training team in his church, and coeditor of a magazine on missional church growth. He is married to Anja, has two boys, and loves to play hockey in his free time.

Bob Whitesel is professor of missional leadership at Wesley Seminary at Indiana Wesleyan University. He is a speaker and writer on the organic church, on missional leadership, and on church growth. He is the author of ten books, including *Preparing for Change Reaction: How to Introduce Change in Your Church* and *Spiritual Waypoints: Helping Others Navigate the Journey*. His book *Organix: Signs of Leadership in a Changing Church* describes emerging and effective leadership changes.

Eric Zander is director for French ministries with the Belgian Evangelical Mission. He leads several alternative expressions of church in a local social network among bikers. He recently finished a MTh in applied theology at Spurgeon's College, London. Eric loves reflecting on contemporary culture and acting to impact it. He also loves motorcycle riding, rock music, running, and good food. He and his wife, Anne, have three children, Samuel, Déborah, and Axelle. They live in Gembloux, Belgium.

Contributor Dedications to Eddie Gibbs

Thank you for encouraging so many of us along the way. Your wise reminder that "Life has to be lived at walking pace" is a countercultural call to a frantic world.

With appreciation, Kelly Bean

Thanks for your humble reminders that Christendom has confused the church's sense of identity, and that our formal ecclesiastical institutions and authority constructs are no longer able to hold up. And yet, in spite of this deconstructive enterprise, your positive impact on students' vision for God's world and our role in that work is beautiful! You're like a great composer. You create a sonic landscape that incorporates the resonance of so many other reimaginers.

Thank you!
Troy Bronsink

From his time as a missionary in South America, through his work with the Bible Society in England—before we gave him as a generous missionary gift to the USA and Fuller Seminary, Eddie Gibbs has been a source of inspiration and wisdom to me and countless others. I will always value his missional thinking about culture and cultural engagement with mission; his refusal to allow church growth to be for anything other than the mission of God in the world; and his stubborn refusal to assume that what worked then must be okay now. I especially love his stubborn refusal to stop learning!

Thank you, Eddie.
Graham Cray

Unfortunately, I never had the privilege of meeting Eddie Gibbs in person, but still I have the impression I at least know a part of him. His books, articles, research, interviews, blogs, etc., have accompanied and influenced me greatly over the past years. For this I am very thankful, and my wishes to Eddie Gibbs for the future are that his openness to new ideas, his wisdom, and his theological foresight may continue to accompany me and many others.

Tobias Faix

I first met Dr. Eddie Gibbs as a student. As odd as it sounds, I wasn't taking a class from him; rather it was Dr. Gibbs who was on a mission to learn from emerging church practitioners. I remember how honored he made me feel when Dr. Gibbs had not only learned of the missional community I was involved with as a young pastor but also wanted to learn from me. I am so grateful to God for Dr. Gibbs, and not simply for his example of faithful service to Christ and Christ's church, with his lifetime of missional leadership on three continents, his commitment to developing leaders, and his passion for documenting his findings so others' kingdom-imaginations might be fueled; I am grateful that in an era when it could be easy to focus on the waning influence of the Western church, Dr. Gibbs explores signs of new life, and he does so with curiosity, humility, wisdom, and genuine openness.

I honor you, Dr. Gibbs; you are my teacher.
Dwight J. Friesen

There are those whose focus on the past has kept us rooted in important streams of Christian traditions. There are others whose commitment to the pressing issues of today's complex world represents a prophetic voice that gives us an appetite for a better world. And yet there are still some, and scarcely so, whose awareness of the past and commitment to the present have propelled them into wondering of the future, hoping to bring about a holistic and kingdom-oriented vision. Eddie Gibbs may be counted among the latter.

Oscar García-Johnson

I started reading on church growth when I found myself as an evangelist in a tough urban environment, asking lots of questions. The first book someone gave me was Eddie's *Body Building Exercises for the Local Church*. His work and input have grown a lot since then. But for many like me he sowed the seeds for a renewed approach to mission.

Steve Hollinghurst

It is an honor to be involved with a volume produced in celebration of Dr. Eddie Gibbs's ministry. To face the challenges before indigenous ministry, it will be necessary to be fearless in innovation and faithful in discipleship. This is, I am convinced, the passion and goal of Dr. Gibbs's work.

> May this volume continue and expand that legacy.
> Mark MacDonald

Eddie Gibbs is a wind catcher noticing the movement of the Holy Spirit and explaining to us the way of the church and leadership during important shifts in our times.

> MaryKate Morse

The writings of Eddie Gibbs have inspired me greatly in my work as a church planting pastor. I have been stimulated to think about church in new ways; and I have been encouraged to walk these ways by reading of those others who were further ahead on the emerging roads. Having the opportunity to meet with Eddie surely confirmed my impression of a warm person with an embracing mind.

> Thank you.
> Andreas Østerlund Nielsen

Although Eddie and I both come from the same country, we only met in 2005. However, I have long admired his scholarship and infectious enthusiasm since his work first introduced me, as a young theology undergraduate in the late 1970s, to the exciting world of missiology. When Eddie went to Fuller in 1984, it looked like a major loss for the UK, but it has been a delight to watch the valuable contribution he has gone on to make in the USA and right around the world.

> Paul Roberts

Eddie Gibbs is well known in Latin America among those leaders (both lay people and missiologists) interested in issues of missional ecclesiology and leadership. His translated books have allowed us for many years to be critical of every "imported" model for doing church from the United States.

> Gracias Don Eddie!
> Osías Segura-Guzmán

I encountered Eddie Gibbs at my first visit at Fuller Seminary as I happened to stumble upon two of his books: *In Name Only* and *Emerging Churches*, which he coauthored with Ryan Bolger. These books became highly influential in my thinking and in my decision to come back to study at Fuller a few years later. To my disappointment, Eddie was at that point not teaching many classes anymore, but through online classes and several great and encouraging conversations over coffee, I have come to deeply appreciate his work and his engagement for the church and its missional task in our time.

Ruth Skree

We all owe Eddie Gibbs a debt because he has been a pioneer of bringing social sciences to the service of Christian mission.

Richard Sudworth

Eddie Gibbs's works continue to challenge me to lead a church as a culture creator integrated in the very lives of the people rather than an institution that tends to be isolated in a one- or two-day weekend activity. Eddie's passion to see the missiological essence of the church lived out in our present society continues to inspire my work, my research, and my leadership at With.

Thanks, Eddie.
Eileen Suico

What I most remember about Eddie is the graciousness of his teaching. I was providing some guest input in his class on emerging church. As the class settled, a young Korean woman sitting at the front of the class spilt her coffee. Highly embarrassed, she desperately tried to remain invisible yet simultaneously mop up the mess, which was slowly dripping between the tiered Fuller seating. Quick as a flash, Eddie began to speak. He told a joke about teaching in South America while chickens ran through the lecture room. The class laughed. The focus shifted from the embarrassed girl to the phenomena of South American chickens. It was a wonderful snapshot of Eddie, quick on his feet, sensitive to others, full of multicultural experiences, and fearless among South American chickens.

Steve Taylor

Years ago Eddie's work triggered me to articulate for the first time my frustration and grief over the status quo of the church. During my emerging wanderings, at several times, he provided stories and ideas that prevented me from slipping into despair and leaving the story of the church altogether.

Nico-Dirk van Loo

Although he does not know it, Eddie Gibbs has had an impact on my ministry and missiology. First, he was always an encouragement when I met with him about entering the PhD program at Fuller. While working in France, I took his course on *Evangelizing Nominal Christians* by distance learning. That course challenged me to begin rethinking my traditional approaches to evangelism and mission in post-Christendom contexts. Through his writing, he has influenced my teaching and research.

Blayne Waltrip

Dr. Gibbs's work gave me permission to leave church to find God. He clearly pointed to what God was doing in the world. For me, it led me to seek God in hip-hop and hear what God was saying through the people and the music. Dr. Gibbs showed me what was emerging, and I found out that God was not restricted to a building. Dr. Gibbs's work was liberation.

Ralph Watkins

Eddie Gibbs not only served as a model but also as a mentor. It was under Eddie's tutelage that I chronicled the organic growth and diffusion of St. Thomas' Church in Sheffield, England. His advice and wisdom greatly aided my PhD research and writing. Eddie's exacting insights, infectious but wry humor, mellow charm, and quest for penetrating what McGavran called the "universal fog" of imprecise analysis, instilled in me and many others an enhanced passion for the *missio Dei*.

Bob Whitesel

Preface

Early in 2009, I began asking in my networks (church growth, missional church, emerging church, and missiology) who they thought were some of the top missional thinkers for the Western world. I asked for thinkers who were both scholars and practitioners—who were vetted both through their writing and their actual experience starting new communities in the West. Some were more on the scholar side, and some on the practitioner, but most all were qualified in both.

I received an initial list of names and then began a second stage of research. I asked these missional scholar-practitioners four sets of related questions:

1. What are the biggest questions/issues/cultural shifts facing the Western church today?
2. How might the church address these issues? In other words, how might the church live missionally/embody the gospel in the post-Christendom West at this time?
3. If you personally have a "big idea" concerning these issues, what is it?
4. Is there someone you know who should be a part of this discussion?

With the first question, I asked these scholar-practitioners to name those issues most significant to the Western church today. This cultural question seeks to get at what issues or themes present the greatest threat to the life of the Western church, especially concerning recent cultural change.

The second set of questions asked how the church might, in its life together, respond to these cultural shifts. What does the church need to do and be at this time? How might the church embody the gospel of Jesus Christ given the demands of our context? A second part of the question deals with post-Christendom, that period in the West where the practice of religion is no longer a cultural expectation but is more of an individual choice. Post-Christendom is that social space where there is a Christian memory, but that memory no longer affects how people make meaning with their lives. Moreover, the institution of church may be looked at with loving nostalgia or with deep suspicion (or somewhere in between), but not as a resource for living. Given this reality—that many of the presuppositions of Christendom are over—how might the church now be the church?

My third question dealt with my responders' "big idea." Some of these scholar-practitioners think a great deal about the church after Christendom, and that is why I wrote to them. What do they think the ultimate challenge is, and what must be done about it?

My fourth question was related to my method of research. I needed to make sure I had all the right people for the study. I asked participants to tell me about others whom they believed had insight in this arena. As they listed these names, I initiated contact with them and the process began again. I would ask these new names the same four questions. I continued this loop until I ceased to hear any more new names. When I heard only repeats, I knew this phase of the research was over; in other words, I had the right set of data.

In all, I asked 137 scholar-practitioners these four questions, and in the end, 76 responded to my request, writing paragraph-long responses to each question. From these 76, I received a total of 273 challenges, responses, and ideas for the Western church today. Fortunately, many of these responses echoed one another. (The book would be a hard sell if it were titled *273 Issues for the Western Church*!)

As I assessed these responses, I focused on challenges that specifically related to our changed context; that is, I paid attention to the important issues for a post-Christendom church. I tried very hard to walk along the theory/praxis nexus. If an answer was simply too far in one direction or the other, I would not work with it. For example, if I received a suggestion of a philosophical nature and could not see how it might affect day-to-day church, I had to let it pass. However, ideas that reduced our challenges to simple strategies or tactics, and that did not reimagine church life considering our present challenges, could not be used either. The responses needed to address current praxis of church in a robust way given our changed culture of post-Christendom.

Where possible, I dug deeper into the legitimate comments. If someone had a particularly novel idea, I followed up with them, asking clarifying questions by email. I did not want to exclude those outliers who really had some wisdom to share, even if not everyone agreed with their opinion.

I grouped the themes into buckets of ideas that needed to be addressed. A common motif in the responses was the need to use our imaginations to interrupt the programming of Western culture. So I separated the responses into six cultural categories, even though there is much overlap among them. Many addressed several of these themes all at once.

- How can we be the church in the midst of an environmental crisis?
- Given globalization and migration, many live between two or more cultures. How can we be the church in this newly created space?
- Secularization is still real as faith is now privatized. Pluralism contributes to an individual form of faith in the West. How might we live our faith communally and in relation with other traditions?
- Given a culture of creativity, how might the church itself live as God's artwork?
- Given that faith is individualized in the West, how do we embody a faith that is not consumeristic?
- We are in a culture of new spiritualities. People want God but they do not want the church. How do we allow for believing without belonging?

Respondents also addressed how the church might transform its internal practices considering these cultural changes and post-Christendom. So in addition to the six cultural categories, I focused on four aspects of church practice. Specifically, how are the Christian practices of (1) worship, (2) formation, (3) mission, and (4) leadership affected by current cultural change?

After creating these ten themes (six rooted in cultural change, four rooted in church practice), I invited ten authors—who had big ideas in these areas and could address the various issues named by others within that theme—to write about them. I also asked them to put their big idea into conversation with the other themes and practices. The selection process was a difficult one, as many of the seventy-six responding authors shared similar "big ideas" (but I couldn't really have seventy-six chapters in the book either).

I also felt we needed a snapshot of the bigger picture, so I asked seven authors to write a chapter on the church after Christendom in particular regional contexts. These scholar-practitioners belong to specific cultural networks and have a good understanding of new faith movements within particular nations and peoples.

In reading other responders, I realized that some have an in-depth view of a particular community, having both started and led new expressions of church life in post-Christendom, and they had gained many insights through these experiences. I asked them to write up these eight case studies of new expressions.

Finally, some of these authors were creating significant change at the denominational level, and I asked them to share their experience of that process.

These five areas—peoples (networks of Christians within a particular people), cultures (six themes), practices (worship, formation, mission, leadership), experiments (case studies), and traditions (denominational change processes)—provide an outline for this volume.[1]

Ryan K. Bolger

---

1. I must say at the outset that in no way is this project exhaustive. There are more than the seven regions of post-Christendom discussed in part 1: whole other chapters could be written on other parts of the world. I chose these particular regions because I felt they would be demonstrative of the challenges faced in the areas hardest hit by post-Christendom. To be sure, there are more cultural themes than the six listed in part 2. I chose the themes given utmost priority by the respondents, the ones I believed to be most pertinent to a post-Christendom church. There were 273 ideas, and I am certain another researcher would come up with a different list. And again, there are more practices in the church than the four listed in part 3, but these are core historic Christian practices that lead to what it means to be church. Eliminate any one of these, and I am not sure we still have a church—at least not for very long. I chose the eight case studies in part 4 based on the stories I received from respondents. Many more case studies could be written, but I felt that these eight studies gave us a reasonable sample of illustrations. Regarding denominational change, I felt the three particular stories in part 5 addressed the challenges presented to denominations in post-Christendom.

Introduction

Ryan K. Bolger

To get a better understanding of church engagements within post-Christendom, we will explore the phenomenon at multiple levels. The structure of this volume moves from large to small and back to large. We begin in part 1 with "Peoples," where our authors examine new expressions of faith within seven nations or regional groups of people. In part 2, "Cultures," we look at six powerful cultural themes and their impact on church life today. In "Practices," part 3, we explore four historic Christian practices as they interact with our cultural themes. Then in part 4 we look at "Experiments," examining eight case studies of new Christian communities in a post-Christendom context. Finally, in "Traditions," part 5, we read the stories of three different efforts, in different parts of the world, of transformation at the denominational level. In the conclusion, I briefly narrate the patterns in this work as a way to respond to my initial questions for the research project.

Peoples

In the first chapter, Osías Segura-Guzmán explores the possibility of emerging churches in a Latin American context. The number of emerging church communities is small, and many go by names other than *iglesias emergentes*. He starts by asking if postmodern people really exist in Latin America, since emerging churches, by definition, are churches within postmodern culture. He also considers whether these postmodern expressions of faith are yet another import from the North or if Latin Americans have made it their own.

Segura-Guzmán's chapter offers three examples of communities that traverse on this Western/non-Western, modern/postmodern divide. He explains that even if church expressions are rooted in the West, Latin Americans modify them and make them their own. Did they do this with these *iglesias emergentes*? His tentative answer is yes. These organic expressions of faith offer simple worship, hospitable community, a commitment to social justice, and flat leadership. Much of their decision making is communal. They are populated by artists, designers, and educated people. Even though they care for the poor, the poor are not yet part of the community.

Steve Taylor, writing in chapter 2 on emerging churches in Aotearoa New Zealand, describes these new communities, beginning with Parallel Universe in 1994, as highly innovative and rooted in the culture. New Zealand is characterized by a population of Christians who no longer find the historic denominations useful, even though they still pursue faith. In this de-churched context faith discussion groups called Spirited Exchanges capture people's imaginations. House churches are a feature of the emergent movement in New Zealand as well.

Some New Zealand fresh expressions have pioneered the use of public installation art as both formation and mission. These multisensory exhibits—especially popular at Christmas and Easter—offer embodied experiences of faith in very accessible public venues. New Zealand also has its share of new monastic communities, with orders committed to an active spirituality expressed through works of justice. In this chapter, Taylor explores the notion of leader as curator. He ends with the question of how much new expressions of church will change as religion continues to be pushed into postmodern choice cultures. Faith expressions online, led by a network of kiwis, have great potential.

Australians are spiritual and anti-institutional, and they value innovation, writes Darren Cronshaw in chapter 3. Although church attendance is dwindling, emerging missional churches do have a future in Australia. Experimental expressions of Christian community such as café churches, house churches, and alternative spirituality groups thrive there. Many of these expressions were influenced by Aussies Michael Frost and Alan Hirsch with their Forge network.

Australian emerging missional churches are dissatisfied with church as they know it. They want the church to focus outside the faith community, to go beyond itself. Incarnational mission in third places is a focus, as they practice an accessible spirituality. Churches in this context create a place for doubt and questioning. Exploring is okay. Who is in and who is out is not considered.

Worship is artistic, participatory, and may focus on justice. Meetings are highly engaging, involving much food and sharing of life together. Collaborative, permission-giving leadership moves away from a pastor-centered structure. The role of the leader is to find peoples' passions and help them develop a ministry in that particular area.

Ruth Skree provides a discussion of the church in Scandinavia in chapter 4. Scandinavia has a folk church of which the majority of the population are members but which few people actively support. In contrast, new forms of church engender high levels of participation. Some of these new churches start accidentally; a meeting might begin among believers within a particular musical subculture, for example, and they grow unintentionally and eventually become a church. No church background is required for someone to fully participate in new churches. Given that for some Christianity is completely new, the church accepts different speeds of spiritual growth among its members. There is no "in" or "out"; everyone is welcome.

Skree offers examples of different practices among the new churches. Regarding worship, artists might lead the time of worship, and the emphasis may be on a meal, on Communion, or on an encounter with art rather than on music. Church might be a church of small groups, and formal discipleship often happens in monastic groups. New monasticism in Scandinavia is a growing movement, and some monastic groups go out and serve beyond their church walls with other communities. Spending time in the culture *is* mission—for example, providing nonviolence training or classes on cross-cultural understanding. They are united by a rhythm of life together; they pray the hours. Leadership is flat, democratic, and empowering, often without one visible leader. The board or elder role is to support the initiatives of the people, and leaders function as guides. Because of the distance between church and culture in the Nordic countries, one leader advises that pastors abstain from full-time church work.

There is a recent increase of interest in spirituality in the Netherlands and Flanders, according to Nico-Dirk van Loo in chapter 5. The private search for meaning and spirituality is common. New expressions start at the margins with little fanfare. A mixed-economy church, although currently not a reality, will be part of the church's future. Evangelical churches were optimistic a decade ago, but now they are in crisis. Incarnational church planting, neomonasticism, and countercultural communities are the way forward.

For many new expressions of church in the Netherlands and Flanders, the sermon is gone. In its place, artistic liturgy occurs but is less frequent than communal meals. There are two types of churches: (1) more anonymous groups with low participation, for example, an inspiring word, music, and media, and

(2) high participation neomonastic communities where communal meals and highly engaging multisensory activities are the rule. Some groups do not use praise choruses but focus on Taizé, Celtic, or Anglican songs. Some rewrite secular Dutch songs for the service. Some eat meals around Dutch food and culture. Their focus is on the life of Jesus and the kingdom of God. In the Low Countries, the Bible is not taught, but is communally discerned. Justice work is mission work. Traditional evangelism has given way to embodied evangelism; the participants' entire lives call out to others to join this community with an alternative story of the kingdom. Often, people outside the church participate in one-time spiritual events. In Dutch new expressions, visionary leaders are suspect, so most communities have egalitarian leadership, with both men and women serving. All people are valued and able to start new ministries.

The Christian situation in French-speaking Europe, on the one hand, could not be bleaker. Not only has Christianity been pushed to the very margins of society, but some sociologists are even calling Christianity incomprehensible to the French. On the other hand, to write off French spirituality would be premature. Although the numbers are small, the French are spiritual people, and some are finding their way back to the church. Those who do convert to Christ are passionate.

In chapter 6, "Fresh Expressions of Missional Church in French-Speaking Europe," Blayne Waltrip discusses the characteristics of some of these new communities of passionate converts. They might desire music that is French or make outside music their own. When they have larger gatherings, multisensory art is a core part of these meetings. Those who have the gift of teaching are the teachers, not necessarily the pastor. A church might have thirty people and function as a network of small groups. The churches meet in homes, and their gatherings are casual and discussion-oriented. Discipleship is done around the table with food. Their outreach is to develop relationships with those outside the community. Church communities both host and frequent many parties. There are no boundaries between "Christian" and "non-Christian" for the church community in French-speaking Europe. They desire to reinterpret Jesus for French culture through art, film, and dance. For those under thirty, no reinterpretation is necessary; it is all new. Verbal proclamation happens in relationship, when someone is asked. The groups have a very flat leadership structure—everyone leads where they are gifted. They envision a network of small groups across the region.

In his chapter on emerging expressions in German-speaking Europe (chap. 7), Peter Aschoff writes that the population is split one-third Protestant, one-third Catholic, 5 percent Muslim, and the rest without ties. Evangelicals form less than 2 percent of the population and are part of mainline Protestantism.

Postmodernity has affected Germany for at least the past twenty-five years. Fresh expressions of church began with the Jesus Freaks in the early 1990s. Today there are several networks, including Emergent Deutschland, which began in 2006. Emerging groups such as Motoki or Kubik are populated by artists, social workers, and educators.

Emerging groups in German-speaking Europe are experiments. Sermons exist, but at the heart of services are Communion and multisensory stations. People can respond in any way they choose. Churches might be located in a pub, a café, an industrial building, or an old church. Diversity, inclusion, and participation are celebrated. The church expressions are networks of small groups. New monasticism is popular. Small learning communities get together to engage in spiritual disciplines. They share, engage Scripture, create and display works of art, meditate, contemplate, pray the hours, and observe Stations of the Cross. Mission is justice work—not just mercy ministry but political action. Not only do they distrust CEO-style leaders, but they shun the pastor as entrepreneur, therapist, or scholar as well. Women are celebrated as leaders. If there are clergy on a team, they are to support the laypeople in significant ways.

Cultures

According to Ian Mobsby (chap. 8), the world is in a time of economic crisis, and humans must begin to take responsibility for the current situation. Humanity's drive for consumption, however, has driven the earth to the brink of destruction. The industrial revolution caused Westerners to forget about the sacredness of all of life. Christians know that the earth is God's creation, but they rarely think of responsibility to that creation. This is not a physical problem per se, but it reveals a deficient spirituality. The Western ego goes unchecked and must develop virtues that will create another set of possibilities for the earth.

People need an eco-spirituality that makes certain the connection between spirituality and creation. Those who have countered the false self are those who create an alternative set of practices for all of life. These monastic communities establish a context for developing creative stewardship of the earth. Corporately they may create worship that invites people into new understandings through sometimes shocking and perhaps unsettling art and stories that can shake people out of complacency. Moot, Mobsby's community in London, has a rhythm of life that advocates for virtues in all of life. These spiritual practices, which form the core of Christian life, create dispositions toward the good, toward treating God, earth, and self well. Christians learn to welcome all others as gifts as they foster a stance of hospitality. This particularly appeals to spiritual questers, those pursuing God directly and not through organized religion. Some monastic communities connect with questers through radical arts cafés and meditative events. Leadership in new monastic communities is based on wisdom and is generally communal in practice.

In chapter 9, "Mission within Hybrid Cultures," Oscar García-Johnson describes the concept of transnationality. He tells the story of Sansei-Peruvian immigrants to Suzuka, Japan. They had migrated from Peru to Japan as teenagers but were cultural hybrids. Their historically Japanese family spoke Spanish and Portuguese. They met at a Brazilian Pentecostal church in Suzuka. They lived in the space between Japanese society, their Brazilian church, and their Peruvian family, but they found that none of those cultures captured who they were—so they started a church in the space of their hybrid-borderline existence, the first immigrant multilingual church in the region. In their church, they have families that share a dual South American/Japanese identity and existence. The church draws Japanese youth as well.

García-Johnson realizes that this dynamic is not unique to this church in Japan; it is happening on a global scale. In Los Angeles, Latino pastors share a similar experience. Their homes travel with them, as they bring their symbolic homeland wherever they go. They transmigrate—rather than immigrate—between home and Home. The vitality of the Global South is traveling to the Global North through these immigrant vessels. Many transnational pastors are mission makers and cultural transmitters. They plant churches that grow rapidly; they lead changes. The local church still exists, but that space is globalized as transnationality occurs at the local level. Neither assimilationism nor essentialism are options for these communities. These are fluid communities, a hybrid phenomenon. Christ is experienced in the center of all these currents. Affirming the diversity of the entire body and the diversity of each person is what the Spirit does. This is Pentecost.

Richard Sudworth begins chapter 10 with the statement, troubling for many, that the modern conception of truth—the idea that truth can be established and authoritative—is crumbling. Christian apologetics was based on the idea of the rational autonomous individual. If our understanding of reality is now rooted in community, practice, and tradition, then how do Christians advocate for truth across communities? In a time of pluralism, sharing across traditions is quite complex, because there may not be a shared base of understanding. What is forgiveness of sins to someone who never felt unforgiven?

Sudworth introduces the idea of being "distinctly welcoming." Christians are rooted in the Christian story, unashamed of their practice and theology of

Christ. At the same time, God may speak to people in any tradition and might be working in ways that are incomprehensible to outsiders. Sudworth describes Sanctuary, a church in Birmingham led by Pall Singh that is culturally eastern, with Indian tunes, Asian sweets, and prayer and devotion to Christ centered in a British Asian context. There is a deep sense of community, and one might be a part of the community for years before one makes a faith confession. Christians must develop the skills to listen to God from within the symbols of other faiths, yet shape their practices around Christian worship and discipline. Leadership must discern the spiritual trek of others using the others' own faith tradition. Christians can no longer be ignorant of other ways of life—they must learn about the texts of other faith communities. Weaving these stories around the Christ event will be a challenge for the church in the future.

Troy Bronsink, formerly of Neighbors Abbey in Atlanta, in "Our P(art) in an Age of Beauty" (chap. 11), writes about communities that follow Jesus by learning from beauty and participating in God's kingdom by becoming art themselves. God dreams for his people and calls his people to fulfill those dreams. The church is the group of people called by God to create a way of life that brings more time, space, and matter into participation with the love of God. All the church's makings and doings are shaped by God's love.

Bronsink writes that some communities "open source" their faith in public and give the rights to interpretation away. This is nothing new; the disciples had to reimagine and reorient themselves over and over again (see the parables). Works of beauty confront people with a new sense of freedom; in this encounter, they become free to overcome those things that limit them and to envision entirely new possibilities for their own lives. Beauty puts us in play, as Troy says. It calls us to get off the sidelines and become an active participant in life. When humans encounter the beautiful, they can praise or confess, nothing else. Troy lists three techniques for communities to become works of art themselves: (1) they must "open source" their translation dilemmas, that is, become transparent with the difficulties involved in communicating the meaning of Christian faith across traditions, thereby letting others interpret the faith; (2) Christians must increase ritual agency, that is, help people become skilled practitioners of Christian rituals; and (3) Christians must create open space for listening, releasing each person's rationale to God's realm, putting themselves in the presence of beauty.

In chapter 12, "Mission among Individual Consumers," Stefan Paas writes about how Western culture has changed from a culture of obligation to one of consumption. In the Netherlands, the Dutch do not have to go to church. They may want to, if they decide to, but it is not imposed on them culturally in any way. They want connection, but they assemble their spirituality themselves, and it is not imposed by any one tradition. For the Dutch, church is like a restaurant. They want what they receive at the restaurant to be good, worthwhile, and meaningful; the chefs (pastors) do not serve just anything, but only what they themselves consider to be of value. Paas clarifies the difference between consumption and consumerism. Consumption is simply the acknowledgment in Western cultures that contemporary people are "choosing" creatures. It is not a pejorative term, but simply a description of how Westerners have been formed. Consumerism, however, is an ethical category—it describes efforts at fulfillment through materialism, experiences, and ephemeral wants and desires. The restaurant provides a place for consumption but not consumerism.

For Paas, worship must both attract and form people. What the church offers to people is a gift—for example, home groups—but it cannot do much more than offer. The restaurant attendees (church visitors) are free to choose their level of involvement. Volunteer commitments, such as doing service in the city, are the most popular part of church life. People today like spirituality and service, but the communal aspect—in other words, the weekly commitment— is difficult for them. For Paas, the leaders must ask the attendees, how can we help you take the next step in your spiritual trek? Ultimately, the leader is not responsible for the attendees; he or she acts more like a guide. In post-Christendom, people want responsibility for their own lives.

Even though sociologists of religion have warned about growing secularization, interest in spirituality has not gone away, writes Steve Hollinghurst in his chapter on the new spirituality culture (chap. 13). In contrast to what popular media may say, people are not running to atheism. Belief remains high, but in Europe it is not Christianity in which they believe. Belief in God changed from seeing God as a personal being to understanding God as a life force. Postmodern culture combines with consumerism to create a mix-and-match faith that meets individual spiritual needs. New spiritualities are client-based faiths in which the adherents are clients of a small group of practitioners who often function as priests.

Worship in new spirituality culture is similar to pagan rituals or rites, and the backgrounds of the converts influence the worship style. Worship will probably revere nature and revolve around the seasons. Dance, drumming, and mystical readings may all play a part. Community life might appear very Eastern. Each participant is on a path; new spirituality encourages changes of direction on that path, but not the need to cross barriers. These communities will allow all seekers to go at their own speed. There might be storytelling circles, meditation gatherings, or other types of groups in community. Following Christ is a part of the journey, but one might start from a different place in another tradition. Mission might take place at New Age fairs and festivals.

Christians may bring part of their tradition to the festival, be it prayer, meditation, or prophecy. They will not be bringing God to these cultures, though,
for God is already there. Leadership in new spirituality communities is flat,
and leaders will probably be unpaid, not serving as part of an institution.
Hollinghurst argues that we need holy Christians in these areas, working
within these cultures.

Practices

Paul Roberts begins the first chapter in part 3, on practices, by explaining
that after Constantine, worship changed from that of a persecuted minority
anticipating future glory to that of a triumphant church holding public celebrations in large civic buildings. He asks if the purpose of worship is to fulfill
the mission of the church in the world. In the early church this was unthinkable: unbelievers were forbidden to come to worship. Missional worship is a
modern phenomenon that occurs when a church in Christendom seeks to lure
a de-churched person back into church (e.g., all seeker-sensitive strategies).

Roberts argues that worship must stay grounded in creation, in the real
material world. The church proclaims God, but this is a real world in which
God became flesh. Worship must be an encounter of each person's humanity
with one another and with God. Part of the challenge of worship is keeping
those practices that are central for Christian identity (such as Communion,
Scripture, prayer, baptism) but letting go of others that are unwelcoming to
new cultures. Worship takes place in a context of beauty: worship space is art
space. Emerging churches return art to the people—creating worship together.
Power structures have changed in the alternative worship movement as they
abandon worship ministry and restrict liturgical roles. They remove all cultural
triumphalism and create worship for those not in power. Radical hospitality
can be a theme of worship in post-Christendom. Christians should not invite
outsiders to come to church, but must dwell in the other's space, even with
their own internal boundaries.

For Dwight J. Friesen (chap. 15), post-Christendom changed the way formation must be performed in the Christian community. During the Constantinian era, many public institutions partnered with the church to form people
in particularly Christian ways, leaving the church to focus on its particular
functions, such as preaching the Word and administering the sacraments. All
the public sectors, administered by the government, were deeply influenced and
staffed by the church. The church could discipline and educate its members
through official sanctions and institutions. However, in post-Christendom the

church's partners in formation no longer push people in Christian directions. So the church must reimagine the activities of Christian formation today. The church needs to tell its story again. Christians must see all of life, not just church life, through the lens of Christ.

For Friesen, Christian hospitality and service must become core practices for today's church, as should stewardship of creation. Christians must underscore the importance of baptism and Communion too. Through the arts, the church can create public rituals, embodying the way of Christ in the surrounding culture. This re-forms the church's collective imagination. Formation after Christendom must commit to a use of space that reconnects with the neighborhood and creates places to walk and a way to know neighbors. Friesen talks about "rooting" and "linking"—keeping the church grounded in the neighborhood and linked to diverse groups beyond themselves. The church's music and art must be prophetic and impart a missional identity, not just a personal relationship with God. Loving God is very everyday, grounded in regular activity. These inviting practices help churches in the task of formation now that they are left holding the ball in post-Christendom.

Mission is synonymous with holistic transformation, according to Tobias Faix in chapter 16. Both shalom (in the Old Testament) and salvation (New Testament) express the transformation of all relationships—God-human, human-human, human-self, and human-creation. Transformation must take place in all spheres of reality, be they economic, social, or political. Transformation advocates for change in small villages and large cities alike. Working for transformation is worship to God. Transformation starts with local churches.

Transformation, in regard to creation, is stewardship. Christians are to advocate for the preservation of creation and work against destructive forces. Transformation as healing, as shown by Jesus, is physical and social restoration. Churches often distance themselves from the ones in society who are most in need of transformation. Do Christians have a middle-class gospel? The best option for transformation in a pluralistic society is dialogue. A transformed church will reflect multiculturalism, in terms of people and culture, and demonstrate economic sharing. People are searching for God and for a community of fellow searchers, and a transformed community, through manifesting the reign of God, can invite them to sing with the church the tune of heaven.

MaryKate Morse, in chapter 17, compares leadership to riding a horse. The rider equates to *conscious* leadership, and the horse to the *unconscious*. Leaders often focus on the rider and ignore the horse, but the horse greatly affects the rider. The unconscious responds to the environment, to stress, to a lack of sleep. In a culture of fear, this can present real challenges, because if a leader feels threatened, the unconscious takes control. Morse offers helpful

xxxviii   Introduction

steps to bring the horse under control: name the threat, reflect on its origin, and pray. Every time a leader feels out of control, he or she must go to prayer and practice spiritual disciplines such as Sabbath keeping.

Morse argues that leaders need to care for their environment, and that men and women do well to share leadership in the church. That is, the church needs them both to create a hybrid leadership structure. Leaders must lead their people into diverse settings. If this feels threatening, they need to be able to calm their unconscious minds. Leaders can use creativity to challenge people and to allow them to create sacred space in which to reenact the Bible story. In a culture in which consumerism is the horse running amok, the leader must pull in the reins and model simplicity. In a culture of fragmentation, the leader must model a spirituality that puts everything back together again—work, home, church are all one in Christ. One manifestation of this desire for spirituality is new monasticism, which forms an integrative spirituality characterized by contemplation, hospitality, and service of the poor. To lead in this context, leaders must be aware of what shapes them. By becoming aware of the horse and rider, leadership may be better equipped to attend to God's plans in the world.

Experiments

Ralph Watkins, in chapter 18, writes about The Underground, a church fully at home in hip-hop culture in southern California. Hip-hop culture arose within urban, African American youth culture in the 1970s. From very early on, however, hip-hop became multicultural. Today, hip-hop churches are filled with Generation Xers and Millennials, those born between 1965 and 1986, as well as those outside the age range who support the culture.

From dress to dance to praise, the church practices in this movement are inherently hip-hop. Worship is led by a DJ and the worship team consists of African Americans, whites, and Latinos. Each person participates in worship as a cocreator—there are no spectators in hip-hop churches. The preaching includes multiple texts. Hip-hop churches are highly missional because they are close to the poor—both in their roots and in current practice. Leadership is transparent, and authenticity is highly important.

In chapter 19, in Andreas Østerlund Nielsen's story of Bykirken in Aarhus, Denmark, we see a "tasty" experiment taking place in a Danish restaurant. Bykirken created a set of small groups that eventually met in a restaurant's downtown courtyard. The new congregation stayed within the Lutheran church but became a "congregation of choice," because church planting is rare in

Denmark. The restaurant was the primary connecting point of the community for seven years. Of the fifty people regularly attending, all but a few had been part of a Christian community before. Their lives were encouraged and sustained by their time at the restaurant. However, when leader Nielsen sought to move the entire church into more active mission, he felt resistance. The church closed after a seven-year run.

Bykirken was a very creative group. Each month they had a "prayer and brunch," with white tablecloths, homemade brunch buffet, and easy jazz as the backdrop to a full church service. It was very participatory and ended with Communion. All service was done in teams, and everyone was part of one. Sunday gatherings formed the participants but never really served as evangelism to unbelievers. The basic unit of the community was the small group—five to eight people meeting twice monthly to share a meal, read the Bible together, participate in discussion and prayer, and serve in mission. Some would form cowalking groups or provide self-help courses for the community. Practical leadership training in the sorts of skills needed for Bykirken was foreign for Denmark. In the end, they had to teach themselves everything.

Nadia Bolz-Weber, who shares the story of House for All Sinners and Saints in chapter 20, is not a stereotypical Lutheran pastor, but she found truth in Lutheran theology and liturgy. She wanted to start a community that looked like her—postmodern urban mystics who live outside the mainstream. She started House for All Sinners and Saints in her living room with seven others.

As they live for one another in the community, participants in HFASS cocreate worship together. During a worship gathering, they may sing old hymns and assemble bleach kits for drug users. Nadia is an adaptive leader, moving and responding to each additional member of the community. They are active in the community with public events that are both unconventional (e.g., beer and hymns in a bar) and identity forming for the members. She understands her authority as a pastor while welcoming a participative community.

After almost giving up on all church models, Eric Zander, director of the Belgian Evangelical Mission, took a leave of absence to discover the church he never knew. He started a degree program in London and interviewed leaders and observed churches throughout Europe and the United States. What he received was encouragement to begin again, with L'Autre Rive ("The Other Bank") in Gembloux, Belgium, which he discusses in chapter 21.

To start, Eric became very involved in the local community, serving in various projects and becoming known as a positive resource to the community. He then began to ask among all his social networks what a church ought to be like that was both local and contextual. He asked both Christians and non-Christians to help him design, even in a tentative way, a new church. The first experiment was the creation of a monthly breakfast for the church community, each time with a different theme. They located themselves in a public social hall, so as to not frighten away the nonreligious. Around a decorated meal, they created a liturgy that mixed the religious with the everyday. Talks from the front inspired conversation around the tables. They used contemporary media and ancient chanting. Zander hoped to create a kind of space that the people had never experienced. It was both Catholic and Protestant in its embodiment. Repeatedly, Zander asks the outside community for feedback. Christians and non-Christians benefit equally from the meetings. Mission may mean local service organizations presenting during the service. During the week, the church does not have Bible studies or prayer, but people are encouraged to reach out into the local community. They look to include nonprofessionals in the leadership of the church. They continue to develop their community one day at a time.

Eileen Suico, who shares the story of her church in chapter 22, started "With" with a group of young Asian American youth in 2003, and they became a self-contained church in 2010. At one point they were so focused on the church community that they lost touch not only with the rest of creation but also with the very present reality of problems in Federal Way, twenty-five miles south of Seattle. The youth became burned out on legalistic ways of leadership and discipleship, but at the breaking point they received a fresh understanding of God's grace and his trinitarian nature.

With was transformed into a relational community, not just within themselves but to the people they serve in Puget Sound. Now they are quite flexible in their life together. One week they might hold a worship service, but the next week they might serve the community (by helping someone move or attending local car shows in their area). They desire to see God worshiped everywhere they go. The church has many groups based on interest, and no one goes to them all, but they do cross-fertilize. They are also quite missional: they may have one group protesting against modern-day slavery and another working for green initiatives. Their hub is Facebook and other online media. Eileen is the pastor and does things differently than male leaders, and that is something that she and With have learned to accept and celebrate. Leadership is fluid in the community, and all are called to lead in areas in which God gives them ability.

In chapter 23 Mark Scandrette tells the story of his progression from youth pastor to leader of the Jesus Dojo, or the Way of Jesus, in San Francisco. He found that youth were not interested in the entertainment style of formation, nor in regular church events. They wanted a way of life together, something active and challenging, something real. With others, he had been asking what form the church should take. That question led them to simply move forward and seek to live out the life of Jesus in present-day San Francisco.

In the Dojo, participants commit to a nine-month curriculum that involves a series of projects and learning labs. Following the Dojo, they may join a Tribe community for a year. Their worship is usually through art forms, poetry, spoken word, or painting. But their focus is always on action, so it is usually tightly connected to the neighborhoods around them. These groups seek to practice the Way of Jesus in community. They agree to a rule of life; it is seasonal, and its spiritual rhythms are in sync with the calendar. Through the Dojo, Scandrette realized he needed to change the type of leadership he practiced to that of the rabbi: modeling, helping, and mentoring an apprentice in a way that helps him or her take on the life of Jesus.

In chapter 24, Bob Whitesel analyzes St. Thomas' Anglican Church in Sheffield, England, specifically focusing on the impact that losing their venue had on the congregation. This church grew into the largest Anglican church in England in a fairly brief period, and Whitesel's essay examines the nature of that growth. The church is a local ecumenical project, in this case a Baptist and Anglican church yoked together. When Mike Breen joined the church in 1993, significant changes came to the community. He created a program called Lifeshapes as well as small groups where primary discipleship happened. Groups of three to seven small groups formed clusters, and these extended families created a midsize space between the small group and the larger congregation. It is at the cluster level where most growth occurred.

In 2000, St. Tom's moved into The Roxy nightclub. Many unchurched joined at that time. They met twice each Sunday at The Roxy and once at St. Thomas' Crookes parish. Multiple subcongregations developed. The next year, The Roxy was condemned, and they had to find a new venue rather quickly. Seventeen cluster groups began to meet weekly all over Sheffield. After a year, they grew to thirty-five clusters with 2,500 members, most under the age of forty. Clusters developed their own culture and leadership. Eventually they created nine celebrations, all distinct, around Sheffield. They soon moved into a huge warehouse, and the numbers of meetings contracted at that point. During the church's history, the quickest growth happened when they lost their venue, but the community continues to grow.

Kelly Bean talks in chapter 25 about her journey to starting Urban Abbey in Portland, Oregon. After raising her kids and living the American dream, she felt something was missing. After finding some like-minded souls, she moved into a poor area of Portland and started a community. She longed for a community where she did not have to make an appointment to see a friend or talk to a neighbor. It began with two couples, and later up to fifteen others joined them.

Urban Abbey became a sustainable place where cars could be shared and members' purchases were understood to be connected to countless other people. They planted a community garden, welcomed artists, and were an intergenerational group of people who came from many different denominations and professions. They were all white, but they were willing to learn. Artists gave their public art as gifts to the neighborhood. Their art served to heal, provoke, unite. They hung out in coffee shops and made friends with all the locals. Urban Abbey became Bean's new dream come true.

Traditions

Mark MacDonald opens part 5, "Traditions," with "Indigenous and Anglican," in which he shares about the effort in Canada to create a native-governed branch of the Anglican Church. The indigenous people did know misery, and many Westerners know that story. What is not so well known is the extent to which native Christian spirituality is thriving. Indigenous people are experiencing a spiritual renewal, but most Western understandings either are ignorant of or minimize this fact. In Canada, the scandals with the Anglican-run Indian residential school program in the 1960s led to reform in the Anglican Church in Canada. By the 1980s, an indigenous council within the Anglican Church began to oversee the Anglican Church's response to the abuse. Sacred Circles were formed in the late 1980s, giving indigenous Anglicans a way to address issues pertinent to them. In 1993, the primate apologized to the native community. A covenant was created to allow for the eventual goal of self-determination for the indigenous peoples. In 2006, the Sacred Circle requested fifteen indigenous bishops across Canada, and their own national indigenous bishop. In 2007, Mark MacDonald became that bishop.

The indigenous consultations practice gospel-based discipleship—a way to meditatively read Scripture in community, similar to *lectio divina*. Scripture infuses the gatherings, as the native peoples do not recognize a sacred/secular split. Gospel jamboree is another native practice spreading throughout native communities—it is a night of singing, prayer, and testimony. There is a hopeful future for native peoples in Canada. The First Nations people might teach the Western church some relational dynamics it needs to understand, such as the nature of individuality within a community and a family, and the necessity of an ecological faith.

In chapter 27, "Turning the Ocean Liner," Bishop Graham Cray discusses the huge changes afloat in the Anglican Church in England. The Anglican Church's report *Mission-Shaped Church* was published in 2004. Its major recommendation was to supplement the parish location-based system with fresh expressions of church. The church created a team, supported by the archbishop, to be a resource to the dioceses. They instituted a pioneer ministry track to ordain pioneer church planters.

Fresh expressions might mean an existing church reimagining itself, or it might translate into starting a new expression in the larger community. Most often these will be new congregations within existing churches. Bishops now encourage the planting of these fresh expressions, so it is both bottom-up and top-down. Rowan Williams came up with the idea of mixed-economy church—a combination of the inherited church and new expressions. The task is to reinvent church for the majority of the English who do not see the church as a resource. In these fresh expressions, leaders decide to follow God and join in God's work. They must die to their own ideas, only to let God come and bring his. Fresh expressions begin with listening, followed by loving and serving, building community, and exploring discipleship. At that point the church might take shape and worship might be developed. Church becomes an event around the risen Jesus long before it is an institution. It is to be God's mission, and it is to be incarnational: it must follow the pattern of Jesus. The Spirit brings the future into the present. Christ is present in the community, fully, yet each community needs all the others to realize the body of Christ.

Markus Weimer (chap. 28) explores the beginning of the fresh expressions movement in Germany, as it takes its inspiration from the Church of England. The church statistics in Germany are dire, as they are in the rest of Europe. These young leaders look to reform the church, but where to start? Weimer begins with a few recommendations.

German church leaders must abandon the fear of change. They must move beyond their fear of failure. The national leadership and the local churches must develop closer levels of partnership, as there is distrust on all sides. National leaders must encourage and support the initiators of new work. The dialogue must be two ways, however, and local leaders should not start things on their own either. They must welcome a diversity of structures in the parish, support the idea of a mixed-economy church, and encourage local initiatives that are highly creative. Already fresh expressions are emerging in Germany. They are characterized by creative worship, service to the environment and the poor, and new leadership training. They hope to work alongside the existing structures.

In the conclusion, I briefly narrate some of the patterns identified throughout the volume and attempt a tentative answer to the questions driving the work.

The Conversation within the Chapters

In addition to the main text by the authors of the chapters, you will notice other voices there as well. In each chapter, the other authors in the book offer comments and connect their ideas to that particular chapter. These comments appear in shaded boxes within the text. The original author of the chapter, in many instances, responds to those comments or questions, and his or her response is embedded in the text in an unshaded box. Finally, Eddie Gibbs's words, through his writings on these topics, are added to the mix as well. His comments appear as sidebars within the text.

Part 1

Peoples

1

Iglesias Emergentes in Latin America

Osías Segura-Guzmán

When we think of a vibrant church in Latin America, the image of a Pentecostal or neo-Pentecostal congregation may come to mind. However, the term "Pentecostal" would probably not be used to describe most emergent churches.[1] Emergent congregations in Latin America are very few in number. They are usually small congregations working under the radar, and they are often stigmatized and overshadowed by larger churches. Finding information about the *iglesia emergente* (emergent church) in Latin America was an enormous challenge because the movement is still very young and small.

When I began exploring the existence of the *iglesia emergente* in Latin America, I contacted my younger Facebook friends throughout Latin America, various vagabond theologians, and some of my former seminary students in Costa Rica. Some of them shared their opinions on the movement and some

---

1. In English, the phrase "emerging church" is usually used to describe a worldwide movement of Christians intentionally ministering among the emerging generation of postmodern people. The term "emergent church" generally refers to one specific kind of church in North Atlantic societies within the emerging church movement. In Latin America, the Spanish term *iglesia emergente*, which would translate literally to the phrase "emergent church," is used to describe both the movement and particular churches within it. There is not a good Spanish equivalent for the term "emerging." Therefore, in this chapter, *iglesia emergente* will be used throughout, but it may refer both to the movement and to a particular local church.

referred me to ministries they knew. Thus to collect data and references I started a Facebook page called "Iglesias Emergentes en America Latina." The challenge, however, is that not all of those who called themselves *emergente* truly fit the criteria of emerging churches, while some who do seem to be part of this group do not call themselves *emergente*. Some perceived their churches as fragile, and maybe not even as churches, and for fear of criticism they resisted providing data for this research. I cannot say that I found as much information as I wanted, but I was able to explore some of what this diverse but very small movement has to offer.

> "Emerging church" is a difficult category concept. It is a recognised term for churches that are reshaping themselves for a postmodern world. But in another sense, hopefully, aren't all churches emerging, in that we are changing and evolving for a new context? If a church self-identifies as emerging I refer to it as such and encourage it to ensure that the reality matches up to the rhetoric. *Darren Cronshaw*

> The emerging church phenomenon's strength lies at the grassroots level at which it operates. Its theory arises from its praxis—and is consequently more diverse and less coherent.
>
> Eddie Gibbs (CM, 36)

It is important to state at the outset that I am a Latin American who has spent most of my time studying the church in this region. Nevertheless, no matter how long I will spend studying the church in Latin America, I believe I will never be able to fully explain it. Perhaps I can only describe it. The church in Latin America is so diverse and mutates so fast that when one thinks one can typologize it, one realizes that it has changed again. Therefore, this chapter is an exploratory work filled with descriptions. I do not know if I am portraying the right image of emerging churches in Latin America, but the approximation in this chapter satisfies me. I seek to answer a series of questions in order to begin to understand *iglesias emergentes*.

> A challenge of mapping small organic-style churches is that they are not as measurable and are more sensitive to the potentially intrusive nature of surveys and research. *Darren Cronshaw*

First, I will begin by exploring the concern of whether *iglesias emergentes* are another "packaged" ecclesiology coming from the North. Second, I will briefly discuss in what ways Latin America is and is not a postmodern society. Third, I will place *iglesias emergentes* within the context of other postmodern churches in Latin America. Finally, I will end this chapter by describing three case studies that illustrate a spectrum of *iglesias emergentes* in Latin America.

Culture

Christianity in Latin America

Colonial and neocolonial forces have exploited this diverse and beautiful region for many centuries. Let us remember that Christianity came to Latin America along with the conquistadors' enterprise. Among these conquistadors were missionaries who were often unaware of the oppression in which they participated simply by their association with the structure of domination in colonialism. Those missionaries belonged mostly to the two main branches of Christianity, the Roman Catholic and the Protestant churches, which came to this region three hundred years apart. First, in the 1500s, the Roman Catholic Church arrived in what is today known as Latin America as the ideological force of the Spanish conquistadors. Then, in the 1800s, the Protestant and evangelical churches came to Latin America as the ideological force of British and United States capitalism.

> The Philippines is also predominantly influenced by the Roman Catholic Church because of the Spanish influence, which lasted for almost four hundred years. The Spanish conquistadors came to the Philippines at almost the same time. *Eileen Suico*

> Yes, there are similarities between the Catholicism in Asia and Latin America. However, Latin American countries became republics and embraced the European enlightenment in the early nineteenth century. This makes this region "Western," although it is part of the two-thirds world. Latin America experienced all three: premodernity, modernity, and postmodernity. *Osías Segura-Guzmán*

While recognizing that Latin America suffered ecclesiological colonialism, we also need to accept the reality that Latin Americans have not been passive recipients. That the Roman Catholic Church and the Protestant, evangelical, Pentecostal, and neo-Pentecostal churches in Latin America look different from the rest of the world is a sign of innovation, demonstrating contextualization, although perhaps at times also religious syncretism. We have locally adopted and innovated all of the "products" we received from global empires. What was once an outside idea becomes our idea. Nevertheless, there is a big difference between innovation and the contextualization of ecclesiologies, and Latin American churches need to work harder on the latter task.

Is Latin America a Postmodern Society?

In Latin America, one can find premodern, modern, and postmodern worldviews coexisting in the same space. Social evolutionists may not agree with this statement because they would argue that in order for postmodern expressions of religion in Latin America to exist, modernity in its full expression must first have flourished in the region. In Latin America, however, the progression through these categories has not been as linear as it perhaps was in the North Atlantic societies. For example, in many parts of Latin America folk-Catholic pilgrimages remain a vibrant part of society, with people from all generations participating together in them. This type of ritual could be classified as a premodern expression of faith. At the same time, within many evangelical churches there is still a strong emphasis on orthodoxy and rational expressions of faith, as evidenced by the sermon occupying at least half of most worship services. Many of these churches continue to operate primarily from within a modern worldview, emphasizing a rigid set of beliefs and practices. As we will see in the case studies below, there is also evidence of postmodern approaches to the practice of the Christian faith. Therefore, within Christianity in Latin America, we see this combination of premodern, modern, and postmodern worldviews.

> Postmodernity presents a missional challenge to the Protestant churches and the evangelical movements that arose in Europe and North America during the era of modernity. Some of these movements go back to the sixteenth-century Reformation in Europe, while others are the product of nineteenth-century Revivalism in North America.
>
> Eddie Gibbs (CM, 20–21)

While it is recognizably oversimplistic, for the purposes of argument, we may label as premodern the Roman Catholic Church presence in most parts of the mestizo population, with its folk-Catholic expressions. Modern churches may be characterized as evangelical (Protestant), Pentecostal, and charismatic congregations. More recently, new postmodern congregations focused on reaching out to young, well-educated populations are beginning to take root.

These postmodern minorities of middle-class young professionals live, paradoxically, in contexts of poverty, violence, and exploitation. They have access to higher education, learn English as a second language, and obtain better-paying jobs than previous generations. Some of these jobs are the result of outsourcing from economic empires (e.g., call centers) and tourism services, among others in the service sector, where they can receive good salaries that may distinguish them as middle or upper-middle class.[2] They may live in gated

---

2. Bernice Martin, in "From Pre- to Postmodernity in Latin America: The Case of Pentecostalism," in *Religion, Modernity and Postmodernity*, ed. Paul Heelas (Oxford, UK: Blackwell, 1998), 105–6, says: "There are a series of recent global processes, which have resulted in the emergence of postmodern cultures and postindustrial economies worldwide. The primary components of this model are: (1) globally circulating objects (i.e., capital, goods, services, information and

neighborhoods, and what they expect of a church is very different from what those in the lower class may desire. This group and the churches beginning to develop to serve them represent a postmodern stream within Latin America.

Experiments

Are There Postmodern Churches in Latin America?

New religious movements within Latin American Christianity continue to bloom, among them many types of new and small congregations trying to reach people in postmodern contexts. Examples of such expressions include satellite churches, internet churches, house churches, theater churches, churches without walls, and some megachurches that are trying to move away from the seeker-sensitive model and prosperity theology. While some of these models, judged from a missiological perspective, are short-term, laughable, and actually painful to see, others may provide helpful ecclesiological options.

The leaders of these postmodern congregations in Latin America, who are generally under thirty-five years of age, were part of traditional denominations and/or may have had some antagonism within megachurches. They may have participated in the first attempts to bring the creative use of arts and music into worship and to indigenize Christian music. Abusive and monolithic leadership structures, weak community building, and doctrinal legalism disappointed them, pushing them to develop something different and nontraditional.

> The monolithic and weak community of the established church in Latin America could describe most of the Anglican Church in the UK, with its top-down directive structure and its, for the most part, nominal attendees. It was amid this environment that John Wimber visited St. Thomas' Church, and soon a focus on small groups (which had for some time been popular in UK churches) was combined with the emphasis on worship encounter within the Vineyard movement. This holistic and healthy structure resulted in growth and eventually gave away to what St. Tom's leaders described as their brittle megachurch organization. They too, like these emerging churches in Latin America, felt a disappointment in their megatriumph. Little wonder that when St. Thomas' Church lost The Roxy as their venue, the leaders seemed genuinely relieved. More research should probably be conducted on anxiety that is birthed from monolithic organizational structures and any sense of relief that occurs once this direction is abandoned in favor of something more flexible, temporal, and mobile. *Bob Whitesel*

communication); (2) mobile subjects (i.e., global labour market involving large-scale migrations of both permanent and temporary sorts at all levels of skill); (3) steady increments of both cognitive and aesthetic reflexivity; (4) and an ever greater individualization in both economic and social life."

What fueled these postmodern churches was probably a combination of some of the following issues: the influence of Latin American theology and missiology professors educated in North Atlantic academia; the writings of theologians and missiologists from North Atlantic countries; the easy access via the internet to global social networks; the creative pastoral applications of the Latin American concept of *misión integral* (integral/holistic mission); young creative leaders who left their traditional denominations or mega-churches looking to develop something fresh and new; Christian university students exposed to postmodern ideas; and Christian artists looking for ways to express their faith within and outside the church. Another influential event was the theological speaking tour of Rene Padilla and Brian McLaren in 2006. Other influences have come from books that have been translated from English into Spanish by authors like John Burke, N. T. Wright, Brian McLaren, Eddie Gibbs, Alan Hirsch, and Frank Viola, among others.

Are There Iglesias Emergentes in Latin America?

Within this historical context, then, it is not surprising that the *iglesia emergente* in some cases may be considered yet another "packaged ecclesiology" that has come through globalization, as Christians in Latin America are exposed to these models through media, blogs and websites, books, and contemporary missionaries. Most of the cases discovered in this small research project had some influence from one or more of these sources. A few cases were actually churches that were planted by US missionaries with a postmodern mind-set, and their churches are linked to emerging churches in the United States. Others, however, were started by Latin Americans who were wrestling with similar issues to those they read about from the sources mentioned above. Nevertheless, as was the case with previous ecclesiologies, innovation, adaptation, and contextualization took place. A small group of churches were started by Latin Americans before they knew the terminology of *iglesia emergente*, and, as such, they could be considered an indigenous expression of this movement. It was only as they read more about this movement that they began to consider that they might be doing something similar.

As in Europe and North America, churches characterized by modernity struggle to engage the postmodern generation. As in France and southern Europe, emerging churches can be perceived as another import from "outside" rather than a fresh expression of Christianity emerging incarnationally. *Blayne Waltrip*

> Most of the Western emergent movement is in reaction to the modern evangelical church. In the context of a majority Roman Catholic culture, where evangelicals are the minority, emergent experiments are often missionary endeavors based on imported strategies, the exact opposite to the original emergent concept. Genuine emergence should rethink church contextually, even if the result is completely different from the North Atlantic versions; and actually by definition it should be as different as the culture is. *Eric Zander*

> Contextualization is a process that involves engaging the biblical text with the local culture for missional purposes. Each community has the task to interpret the text and the context in different ways and at different levels, and to discern the Spirit to find out how to respond to one or more challenges in the local context. Who are we to judge what is genuine emergence or not? Is there a cross-cultural rule of thumb for the emerging church that applies to two-thirds-world churches? *Osías Segura-Guzmán*

Latin American missiologists and theologians continue to debate whether the *iglesia emergente* is another imported ecclesiology. This is a very important complaint to understand. Latin Americans have seen many religious colonial trends throughout the centuries. First, there was the Roman Catholic Church; next, the Protestant ethnic congregations for expatriates; and then the evangelical churches, including the Pentecostal and now the neo-Pentecostal congregations, with their multinational television networks.[3] Allow me to be poetic in order not to sound rude in judging these movements: all these seeds were imported. Once planted, they grew and gave their fruit. They tasted good and became our fruit. However, ultimately, they do not satisfy our nutritional needs. Latin Americans are not always able to contextualize these expressions of the church to meet our own deepest spiritual and ecclesiological nutritional needs.

> This concern, that emerging expressions of church may be the result of ecclesial colonialism, was felt by the leaders of St. Tom's Church in Sheffield, England, too. It had been the influence of southern Californian John Wimber that started St. Tom's Church on a trajectory to become England's largest and youngest Anglican church. St. Tom's created upon this southern California influence their own indigenous forms. For example, the music early on had a sound and style that was reminiscent of the Vineyard worship music (a strength of the Vineyard movement was not only signs and wonders but also their heartfelt musical genre). More recently, I noticed that their musical genre is now more heavily influenced by the band

3. In Latin America there is a conceptual difference between the evangelical and Protestant movements. "Protestant" usually refers to historical churches born before 1850 in the United States and Europe that then came to Latin America, such as the Episcopal Church. The evangelical church refers to all other denominations that came during the missionary movement from the United States in the early 1900s.

U2. One worship leader said that U2 had such an impact on the Commonwealth that it had become a native style and was thus reflected in most of the music. Even signs and wonders that had often characterized Vineyard churches seemed to be exchanged at St. Tom's for a more "Pentecostal" prophetic ministry. So it appears that, over time, these British Christians tailored and adapted potential colonial influences, making them distinctly their own. *Bob Whitesel*

It seems evident that there are *iglesias emergentes* in Latin America. The difficulty comes in knowing how to identify them. As already mentioned, some call themselves emergent but they are not, while others do not call themselves emergent but they are. So it becomes difficult to identify these churches. There appears to be a spectrum upon which churches fall, including those that self-identify as *iglesias emergentes* and those that have the characteristics of *iglesias emergentes*, whether or not they call themselves by this name. This spectrum will be illustrated by three case studies drawn from the churches and leaders who participated in the small study done for this chapter.[4] These case studies give a small glimpse of how the emergent church may look in Latin America at this point in time. I will present information from all three case studies pertaining to their worship practices, community values, missional activities, and leadership structure.

Interludio (Interlude)[5] is a community that includes people from both evangelical and Roman Catholic backgrounds, and it is under the accountability of the Vineyard movement of churches. Its pastor, José Chacón, started this community with his wife in April 2008. After much prayer, the Spirit guided them to leave their previous church and begin the journey of developing a new kind of congregation with a different ecclesiology.

The international influence of the Vineyard movement may be understudied and underappreciated. The Vineyard movement exemplified an early postmodern, experience-driven but rationally supported authentic spirituality. In many ways, John Wimber's quest to distance himself from the more intellectual and less supernatural confines of the Calvary Chapel movement may have made the Vineyard movement more appealing around the world. *Bob Whitesel*

The second church is a house church. Several years ago, the teenage children of Alexis Valverde told him they did not want to go back to their megachurch. They wanted an extended devotional time as a family in which they could invite

4. The emergent church leaders who participated in this study, among other informants, were Marco Andrade (Ecuador), Anyul Led Rivas (Venezuela), Angel and Claudia Monzón (Guatemala), Gustavo Frederico (Brazil), Natanael Disla (Dominican Republic), Lustein Lopez (Mexico), Alexandra Mantilla (Costa Rican missionary in Uruguay), and Pablo Moran (Panama).
    5. For more information see http://interludio.ning.com.

some friends to join them in worship. Valverde himself was not very happy in the megachurch, so as a family they decided to pray about this change. After a few weeks of meetings, friends with a similar interest of looking for a new way to follow Christ joined this house church. Today, approximately twenty people participate in the group. Most of them came from megachurches, where they burned out because of spiritual abuse and a lack of pastoral care. This house church is part of an informal network of five or more house church congregations that have been exchanging experiences for the past ten years.

The third church is the Iglesia Punk in Argentina. The leader and pastor, Juan Granado, gathered a group of thirty ex-punks in a house in 2003. After a while, the group considered Juan's leadership and changed its direction toward a more open and welcoming church. After that, they met in larger homes or parks, and they currently meet in a Baptist church building.

Practices

Worship

For worship gatherings, Interludio meets on Monday nights (because some of its people work on Sundays). They start by eating a light meal brought by the people themselves. The majority of the attendees are artists, graphic designers, and video producers, as well as musicians. Not all songs are Christian, but they "motivate people to connect to God."[6] In between songs, they project quotes from famous thinkers. A video clip often promotes a discussion as part of the worship experience, and at the end a teaching speech (or sermon) is given.

> One of the reoccurring themes I noticed in emerging churches is a desire to give artists of all disciplines access to worship and participation. Whether it is the artist corner at Vintage Faith Church in Santa Cruz or the art galleries that characterize many other emerging churches, these congregations seem intent on making all artists, not just musical ones, welcome. *Bob Whitesel*

Worship at the house church starts at the table of hospitality with coffee and bread. After approximately thirty to forty minutes, someone begins to play a praise song and the singing starts. While singing, anyone may pray, read the Scripture, or share a thought or homily, and another person may share a deeper study that may or may not have been prepared in advance. The

6. José Chacón, interview by Osías Segura-Guzmán, September 27, 2010, on Interludio community as emergent church.

group is not Pentecostal in nature, but "the Spirit guides the worship time, determining when to end."[7]

The Punk Church meets on Sundays for three hours for conversation, debate, prayer, and listening to a Bible teaching, and again on Tuesdays for Bible study. They present worship as something simple, creative, and closely linked to the primitive church in Acts. There is no praise music, although sometimes there is music if they feel like singing. There is no pulpit, no temple, and no tithing; but there is a teaching moment, they meet in a "borrowed" temple, and they voluntarily financially support the church. "We don't have any traditional structure except baptism, Holy Communion, and weddings."[8]

Community

The house church develops its ministries of justice, evangelism, and discipleship not as a program, but as something that "flows out of our daily lives, according to the gifts of the Spirit."[9] Evangelism happens when the members of the house church are invited to visit their family members' homes. Food, singing, and Bible study are simple and located in an inviting atmosphere for nonbelievers. The idea of the meeting is to allow nonbelievers to participate, experience the gospel, and to feel convicted of sins. They also do evangelism by inviting university students to participate in their regular meetings. The house church creates a space for them to ask questions and then receive discipleship in a natural flow. Some of the members participate in poor neighborhoods with ministries that serve children at risk. They take offerings mostly to help those in need. Thus the church community affects even the neighbors, especially those going through tough financial situations. All who are being touched by the gospel are reached in an integral way (i.e., personal, familiar, and through neighborhoods).

Juan Granado, pastor at The Punk Church, states that "our mission in the beginning was to make the church understand that God does not exclude certain people, and that God can lift up anyone, no matter his or her looks."[10] The church requires theological training for those who want to serve:

> The whole church studies four years in a seminary. . . . The discipleship is short, but from there to the seminary. . . . Everyone must study; they must be teachers,

7. Alexis Valverde, interview by Osías Segura-Guzmán, October 21, 2010, on Ekklesia House Church as emergent church.

8. Juan Granado, interview by Osías Segura-Guzmán, June 26, 2011.

9. Valverde, interview.

10. Granado, interview.

and we give them the tools to become ministers because they are heavy punks and rockers. We want to prepare them for the time that is coming. . . . We are to serve everyone, our brothers and sisters, and even more those who do not belong to the church.[11]

Mission

Interludio's various groups organize artistic events, social activities, home visits, hospital visitations, and trips as ways to create community and strengthen hospitality. These activities allow newcomers to be incorporated easily into the hospitality of the congregation. In addition, every week the congregation collects food, clothing, and other items to be distributed among nongovernmental organizations (NGOs) to help poor families. For instance, "Interludio is committed to Love146 [www.love146.org] and their fight to end sex slavery and trafficking," as well as to projects to protect the environment.[12] Close friends of José Chacón who are also a part of the Vineyard movement share the same concerns and burdens. For this reason, another Interludio was to start in Mexico by the end of 2011. In Panama there is already a group of twenty people, and in Brazil another group; both groups celebrated their official Interludio kick-off in January 2011.

Leadership

Interludio practices inclusivity and overcomes the separation of the secular and the sacred. These values led to what might be called a "flat" organization in terms of leadership. They follow what José Chacón and his team call an "open theology." They describe this as being Christ-centered—following Christ as the center of the Christian faith—and including people from any denominational background. For instance, "the leadership team at Interludio is made up of Roman Catholics and Evangelicals," both of whom remain spiritually as such.[13]

> Emergent churches are open and welcoming to everybody, whatever their background. But a common downfall of such openness is the refusal to challenge erroneous beliefs from the original context. Living in a Catholic country, I am very sensitive to common Roman Catholic practices that are hardly compatible with the evangelical faith. So considering Roman Catholics "remaining spiritually as such" as part of a leadership team raises serious objections. *Eric Zander*

11. Ibid.
12. Chacón, interview.
13. Ibid.

The house church, in its organic "organization," also conceives of itself as a flat organization. "Christ is the head of the church; he gave us his Spirit and his gifts to make decisions in consensus. We are all priests from whom the Spirit raises elders, with character, good testimony, and wisdom."[14] This authority is functional and not positional; decisions are made in community. "Love and unity are more important than doctrinal consensus," Valverde says. The house church's values of love, mercy, unity, solidarity, and service are expressed around the table fellowship and hospitality. This house church seeks to develop "an organic church, not an organization."[15] These values came from a deeper study of the Scriptures and the study of the works of Gene Edwards, Frank Viola, and Steve Atkerson, according to Valverde.

The Punk Church heavily criticizes the emergent church movement and does not see itself as part of it.

> The emergent movement pretends to build a better church for the postmodern society, but it is trying to do this through human strategies. . . . The church needs to go back to the Scripture and its roots. It needs a gospel with power, a biblical gospel, [and] not bland strategies.[16]

This church does not believe that the church needs to adapt itself to the culture. It believes that the church is "something simple and natural."[17]

> Our values depend totally on grace. We don't judge anyone; we are messengers of the gospel of reconciliation. . . . I am the pastor, and I have a group of elders, who I call my conscience because they correct me and consult with me when I make a mistake.[18]

It is quite interesting that a community choosing to add "Punk" to "church" in their own identification refuses the cultural adaptation idea. *Eric Zander*

I found many similarities with emerging communities in Europe. For example, when Interludio starts church at the table of hospitality with coffee and bread, I am reminded of the Vintage Community and the Brie Church in France. The Punk Church reminds me of the Jesus Freaks in Germany. Like many of the emerging churches in Germany, they meet for conversation, debate, prayer, and listening to a Bible teaching. Reminiscent of the emerging European churches, the emerging churches described by Segura-Guzmán

14. Valverde, interview.
15. Ibid.
16. http://www.iglesiapunk.com.ar/iglesia.html (accessed June 25, 2011).
17. Ibid.
18. Granado, interview.

are simple, creative, and closely linked to the ancient church in Acts. They all (Latin American and European) are moving away from organization to organic ecclesiological structures. Furthermore, both European and Latin American emerging churches are inclusive communities. They also live out evangelism/mission as a lifestyle. The leadership in these three *iglesias emergentes* is flat and empowering. The question that I have is, Are these similarities simply packages of church imported by North American, British, and Australian perspectives of postmodern Christianity, or are they organically emerging from a growing postmodern society, and thus truly indigenous? I suspect that the truth is somewhat in between. I agree with Segura-Guzmán that further research is needed and welcomed. Blayne Waltrip

The heart of the emergent church is its contextualization in postmodern settings. Postmodernity may be expressed differently in Latin America, but the phenomenon is the same. Contextualization takes many shapes in different regions, cultures, and social classes. Peacemaking, poverty, gender relations, human trafficking, urban ministries, children at risk, folk religions, Islam (interfaith dialogue), development and relief efforts, AIDS, holistic evangelistic and discipleship efforts, and a more missional church are among other aspects that require engagement, and not all the churches in Latin America are accustomed to dealing with these crude structural realities.

The *iglesia emergente* may be attempting to do this more than previous expressions of the church, but it is not an ecclesiological panacea for the region. This kind of church does not *yet* seem to be an option in Latin America for the economically disenfranchised, the drug addicts, the politically marginalized, the immigrants, poor women, modern slaves, and children being trafficked and sexually exploited. Emergent leaders talk about these people as those "out there" who need the gospel, but not yet as those "within us." In other words, Latin America needs emerging churches for those who are socially and economically marginalized.

There may be some emergent churches in Latin America that are a "copy-paste" model from what is being constructed in North Atlantic nations. However, in other cases there is a move of the Spirit to refresh our understandings of what it means to be the church of our Lord among new generations. Are emergent churches another "packaged" church from the religious empire of the North? Alternatively, is the emergent movement in Latin America a *criollo* (autochthonous) movement? Both questions are valid, and more research needs to be done to make a fair judgment. In Latin America, the emerging movement is growing, but it does not yet appear to be a strong Pan-American movement.

Bibliography

Bastian, Jean Pierre. "Para una Aproximación Teórica del Fenómeno Religioso Protestante en America Latina" [Towards a Theoretical Approach of the Protestant Religious Phenomena in Latin America]. Revista Cristianismo y Sociedad, 1986.

Cleary, Steve, and Hannah Stewart-Gambino. *Conflict and Competition: The Latin American Church in a Changing Environment*. Boulder, CO: Lynne Rienner, 1992.

Introvigne, Massimo. "Nueva Religiosidad y Contexto Postmoderno." Pages 243–69 in *Comprender la Religión: II Simposio Internacional Fe Cristiana y Cultura Contemporánea*, edited by Javier Aranguren. Pamplona, Spain: EUNSA, 2001.

Klaiber, Jeffrey L. *The Church, Dictatorship, and Democracy in Latin America*. Maryknoll, NY: Orbis, 1998.

Martin, Bernice. "From Pre- to Postmodernity in Latin America: The Case of Pentecostalism." Pages 102–46 in *Religion, Modernity and Postmodernity*, edited by Paul Heelas. Oxford: Blackwell, 1998.

Miguez Bonino, Jose. *Faces of Latin American Protestantism*. Grand Rapids: Eerdmans, 1997.

Padilla, Rene. "La Teologia en Latinoamerica." *Boletin Teologico* 2 (1972).

Smith, Brian. *Religious Politics in Latin America: Pentecostal vs. Catholic*. Notre Dame, IN: University of Notre Dame Press, 1998.

Westmeier, Karl W. *Protestant Pentecostalism in Latin America: A Study in the Dynamics of Missions*. Madison, NJ: Fairleigh Dickinson University Press, 2001.

2

Emerging Churches
in Aotearoa New Zealand

Steve Taylor

Culture

Situated on the Pacific ring of fire, New Zealand (called *Aotearoa* by the indigenous people) enjoys a reputation for spectacular scenery, natural beauty, and a peaceable nuclear-free stance. And hobbits! To understand the shape of emerging fresh expressions in New Zealand one must begin not with the pioneering zeal of black-suited European missionaries but with indigenous people (Maori) and their holistic worldview that integrates sacred and secular, values people and place, and prioritizes *awhi* (respect, embrace) and *aroha* (love). European contact began with Captain Cook in 1769. In 1814, the first British missionaries (Church Missionary Society) landed in the Bay of Islands. "It being Christmas Day, I preached from the second chapter of St. Luke's Gospel and the tenth verse—Behold! I bring you glad tidings of great joy. The Natives . . . could not understand what I meant."[1] While missionary

1. Allan K. Davidson and Peter J. Lineham, *Transplanted Christianity: Documents Illustrating Aspects of New Zealand Church History* (Auckland: College Communications, 1987), 1.3, Marsden's account of "The first Sabbath-day observed in New Zealand," 24.

momentum was initially slow, the 1840s saw significant levels of response among indigenous Maori.[2]

A defining moment in New Zealand history was the signing of the Treaty of Waitangi in 1840. It became New Zealand's founding document, recognizing the right of indigenous people to own land and giving them rights as British subjects. The treaty was needed, for by the turn of the century settler numbers had soared twentyfold, from 37,706 in 1851 to 772,719 in 1901. Settlers brought a vision of New Zealand as a secular state. In the nineteenth century, church attendance averaged 26.3 percent of the population.[3] An eyewitness noted: "When you enter a church you do not get the impression that zeal for God's house is eating us up. Congregations are small, collections very small, and a majority of those present are not young."[4]

Life was more buoyant for the church after World War II, with church attendance increasing and the steeples of new church plants springing up in ever-expanding suburbs. However, cultural and theological shifts in the 1960s brought a sea change in religious identity. Census returns showed an increase in "No religion" from 1.2 percent in 1966[5] to 32.2 percent in 2006.[6] Such trends— honoring a bicultural past and a multicultural future, finding responses to historic patterns of religious apathy, and the need to find a religious identity rooted in the soil of Aotearoa New Zealand—have major implications for the conceiving of religious life in a new millennium.

> Lord, Holy Spirit,
> You blow . . . in a thousand paddocks[7]

This chapter describes a number of recent experiments in the church in New Zealand. It explores how worship, formation, mission, and leadership are expressed and outlines the recurring challenge of negotiating "faithful

2. "Geoff Clarke estimated that in 1845, out of a population of 110,000 Maori, 42,700 regularly attended Anglican services, 16,000 Methodist services and 5,100 were associated with Roman Catholics" (Allan K. Davidson, *Christianity in Aotearoa: A History of Church and Society in New Zealand* [Wellington: Education for Ministry, 1991], 14).

3. Ibid., 50.

4. Davidson and Lineham, *Transplanted Christianity*, 5.7, "Religion in New Zealand in 1940," 255.

5. Figures drawn from Allan K. Davidson, *Aotearoa New Zealand: Defining Moments in the Gospel-Culture Encounter* (Geneva: WCC Publications, 1996), 43–44.

6. "QuickStats About Culture and Identity." http://www.stats.govt.nz/Census/2006Census HomePage/QuickStats/quickstats-about-a-subject/culture-and-identity/religious-affiliation.aspx. Accessed May 18, 2012.

7. Excerpt from James K. Baxter, "Song to the Holy Spirit," in J. E. Weir, ed., *James K. Baxter: Collected Poems* (Oxford: Oxford University Press, 1979), 572.

transmission" of the gospel with specific reference to dwelling among postmodern cultures of choice.

Given the focus of this book on new forms of church, it seems appropriate to now offer a distinctive local story from within Aotearoa New Zealand, one that exemplifies experimentation, depends on the breath of wind, and emerges from the paddocks that dominate the visual landscape of clean, green New Zealand. It was March 31, 1903, a sleepy Saturday in the south of New Zealand. Neighbors were roused by an engine roar and astonished to see a winged contraption, complete with tail, emerge from a local farmer's shed. Nine months before the Wright brothers flew at Kitty Hawk, local farmer and engineering experimenter Richard Pearse flew his winged contraption some 150 meters.[8]

It was a moment of experimental innovation that provides an analogy for understanding the shape of emerging churches in New Zealand as early adaptations of experimental innovation that need to be sourced by a missional pneumatology and to follow the wind of the Spirit, who blows inside and outside the fences of church and culture.[9]

Experiments

Emerging History[10]

> Lord, Holy Spirit,
> You are the sun who shines on the little plant.[11]

The emerging church scene in New Zealand roared into life in 1994. This could be called the "making waves" period. Mike Riddell, Mark Wooley, Mark Pierson, and Jen Long began Parallel Universe, a church community whose worship byline was "on and off the wall." They offered a monthly Sunday

8. "Pearse himself, in two letters, the first to Dunedin's *Evening Star*, published on May 10, 1915, the second published in the *Christchurch Star* on September 15, 1928, didn't believe, by his own rigorous standards, that he had achieved 'proper' flight. For him this meant a powered take-off followed by 'sustained and controlled flight.' Pearse's flights, characterised by powered take-offs followed by erratic descents, failed to meet his own criteria." "Richard Pearse: First Flyer," http://www.nzedge.com/heroes/pearse.html.

9. Two places to gain a global overview of the emerging church are in two journals, *Zadok* (February 2006) and *International Journal for the Study of the Christian Church* 6, no. 1 (March 2006).

10. Relevant parts of this section were sent during November–December 2007 to David Allis, Alan Jamieson, Jenny McIntosh, and Mark Pierson for comments and additions. These were integrated and edited and then resent for comment.

11. Adapted excerpt from Baxter, "Song to the Holy Spirit," 572.

evening service aimed at twenty- to forty-year-olds who had either dropped out of the church or who had never seen the church as worth exploring. Working out of a nightclub, they sought worship that might connect with contemporary postmodern cultures. This involved an outpouring of intense creativity and frequent use of multimedia. Bottles of chardonnay descended from the ceiling and large gas flames were lit at Pentecost. Much of this is described in Riddell's *Threshold of the Future* and *The Prodigal Project*.[12]

Parallel Universe became an imaginative fire starter. In the years following, various worship expressions and communities took shape around the emerging church values of participation, cultural engagement, and creativity. Some examples included Cityside Baptist and Graceway Baptist in Auckland, Ilam Baptist and Side Door in Christchurch, Urban Vision and Jireh in Wellington, Soul Reason in Greymouth, and Soul Outpost and Out of Bounds in Dunedin. Ethnographic research showed that these communities were nourishing the faith of postmodern people through creativity, with community, and in the way they engaged with contemporary culture.[13]

> Creativity . . . requires a pioneering spirit. Creative leaders don't procrastinate or seek safety by doing the least amount necessary to get by.
>
> Eddie Gibbs (LN. 141)

Most early groups existed on the edges of churches and denominations. Considerable energy was spent in responding to critique from the existing church. Over time, durability and sustainability proved problematic, and a number of these communities ceased to exist. Anecdotal evidence suggests this is an issue in general with regard to entrepreneurial start-ups in New Zealand.

> I guess the question of entrepreneurial problems is connected to preconceived values about the costs of failure (or success, for that matter). Small experiments that are short-lived and yet equip people to make new steps may be highly effective uses of a Christian community's resources. Many forms of performance art value the presence of the moment as sufficient. Take for example the installations of Andrew Goldsworthy, whose naturalist pieces may last only that specific day. Some faith collectives are willing to invest in one-offs that may change the ritualized agent or the narrated worshiper forever thereafter. Micro

---

12. Mike Riddell, *Threshold of the Future: Reforming the Church in the Post-Christian West* (London: SPCK, 1998); Mike Riddell, Mark Pierson, and Cathy Kirkpatrick, *The Prodigal Project: Journey into the Emerging Church* (London: SPCK, 2000).

13. Steve Taylor, "A New Way of Being Church? A Case Study Approach to Cityside Baptist Church as Christian Faith 'Making Do' in a Postmodern World" (PhD thesis, University of Otago, 2004).

and short-term faith groups can do this as well—so long as healthy communication takes place at the onset. *Troy Bronsink*

The De-churched

Another form of emerging church in New Zealand stemmed from the conversation about the "de-churched." Research by Alan Jamieson in the 1990s identified a wide open back door among evangelical, charismatic, and Pentecostal churches and demonstrated that many people who leave these churches were in fact not losing their faith. Rather, they were looking for a deeper faith, for more authentic responses to the often painful experiences of life, for Christian practices that were plausible beyond Christian circles, and for the ability to integrate their faith with the whole of life.

In the Gospels, a shepherd of lost sheep is one of the images used to describe the mission of Jesus. In Luke 15, the lost are identified as sinners, while in Matthew 18:10–14, they are identified as the little ones within the church who have stumbled. This suggests that gospel mission needs to include not only those outside the church, but also those who feel hurt or wounded by their experiences inside what they perceive as the fences of the church.

An emerging mission for the de-churched in New Zealand took shape around a movement called Spirited Exchanges. Groups began in various cities as places to share and learn from the spiritual journeys of others. This was not mission as conversion, but mission as walking alongside and offering safe, nonjudgmental, open-ended discussion forums in order to enable people to process and explore issues related to faith, church dissatisfaction, and dissonance. Such groups were designed to be a space for transition rather than an end point where people can live out their faith long-term.

Alan Jamieson's original research took on longitudinal strength when the original church leavers were reinterviewed five years later.[14] The need for places like Spirited Exchanges was strongly affirmed, as was the conclusion that those who left were not returning to the churches they had left originally. Despite this research, Spirited Exchanges began to struggle in New Zealand. It was difficult to find appropriate pathways into, and beyond, the safe spaces that Spirited Exchanges created. The movement also struggled with a wider cultural shift, a general trend away from voluntary associations and toward an increasingly individualized spiritual search, which could be sustained not by group attendance but by an ever-increasing range of internet resources.

14. Alan Jamieson, Jenny McIntosh, and Adrienne Thompson, *Five Years On: Continuing Faith Journeys of Those Who Left the Church* (Portland Trust: Wellington, 2006); sequel to *A Churchless Faith*.

Online Faith

Another manifestation of emerging church in New Zealand was the exploration of faith online. In the early days of blogging, leadership came from New Zealand Christians including Rachel Cunliffe, Paul Fromont, Steve Taylor, and Andrew Jones. Tim Bulkeley, lecturer at Carey Baptist College, set up the PodBible website to enable the mobile internet generation to access daily online Bible readings.[15] Churches like Opawa Baptist explored preaching using online video and the use of cell phones during Communion. Mark Brown, who in real life was the CEO of the New Zealand Bible Society, planted an online cathedral in the virtual world of Second Life, a space in which millions of residents exist as "avatars," or 3D representations. In this digital mission field, Mark began to offer a weekly online church service, including a sermon that could stream into members' computers, along with opportunities for people to interact and pray.

> Innovation can also be scary and risky. Innovators are gifted with the power of imagination, but all of those vivid mental pictures must be translated into reality. Invariably, innovators are restless people. An innovator's vision is constantly unfolding and evolving.
>
> Eddie Gibbs (LN, 167)

Such innovation was one response to the fact that the internet is a place of spiritual pursuit presenting huge challenges and opportunities for the future of Christian faith. A recent Pew Research Center study of American teenagers noted that 55 percent use on-line social networking sites, while 89 percent of teens and 71 percent of their parents believe the internet and technology like cell phones make life easier.[16] The internet as a mission field was generating a new vision for New Zealand churches.[17]

House Churches

Another manifestation of the emerging church in New Zealand is that of house churches. Because such groups generally choose not to advertise or meet publicly, it is difficult to quantify the extent of this network or to assess their missional effectiveness. Anecdotal evidence suggests perhaps five hundred house churches exist in New Zealand.[18] The hope is that by freeing

15. http://www.podbible.com.
16. http://www.pewinternet.org.
17. For a more thorough discussion see Paul Teusner, "Christianity 2.0: A New Religion for a New Web," http://paulteusner.org/docs/aoir8paper1.pdf; and idem, "IT, Culture & the Church," *Stimulus* 12, no. 3 (August 2004).
18. Estimate from David Allis, http://www.edgenet.org.nz, December 2007.

resources from buildings, public worship, and paid pastoral staff, deeper relationships and greater participation might result. However, time has shown that the strength of house churches is also their weakness. While a home is undoubtedly a relational place, it is also a place that can be entered only by invitation. Hence, house churches work best by networking through existing social networks, while the missionary crossing of subcultural barriers requires a greater degree of intentionality.

> This clarifies our experience at Neighbors Abbey. We were a house church for the first three years, doing community work in borrowed spaces the rest of the week. But the worship gathering presented challenges: it involved crossing multiple barriers because it was held in different homes every week. We've moved into a fixed building for the first time in hopes that it will invigorate this expansive, boundary-crossing impulse of good-news communities (aka evangelicalism). But it's too early to tell how much of that house church MO has irreversibly entered into the DNA of the Abbey. *Troy Bronsink*

Installation Art

A final example of the emerging church in New Zealand is seen in the development of installation art as mission through spiritual formation. In 1993, Mark Pierson, then pastor of Cityside Baptist Church, suggested to his congregation a project titled "Stations of the Cross: Contemporary Icons to Reflect Easter." People were invited to enter into the journey to Easter by choosing a historic Christian station and presenting it in a contemporary fashion and in a form that others would be able to reflect upon.

> This is not the time for conformity but rather for creative thinking and innovation organized around an inspiring and inclusive vision.
>
> Eddie Gibbs (LN, 167)

What started as an outlet for the creative expression of those who attended Cityside Baptist has had considerable ongoing spiritual impact. Research of individuals who engaged one Stations of the Cross installation found that the experience often resulted in what these "pilgrims" described as significant encounters with God.[19] Other churches in New Zealand and around the world also began to embrace this form of missional engagement.

A significant development began with the desire to take this installation art outside church "fences" and into public spaces. In Christchurch, Peter and Joyce Majendie gained city council permission to place shipping containers in

19. Mark Pierson, "Stations of the Cross 2003: An Analysis of a Liturgical Experience and Its Relevance for Spiritual Formation" (MMin thesis, Melbourne College of Divinity, 2007).

central city tourist locations. (Using shipping containers ensures a secure and safe space in which to house art installations.) The containers were wrapped in nylon fabric, both for aesthetic reasons and to suggest the shape of a (very large) Christmas present. In 2005, over eight thousand people walked through, making the Christmas Journey the largest "Christmas church" in New Zealand (aided by the fact that Christmas falls during summer in the Southern Hemisphere).

Then in 2007, shipping containers gave way to a thousand straw bales, laid out in a central city square in the shape of a large-scale labyrinth. At various points on the walk through the labyrinth, art stations were placed to invite a tactile interaction with the Christmas story. For example, a "Peace with the Environment" station reflected on the environmental costs of dairy farming, while a "Peace with Myself" station invited people to confess a secret sin. At the centre of the labyrinth was (in true C. S. Lewis fashion) a lamppost, a stable, and the words "God with Us." Here was Christmas being returned to its original location, being celebrated not in church but in the middle of a bustling town.

One way to analyze the emergence of all these experimental forms of church is through the framework provided by Andy Crouch. He suggests a range of Christian stances toward culture: condemnation, critique, copying, and consuming, in which "most evangelicals today . . . simply go to the movies . . . [and] . . . walk out amused, titillated, distracted or thrilled, just like our fellow consumers who do not share our faith."[20] Instead, Crouch urges Christians to be culture makers, "creators—people who dare to think and do something that has never been thought or done before, something that makes the world more welcoming and thrilling and beautiful."[21] This provides a way to understand the various forms of the emerging church in New Zealand, as expressions of "culture making," as experimental innovations that seek to take forward the mission of God.

Practices

> Lord, Holy Spirit . . .
> Driving us out like sparks to set the world on fire.[22]

Given this historical overview, the task of this next section is to offer a number of action stories. Utilizing the headings of worship, community, mission, and leadership, the stories are chosen to allow reflection on an ongoing

20. Andy Crouch, *Culture Making: Recovering Our Creative Calling* (Downers Grove, IL: InterVarsity, 2008), 89.
21. Ibid., 97–98.
22. Excerpt from Baxter, "Song to the Holy Spirit," 572.

missionary question, that of "faithful transmission" of the gospel in the midst of an increasingly individualized, consumer-oriented culture.

Worship

One of the features of the emerging church in New Zealand is the desire to explore worship that is tactile and experiential. This is shaped by the call of Jesus to love God and neighbour with body, mind, and soul.[23] It invites a whole-bodied Christianity, a faith making sense through, in, and with all the senses. One story, among many, is of the Stations of the Cross exhibition offered over recent years by a Christian art collective in the Hamilton Public Gardens.[24] The creative process is described by the organizer, Dave White, as one of collective dialogue.

> Individual [ideas] are brought to the table and negotiated, mocked, discussed, and prayed. Sometimes an idea mutates with the collective involvement into something worthy. Sometimes an artist's original idea is farmed to another artist. Artists sometimes work collaboratively.[25]

Attendance at the stations has grown from three hundred to three thousand, making it, by New Zealand standards, a large "Easter church."

The aim of Stations of the Cross is to invite people into a tactile, experiential, and multisensory engagement with the Easter story. White provides one example:

> From a street-type ice cream cart, a woman in a white coat offers an ice cube with a curious greenish centre. You take it. You hold the ice cube in the palm of your hand, your fingers curled around it on a cold [evening in Holy Week]. [It] melts painfully in your palm, leaving a moist leaf cut in the shape of the cross, as you journey the path. That is an engaging experience of Jesus carrying the cross. It's personal, experiential, creative. And the leaf is from our backyards. Our backyards. Christ's bearing of the cross is for Kiwis in the South Pacific too.[26]

This worship expects a whole-body engagement. It demands that the process of Christian formation not be "seeker sensitive," but instead involve

23. Matt. 22:37–39.
24. This is told fully in Dave White, "Depth a Close Friend but Not a Lover," in *Curating Worship*, ed. Jonny Baker (London: SPCK, 2010), 80–86.
25. Ibid., 83.
26. Ibid., 85.

personal work, utilizing all five senses. It is based on a willingness to risk holding an ice cube and a giving of time to make connections as a result of the experience.

> I appreciate your emphasis on "work" in worship. Some of the most evocative art asks the participant to take responsibility for the engagement. Since the revivals of Charles Finney and the Great Awakenings, the church has been taking too much responsibility for the participant, which naturally leads to the "seeker-sensitive" movement. Community organizers like Peter Block have noted that real empowerment requires leaders who confront the citizen with their freedom. *Troy Bronsink*

Such an approach simultaneously accepts and subverts consumer culture. It offers an engagement with the Easter story that is essentially privatized and individualized, potentially detached from any experience of Christian community. It is offered by a community in the shape of an artist's collective, but a community that makes no offer of ongoing longevity. At the same time, the stations present an experience of Christianity that refuses to be easily digestible, or commodified, and that encourages the individual to take ownership of their own spiritual search.

> Worship leader as curator is an imagination-grabbing model of ministry. "Curators" in museums or art galleries set up the displays and experiences, and create an ambience for people to be guided through the experience of enjoying and honouring what is on display. In our local church at Auburn Baptist, we invite worship leaders to see their role as a "worship curator" to lead us through an experience of enjoying and honouring God and encouraging one another on a Sunday morning. We give curators permission and encouragement to let their creativity loose. *Darren Cronshaw*

Community

> Lord, Holy Spirit,
> In the love of friends you are building a new house.[27]

Another story—that of a faith growing by community, rather than by privatized encounter—opens up a different angle on the challenge of discipleship in an age of consumption. In 2005, a young woman phoned a local church (Opawa Baptist) and arranged to meet the pastor, Steve Taylor. On meeting him, she briefly explained that she was on a spiritual search and then proceeded to outline a range of questions she had about Christian faith. As the time

---

27. Excerpt from Baxter, "Song to the Holy Spirit," 572.

ended, she noted how helpful the environment of mutual dialogue had been. She expressed a desire to keep meeting and indicated that she had friends who also had questions and appreciated a conversational approach to learning.

One response would have been to invite her to a regular church service or into a discipleship process. Instead, the pastor invited her to help experiment with a new form of church.[28] The result has been that every Tuesday for the past six years people have gathered on a circle of couches in the foyer of Opawa Baptist Church, in an expression of church called Espresso. In the center sits a bowl filled with questions. Most weeks a question is taken and discussed. (Other weeks involve the telling of stories and sharing of Communion, or an opportunity for outward missional service.) There is no space for sermons. Instead, time is given to probe experience, to question inherited ideas, and to engage in robust conversation. A set of ground rules is used to foster listening and dialogue. It is an open space, with people coming and going over time. It is also a communal space, in which the search for truth is shared among a questing community.

> Participants of missional experiments in Australia who meet in cafés or bistros similarly say they find the casual conversational approach to meeting significantly formative. One participant of a congregation meeting in a bistro said, "Talking about faith dilemmas over coffee and cake over the last year has been more formative than five years of sermons and singing." *Darren Cronshaw*

One way to understand Espresso would be to appreciate the resonances with aspects of the Emmaus Road encounter in Luke 24. Both began with honesty and were catalysed by questions. Both made the journey together a priority and found that in sharing around a table, in relationships and over food, encounter with God occurred.

Espresso enabled an engagement with the new yearnings for spirituality in contemporary culture, particularly among those with the skills to learn through conversation. Over time, primarily through the practice of being community, people have grown in relationships with one another, with God, and with the church. But not all people are as fortunate, as educated, as those who gather at Espresso. What of God's mission to the poor?

> Australian experiments meeting in cafés or bistros face the same question. One church that met in a bistro also hosted a soup-kitchen style "Dining Room" but did not expect the guests at the Dining Room would easily come to the conversations at the bistro. *Darren Cronshaw*

28. Discussed more fully in Steve Taylor, "Emerging, Established or Re-emerging? A Trinitarian Reflection on Church and Ministry Today," *Ministry Today* 38 (November 2006): 24–34.

Mission

> Lord, Holy Spirit . . .
> You are singing your song in the hearts of the poor.[29]

Urban Vision began in 1996 as a group of people committed to serving the inner city of Wellington through acts of incarnational mission. Its origins were in a shared set of friendships, a suburb (Berhampore), and a commitment to quietly follow Christ among the poor and marginalized. An important ministry feature was "the Castle," an intentional community where people from the street could experience belonging and equality. There was also a willingness from individuals to deliberately relocate into public housing areas in order to support refugees and migrants.

Over the years, Urban Vision grew and morphed in strength and outreach. It has seeded teams into other urban poor and marginalized suburbs around Wellington. Then in 2007, Urban Vision decided to reform itself as a contemporary independent order centered around a set of shared values. These include

- a prophetic call to seek justice
- a willingness to be sent as good news
- an action/reflection spirituality
- a commitment to simple lifestyle and
- discipleship formation

To quote from their website:

> We're not simply copying something from the past. . . . [Rather] this similarity to the old missionary movements has come about because of the contexts we live, because of the times we live in and the prevailing culture of society and the church at this point of history in Aotearoa/New Zealand.[30]

This commitment to radical discipleship, along with their durability over a decade, makes Urban Vision a fine example of experimental emerging praxis, of giving concrete expression to the wind of the Spirit who yearns to whisper God's "songs in the hearts of the poor."

These stories raise the question of what type of leadership is needed to foster such emerging praxis, to encourage art collectives into action, to set up

---

29. Excerpt from Baxter, "Song to the Holy Spirit," 572.
30. "New Monasticism?," *Urban Vision*, http://www.urbanvision.org.nz/covenant-dedication /new-monasticism (accessed December 21, 2010).

conversational forms of church in which the leader is only one voice among many, or to lead people into costly mission among the urban poor. We turn to these issues of leadership in the next section.

Leadership

On September 14, 1997, Mark Pierson, faced with the task of revitalizing a dying inner-city church in the centre of Auckland, journaled the following:[31]

> I'm beginning to understand worship and . . . myself . . . as a worship curator—someone who takes the pieces provided and puts them in a particular setting and makes a particular arrangement of them. . . . A maker of context rather than a presenter of content.[32]

Mark has gone on to explore the notion of leadership as the art of curation, embodied in a set of practices that value participation over monologue, open-endedness over certainty, a slow spirituality over quick results, integrity over appearance, failure over success, and questions over answers.[33]

> The church that sees itself as curator is free to entrust the invitation or the inspiration to the unknown space of God's realm, as well as the unknown space of the other—the individuals we encounter with curiosity who are unique and different from any projection of our best or worst selves. Rather than seeking to realize a perfect projection of truth, beauty, or justice (a la Crouch) we can make open environments where rituals and narratives emerge and others are free to act on them. *Troy Bronsink*

The notion of "leader as curator" offers a distinctive praxis for the emerging church in worship, community (ecclesiology), mission, and leadership. This type of leadership crafts contexts so that individual artists become an art collective for Easter mission, or forms Espresso in dialogue with the heart murmur of a spiritual seeker, or helps passionate urban missionaries frame themselves into a contemporary order of mission. It assumes a deep trust in God's work among people and a willingness to follow the wind of the Spirit, both "inside and outside the fences."[34]

---

31. The story of the church, Cityside, is told in extensive detail in Taylor, "A New Way of Being Church?"

32. Mark Pierson, *The Art of Curating Worship* (Minneapolis: SparkHouse, Augsburg Fortress, 2010), 7–8.

33. Ibid., 68ff.

34. Excerpt from Baxter, "Song to the Holy Spirit," 572.

> The best curators will be conscious of creating space for worship that is engaging for people of all ages, all stages of faith, and different cultural backgrounds. At Auburn Baptist we encourage our curators to foster engagement for all ages, inviting input and interaction from children as well as adults. And to remember that different people are at different stages of faith (or no faith), so don't assume we are all in the same place with God. Also think of celebrating our multicultural congregation and neighbourhood—and include PowerPoint slides, Bible readings, or prayers in Pidgin, Romanian, or Chinese. Darren Cronshaw

In this chapter we explored five expressions of the emerging church in New Zealand. In making waves, through Spirited Exchanges, in offering faith online, through house churches, and in installation art, there has been a history of innovation, along with a challenge to existing church structures regarding their ability to engage in effective partnership with experimental mission. A number of stories, clustered around themes of worship, community, mission, and leadership, have also been told. Together these stories suggest that the emerging church in New Zealand has neither accepted the cultural status quo nor chosen to become an alternative subculture. Rather, it has sought culture-making transformation, whether of the internet, of city squares, of networks, or among the urban poor.

This, as with all missionary encounters, raises the vital question of "faithful transmission" as the Word seeks to become flesh in ever-changing cultures. In New Zealand, such a mission question applies specifically to the challenge of dwelling incarnationally among "postmodern cultures" of choice. Given that notions of leader-as-curator encourage individualized spaces, as seen in installation art, what are the pathways by which individual experiences—whether online or at art installations—become integrated with kingdom, communal discipleship? Given that communities such as Urban Vision and Espresso both emerged because individuals claimed space outside the "fences" of existing church practice, how do they form relational and networked communities of Christian practice in the midst of an individualized, experiential culture?

Such questions can be addressed empirically, and research has begun on a longitudinal study of the emerging church ten years on.[35] The questions can, equally, be addressed theologically. In that light, it is helpful to consider the notion of faithful transmission in light of the ministry and mission of Jesus. He told stories of the kingdom of God that drew on organic metaphors of mustard seeds that become trees, and of new wine needing new wineskins.

35. For more information, contact Dr. Steve Taylor, Flinders University, steve.taylor@finders.edu.au.

Such images provide an example of experimentation and innovation without losing the DNA of the kingdom. The fundamentals are retained, even while new forms are welcomed. These organic images provided by Jesus are one way to sense the experimental history and innovative praxis of the emerging church in New Zealand, as it has sought, in the spirit of Richard Pearse, to respond to the Wind of the Spirit as it blows inside and outside the fences of church and culture.

Bibliography

Jamieson, Alan. *A Churchless Faith: Faith Journeys beyond Evangelical, Pentecostal and Charismatic Churches*. Wellington: Philip Garside, 2000.

———. *Called Again: In and Beyond the Deserts of Faith*. Wellington: Philip Garside, 2004.

Jamieson, Alan, Jenny McIntosh, and Adrienne Thompson. *Five Years On: Continuing Faith Journeys of Those Who Left the Church*. Wellington: Portland Trust, 2006. Sequel to *A Churchless Faith*.

Pierson, Mark. *The Art of Curating Worship*. Minneapolis: SparkHouse, 2010.

Riddell, Mike. *Threshold of the Future: Reforming the Church in the Post-Christian West*. London: SPCK, 1998.

Riddell, Mike, Mark Pierson, and Cathy Kirkpatrick. *The Prodigal Project: Journey into the Emerging Church*. London: SPCK, 2000.

Taylor, Steve. *The Out of Bounds Church? Learning to Create a Community of Faith in a Culture of Change*. Grand Rapids: Zondervan, 2005.

3

Emerging Missional Churches in Australia

Darren Cronshaw

Culture

Australians place a high cultural value on innovation and ingenuity, which explains why innovations in church life are welcome in Australia. A British general commented in World War I that if the world fell apart tomorrow, an Australian would put it back together with three bits of string and a length of fencing wire. He had seen Australian creativity in the face of hopeless odds and learned to appreciate it.

Today Australians long for new expressions of church rather than reliance on an imported denominational heritage from Europe or the latest models from North America. Australians value authenticity and show a fair share of anti-institutionalism, a leftover from our colonial past. We value religion that makes a difference in society and expresses itself in meaningful service beyond the walls of the church. Historically, Australia's relationship between church and culture has been more distant than in North America. It could be said that Australia started almost as a post-Christendom settlement where the church has always struggled to be at home. There is a pressing need to foster creative ways to connect the church with Australians.

> True for the Netherlands too. A Dutch church planter's prayer might be. "Deliver us from our US church models." *Nico-Dirk van Loo*

There is a search for spirituality in Australia, and even an attraction to Jesus and his subversive and unconventional ways.[1] Yet this burgeoning interest in spirituality does not mean flourishing churches. Like elsewhere in the West, church attendance is declining and a diminishing percentage of younger generations is involved. Fifty years ago 41 percent of the Australian population attended church monthly; by 2009 it was 15 percent.[2] Moreover, in 2006 among Australians age fifteen or older, 43 percent of the population but only 25 percent of church attenders were under the age of forty. Yet while only 23 percent of the population was over sixty, this group made up 42 percent of churchgoers.[3] Education, career, financial success, leisure, and home ownership are all-consuming goals. Consumerism drives much of society and offers as much competition to Christianity as other religions and alternative spiritualities. In this diverse marketplace of religious and lifestyle options, Australian churches have a fresh challenge to communicate their message.

Experiments

New Forms of Church in Australia

I am encouraged by "emerging missional churches" (EMCs) pointing in new directions. Over the last six years I have studied EMCs in Melbourne and around Australia.[4] My family and I joined Connection Community, a reinvented Church of Christ, in discussing faith issues over coffee and cake in a family restaurant. We visited Solace Community, an alternative network focused on encouraging Christians to relate faith to their everyday lives. We were inspired by Urban Life, a Pentecostal congregation that had recently

1. Julia Baird, "The Dude Is Back in the Building," *Sydney Morning Herald*, December 23, 2005, http://www.smh.com.au/news/national/the-dude-is-back/2005/12/22/1135032135729 .html?page=full; Darren Cronshaw, *Credible Witness: Companions, Prophets, Hosts and Other Australian Mission Models* (Melbourne: Urban Neighbours of Hope, 2006), 23–26.

2. Peter Kaldor et al., *Build My Church: Trends and Possibilities for Australian Churches* (Sydney: Openbook, 1999), 22; Survey of Australian Social Attitudes (2009).

3. The Australian Bureau of Statistics National Census: http://www.abs.gov.au/census (2006); The Australian National Church Life Survey: http://www.ncls.org.au/ (2006).

4. Fuller details of the EMCs and the research methodology, interview sources, and primary documents on which this chapter draws are accessible in Darren Cronshaw, *The Shaping of Things Now: Emerging Church Mission and Innovation in 21st Century Melbourne* (Saarbrücken: VDM Verlag, 2009).

relocated, transitioned leadership, changed its name, and reinvented itself around community and mission. Inspired by Michael Frost's *Exiles*,[5] we hosted a neighbourhood expression of church called Bimbadeen Tribe that had a missional interest in our neighbourhood and school networks, and a desire to celebrate faith and friendship over meals. Bimbadeen Tribe joined with Eastern Hills, a church plant of young adults characterized by alternative worship and social justice.

Around Australia I have seen a groundswell of café churches, missionary networks, house churches, pub churches, soup kitchens, and thrift stores, seeker studies, alternative spirituality groups, ancient worship gatherings, grassroots community development, and missional churches starting in schools, workplaces, and shopping centers. These experiments are representative of EMCs in Australia whose imagination is captured by mission and cultural engagement.

> A church that is missional understands that God's mission calls and sends the church of Jesus Christ to be a missionary church in its own society and in the cultures in which it finds itself.
>
> Eddie Gibbs (CN. 51)

The main catalyst for missional conversation in Australia is the Forge Mission Training Network. Started by Alan Hirsch and Michael Frost in the mid-1990s, Forge links colleges, churches, and emerging leaders in a yearlong action-reflection internship around a mission placement, missional coaching, intern clusters, and three weeklong intensives. Forge also hosts "Postcard" events to share stories of missional experiments, and "Dangerous Stories" conferences to bring mission-hearted people together from around the country, all to cultivate missionary identity and pioneering leadership skills. Forge applies cross-cultural mission principles to the Western world and exegetes popular culture, challenging the church to move beyond consumerism.

Frost and Hirsch wrote what has become an influential textbook for Australian emerging/missional church life, *The Shaping of Things to Come*.[6] It urges churches to experiment, risk failure, foster radical change, and plant new communities among diverse subcultural groups. The authors espouse "incarnational ecclesiology," which infiltrates community networks; "messianic spirituality," which engages culture and everyday rhythms of life; and "apostolic leadership," which pioneers new and innovative mission.

Other organizations that enhance the emerging conversation include Oikos house church network, coordinated by Bessie Periera, the Anglican Fresh

5. Michael Frost, *Exiles: Living Missionally in a Post-Christian Culture* (Peabody, MA: Hendrickson, 2006).

6. Michael Frost and Alan Hirsch, *The Shaping of Things to Come: Innovation and Mission for the 21st-Century Church* (Peabody, MA: Hendrickson, 2003).

Expressions initiatives that are gaining momentum under Wayne Brighton's leadership, and the National Church Life Survey Innovations Project with Ruth Powell researching new initiatives.

Case Studies of Australian Emerging Missional Churches

Emerging missional churches are learning organizations.[7] Many are not reaching as many unchurched people as their ideals suggest, and some of their change processes are haphazard. But this gap between ideals and experience provides a creative tension that invites ongoing evaluation and learning about the shaping of mission and leadership for the twenty-first century. The remainder of this chapter introduces three case studies and how they foster authentic worship, inclusive community, incarnational mission, and empowering leadership.

EASTERN HILLS, MELBOURNE

Eastern Hills Community Church was planted in Melbourne in 2003 by Toliu and Emma Morgan and an eager nucleus of young adults from a permission-giving parent church, Templestowe Baptist. Their pastor at Templestowe encouraged them to experiment: "The church is dying; do whatever you can." They dreamed together for a year, inspired by Rodney Clapp's and Tom Sine's books on countercultural church community and Tom Wright's book on Jesus.[8] Claire[9] recalls making lists of what they hated about church and why, and what the Gospels say about those things. Not every Eastern Hills member was dissatisfied with the existing church, but discontent is a common theme for those who started Eastern Hills and other EMCs. They did not set out to start an "emerging church" or for it to be styled that way, but sought to "be church" together in ways they were persuaded God wanted them to be, expressed in their mission statement, "Creating lives which reflect the kingdom of God."[10]

> Leadership training has to move beyond the pastoral care of the flock to an equal or greater emphasis of ministry to the world.
>
> Eddie Gibbs (LN. 203)

7. Peter M. Senge, *The Fifth Discipline: The Art and Practice of the Learning Organization* (Sydney: Random House, 1992), 75–104, 378–90.

8. Rodney Clapp, *A Peculiar People: The Church as Culture in a Post-Christian Society* (Downers Grove, IL: InterVarsity, 1996); Tom Sine, *Mustard Seed versus McWorld: Reinventing Life and Faith for the Future* (Grand Rapids: Baker Books, 1999); N. T. Wright, *Jesus and the Victory of God* (London: SPCK, 1996).

9. Throughout this chapter I mention several statements and personal stories from participants in the churches discussed here. Most personal names, other than pastors', are pseudonyms.

10. http://www.ehillschurch.com.

URBAN LIFE, RINGWOOD

Sometimes new movements arise out of anger and frustration in reaction to the ponderous nature of existing institutions. For the most part, though, younger church leaders are not characterized by attitudes of rebellion and defiance. Many fully appreciate the tradition that formed them, expressing a cultural trend described by some as "retrofuture" [Gerard Kelly's term].

Eddie Gibbs (LN, 145)

Urban Life is a reinvented Christian Revival Crusade (CRC) Pentecostal church. In 2005 they left their four and a half acres on the outskirts of suburban Ringwood because they did not feel engaged with their city. Instead they leased an old nightclub in the centre of Ringwood, a journey they describe as "from the country club to the nightclub." Their new space, The Urban, is a café, community centre, and children's play area that also has church on Sundays. It offers what Frost and Hirsch term a "proximity place" for bringing the church into closer connection with those outside church.[11] Urban Life participants say that the geographic move reminds them that the church is not mainly for their needs but is a place to interact with their community: "Church is not just us tucked away in a nice, safe, little place." They are continually asking themselves how to be "living for the well-being of our community."[12]

Intentionally focusing on the welfare of the community seems a key factor for the survival of a church plant in the Netherlands. *Nico-Dirk van Loo*

SOLACE, ALPHINGTON

Solace was one of the first emerging churches inspired by Forge, and it was started by Olivia Maclean in 2000 as an additional congregation of a large Anglican church. The group since branched off on its own, but it has always offered space for theological questioning and interactive worship for all ages and all stages of faith. The participants focus on celebrating everyday spirituality and the mission and vocation of all their members. Solace sees itself as an interactive network more than a group that centers on Sunday worship. Their book, *Remaking*,[13] and its seven ways of Jesus-centered spirituality, show how they seek to nurture people for mission in the workplace and everyday life.

11. Frost and Hirsch, *Shaping of Things to Come*, 24–25.
12. http://www.urbanlife.org.au; see also Darren Cronshaw, "Urban Life: A Case Study of a Pentecostal 'Emerging Missional Church,'" *Pentecostal Charismatic Bible Colleges Journal* 2 (October 2006), http://webjournals.ac.edu.au/journals/PCBC/200602/02-urban-life -a-case-study-of-a-pentecostal-emergi.
13. Solace, *Remaking: A Workbook for Spiritual Formation, A Collaborative Project of Solace*, ed. Stuart Davey (Melbourne: Solace EMC, 2006); based on spiritual traditions from Richard Foster, *Streams of Living Water: Celebrating the Great Traditions of Christian Faith*

The pastors help people reflect on their dreams and passions. They celebrate how members develop as better friends, entrepreneurs, teachers, nurses, and environmental stewards. Their purpose is "to enable a people to thrive as followers of Jesus, celebrating and re-making their everyday world."[14]

Practices

Alternative Worship

Eastern Hills encourages creativity and engagement with God through alternative approaches to worship. The Sunday-morning gathering sits people at tables with space to write or talk with others in a café-style environment. A volunteer prepares a "vibe" beforehand as a visual and environmental experience—usually objects, photos, and thought-provoking quotations arranged on a table. Worship gatherings often appear as art installations with a justice emphasis, sometimes incorporating short stories, poetry, dance, newspapers, yoga, and diverse media. Prayer was introduced one morning with singing "Lord, Have Your Way" followed by voicing global concerns. People mentioned Iraq, slavery in Uganda, indigenous communities, East Timor, world leaders, "my classroom," and people in prison. After praying for these marginalised people and trouble spots, the leader concluded with a "by the way, God" prayer for families and friends. (Normally the "by the way" prayer is for the broader world.)

> When we come near to the heart of God in worship, we cannot but feel God's heartbeat for the world.
>
> Eddie Gibbs (LN, 77)

Solace started with a focus on interactive worship—for all ages and stages of faith and different learning styles. Its gatherings are highly interactive, with people seated around lounges, with coffee, candles, and crayons available. Each person has the freedom to opt in or out of activities. Olivia, the leader, says worship at its best is like a game of hacky sack: anyone can contribute to conversation, people learn by doing, and the game is not successful until everyone participates. The community also hosts worship at monthly Taizé services, at an annual festival weekend, on Tuesday nights over a meal, and at monthly Pancake Sundays for young families. Through an email network

---

(London: HarperCollins, 1999) and "transforming grace" from Dallas Willard, *The Divine Conspiracy: Rediscovering Our Hidden Life in God* (San Francisco: HarperSanFrancisco, 1998).

14. http://www.solace.emc.org.au; see also Darren Cronshaw, "Mission and Spirituality at Solace EMC, an Interactive Network for Everyday Faith," *Australian Journal of Mission Studies* 2, no. 2 (2008): 38–44.

members are invited to participate wherever is helpful, without having to commit to Sunday stuff. Solace started with a vision for the unchurched but found that it attracted a lot of de-churched and over-churched people who appreciated the space and freedom to question and explore their faith dilemmas, and for whom traditional sermon and worship styles (a sing and a talk) did not fit.

Inclusive Community and Hospitality

EMCs espouse authentic and inclusive community and advocate a "centered-set" approach in helping people grow toward Christ.[15] Inviting people to belong to a church community, even before they may believe, is a path that arguably suits many postmodern people, including many of the young adults who have been attracted to these churches.

Eastern Hills started with the intention of being "more than Sunday." The group wanted to counterculturally confront individualism and foster strong community and relationships. Worship gatherings include space for conversation and coffee and lunch together afterward. Participants often play and create together too. For example, at Christmas they organised a food hamper collection, a berry-picking afternoon, a gift-making day, and a Christmas feast to celebrate the season. The group has involved others in sport, cooking classes, working bees for a women's refuge, a nursing home concert, make-a-movie nights, court parties, belly dancing, and worship services. The church has helped them to belong even while they are yet to come to a place of belief.

> Whereas a clique closes its ranks and faces inward, authentic community turns outward to welcome and serve others.
>
> Eddie Gibbs (LN, 106)

Urban Life describes community as "doing life deeply together,"[16] especially through their small group structure, "Get-Togethers" (GTs). Tired of traditional Bible studies and their failure to connect with newcomers, they decided they would host a big table with good food and lots of laughter while carrying one another's burdens. In GTs they seek to mirror the picture of the church in Acts, whose members would bleed for one another: "They would do whatever it took to see the other person get on and do well."[17] Since introducing GTs Urban Life's levels of small group

---

15. Frost and Hirsch, *Shaping of Things to Come*, 47–51, 206–10; Olivia Moffat, "What Kind of Church?" (paper presented at the EFAC conference, 2001), http://home.vicnet.net.au/~efac/whatchurch.htm.

16. Borrowed from Bill Hybels, *Courageous Leadership* (Grand Rapids: Zondervan, 2002), 74.

17. Anthea Smits, "The Story of Urban Life," Forge Missional DNA Conference, Brisbane, June 15, 2006.

involvement and engagement in community mission have markedly increased.

EMCs value the importance of inclusive community, and Solace participants love that their church culture makes space for people of any stage of faith, including those with no faith. Diane comments:

> The Church must constantly reaffirm its own distinctive nature, recognizing the extent to which it has been subverted by the cultural values of individualism and narcissism.
>
> Eddie Gibbs (LN, 100)

> I don't know if our church does it perfectly, but one thing our church does well is to allow people to come in and explore God and spirituality without commitment or criticism, and to leave when they are ready or to stay and ask questions. No question is silly!

Traditional boundaries of who is "in" and "out" are not so important. Nigel attends with his family but explains he is not a Christian because he has not had a convincing experience of God. But he participates regularly, contributes practically, and helps teach about his experience of meditation. It has been helpful for a young person grappling with her inherited faith to ask Nigel, "So why are you not a Christian?" and talk through issues of faith and doubt.

> An incarnational community that talks through issues of faith and doubt in this way is stripped of the quick persuasive "sales" appeal of evangelistic campaigns, and will naturally involve a longer time perspective for the unchurched to become followers of Christ. However, the authentic grappling with these questions will also provide the time to mature into a faith that hopefully is more holistic. The tension then remains in the faithful living and waiting. *Ruth Skree*

Incarnational Mission, Engaging the World

Rather than using the term "emerging church," Forge and many Australian fresh expressions use "missional church" or "emerging missional church" (EMC). Alan Hirsch suggests that the Northern Hemisphere emerging church conversation is sometimes more of a renewal movement of postmodern worship and spirituality than it is mission-shaped.[18] The term "emerging *missional* church" implies that emerging is for the sake of mission and that mission is central.

Australian EMCs focus on an incarnational mission that goes to people in their networks and "third spaces" and does not wait for people to come to

18. Alan Hirsch, *The Forgotten Ways: Reactivating the Missional Church* (Grand Rapids: Brazos, 2006), 17, 71–72.

church. They demonstrate a commitment to holistic mission through mercy, justice, and evangelism, and they explore how to promote the mission of the whole people of God. For example, Eastern Hills understands itself as a sent people: "We believe the Holy Spirit sends us to our homes, local community and wider world and empowers us to bring about love, truth, hope, healing, beauty and justice."[19] A "Simon doesn't know" (a five-minute interview of someone in the congregation about how his or her life and faith connect) helps participants get to know one another but also explores how faith relates to everyday life. Prayer journeys help reflect on where people are "sent to bring life" throughout the week. As a church Eastern Hills expresses missional engagement in diverse and creative formats—nursing home art classes, moviemaking groups, school outreach, a soup kitchen team that turned into a sports team, a creative group for people with mental illness, rent relief and assistance for asylum seekers, indoor soccer for migrant teenagers, and basically anything else people want to get involved in. One of their first socials was the harbor-deepening protest rally, which they went to out of a keen sense of social justice *and* because one of their members felt passionate about it. Eastern Hills's engagement with the world embraces a longing to help make it more in line with God's dream for it—the kingdom of God.

> The emerging church must remain intentionally and intensively missional; otherwise it will retreat in search of safer and more familiar ground.
>
> Eddie Gibbs (LN, 112)

Urban Life describes mission as "being found about our Father's business." In addition to their global mission, they look at ways to serve and reach their own community through a soup kitchen, high school ministry, a craft group, book club, Prime Timers social group (for fifty-plus adults), role-playing games, and an exercise group. They invite their broader community to join them in alleviating poverty—locally and in Cambodia. Their new mission statement is "living for the well-being of our community." The leadership knew they were changing their culture when the worship team ran out of volunteers because so many volunteered for newly focused soup kitchen and school ministries.

Solace's main focus is not postmodernizing worship or rethinking theology for its own sake, but helping Solace participants live out the ways of Jesus, "to enable a people to thrive as followers of Jesus, celebrating and re-making their everyday world." They wrote an art- and story-filled book called *Re-making* (mentioned above), about seven ways of Jesus-centered spirituality.[20]

---

19. Eastern Hills Community Church, "About Eastern Hills—Our Core Values," http://www.ehillschurch.com/about, accessed May 16, 2012.
20. Solace, *Remaking*.

For example, the first of the seven ways focuses on the sacramental tradition of celebrating God in the ordinary events of everyday life and work:

> *The Way of the Everyday* is about acknowledging that God is both above all things and in all things—that there exist no separate categories of spiritual and unspiritual, and that God can be found, and has an integral interest, in all that happens in the world.[21]

Solace is most fruitful, members believe, when they are reflecting on and expressing their faith and mission in their workplaces, neighbourhoods, and relationships broader than the church.

> For younger leaders, the greatest concern isn't how to get people to come to church but how best to take the church into the world. Their emphasis is not on extraction from the world but on engagement with society.
>
> Eddie Gibbs (LN. 44)

Empowering and Shared Leadership

Australian EMCs exercise an empowering and shared approach to leadership. The default seems to be a collaborative, affirming, and permission-giving leadership style that encourages people to foster their creativity and passion in mission.

> This is the default in the Netherlands too. *Nico-Dirk van Loo*

Part of Eastern Hills's initial dream was to share responsibilities rather than become pastor-centered. The community involves lots of people in leadership and opens leaders' meetings to anyone who wants to contribute. As a group comprising mainly young adults with high levels of trust in one another, it finds decision making easier and risky change more acceptable. Empowering leadership is part of the culture. Members appreciate that if they have a passion for something, the church is supportive. Claire wanted to start a soup kitchen, and the other leaders supported her. Pria offered to serve a local school, and others offered to paint drama backdrops and sew costumes. The church invited a person with a passion for environmentalism to teach about it, shaping the program around his interest rather than recruiting him first to fill out a roster. The group tends to go with people's passions as a guide for what ministries to develop. Emma and Toliu's leadership style as pastors is to draw out people's passions, funnel them into appropriate service, and help them gather necessary resources to be successful.

21. Ibid., 22.

> Participation is key to community building. Transformation itself happens in the midst of participation. *Eileen Suico*

A radical part of Urban Life's remissionalisation story is that of fifty-year-old Doug Faircloth who handed over leadership to his associate, thirty-five-year-old Anthea Smits. Doug continued in a two-days-per-week coaching role. Anthea, recruited from a business background, reports that Brian McLaren's reflections on Dorothy and *The Wizard of Oz* inspired her to move away from CEO-style leadership and to instead invite people on a journey and help them maximise their strengths.[22] She is passionate to lead and "awaken the missionary in people." Oliver wanted to use the café area for a role-playing games venue, and Anthea applauded him. He wondered why she was excited. She explained that his group and its community connections are what Urban Life wants to prioritise, and that no other churches in the area are engaging with youth playing those games.

> It is worth noting here that despite the above criticism of the North American emerging church, here is a positive example, via Brian McLaren, of it shaping an Australian church toward mission. *Steve Taylor*

Solace practices extensive collaboration in dreaming and decision making, stretching to also include the broader community in dreaming about how to improve its neighbourhood. One big dream the church explored was "SPACE," a group involving St. Paul's and SolACE people to investigate how to develop and use their shared space at St. Paul's. Their discernment followed a community development approach, and they started their meetings with an hour of discussion around these topics:

- things to cheer
- changes to be part of
- crisis/conflict in which to be a peacemaker
- celebrations to join in
- crowds or coincidences to pay attention to
- conversations that lead somewhere

> This is such a rich list, and seems to offer a language for all folk, not only church folk, to participate in. *Steve Taylor*

22. Inspired by Brian D. McLaren, "Dorothy on Leadership or 'How a Movie from Childhood Can Help Us Understand the Changing Nature of Leadership in the Postmodern Tradition.'" *Rev Magazine* (November/December 2000), http://www.brianmclaren.net/emc/archives/imported/dorothy-on-leadership.html.

During the second hour of the meetings, they discussed their building needs, but they wanted to ensure any building redevelopment enhanced and built on their openness to their community.

The experiments of emerging missional churches in Australia point in hopeful directions. They are "creating lives which reflect the kingdom of God," inspiring people to be "living for the well-being of our community," and "[enabling] a people to thrive as followers of Jesus, celebrating and re-making their everyday world" (Eastern Hills's, Urban Life's, and Solace's mission statements). These experiments are not sourced in clever leadership or creativity, but are part of a shaping process at work in these churches. The mission of God is active in the variety and advocacy for justice at Eastern Hills, the courage and refocusing of Urban Life, and the networks and everyday spirituality of Solace. These are windows into how God is at work in the shaping of things now and the shaping of things to come.

4

New Expressions of Church in Scandinavia

Ruth Skree

Culture

The Scandinavian countries have a long Christian history going back to the ninth century. However, in the twentieth century the development is marked by a growing secularization, and the church has been pushed to the margins of society. Today the Nordic countries are considered among the most secularized nations in the world,[1] and missionaries now come to Scandinavia from the countries that once were on the receiving end of mission.

The majority of the Scandinavian population consists of nominal members of the national folk churches; in Denmark 80 percent of the population are members,[2] in Norway 78 percent,[3] and in Sweden 70 percent.[4] At the

1. See Gallup poll from 2005, https://worldview.gallup.com/default.aspx, accessed September 1, 2011, and The European Commission Eurobarometer Poll: *Social Values, Science and Technology* (June 2005), http://ec.europa.eu/public_opinion/archives/ebs/ebs_225_report_en.pdf, accessed September 1, 2011.

2. http://www.km.dk/folkekirken/statistik-og-oekonomi/kirkestatistik/folkekirkens-medlem stal.html, accessed September 1, 2011.

3. http://statbank.ssb.no/statistikkbanken/Default_FR.asp?PXSid=0andnvl=trueandPLan guage=0andtilside=selectvarval/define.aspandTabellid=06929, accessed September 2, 2011.

4. http://www.svenskakyrkan.se/default.aspx?id=645562, accessed September 11, 2011.

same time only a small minority participate in church services[5] or believe central Christian doctrine.[6] This creates an odd reality, where a society that no longer considers itself Christian still has a national folk church that few actively support. The Swedish church formally cut the ties in 2000,[7] but Denmark and Norway are still discussing how to dissolve the tight connection between the state and the church. Missional engagements in post-Christendom societies wrestle with the tension of an increasingly secular society and at the same time a resurgence of religiosity and immigrants with a vibrant faith.

> It sometimes requires the critique of non-Western societies to make Christians aware of the extent to which secular thinking has not only marginalized the church from society, but has itself permeated the belief system and institutional life of the church.
>
> Eddie Gibbs (INO, 165)

Experiments

Nedre Glomma Frikirke, Sarpsborg, Norway

After years of ministry in a wide variety of contexts and churches, Dag W. Stang found that the common language and way of practicing faith often functioned as a barrier rather than a help for people on their journeys toward Jesus. As Christian faith became marginal in Norwegian society, traditional churches seemed to be totally out of touch with the average person. After ending his association with a national Christian ministry in 2003, Dag started a conversation with the Evangelical Lutheran Free Church of Norway. He explored how to start a missional church that welcomes rather than excludes the average Norwegian.

What began as a group of eight people grew into a fully acknowledged church by March 2007. Dag believes that pastors should not be employed exclusively by the church. Everyone in the church ought to fully participate in society, work, and life, and not retreat into a Christian isolationist subculture. Nedre Glomma Frikirke today consists of five small groups that meet in homes every other week, and it holds café services on the other weeks.

Relationality in every area of ministry is the guiding principle. The central philosophy is to include people wherever they find themselves in regard to Christian faith. When they started meeting together in 2003 as a small group,

5. In Norway this is down to below 3 percent on any given Sunday, http://www.ssb.no/emner/07/02/10/kirke_kostra/, accessed September 9, 2011.
6. Bent Reidar Eriksen et al., *Norsk Håndbok for Kirke og Misjon* (Oslo: Lunde Forlag, 1990), 6.
7. http://www.svenskakyrkan.se/default.aspx?id=656230, accessed September 11, 2011.

> In the urban context, the church has to become a counterculture movement, not in the sense of withdrawal, but of engagement with the wider society. The church must act prophetically by demonstrating authentic community based on networks of small groups. The small groups help to contextualize the kingdom of God in different working and living environments.
>
> Eddie Gibbs (INO, 164)

sharing the Christian life and teaching one another, the community started courses for couples on relationship issues, regardless of the participants' beliefs and social status (married or couples living together). The church connects with many people struggling in the aftermath of divorce and facing other issues in their faith. The parable of the welcoming father serves as a focal point for understanding how God seeks relationship with people whether they find themselves as the prodigal or the older brother at home. "We evaluate what we are doing based on other criteria than what is normal for churches around us," Dag says. He cannot emphasize enough the importance of a relational church. His conviction is that the church should never grow so big that they risk not noticing whether people are coming to gatherings or not. "We choose to be at a vulnerable size to continue to be in relationship with each other. We would rather grow into several communities before we grow too big as one congregation."[8]

In Bykirken we declared that the "level of relations" was more important than the "level of activity." We are made disciples of Jesus in community. *Andreas Østerlund Nielsen*

A former UK megachurch, St. Tom's Church in Sheffield, developed dispersed expressions of church after the loss of their mega-venue. This resulted in new expressions that intrigued and attracted many cynical English churchgoers, with an emphasis on discipleship in "small groups," an extended family feel in "clusters" of three to seven small groups, and culturally distinct celebrations (composed of multiple clusters). *Bob Whitesel*

Because the people involved in the church come from an unchurched background, discipleship starts at a different place and moves at a different pace than in many other churches. The services are a safe space where people can come and know what to expect even without having faith. The services consist of extended teaching in an open conversational style; they start where people are, and they wrestle with theological and spiritual questions. As Dag distances what he is doing from conventional cultural Christianity in Norway, he asks whether what they are doing is even Christianity as we know it. The

8. Dag W. Stang, interview with Ruth Skree, September 28, 2010. Unless otherwise marked, all quotes and citations are translated into English by Ruth Skree.

focus is centered on following in the Way of Jesus, rather than tending to institutional religion.

> I find myself asking similar questions about the distinction between the simple quest to follow the Way of Jesus and the conventional practices of institutional religion. I wonder whether the rituals and practices that characterize public religion actually help participants to be formed and transformed by the living reality of Christ and his kingdom. *Mark Scandrette*

> This resonates with the new monastic commitment to follow Jesus radically—to love God, love self, and love others. The emerging church commitment to follow Jesus in this way resembles what the monks and friars have done ever since the early church mothers and fathers went into the desert. *Ian Mobsby*

> St. Tom's Church in Sheffield, England, found that the "safest place" for visitors to connect with the church was not amid one of the seven culturally different celebrations or even in one of the many small groups of the church. Rather, St. Tom's leaders discovered that it was in the relative anonymity yet connectedness of "clusters" of three to seven small groups (which they called midsize missional communities) that most newcomers said they bonded with the church. *Bob Whitesel*

Mosaik, Aalborg, Denmark

In Denmark, the highly secularized culture creates a church that is a marginal and private phenomenon. While there is not an emerging movement in Denmark, beginning in the early 2000s conversations on the topic were held in various forums. No one was speaking out loud about new expressions of church, but like-minded people blogged and formed relationships among themselves, in addition to reading various resources and making connections with people involved in the conversations taking place in the United States. Henrik Holmgaard, pastor of Mosaik in Aalborg, explains how American participants in the emerging conversation came to visit Denmark. The conversations proved helpful in deconstructing faith, but the reconstruction needed to take place on Danish terms. When it comes to engaging the Bible, Henrik says, "We live in a country that is so deeply secularized that even the Christians stopped reading the Bible, so we start at another place than an American culture where the Bible still has a voice in the conversation."[9]

Many of the newer expressions of faith in Denmark take their impulse from the United Kingdom, from the fresh expressions movement as well as the new monastic orders within the structures of the Church of England. "We

9. Henrik Holmgaard, interview with Ruth Skree, September 30, 2010.

have found our way of thinking about discipleship that still maintains belief in an institution, as well as an awareness that institutions cannot provide everything, and, in the same way, that the network can provide something, but not everything," Henrik says.[10]

> In Denmark, national religion is "culture Christianity." Even though more than 80 percent are members of the Lutheran Church, and the Christian heritage is still woven into many parts of the society, faith is marginal to most peoples' life-worlds. *Andreas Østerlund Nielsen*

The story of Mosaik began in 2005 as a fellowship of students who were then called Re:Search. Emerging from the Apostolic Church in Aalborg, they established a community as a church for students. Many students saw the relationship between their studies, science, church, and God as something that created tension and complexity. Life was compartmentalized and lived differently in their different worlds. Henrik says:

> When we read the stories about Jesus, how He said quite simply "Come, follow me," how he changed people's lives, taught them to be disciples and sent them out as servants into the world, something told us that the church had turned into something too complicated. To be a Christian was no longer quite as simple as we read about in the Gospels.[11]

Re:Search started on a journey, with the Bible as the basic story and Jesus as a model for their practices, to find a solution that did not contribute to further complexity. "We had to address the question: 'How can the personality, life and teachings of Jesus bring greater simplicity in life as followers, so it can be learned, lived and transform human life?'"[12] Over time this community evolved into something more than a student group, and eventually the idea of planting a new church began to take shape. Mosaik emerged as a church in early 2009.[13]

> Confronting individualism, hybridity, and compartmentalization will be essential for mission in the Western world. Christian communal life may well become the primary public witness to gospel-enabling transformation and discipleship. If this is so, new monasticism points to the future. *Andreas Østerlund Nielsen*

10. Ibid.
11. Ibid.
12. Henrik Holmgaard, Bettina Poulsen, and Anne Storgaard Larsen, *Mosaik Bogen: I Fælleskab at Udleve Jesu Livsstil* (Aalborg, Denmark: Mosaik, 2010), 71–72; online at http://www.muckup.dk/MOSAIK/mosaikweb.pdf, accessed September 10, 2010.
13. Ibid., 70.

> It was in a similar quest to address spiritual complexity that Mike Breen, former rector of St. Tom's Church in Sheffield, England, developed the icon-based discipleship tool Lifeshapes. Each of the six icons emphasizes the daily praxis between faith and life. *Bob Whitesel*

One of the important but most difficult challenges for Mosaik was to articulate in a positive way what they believe and how they will live it out. Henrik explains:

> In a time of many changes it is easy to look at dead tradition and go bitter, to deconstruct reality and ultimately end up with a theology and practice that is defined on negative terms—all the things that we do not believe or will not do anymore, but we have seen the importance of simultaneously reconstructing a new understanding. The story of Re:Search can be summarized as a time of deconstruction and reconstruction of our understanding of what it means for the church to encounter a changing culture.[14]

> What has been described as the phenomenon of the emerging church might be better thought of as a prophetic movement within the larger church. It has taken time for these groups to move from deconstruction and critique to a constructive practice. Yet I don't think that the seasons of deconstruction have been insignificant. There is a time for lament and the acknowledgment of failure and mistakes. The containers that allowed for this deconstructive lament to take place might not be the best for reconstruction—but I see encouraging signs worldwide of reorganizing for a more constructive phase. I've noticed that leaders who are just coming of age today are much less deconstructive than those of us who stepped into leadership ten or fifteen years ago. I think this is partly because new permission and space has been created through the struggles and explorations, new expressions, and the writing of the past ten to fifteen years. As a pattern, many younger front-edge leaders and communities are deeply committed to place and geography as an organizing principle through which to explore embodied kingdom theology. *Mark Scandrette*

SubChurch, SubStans, Oslo, Norway

In 1997 a small group of Christians with an affinity for playing alternative, goth, and punk music started meeting up in Oslo. Stian Kilde Aarebrot joined after about three months, and he tells how a church that did not want to be church started:

> We only met every other week, and [we still] encouraged people to go to their home churches—our purpose was never to take people away from their churches,

14. Holmgaard, interview.

but [to] provide a place where we could share our passion for alternative music and not feel different because of our style. We had no idea that this kind of alternative church thing was happening [in] other places as well; we just wanted to be a hub where we could talk about our bands and support each other. It was not really about not fitting in when it came to faith as much as it was about style.[15]

But after two years people started realizing that none of the people who attended actually went to other churches anymore. This group that functioned as a church needed to acknowledge and call what they were doing "church"— and thus SubChurch came into being.

SubChurch emerged among people that did not feel at home in the traditional Christian culture. We wanted to create something new and different, and express ourselves in ways that were not common in other Christian churches, and in the rest of the mainstream culture. SubChurch wanted to continue to build on this heritage.[16]

> This style of localized artistic expression developed at St. Tom's Church in England among the "clubbers" who frequented the popular disco club scene in Sheffield. Their all-night techno raves contributed to an indigenous worship expression similar to SubChurch. The difference in Sheffield was that their gathering remained part of a diversified larger congregation. This gave the lower-income clubbers the fiscal base and a spiritual connection to a larger faith community. *Bob Whitesel*

From the start Sub had a conservative Christian faith, with most of its participants playing in rock, goth, metal, and punk bands. The church was and is interdenominational, emphasizing the unifying elements of faith over theological and ecclesiological differences. Over time the church evolved into much more of a patchwork of people and made a theological shift. Stian says:

In 2001 when we got our own space, we grew very fast. In a month we went from about thirty to about seventy in our gatherings, and the older "sub-ers" started complaining about these mainstream people entering the church. We had some church-shoppers come by, and many people other than the typical "sub-person" stayed as they found that what we were doing worked for them. This essentially shaped us to gradually shift our core identity from style and music towards our faith. Our calling is to have a heart for the subcultures, and for the people falling outside of the regular churches.[17]

15. Stian Kilde Aarebrot, interview with Ruth Skree, November 11, 2010.
16. SubChurch, *SubManifest: Med Gud-Mot Strømmen* (Oslo, Norway, 2008); online at http://www.subchurch.no/, accessed May 27, 2010.
17. Aarebrot, interview.

Today SubChurch has about a hundred people at a gathering, and roughly two hundred would consider Sub their church. They are situated in the very centre of Oslo, renting a venue that used to be a gay bar. Here they run Sub Scene and Sub Café, which draws a big crowd of teenagers. Several of them have come to faith; others hang out in the café during the service or pop by. "The younger 'sub-ers'[18] often hang out in the café with the teenagers, and the gap between the church crowd and the café crowd is diminishing."[19] The café also partners with the city in being a safe, alcohol-free space for teenagers and has become a way of connecting with the larger culture.

After spending a year with Re:IMAGINE in San Francisco, California, Stian initiated "SubStans,"[20] which is a way of engaging people in more focused discipleship processes, inspired by Mark Scandrette's Jesus Dojo.[21] Over six weeks, a group of people commits to go through a program together, focusing on one aspect of discipleship, such as simplicity.

St. Tom's Church counters the influence of "mainstream people entering the church" by creating a network of seven linked but culturally different worship communities (which they call "celebrations"). Subsequently, when visitors are attracted to a celebration, but find it not completely to their mainstream liking, the visitors have six linked alternative celebrations they may choose instead. Thus mainstream curiosity does not need to end in parasitical incursion (to colonize emerging expressions) or in group exit. Since at St. Tom's the SubChurch culture is part of a network of six other celebrations (with forty-plus extended family clusters), when inquisitiveness wears off various alternative expressions are available. *Bob Whitesel*

Maintaining the original vision as different people get attracted is apparently always a difficulty. Still, the "homogeneous unit principle" has its problems if such units are too loosely attached to the larger body of Christ. In any case, shifting from style to faith doesn't sound too bad. *Andreas Østerlund Nielsen*

Oikos Kommuniteten, Hamarkullen, Sweden

Throughout Scandinavia a wide variety of communities and collectives in the new monastic fashion are emerging across a broad spectrum of theological traditions, denominations, and movements. The writings of Shane Claiborne and The Order of Mission from St. Thomas' Church in Sheffield have been particularly influential. These influences are usually combined with

18. A person who considers himself a part of SubChurch.
19. Aarebrot, interview.
20. A Norwegian word meaning both "substance" and "sub-stop."
21. For more information on the Jesus Dojo, visit Re:IMAGINE's website, http://www.reimagine.org/node/32, accessed October 30, 2010.

various impulses from different monastic movements, both contemporary and throughout church history. Sweden in particular has experienced a resurgence in monastic communities in recent years that builds on the experiences from the people involved in the Jesus movement and different forms of communal living in the seventies.

> The Order of Mission (TOM) is growing in Germany. Some of the members are deeply involved in the reform movement within the established church. *Markus Weimer*

> St. Tom's Church recognized its responsibility to resource other fresh expressions since former rector Mike Breen's "Ephesus" vision. Breen understood this vision to mean that St. Tom's would be a fresh expression of Ephesus, where Paul trained leaders and "the word of the Lord spread widely and grew in power" (Acts 19:20). In response, every June St. Tom's hosts a "Pilgrimage Week" where leaders from across North America and Europe are invited to learn about St. Tom's history, its Order of Mission, and its innovative missional structures. *Bob Whitesel*

Oikos Kommuniteten (The Oikos Community) in Hamarkullen, Sweden, is a new ecumenical community with fifteen members. The participants in this new monastic community come from different traditions and movements, but as a community they choose to be affiliated with an existing denomination (The Swedish Church/EFS). This association helps the community to stand rooted in the Christian tradition while simultaneously exploring what it means to be a Christian community in Hammarkullen today.

Oikos as a community is inspired by impulses from Christian movements through history that emphasized living life in close community, from Catholic orders to the Anabaptist movement. "The Oikos Community started from various . . . loosely connected communities that chose to join together to live in community," says Tobias Herrström, the priest of the Oikos Community. "We missed having a community that was church, instead of simply going to church. We also missed being part of a community where the love practiced in everyday life would help us become better disciples of Jesus."[22]

"Instead of having a lot of activities we would rather be a community that went to other activities and was active there, and in that way to be there as the church. Instead of inviting people in to come to us, we decided to go out," Herrström says. The community does not focus on Sunday services, but encourages people living in the community to contribute to other churches. There are sixteen people who do not live in the community yet still come to the Tuesday meal and participate in their rhythm of praying the hours. Core

22. Tobias Herrström, email interview with Ruth Skree.

values for Oikos are nonviolence, commitment to their rule of life (made annually), and a consensus-led community where every decision is made by the whole community.

A central theological ethos of the Oikos Community is the kingdom of God as something that is present now but will one day fully reign. The church is called to give signs or symptoms of this kingdom.[23] Tobias emphasizes that the church is called to be different and live out the Sermon on the Mount. They strive to provide a vision of church as the people together rather than church as an organization or building.

> One thing I think is important to note about Oikos Community is that it is situated in a predominantly Muslim neighborhood on the outskirts of Gotenborg. In so many cities across Europe and America, friendship and dialogue across cultures and religions is such an important task for the church—made especially poignant by the current trend of xenophobia, fear, and violence. *Mark Scandrette*

Practices

Worship

Dag W. Stang in Nedre Glomma Frikirke describes the church's philosophy regarding their worship practices:

> I would rather have a worshiping church that doesn't know how to sing than a singing church that doesn't know how to worship. This is why we have chosen not to sing as our primary way of worship in our services. Music is such a powerful inclusive force, and on the opposite, a way to make people feel excluded and as outsiders. To us we stress that worship is a lifestyle and has more to do with how I treat my children and work colleagues than knowing the right songs.[24]

In this way the participants in the community honor God by seeking to grow in love as a hospitable people.

> It often seems that our proficiency with religious words and ritual worship practices is in inverse relationship with our skills and ability to actually do the things that Jesus said and did in the gritty details of our lives. Communities of resistance, like Oikos, address this disparity. *Mark Scandrette*

23. Ibid.
24. Stang, interview.

Creative expressions are encouraged in Nedre Glomma Frikirke. Artists
and writers meet on a regular basis, sharing and encouraging one another's
creative processes, both in music and texts. These texts per se are not necessarily intended for corporal use in the church, but are often performed as
artistic expressions that reflect on faith as well as life. "The early church
was probably more shaped by the meetings in the synagogues focused on
reading of Scripture and teaching than contemporary worship services,"
says Stang.[25]

For Oikos as well as Nedre Glomma Frikirke, Holy Communion is a central
practice that is celebrated weekly. In Oikos this takes place in combination
with a weekly meal. "These two practices are an integral part of our theology,"
Tobias Herrström says. "Food is important for our community and a clear
feature in the early church as well."[26] Because relationships are highly valued
as places, not only for discipleship, but also for worship, these communities
value smaller arenas and do not separate worship from everyday life. "Worship to us is just as much hanging out with the teenagers in the café as [it is]
coming together on a Sunday," Stian Kilde Aarebrot says.[27]

From the beginning, SubChurch broke out of the common conventions of
what people connect with worship. When they worship, whether on a Sunday
or at another time or place, it normally doesn't sound or look like traditional
church. Stian says, "But it doesn't really matter how it looks from the outside;
everything is worship when we worship God with and through all of our
lives."[28] Mosaik shares meals and does Communion in their neighborhood-
based clusters that meet every other week. Coming from a tradition that
limited worship and the Christian life to primarily the Sunday service, Mosaik
sought to find a new way and a new language.

> We merely found that the experience of the Sunday service as operating system
> for us did not adequately respond to our questions about discipleship prac-
> tices and simplicity. We had a feeling that there was something we had to try
> to change, but we lacked the language that could describe our new practice.[29]

In this process they did not do away with the Sunday gatherings, which still
might have a somewhat traditional look, but these meetings are no longer the
primary expression of their worship.

25. Ibid.
26. Herrström, interview.
27. Aarebrot, interview.
28. Ibid.
29. Holmgaard, Poulsen, and Larsen, *Mosaik Bogen*, 72.

Oikos's worship practices involve praying the hours four times a week as a community as well as trying to find a breeding ground for a healthy, earthy, charismatic expression. Tobias Herrström emphasizes how central it is to form inclusive practices in which everyone contributes with their gift. "Everyone's participation is essentially about how everyone finds a place and function in the community as a whole, not primarily in the worship service."[30]

> I had a chance to participate in the Korsvei Festival in Norway and I was impressed with the passion and holistic and embodied nature of the festival and Korsvei network. I'm intrigued by the signs of life evident in the renewal movements within the state churches in both Norway and Denmark, with Sunday morning worship being maintained by the paid clergy and other more grassroots and participatory gatherings happening throughout the week. *Mark Scandrette*

Community Formation

Relationships are the core ingredient of Nedre Glomma Frikirke. People are welcomed to be a part of the community no matter where they are on their journey of faith. "We are not a church focused on speed and growth, but on slowly moving in the right direction," says Dag. He continues:

People are allowed to be who they are and where they are, which implies a different view on membership than our church tradition normally holds. We stress orthopraxy over orthodoxy, that people seek to live out their faith in their everyday practices, such as giving, spending time with people that are seeking faith, participating in the relationships and groups in the church over believing the right doctrinal statements. Right now we have a gay couple who are a part of our community, whom we might not send out to participate as national representatives in our denomination, which might not approve of our ways, but they are of course welcomed and included as a part of our community.[31]

Oikos functions as a new monastic community committed to a common rule with a rhythm of discipleship. There are small groups of three to four people who meet once a month to share questions about discipleship, how to live the vision, and what it means to live according to the values. Tobias explains:

The community is there to train us in discipleship, which is at the centre of our existence. We also have a strong commitment where members commit for one year at a time, [and] we invite each other to exercise discipleship. The focus,

30. Herrström, interview.
31. Stang, interview.

however, is that it is an exercise; we will fail living up to the vision and our values, but this is okay because we are practicing together as a community. Here our prayer rhythm is important as well; prayer and work must be kept together. Without our life of prayer we would not exist.[32]

> John Wesley might be amused to see his "band meetings," intimate groupings of less than eight for discipleship and accountability, being reflected in Scandinavian monastic gatherings. For Wesley, the band was the principle confessional/accountability unit of his methodology. *Bob Whitesel*

> In our community in San Francisco we've noticed a tension between belonging and becoming. Even if we say we want to be about shared practices and radical action, it is much easier, and perhaps instinctual, to gravitate toward socializing and shared entertainment. For most of us, especially at certain life stages, belonging is such a strong impulse that it can squelch our initiative toward Christ-inspired action and practice. We like to say that a sense of community is a by-product, not the goal, of a shared journey of formation and mission. Jesus was a rabbi with a clear agenda for change, not just a buddy to his disciples. So we've had to wrestle with how to be a community that offers a sense of belonging, but more important, momentum toward transformation. *Mark Scandrette*

Mission

The central focus of many of the new expressions is the emphasis on a missional life. The new expressions in the Scandinavian countries are motivated more from the *missio Dei* than from critiquing the deficits in the existing churches and denominations around them. This doesn't mean, however, that they do not critique a Christendom model and the state church concept as both unbiblical and impossible in a pluralist, postmodern society. The latter half of the twentieth century in Scandinavia is marked by economic growth as well as a drastic decline in religious involvement. Secularism remained strong, and Christian faith became private and nominal at best. The different communities realize that Scandinavia today has little to no communal Christian memory anymore. From this springs a deep commitment to God's mission in their local communities. Dag Stang, who worked in full-time ministry for many years prior to starting Nedre Glomma Frikirke, says:

> If God is already where people are, then I as a pastor need to know this world and be a part of this world. The church leaders in Norway tend to be so culturally removed by working full-time for the church that they do not speak the same

32. Herrström, interview.

language as the average Norwegian. Missional living means living with people where they are; it is all about relationships. This is why I never again want to work full-time inside the church.[33]

> To point to the deficits of the existing parochial structure is important. To question its effect in a pluralistic society is necessary. To call it unbiblical stretches the point. Is there any single biblical approach? *Markus Weimer*

> The emphasis in Scandinavia—to focus on the *missio Dei* more than to criticize the existing church—is also evident at St. Tom's Church in Sheffield, England. This may in part be due to the state church's political power and influence in these countries. *Bob Whitesel*

As Scandinavian countries had several waves of immigration during the twentieth century, particularly from the Middle East, the former monocultures changed drastically. Now the neighbor next door might be Muslim, Sikh, or Hindu, and so loving our neighbor may be fraught with tension. Oikos in Hamarkullen, Sweden, has offered practical courses in nonviolent conflict resolution and will continue to train people who can in turn train others. This is not primarily seen as an activity, but as a central part of their missional living as those sent to the community around them.

SubChurch in the same way has had a growing awareness of social issues as a core part of their understanding of what mission really is. The Jesus Dojos are ways in which they try to move forward in this direction, but Aarebrot admits that the church is just exploring what this might mean for how discipleship will look in the future. The Scandinavian countries are not at the forefront when it comes to awareness and working for fair trade and other justice issues. SubChurch and Oikos have a growing concern for a more holistic understanding of mission and the kingdom of God. Common for Oikos, SubChurch, Mosaik, and Nedre Glomma Frikirke is a foundational understanding of being sent to their local context. Today a rediscovery of missional living in the Nordic context is crucial for the continuing existence of the church in the future. Stian Kilde Aarebrot says mission is at the heart of SubChurch:

> The moment we stop, and just become a church that is a church, and has no involvement or calling to the subcultures and the people falling on the wayside of regular church, then we stop having a reason for existence.[34]

> There is a danger of attaching a (hyped) missional ecclesiology to a (traditional) theology of maintenance. To become healthy missional churches we need to generate sound missional

---

33. Stang, interview.
34. Aarebrot, interview.

theologies. Every newcomer with a church background needs to be carefully introduced to it. *Andreas Østerlund Nielsen*

Leadership

As new expressions of faith emerge in Scandinavia, there are some common patterns when it comes to leadership. With the hierarchic and episcopal state churches as their backdrop, almost all of these new expressions employ a flat leadership structure, even if the national leadership in their denominations function in another way.

The flat leadership structure at St. Tom's Church is described by them as turning the leadership pyramid upside down. By this they mean they embrace the idea that the upper echelon of leaders is there to serve the base of congregants, rather than seeing the church as a large base of congregants that is there to support an elite apex of leaders. *Bob Whitesel*

SubChurch has seen both the benefits and the drawbacks of a flat leadership structure. The church is led by a board both in pastoral as well as in practical matters. Board members are elected once a year at the annual church meeting. This is done in a democratic way, and people can be on the board for a maximum of four years. For many years the church has not had a centralized leader in the form of a head pastor. The pastoral leadership is taken care of by the board, and even when the church had a pastor, he was a volunteer and an equal member of the board. "We have never had a very visible leader," Stian Aarebrot says. "One of the biggest strengths of this flat structure is that we have a group of almost ten different people in a church of about 150 people that will speak at a Sunday service. The challenge is to keep a steady direction in where we are going."[35]

SubChurch has found a way to keep participation high. People are encouraged to move forward with their ideas, and the church as a body will support it. In this way there is a lot of informal leadership taking place, and the role of the board is to maintain some sort of control and guide the initiatives from taking a wrong turn. There is therefore a short distance between being a leader and being a member in the church, and the line is blurry. Stian admits, however, that the board in recent years has not always been great at communicating their role as primarily backing and supporting initiatives, and therefore it is not functioning in an optimal way. Tobias Herrström from Oikos resonates with the challenges of flat leadership: "A relationship-based church is moving

35. Ibid.

and messy. It is partially liquid, but needs boundaries in order to keep together relationships and structures that are not solely based on friendship."[36]

> Dare one say: based on Christian love? Due to its own fallibility, true love establishes structures to sustain its loving self-surrender. Though, such structures are not mainly centers of retreat nor protecting borders; rather they are edifying processes of interchange (read: mission). *Andreas Østerlund Nielsen*

Nedre Glomma Frikirke holds to an ideal of a flat structure in theory and theology, but in real life the leader is the problem, Dag W. Stang admits. As one of the central leaders starting the church, he struggles with letting go and not always being in control as the leader. "It is not easy to lead with a flat structure with a lot of broken people in the community."[37]

> Leadership is inevitably entangled in so many personal issues. Without recognized leadership, power is just invisible and out of control. Maybe it is time again to liberate ourselves by submitting to moral and spiritual authority? *Andreas Østerlund Nielsen*

A common understanding is that leadership is a function in the body rather than a position to be filled. In Oikos leadership is shared and all decisions related to life in the community are made by consensus. This process has certain specific guidelines to preserve and value every individual's unique contribution as well as the group's interests. The priest, Tobias, holds no power over others; he functions as a guide. "We try to serve each other and increase loyalty to Jesus," Tobias says. For both Oikos and Mosaik, leadership is deeply rooted in a commitment to follow Jesus as their leader. Leadership in Mosaik is about following in the way and living out the life of Jesus so that others can follow. According to Henrik:

> We all model our lives after different images and models that surround us. In the various relationships and communities where we belong, there are also people who look to us, to our life and practices. We are all both apprentices and leaders at the same time: From the front we all look like sheep. From behind we all resemble shepherds.[38]

> I think in groups where "flat" leadership is valued, the clearly defined and articulated values and structures of the community take on some of the role often reserved for leaders. Even in participatory and consensus-based communities, some people have more vested

---

36. Herrström, interview.
37. Stang, interview.
38. Holmgaard, Poulsen, and Larsen, *Mosaik Bogen*, 22.

interest, earned credibility, wisdom, and the weight of influence. So there is actually implicit leadership. As I get older I see that one of the "mistakes" I've made was reacting to the abuse of leadership I had experienced by trying to make things completely flat—the vacuum of leadership I created by my hesitancy and insecurity actually created a lot of pain for the group. No leadership is not the solution—but we can work toward new models and practices of leadership. Mark Scandrette

Bibliography

Holmgaard, Henrik, Bettina Poulsen, and Anne Storgaard Larsen. *Mosaik Bogen: I Fælleskab at Udleve Jesu Livsstil.* Aalborg, Denmark: Mosaik, 2010. Online at http://www.muckup.dk/MOSAIK/mosaikweb.pdf. Accessed September 10, 2010.

Kommuniteten Oikos: http://www.kommunitetenoikos.se.

Kommuniteten Oikos. *Regel.* Hamarkullen, Sweden, 2009. Community bylaws. Tobias Herrström, emailed to author, November 14, 2010.

Mosaik: http://mosaiknet.weebly.com.

Nedre Glomma Frikirke: http://nedreglomma.frikirken.no/wordpress.

SubChurch. *SubManifest: Med Gud-Mot Strømmen.* Oslo, Norway, 2008. Online at http://www.subchurch.no. Accessed May 27, 2010.

SubStans: http://jesusdojo.no.

5

New Expressions of Church in the Low Countries

Nico-Dirk van Loo

When our time is seen as post-Christian usually the kerygma is confused with its realization.

J. C. Hoekendijk, 1948[1]

More than sixty years after Hoekendijk penned these words they are strangely comforting. While he spoke in the aftermath of World War II, we live in a new century that feels betrayed by the promises of modernity and experiences a spirituality beyond the secular.

New expressions of church in the Low Countries (Belgium and the Netherlands) rediscover the realization of the kerygma by leaving the Christian subculture and finding their way again in a homeland that shifted beyond Christendom and beyond modernity. This chapter offers a short overview of these new churches. After a brief introduction to the historical and contemporary context of these new expressions of church, I will identify the characteristics of these communities through an examination of their worship, community life, mission, and leadership practices.

1. "Kerk en volk in de Duitse zendingswetenschap" (PhD thesis, Utrecht University, 1948).

Culture

Reformed Christendom rose during the sixteenth century, and it was stabilized when the state ordered the Synod of Dordrecht (1618–19). The Reformed Church lost its privileged position during the nineteenth century and lost a lot of ground during the latter part of the twentieth century. Despite all this, God arose in the twenty-first century after a premature burial by secularism. Recent sociological studies show an increase in spirituality. God is back in an impressive rise in private spirituality and the search for individual meaning. Reformed Christendom is gone and only a small Christian subculture remains—a subculture that is still pretty strong although it is marginal in the Dutch society at large. In Flanders, Protestantism was suppressed during the Spanish War (1568–1648) and has remained marginal since then (despite the Belgic Confession!). Catholicism has been firmly established for a long time.[2]

Experiments

New Expressions of Church

The relationship between new expressions of church and the rest of the body of Christ is both difficult and easy. It is difficult because virtually all emerging

2. It may be helpful for non-Dutch readers to understand the following demographic information and assessment provided by Stefan Paas: The Netherlands, home of 16 million Dutch speakers, shares its southern border with Belgium. Historically, these two countries belonged together as the Northern and Southern Netherlands. However, after the war with France (seventeenth century) the Southern Netherlands were separated, and after a brief interval in which the two countries were reunited, the Southern Netherlands became independent for good. Since 1830 it has been called the Kingdom of Belgium.

Historically, the northern provinces of the current Kingdom of the Netherlands are Protestant and the south is Catholic. Belgium shares its northern border with the Netherlands and has 11 million people. The northern part, Flanders, is Dutch-speaking and the southern part, Wallonia, is French-speaking. Belgium is predominantly Catholic.

The Netherlands has never known a state church like England. The Reformed Church during the seventeenth and eighteenth centuries became a "public church." It was privileged but other churches were tolerated. Still, 20 percent of the population are members of one of the Reformed churches. As for the southern part of the Netherlands and Belgium, the Reformation was chased away by the Inquisition. Today, about 70 percent of the Belgians are nominally Catholic.

(Post-)Catholic Belgium is more hierarchic, more family-minded, more suspicious toward government, new religious groups, and so forth, whereas Protestant Holland is generally more inclined to a political and public culture of trust and idealistic enterprises. The evangelical movement has made far deeper inroads in the northern regions of the Netherlands ("Holland") than in the southern part and in Belgium, partly because of this cultural setup. Also, Holland is more deeply secular and rational because of its Protestant history.

leaders were "born" out of frustration with the status quo by the end of the last century and then had a three- to four-year pilgrimage inside or outside the church. The relationship is also "easy" since it never did lead to high tensions between new expressions of church and the rest of the body of Christ, for three reasons. First, most new expressions intentionally stayed "below the radar" and preferred the margin of the Christian subculture. Second, many churches mind their own business. Third, several Reformed denominations developed an awareness that something must change. "We are sinking like the Titanic," a leader recently said. Most denominations support experiments within their denomination while they prefer the wildly innovative experiments to remain outside their denomination.

Due to an awareness of the crisis, combined with a positive view of church experiments, an informal mixed-economy church may be possible.[3] Pushing for a formal mixed economy may be a bridge too far. This informal mixed economy will not save the Titanic in the coming decade, but it may help to build some additional lifeboats.

> A formal mixed economy (for church) will be workable in the end. An informal mixed economy is actually already the case in most Dutch denominations. It is just a matter of formally recognizing the altered state of the church in this country. In some denominations this formal recognition is happening already. As for Belgium, the situation is different, given the strong Catholic monoculture. However, within the Catholic Church of Vlaanderen there are voices pleading for a kind of mixed economy (for example, pioneer leaders like Paul and pastoral leaders like Timothy). *Stefan Paas*

New expressions of church are recognized by many as experiments for the church in the next decades. Some attempt to leave the Christian subculture but few fully succeed.

Theologically and philosophically, it may be possible on paper to contextualize the biblical narrative in post-Christendom and postmodern society, a society that lost knowledge of the Christian narrative and faith in the secular narrative. However, the Dutch society is fragmented and driven by conflicting desires; some are modern, some postmodern, some secular, and others deeply religious, making contextualization a messy endeavor.

A decade ago the Christian subculture was much more optimistic than today. Many Christians now fear both secular and Islamic rule and feel more marginalized than ever. Large evangelical churches in midsize cities grow larger to the

---

3. "The mixed economy refers to fresh expressions and conventional churches working side by side." See http://www.freshexpressions.org.uk/news/changingthelandscape11, accessed May 17, 2012.

detriment of smaller churches. The Protestant church[4] collects gray hair and closes a church a week while several large evangelical churches postpone or cancel their new building projects. Only large national and interdenominational conferences and events create short bursts of optimism for the Christian subculture, but this just disguises the church's irrelevance to the Dutch society at large.

> The collapse of institutional Christianity correlates to an increase of pilgrimages and retreats ("festive" religion), prayer nights, and home groups. To be sure, in this change churches lose members, and probably many of those not on membership rolls will not appear in the other activities mentioned. Nevertheless, there is a change to less institutional forms of belief. I reflected a bit on this in my chapter (under the heading "From Obligation to Consumption"). *Stefan Paas*

Also the Dutch society lost much optimism. The events of 9/11, the murders of Pim Fortuyn (a politician murdered by an animal rights terrorist) and Theo van Gogh (a filmmaker murdered by a Muslim terrorist), and the economic crisis created a fearful society where many blame politics and immigrants.

A Brief Timeline of New Expressions

New expressions incarnate the narrative of God's kingdom in our present-day context. But there is no official "emerging church" in the Netherlands or in Flanders, and it is not foreseeable in the near future. The following case studies entail churches and projects that have a missional focus and contextualize their practices to a present-day post-Christendom and postmodern society. In this regard, these case studies resonate with the international usage of the term "emerging church." By conservative estimation this would cover twenty to thirty churches or church plants to date. New expressions of church lack any connecting formal structures; they are a small relational network of individual leaders.

GENESIS (2000–)

The roots for new expressions of church were planted in the 1990s when several now-emerging leaders were involved in youth ministry. Many projects did not work out well due to cultural differences between "old" Christians and "new" Christians, and out of these cultural differences arose theological

4. This is the largest Protestant church in the Netherlands (Protestantse Kerk in Nederland), a merger of several smaller denominations (among which is the former public Reformed church). It has approximately 2 million members. Next to the PKN there are smaller Protestant denominations, Reformed as well as evangelical (free church). Generally, these smaller denominations fare somewhat better in terms of numbers than does the PKN. Again, thanks to Stefan Paas for providing this information.

debates. It became clear that church-as-we-know-it was missionally out of touch with a postmodern and post-Christendom society.

The earliest public expressions in the Netherlands of "all things emerging" date to around the turn of the century. These experiments were part of a broader momentum of church planting in the Netherlands. Most denominations showed renewed interest in missionality and chose as a part of their strategy to initiate some church plants.

Most church plants are in urban contexts and are committed to incarnational living in their context. Some focus on poor urban areas and develop a multicultural (Villa Klarendal, Arnhem) or ethnically white ("In the Doctor's Office," The Hague) or Caribbean church (Thugz Church, Rotterdam). Other church plants focus on creative young urban professionals (Oase/Oasis, Soest; Via Nova and Stroom/Stream, both Amsterdam).

> There is an urgent need to engage in *critical contextualization* through ongoing dialogue with popular culture, which will bring questions, old and new, to the Scriptures. Such engagement will enable us to read the Bible in a new light as we seek insights in response to the challenges of ministry and mission in postmodern contexts.
>
> Eddie Gibbs (CN, 31–32)

DIALOGUE (2005–)

Halfway into the decade an informal network of church planters emerged with blogs as centers of dialogue. A network developed with different "hotspots" based on their inspirational sources such as Redeemer (Tim Keller), urban expressions (Stuart Murray), or emerging (Brian McLaren, James K. A. Smith, Carl Raschke, N. T. Wright, John Howard Yoder, Stanley Hauerwas, Walter Brueggemann). In Flanders, the emerging dialogue started not with church plants but with young theologians discussing the same books as the Dutch emergers. This dialogue started at the fringes of the evangelical subculture but has recently reached its center when its instigator, Filip de Cavel, got a leading role in one of the evangelical denominations in Flanders.

> Emerging church innovations in the Western world almost exclusively happen in post-Protestant/evangelical cultures. I suspect it is because alternative expressions "parasite" the institutional church, drawing from disillusioned Protestant/evangelical Christians and on the resources they are willing to invest in a new project. Post-Catholic contexts (like Flanders here, but also Wallonia, France) seem to produce discussions and debate, but very few concrete new experiments. Is it a matter of time? Or because of limited resources?
>
> Eric Zander

NEW EXPERIMENTS (2008–)

By the end of the decade several books were published by key players in church planting or the emerging dialogue, books with fresh theology, real-life stories, and the beginnings of a comprehensive approach to church planting. In addition to the books, there were seminars, retreats, and national church-planting meetings. During these years new projects started and others continued their lifecycle or ended prematurely. Maturing church plants forged surprising relationships with denominations, while others continued independently. Some denominational tensions surfaced with maturing denominational church plants.

In the second part of the decade new developments arose. First, simple churches began where members relocated to a neighbourhood to live there incarnationally (Utrecht). Second, there was a strong impulse toward neomo-nasticism: the formation of countercultural communities desiring the kingdom ("the seventh rule"). Finally, there was the start of some open-space environments: these are intentionally created environments where different narratives of meaning (Christian, secular, Islamic, or otherwise) can interact toward a common goal, whether artistic (RuisFactory) or for the well-being of the city (Blooming People).

Practices

Contextual Worship

Alternative forms of worship are the most visible marker of new expressions of church and get most of the media attention. New expressions remove the sermon from the worship service. This does not mean that these communities are theologically naive; on the contrary, they are stronger in biblical theology than most traditional churches. These communities share the conviction that people do not change during sermons but only when lives are shared in community. Worship events are less frequent, and more time is given instead to sharing meals and fellowship.

> This is a very post-Protestant approach of worship! First, "worship" is identified with "listening to sermons," and second, the goal of worship is defined as "changing people." In Via Nova, we tried to work out a slightly different approach: worship is primarily about giving worth to God and setting our priorities right. Going to church in a weekly rhythm, overruling our agendas, meeting people we would never choose to hang out with in the rest of our week, and yes, singing songs and listening to sermons, using the sacraments . . . all this will *not* produce immediate results of change. But we do believe that it teaches people

(albeit more caught than taught) to direct themselves from concerns with their own comfort to concern for God and their neighbour. Of course, more is necessary than this (Nico-Dirk is very right to emphasize this), but there may be more in this seemingly "unproductive," "functionless" worship service than we assume. We are embodied creatures, "liturgical beings" (James Smith), and I think there is no way to escape this. Instead, we should embrace it and think of simple, steady, sustainable ways to lead people into liturgy/worship on a regular basis. *Stefan Paas*

Within new expressions of worship there are two directions of development. Both are missionally driven, but one requires participation while the other does not. The difference is determined by how visitors in that particular context experience safety. Low-participation projects include experiments among young urban professionals where the worship service is minimal, providing music and live media and creative preaching in a larger venue (one hundred-plus seats). These services function as a public expression of a network church. If a low-participation church creates a high-participation service, they will let the community know beforehand.

The traditional church mind-set often limits teaching to the unidirectional transfer of knowledge from the professional performer to the silent auditors. Contemporary pedagogy has shown for years the effectiveness of collective apprenticeship where learners explore together. Worship becomes the collective discovery journey, the leader serving as a tour guide encouraging communal inspiration and collective interpretation. *Eric Zander*

High-participation new expressions meet in smaller venues and include meals in their gathering. Their worship events invite all to physically participate in a multisensory holistic worship service. These services welcome silence and mystery. These high-participatory worship services are identical be it upper-class white churches or lower-class multicultural churches.

Many new expressions incorporate the arts, social media, and multimedia during worship. Most hesitate to use classical praise and worship songs; instead they feature secular, Celtic, or Anglican songs. They sing Taizé songs or newly translated and composed psalms as well. Two emerging churches write new songs for their worship services. Several inner-city church plants use popular Dutch pop songs and rewrite the lyrics. These various worship developments nurture a deep Christian spirituality within a specific cultural context.

As for Via Nova, we would use all these kinds of music but also worship and praise music, as long as it is done well. Quality (textual and musical) is essential; the rest is not. We are thoroughly eclectic. *Stefan Paas*

> Fresh expressions of church find a way to express their faith in their own words, rhythm, and style. *Markus Weimer*

Communities of the Kingdom

Traditional Dutch church culture is not known for good food and shared meals, and in this sense these emerging churches are rather countercultural. New expressions of community equate to small groups and food. Virtually all events include food, usually organic and fair trade. After-dinner coffee or wine becomes a main instrument of discipleship, when friends share life together. New expressions are not churches with small groups; they are networked small groups that may or may not have a central worship event.

> As may appear from my piece on Via Nova, our situation is less clear than this. There is a group of people for whom the worship service is essential, whereas others prefer the small groups. From the leadership perspective, we value them both equally. In the worship service some things can be done that cannot be done in the small groups and vice versa. I feel very uncomfortable if we have to choose between worship service (liturgy, the people of God meeting publicly in an accessible building) and the small groups (building community). By "choosing" I mean I would not like to prioritize one or the other. *Stefan Paas*

Small groups and missionality do not always mix well. The intimacy of sharing life together locks out newcomers when the shared dream turns inward. However, replication and being part of a larger local network are essential for healthy missional, psychological, and social small group development.

> In a consumer culture, it remains important to have a public and accessible worship service. *Stefan Paas*

> Neighbors Abbey began as a house church in downtown Atlanta, Georgia, in 2009. Our love-hate relationship with the issue of inward dreams and outreach health followed us during the first three years of our community. Intimate communities must face difficult internal work before they have the courage to critically examine the external work. *Troy Bronsink*

The heart of teaching lies within the small groups when they read Scripture and interpret it communally. Some see their community as a part of a larger and living historic and hermeneutic tradition. New expressions add to this historic tradition a renewed emphasis on Jesus and the kingdom of God. They leave behind a Jesus who saves people from their sins and ushers them into a heavenly kingdom. Instead, new expressions stress the incarnate God, who will renew both heaven and earth. Until the eschaton the church is the people of God desiring the kingdom, a contrast community telling and living out a story. Churches are seen as communities carving out little signs of God's kingdom.

> To what extent is communal Scripture reading and interpretation a post-Protestant phenomenon? How would this work out in Belgium, with its strong Catholic, hierarchical tradition? It is far more difficult to set up participatory and egalitarian forms of Scripture interpretation in Catholic areas. This leads to a question of contextualization: Is this picture a biblical necessity or a (low-church) Protestant tradition? Would it be a must to set up something like this in Catholic areas, or might we rather rely on embedded hierarchic patterns (including a "priest" or an "expert" who does the teaching)? *Stefan Paas*

> One of the stark differences between French-speaking and German-speaking cultures is the importance of relationships and food. In French-speaking and southern European (e.g., Portuguese and Italian) culture, life happens around the table with food and wine. However, in the Netherlands and Germany they also emphasize the importance of life relationships in community around the dinner table and in small groups. As these fresh expressions become countercultural vis-à-vis a secular Western culture that is influenced by the individualism of modernity, they return to the heart of hospitality and community. Postmodern Dutch and German Christ-followers welcome the other to share life intimately around the table, and this lifestyle is a fresh countercultural witness in parts of Europe where hospitality may be less obvious. *Blayne Waltrip*

> That is an example of an inaugurated eschatology. *Markus Weimer*

Many new expressions feel that evangelicalism in the Netherlands has lost its countercultural bite. These new voices search for countercultural practices and rituals that help "convert" themselves toward desiring the kingdom as shown by Jesus. Both "urban expressions" (inner-city church planting) and "the seventh rule" (a new neomonastic order) experiment with morning and evening prayers and formulate monastic values, virtues, and vows. The seventh rule incorporates social media and, through virtual networks, video streams morning/evening prayers into its small groups.

> Is this picture prescriptive for the whole church, or rather a specific way of being church (together with other, less-demanding ways)? I am thinking of the traditional pattern in Europe, where churches and monasteries (or other types of intensive, dedicated religion) work together in mutual respect, ideally working for the same mission. One emphasizes the "against the world" and "out of the world," the other emphasizes the "in the world" and "for the world." Would the church not always need this sense of different callings or even different levels of intensity (in terms of communion and discipleship)? There is a wideness

in God's mercy, as reflected by the extensive people's churches of Europe, but also a depth that is reflected in the monastic way of life. *Stefan Paas*

The community with small groups at the center is the place where following Christ is embodied in a community of the kingdom and others are invited to join. These communities of the kingdom are pretty messy; people join because of friendships and food combined with some interest in Jesus. There is no step-by-step discipleship strategy: people eat, pray, love, and live life, and somewhere along the line Christ and God's kingdom materialize and lives change.

Mission as Living Hope

New expressions are subversive communities, and this works quite differently for the inner-city churches than for the young urban professional churches. The inner-city church Villa Klarendal (Arnhem) not only provides preaching and prayers but also facilitates computer lessons to older migrant women. Thugz Church (Rotterdam) is an unintended spin-off of a local government-funded welfare program for Caribbean teenagers. Because of government funding, the social work is formally separated from the "church work." These programs might be for empowerment, coaching, debt management, latch-key kids, a buddy network, cultural diversity, or homework tutoring. In most cities, (in)formal networks of welfare organizations and churches work together to carve out little signs of the kingdom. Government funding for Christian welfare organizations is a debated subject in Dutch politics, and whether it will continue on the long run depends on the wisdom and sensitivity of the Christian organizations in a post-Christendom society.

When the major chocolate company in the Netherlands became fully fair trade, a festival was held at the national monument remembering slavery in Amsterdam. Members of Oasis (Soest) played onstage. Members of emerging churches are neighborhood mediators; they help with food banks, participate in buddy networks, and intentionally go the extra mile in local social life and hospitality.

New expressions disappear into the margins of justice and missions work compared to two bigger communities. First, the Salvation Army is an impressive organisation that has a rock-solid image in a post-Christendom society and is rediscovering its Christian heartbeat. Second are the many new migrant churches. Most of them are not emerging in the sense of theology and post-Christianity, but they are highly contextual toward their particular ethnic groups. They present the risen Christ and God's kingdom in parts of society unreachable by virtually all other churches. Migrant churches are among the strongest defenders of undocumented migrants and fighters against human trafficking.

Leaders of new expressions are critiqued for too much social service: too much "horizontal" salvation and not enough "vertical" salvation, too many "cups of water" and not enough preaching, worship, and discipleship. The difference for emerging churches is in the framework of salvation: Are human souls center stage or is creation center stage? For emerging churches the latter is the case. Most new expressions have basically no evangelism in the traditional sense. As a part of a post-Christendom they see themselves as embodiments of an alternative story. In secular terms this is a specific story of the "good life," namely the Christian one.

> In a society where the Christian story is no longer known it cannot be merely embodied. It must be told as well. If new expressions do not evangelize (i.e., tell the story), they will go the way of many Dutch Christian organizations in the last decades: they will lose their ability to articulate what they believe and thus become speechless. The Netherlands are full of formerly Christian groups and organizations that started out of idealistic motives (a world-formative Christianity) but have become thoroughly secularized. Evangelization is not just a matter of recruitment for the church. It is a resource of language and symbols for a society that is less and less capable of giving words to what they experience. This also affects the so-called new spiritualities. If we believe that God is not far from us (as Paul declared on Mars Hill) we may believe that he will be involved in the lives of people. However, one of the main problems of secularized societies is that people no longer recognize or affirm God in their lives, by a lack of concepts and language to recognize him. If we don't articulate what we are doing and why, but just show the Christian life, people will explain this with the help of other competing and secular stories (coming from psychology, sociology, new age beliefs, and the like). The Name must be named; there is no alternative for that. *Stefan Paas*

> Evangelism is an artificial and superficial attractive event. It sadly separates mission from church community life. The gospel should transpire through the lives of the believers, both individually and corporately, in whatever they do. Typical evangelism often serves as an excuse to avoid incarnation, both individually and corporately. *Eric Zander*

For these new voices the story of the kingdom is their addition to the marketplace of narratives of meaning; it is a story that is eschatologically different from the secular society and as such will always critique it. Given a capitalistic society driven by consumption (aka greed), they pray their words and actions are the call for the justice as told in Scripture: a call that invites others to enter into an alternative community and into obedience to a different Lord.

Leadership: Everyone Plays

"Everybody gets to play," John Wimber famously said: all believers are Spirit empowered. Emerging churches take this one step further: "*unless* we all play." It is a different approach to community formation and leadership. Both the inner-city and young urban professional communities are allergic to directive leadership. They do not trust visionary leaders with their "big words" or any other style of leadership that will allocate you as a resource to their "God-given" vision.

> There are good reasons for these emerging critiques. Instead of remaining here, the developments in the UK reveal that there should be a time of repentance. It is not helpful to remain in such an "against" attitude. A positive approach that involves the visionary leaders of the huge churches will provide good soil for future developments in the kingdom of God. *Markus Weimer*

"Unless we all play" means that the vision is communal; it is a shared desire that emerges out of the community, because all Spirit-empowered people get to play. The team of leaders may have a coordinating and supportive role here but they do not own the vision; the community owns the vision. Because "everybody gets to play," the church community should live in such a way that it will fail "unless we all play."

All new expressions have teams in leadership; it is never a one-man show. Most new expressions have strictly egalitarian leadership teams both in the sense of gender and hierarchy within the team. This leadership style fits well with the Dutch society, which is one of the most egalitarian in the world. Most new expressions do not see this conflicting with Scripture or their tradition.

> In today's world, leaders must be skilled at bringing people together in order to pool knowledge and skills. They must struggle to create the right "chemistry" of human relations, so that those they lead spark ideas in one another, urging each other forward in ministry and outreach.
>
> Eddie Gibbs (LN, 106)

"Unless we all play" respects the unique contribution of any member to the community. The unique contribution of a biblical theologian, a ten-year-old streetwise kid, a social worker, a manager, or a mom of four is to be respected. Their contributions are seen as a set of different expert opinions. These voices represent the unique Spirit-given contributions (charismata) to the community, and therefore the body of Christ is to accept these with gratitude.

This different approach to leadership is no safeguard against power plays and emotionally unhealthy communities; a church just may substitute one bad leader with an entirely unhealthy community. Nor is it an easygoing approach to church discipline. Emerging churches are centered-set churches—communities that invite all to a central set of values and virtues that embody the communal understanding of the kingdom and Jesus our Lord who lived it.

> I'm convinced by Doug Pagitt that there is a third option to centered-set or bounded-set called relational set. Many emerging and neomonastic expressions of church in the United States privilege the shared relationships over a central idea, person, value, or practice. This is much like the Eastern Orthodox position of our "participation in the love of God." What follows, in the United States, are affinities within the amoeba-like church who see their unique participation as a facet of the whole body, rather than seeing worship attendance or leadership as central. So the yoga attendee or the community action person is as significant a part of the church body as the music leader (much as you have described diversity in biblical interpretation). *Troy Bronsink*

> The future task for the leaders of the new movements and the established churches will be to reconnect the center with the edge. *Markus Weimer*

Some new expressions of church learned the hard way that people *must* talk about and live out *all* values and virtues over and over again; the values that touch "communal safety" especially need to be in the open over and over again. Doing so makes people join or leave, and not doing so makes the community fall apart. Bringing up and living out the communal center-set authentically as a "broken vessel" may be the only job left for an emerging leader; it just happens to be a very big job indeed.

In the wastelands of the Christian subculture and the society at large, Hoekendijks's statement (quoted at the opening of this chapter) holds true. The kerygma is not gone, the realization of it needs to be rediscovered. New expressions of church are small experiments that do just that. Living between these two cultures, Christian communities embody hope. They are communities living to be the prayer "Thy kingdom come. . . ."[5]

5. The author would like to thank Filip De Cavel, Miranda Klaver, and the community of "emergers" for their input and corrections.

6

Fresh Expressions of Missional Church in French-Speaking Europe

Blayne Waltrip

Culture

While secularization continues its march through French-speaking Europe, Christian communities arise in new places. In this chapter I present the culture, experiments, and practices of fresh expressions of missional church in French-speaking Europe.

In 2006, David Bjork wrote "The Future of Christianity in Western Europe," based on writings by the French sociologist Danièle Hervieu-Léger. Hervieu-Léger writes that Christianity is incomprehensible to contemporary French. She refers to an "exculturation of Christianity" from European secular culture.[1] She continues to say that we must "go beyond the simple recognition that Christianity has lost its influence in French society and been exiled to the outer limits of the public sphere through the process of secularization."[2]

---

1. Danièle Hervieu-Léger, *Catholisme, la fin d'un monde* (Paris: Bayard, 2003), 97.
2. David Bjork, "The Future of Christianity in Western Europe: The End of the World," *Missiology: An International Review* 34, no. 3 (July 2006): 312–18, quote at 309.

While 81 percent of the French who were fifteen years of age or older in 1986 considered themselves Catholic, only 69 percent of the French did so in 2001. In 2002, only 7 percent of French adults who identified themselves as Catholics practiced their faith, and 44 percent stated that they never attend church services. The French are more attached to humanistic values that they find in their faith than they are to the doctrines and dogmas of their religion.[3] For many, Christianity is "now understood in terms of 'personal well-being,' 'wisdom,' or 'inner life.'"[4] Moreover, Bjork writes:

> The secular mind-set represents a worldview which considers this world as a closed, self-sustaining system and regards humans as autonomous beings, answerable to no higher authority.
>
> Eddie Gibbs (INO, 166)

> In a study done in 2003 which asked the same questions of the French that had been asked ten years earlier, all of the indicators of Christian belief had dropped. That survey revealed that fewer of French believe in the existence of God and in the primary Christian beliefs than was formerly the case. They attend church services less, pray less, and fewer of them claim that Christian faith plays an important role in their lives than was true ten years earlier.[5]

Twenty percent of the French claim that they are agnostics. Furthermore, the largest percentage of convinced atheists (i.e., 14 percent) in Western Europe resides in France.

> Western Europe is a religious disaster area. Secularization in France has reached an advanced stage. The established church must rethink its current approach and invest in new ways of being. *Markus Weimer*

The French have not given up on spirituality, however. In fact, French churches (e.g., Catholic, Lutheran, and Reformed) are faced with the problem of how to evangelize people who desire to enter the church. Evangelical Protestant churches experience growth through the conversion of French men and women as never before in the history of their work in France.[6] Although French-speaking Europeans are not actively looking for God, they do become convicted by an encounter with a convert or a group of converted Christians.[7]

---

3. Collette Muller and and Jean-René Bertrand, *Où sont passé les catholiques?* (Paris: Desclée de Brouwer, 2002), 24–25.
4. Bjork, "Future of Christianity," 311.
5. Ibid.
6. Ibid., 315.
7. Ibid., 319.

Church congregations in France normally consist of believers and converts.[8] The socialization process of believers is based on tradition and continuity, whereas the socializing process of conversion is based on the principle of rupture and discontinuity. Converts speak of a second birth and a "change in life." They have a stronger commitment to Christ than do the socialized believers, so they find it challenging to find satisfaction in many churches. Unlike the believer, the convert experiences a complete reorientation of his or her life in which religious faith moves from the periphery to the center of reality. Rather than a decline, a growing number of French postmoderns feel like they belong to a religious group and affirm a belief in God.

> Did Bjork mention Catholics? This strikes me as strange that they should be "confronted with the problem of knowing how to evangelize people who desire to enter the church and be incorporated into the communities of faith." I thought this would be the problem of evangelical churches only. *Matthias Radloff*

> Bjork addresses European Christendom (Catholic, Protestant, and evangelical) when he describes "believers" and "converts." Catholics now too are faced with the challenge of incarnational evangelism in post-Christendom Europe, and for this reason Pope Benedict XVI calls for a "reevangelization of Europe." The challenge of losing "believers" and the hope of incorporating "converts" are shared by all denominations. The missional call to incorporate "converts" who have life-changing experiences with God sounds for the whole church—Catholic, Lutheran, Reformed, Anglican, evangelical, Pentecostal, and emerging. *Blayne Waltrip*

> The big difference with evangelical churches in a Catholic context is that they have always lived on the margins. They don't share that new feeling of being pushed to the margins like

---

8. Bjork and Hervieu-Léger describe three basic ways in which French-speaking Europeans relate to Christian faith based on an understanding of the nature of the church and its place in society. The models communicate a perspective of how people enter into relationship with God and thus how Christian faith is transmitted. This typology includes the "believer" (i.e., "le pratiquant," per Hervieu-Léger), "pilgrim" (i.e., "le pelerine," per Hervieu-Léger), and "convert" (i.e., "le converti"). They explain that becoming Christian in most European societies has been understood as a process of socialization. Many Europeans have identified themselves as Christians because they participated in a liturgical process in a church that dominated religious life in their country. For many, their mother and father were members of a church, so they were baptized into the church as infants and went through the process of "catechism" and later were "confirmed." According to Bjork, one out of four French adults goes on a pilgrimage each year. During their pilgrimage, these people feel the freedom to gather, to express themselves in a temporary way with others, and to distance themselves from reality, or the social status quo. Pilgrimages are not tied to religious rituals from the past and have become a societal phenomenon in Europe. Bjork, "Future of Christianity," 312–18; Hervieu-Léger, *Le Pèlerin et le Converti: La religion en mouvement* (Paris: Flammarion, 1999), 89–155.

> most evangelicals do in Protestant/evangelical contexts. The main evolution is that they are now joined by the Catholic former majority . . . but not yet completely. *Eric Zander*

We need to develop and mobilize communities of "converts."[9] Fortunately, there are missional Christians in French-speaking Europe, such as Matthias Radloff, Henri Bacher, Matthew Glock, Jean Hassendorfer, Gabriel Monet, and Eric Zander, who advocate moving beyond the church of Christendom (i.e., churches of socialized believers) and call for creating fresh expressions of missional church (i.e., incarnated churches of converts).

> Churches on the margins, like the French evangelicals, tend to protect their identity from the negative influence of "the world" by secluding themselves from the secular dominant society and developing their own microcosmic culture and relationship network. The disruptive process of conversion, at the heart of the identity of these churches, not only introduces the "born again Christian" into a new commitment to Christ but sadly often to a new segregated culture and network. Not only do they learn a new relationship to God, but also a new vocabulary, music, postures . . . and their "worldly" relationships are replaced by "brothers and sisters" exclusively. Here lays the big challenge of the margins: protective seclusion or influential infiltration. *Eric Zander*

> Great observation. This is a big challenge for converts on the margins. There is a tendency of evangelicals in Europe and North America to seclude themselves from "the world" (i.e., a "Christ-against-culture" perspective). *Blayne Waltrip*

Experiments

I will explore two fresh expressions of missional church in French-speaking Europe. (A third community, L'Autre Rive, is described in chap. 21 by its founder, Eric Zander.) Both of these missional communities are in the Paris area—Vintage Church in Paris and Brie Church in Solers. Their stories reveal two examples of living out church in a fresh way in France.

Vintage Church

Frank Wilder came to Paris almost a decade ago with a leadership team of nine people sent by Christian Associates International (CAI) to plant a missional church in the emerging culture of Paris. When Wilder and the CAI

9. Bjork, "Future of Christianity," 315.

team came to Paris, they wanted to learn and understand the culture. Wilder did not want to impose a "prefabricated formula on the culture."[10] As a result, they asked questions and developed a network of relationships. In the past few years, the community has expanded and decreased. Many of the original nine leaders have returned to the United States. Nevertheless, though the size of the community has gone up and down, the indigenous leadership core has been consistent. Although their origins are not native to Paris, Vintage Church embodies a multicultural, international, and very French Christian community in the Parisian context.

Brie Church

Lorenzo and Marie-Alice Monge are the founders and leaders of the Brie Church.[11] Lorenzo is a song composer and the coordinator for Brie. As a guitar player, singer, and composer, he has a band by the name of "Les Passagers." The Monges have been with France Mission for over ten years. In 2007, they began meeting together once a month with a group of friends for a home Bible study. In the second year, they decided to continue the Bible study along with initiating activities for children, "Bi-Dieu-Dul." The Monges and their friends were all young families with children. Consequently, they started something "artistic" for the children.

Brie Church is a French missional community in Solers, which is a village outside (southeast) of Paris, France. Solers is in the region of the Seine and Marne rivers, which is known as Brie. As a result, the church's name is L'Église de la Brie (the Church of Brie). However, Marie-Alice Monge points out that the name is a play on words.[12] In French, the term "la Brie" sounds like "l'abri," which means "shelter." The Church of "l'abri" is where people can come to find shelter and rest—"to have peace."

Practices

Worship

VINTAGE CHURCH

For the first year, the Vintage Church gathered on Friday evenings. In that meeting, they taught the Bible and worshiped through music and song. Wilder

---

10. Frank Wilder, interview by Blayne Waltrip, Paris, France, June 9, 2008.
11. Brie Church: http://www.briechurch.com/bienvenue.html.
12. Lorenzo and Marie-Alice Monge, interview with Blayne Waltrip, Solers, France, June 8, 2009.

describes it as a "traditional church thing."[13] Each home group took responsibility for the meeting once a month. Because people came from various backgrounds, the expressions were diverse. After a year, the gathering "ran its course," so they decided to stop the monthly meeting.

Though the gathering ceased, they continued with three weekly home groups. When people left one group, it disbanded and melded into the other two home groups. One group meets on Sunday evenings and is French-speaking, and the other is an English-speaking group that meets on Monday evenings. Both groups are very casual and hospitable. The French group eats dinner together and spends the time talking. There is a strong communal feeling in this group. During the study, there is a lot of discussion and reflection as well. The Monday evening group also eats and speaks together. Both home groups are very relational. The Bible studies in the two home groups are casual and fluid and emphasize discussion.

> European postmoderns make life happen around a beer, or maybe a glass of wine. *Eric Zander*

BRIE CHURCH

Like Vintage, the Brie Church did not begin with a church service. They were planning to launch a "celebration service" that would be a larger gathering of small groups to give back to God in worship. However, the service would not contain a traditional liturgy. According to the Monges' plans for the celebration services, they were to start with new worship music (e.g., new songs in French). For Lorenzo, music is a tool "so people can feel great in worshiping God."[14] The celebration service would be rooted in art as well. They were planning on multisensory worship, using painters and dancers. La Brie strives to be "open and creative." The focus of their worship "will be on Christ in the midst of community, not community in the midst of a building."[15]

Brie Church features a Bi-Dieu-Dul service. The name "Bi-Dieu-Dul" is a play on words in French. The word *bidule* is slang for "thingy" or "what do you call it." It is a catch-all word for "stuff." The Monges explain that when "Dieu" (God) is put in the middle of the word, a word is created that means "God-thing" for children. Unlike the small groups, the Bi-Dieu-Dul service is open to all the families in the village, and their goal is to engage the children with the message of who God is and how he cares for them. By using drama, music, games, and art, they "draw children into the life of the church."

13. Wilder, interview.
14. Monge, interview.
15. http://www.briechurch.com/ways.html.

The Bi-Dieu-Dul service attracts children and parents from all over the Brie region. It is a similar concept to Disneyland. Parents and children have fun together, but the stories and themes of the drama and games have a distinct (in their case, Christian) message. The message is transmitted in a format that is fun, such as "funny hats, glasses, etc." For example, they had someone dress up as Spider-man and tell the children that he was cool and strong, but God is stronger. The show is also "mysterious." After each show, they do crafts with the children. Parents also have cards to discuss the theme of the night at home.[16]

> The challenge is to present a high-quality performance without imprisoning spectators into passive consumerism. I appreciate their efforts to involve people concretely. They will need to find ways to integrate participants in the production process to evolve from a show to a church. *Eric Zander*

Community Formation

VINTAGE CHURCH

Vintage Church consists of twenty to thirty people, approximately ten of whom are French. They purposely keep the international feel. They are not defined by boundaries, such as "Christian and non-Christian"; they are "center set" rather than "boundary set." They are not "French-speaking" or "English-speaking." Rather, they are defined by their center—their values and purpose. Vintage's expressed purpose is to reinterpret Jesus for Parisian culture. They reinterpret Jesus through art, film, dance, parties, food, relationships, friendships, and "all that stuff." According to Wilder, the Parisians know about God/Jesus, but need him reinterpreted.[17]

> Fascinating! In urban Netherlands, God/Jesus is totally unknown, and it is only in rural Netherlands where such a reinterpretation is needed. In urban Netherlands you start from scratch. *Nico-Dirk van Loo*

> I found it fascinating as well. I think that it has a lot to do with the various ages of the community. I think God/Jesus is unknown to the Parisians and other French urbanites under the age of thirty years. For the younger set, you have to start from scratch. For those over thirty, you have to reinterpret Jesus because of the misunderstandings developed from years of Christendom. In either case, the church does need to be reimagined. *Blayne Waltrip*

---

16. Monge, interview.
17. Wilder, interview.

> What the French know about God or Jesus is quite limited. And they do not desire more theological knowledge. The clever thing here is to use indirect communication: art, relationships, parties . . . that mention God and Jesus. *Matthias Radloff*

> I appreciate the integration dynamics blurring the identity boundaries between so-called Christians and non-Christians, which is by the way a typical church distinction (people rarely identify as "non-something"). But I am afraid that a culturally all-inclusive approach, based on values and purpose but denying essential cultural barriers (like language), will not reach a typical cultural group, like Parisians in this case. But Parisians may be especially culturally open compared to other cultural groups. *Eric Zander*

Reinterpreting Jesus means reinventing church. The French know what the Catholic Church is, but do not know what real life in church is. Most churches in Europe offer little community.[18] As a result, Vintage strives to live as an incarnated community that confronts the French "with Jesus by living out BELLS."[19]

First, "B" in BELLS represents "to bless." For Vintage Church, "B" means that each person in the group tries to bless at least three people during a week. "E" means "to eat." In French culture, ministry happens—in fact life happens—around the table.[20] For postmoderns, life happens over a cup of coffee. Vintage lives out the "E" by making an effort to eat with others at least three times a week. This could be lived out by having coffee together or going out to dinner with someone. The purpose is to spend time with people. The first "L" in BELLS is for "learning." Vintage strives to be a learning community by sharing books, resources, Scripture, and so on. They covenant together to read one of the Gospels, a New Testament book, and another book in the Bible three times a week. The second "L" is "listen." Accordingly, Vintage endeavours to listen to God by encouraging everyone in the community to take at least one hour of quiet time each week to focus and listen to God. This is beyond regular prayer time. Last, "S" means "sent"—"wherever we go, we're sent." We are sent by God to be his agents in the culture. It means being missional. If you are Christian, "you are missional."[21] We cannot *not* be missional.

> The church is missional by definition but we certainly need fresh expressions of church (like Vintage) as an example of how a missional DNA can look. *Markus Weimer*

18. Christian Associates International, http://www.christianassociates.org/?p=13.
19. Wilder, interview.
20. This corresponds with Lorenzo Monge's observations—i.e., life happens at the dinner table.
21. Wilder, interview.

The Vintage Church has added "T" for "throwing parties," which creates the acronym T-BELLS. The community loves to throw parties and theologically explains the practice by referring to when the apostle Matthew confronted Jesus by throwing a party (Luke 5:29).[22] As a consequence, the community hosts and goes to many parties. The goal is to be with people and develop relationships.

> Relationships are being built by "doing things together," be it to eat or to party, to practice team sports or to go to the same pub regularly. "Belonging before believing" is an important principle. *Matthias Radloff*

> "T-BELLS" . . . It really sounds hard to adapt and present to non-English, non-American, local believers. To have these locals appropriate the new church concept, I guess they will have to find a way to translate, linguistically and culturally, these values in order to make them part of the DNA of the project. *Eric Zander*

> As an international/bilingual/French community of faith, Vintage strives to bless, eat (or drink), learn, listen, serve, and find neutral space within Parisian culture. Rather than impose a foreign "T-BELLS" idea from the outside, they live it out in the context. The English "T-BELLS" terminology is used only internally among the leadership (i.e., a French and international leadership) to express kingdom values. I agree that how it gets lived out must be very French. *Blayne Waltrip*

The community's discipleship is done primarily in the home groups. Each group has its own leader. What happens in the groups is decided by the group members themselves. For example, the groups have their own events, parties, and so on. Nevertheless, the two home groups come together once a month as a community. They also have discussion groups where Wilder encourages the gifted teachers to teach. Teaching is not a "top-down thing"; the "teachers" are encouraged to teach. Since leaders serve as mentors, discipleship is more relationally intimate and organic.

> Also in the Netherlands, home groups are the key. Church is a kind of organized network. *Nico-Dirk van Loo*

BRIE CHURCH

There are approximately sixty people who are a "little involved" in the Brie Church (involved in small groups or the children's ministry). The majority of

---

22. Connecting and living life by having and going to parties were not only prevalent with Vintage, but also Brie and all the case studies in my research (i.e., four French-speaking and four German-speaking emerging missional churches/gatherings).

those in the Brie Church are young families whose parents are between the ages of thirty and forty-five years. For the Monges, church is the people, not a building. France does not need another building with a cross on top, but rather communities of believers who incarnationally live out their faith in an authentic French way.[23] As community, church is a lifestyle. Because France is a very communal culture, church is all about relationships and friendships. The Monges spend a lot of time around the table eating together with those in their community and village.[24] They have parties together. They help one another with their children. They "have life together."

> We see here another big challenge for an emergent French church in going against the traditional identification of a church with a specific building. They have to go beyond the diffusion of Christian individual influence, and find a way to identify the Christian community, where people will belong. I appreciate that the gatherings make the church, not the meeting place. Eric Zander

Small groups are a natural outflow of these relationships. Brie is an "organized community of small groups."[25] Small groups are the heart of La Brie. The small groups of the church are organized as a network. As community, there is a mutual submission, trust, and desire to grow together. The groups form a united body. Through small groups, the Brie Church lives out the life of the church in their villages and communities and "then gather[s] all the groups (temple courts) for joint worship, teaching and service."[26] In the small group, Brie is living "a deep thing in God, praying and reading the Bible together."[27]

Discipleship at Brie Church is a lifestyle. Brie forms disciples by encouraging, supporting, teaching, and accompanying others so they can grow in their relationship with Christ. Disciples are encouraged to follow Christ on their own. The small groups are the principal context for discipleship. In the small groups, the Monges pray and study the Bible together with the participants. In the lifestyle of making disciples, it is about living life in relationship with God and one another. The goal is to encourage and teach others

> The term *missional* . . . draws attention to the essential nature and vocation of the church as God's called and sent people. It sees the church primarily as the instrument of God's mission.
>
> Eddie Gibbs (CN, 51)

23. Monge, interview.
24. In France, life happens around the table. A church which will be authentically French needs "to have at its core this convivial gathering around the table." Ibid.
25. MongeWorld: http://www.mongeworld.com/MongeWorld/Eglise_de_la_Brie.html.
26. Ibid.
27. Monge, interview.

to live out their own spiritual growth. Mentoring is essential for discipleship. The leaders mentor disciples in their faith journey. For example, discipleship is done around the table. It is done when neighbors come to visit, ask questions, pray, and study the Bible together. The mentors model the Christian life for the neighbors. This lifestyle requires transparency, sincerity, and honesty.

Mission

VINTAGE CHURCH

As they live out evangelism, the participants at Vintage Church find creative ways to share Christ. For example, someone in the community developed an idea called "fill 'er up." The idea is to go out with change in one's pocket and give it out to people. Wilder told a story how one time they had their pockets full with about twenty-four euros in change. A woman came up to ask them if they had any spare change, and they gave her their pocket money. She was quite surprised. Subsequently, they did it every week. As a result, Vintage Community develops relationships with the people on the streets by giving change frequently.

> A great idea to get in touch with people who would definitely not attend a well-performed seeker service. *Markus Weimer*

They develop relationships on established holidays or events. On International Neighbors' Day, each person or couple in Vintage hosted a party in their home and invited all their neighbors. The original International Neighbors' Day was launched by a former vice-mayor of their *arrondissement* (i.e., civil administrative district) who wanted the city to be human again by people saying "hello" and talking with one another. When the Wilders planned their party, the neighbors were too busy or suspicious to come. As a result, Frank Wilder and his wife baked cakes and went to each neighbor in their building with their children. When a neighbor answered the door, they wished the person "Happy International Neighbors' Day." The neighbors began to send flowers, gifts, or cards, and they began to invite the Wilders to their homes. It was revolutionary in their apartment building.[28]

> For a smaller group, it is essential to find the ways that connect both with the makeup of the people as well as the makeup of the neighborhood. Vintage seems to do this well by redefining and reusing what is already present. *Ruth Skree*

28. Wilder, interview.

Vintage is deliberate and creative in developing relationships. When the original CAI team came to Paris, they developed many relationships in the cities, mainly by having parties and by focusing on loving and serving people. Vintage adopted a pub named Wide Open Spaces. By adopting it, they determined to bless the owners and customers of the pub. They were going to the place as often as possible, and they were even holding their leadership meetings there. They were even having Bible studies in the pub. The people involved with Vintage consider themselves emissaries of Christ. As a result, the pub owners were amazed at their kindness and are now friends. As Wilder asserts, this is where Jesus would go if he were in Paris—to the pubs and cafés.

> No prepackaged "gospel presentations" and "seeker-sensitive" worship services will constitute adequate responses to the challenge presented by the post-Christian, neopagan, postmodern generation.
>
> Eddie Gibbs (CN, 30)

BRIE CHURCH

The Monges do not like the words "evangelism" or "evangelization." In traditional churches, there is an imposed guilt about evangelism. It becomes an activity. In their opinion, it is killing the church. People in the churches are living with guilt to evangelize more. As a result, a Christian is afraid to talk with someone because they know that during the conversation, they will have to share the gospel. It is a system that "becomes unnatural." The conversation is often strained, and the other person becomes suspicious of the Christian's motives.

In contrast to this unnatural process of evangelism, the Monges promote relational evangelism that is more incarnational and organic. Marie-Alice Monge says, "It is important that the people in the village know who I am, such as where I work."[29] It is important to work beyond the church, "so people know who I am and what I do."

Lorenzo Monge insisted that we have to live the faith. "If you're living your faith, you will eventually talk about your faith. People will ask questions." When people around us see that we are authentic, simple, and sincere, they will ask questions. When they started the church, the Monges never initiated conversations about faith when attending parties or other events. However, they became excited because others always initiated the conversations with them about God, "always, 100 percent of the time!"[30]

> I have seen this many times too: never start talking about Christ, others will do it.
> Nico-Dirk van Loo

29. Monge, interview.
30. Ibid.

Leadership

VINTAGE CHURCH

Vintage built a flat leadership that is a "less hierarchal leadership structure."[31] To explain his leadership philosophy, Wilder refers to the book *The Starfish and the Spider* by Ori Brafman and Rod A. Beckstrom. The starfish is like a flat leadership structure; when one of the legs is cut off, the starfish will grow another. However, when a spider has a leg cut off, he will not grow another. In the Vintage community, Wilder prefers the whole body to lead.

> This is *so* true, yet a very messy, chaotic, and slow process. It is very inefficient in time and resources in the short run but also a great way of "riding together," so probably efficient in the long run. In an arts collective, it is the only way of leading. *Nico-Dirk van Loo*

> In many fresh expressions, the whole body leads. Body leadership was prevalent in almost every case of my research. It is true that it is often very messy and chaotic in the short run. That is why it is often criticized by traditional churches. Van Loo has a good point that leading as a body becomes more efficient in the long run, especially as emergents are the ones leading. The early chaotic nature may be why the apostle Paul took a greater lead when he initiated communities of faith in the first century, but empowered the communities to lead together as a body. In such cases, apostolic leaders must resist the tendency to control. Monge, Wilder, and Zander are great examples of such leaders. I saw very positive examples of leadership in Germany as well (e.g., Hope-Berlin, Kubik Community and the Jesus-Freaks-Eppingen). *Blayne Waltrip*

As they moved away from a hierarchical leadership structure, they moved toward a "fivefold" leadership. First they identified the fivefold ministry in the leadership team by distinguishing the prophet, the evangelist, the apostle, the pastor, and the teacher. Then they used a profile test developed by Alan Hirsch and someone from Gallup. The test identified a person's top two roles. As a result of taking the test, everyone in leadership knows his or her role at Vintage. Incidentally, they found a lot of pastoral people on the team. Thus they are in the process of understanding what it means to be a shepherd and who in the group brings the apostolic voice, the prophetic voice, the teaching voice, and so on.

BRIE CHURCH

The Monges are the leaders of Brie. The leadership is flat, empowering, and antiauthoritarian. Leadership recognition is more organic and relational.

---

31. Wilder, interview.

They recognize a potential leader in the context of relationship. As leaders are developed, they envision a network of leaders initiating small groups throughout the region of Brie. These small groups with trained and healthy leaders will be "seasoning" villages with the gospel.[32]

At Vintage and Brie, leadership is organic and flat. Leadership that is hierarchal and authoritarian is rejected. Vintage emphasizes the whole body leading. The leaders at Vintage and Brie allow others to share in decision making, an important value in their leadership philosophy. They also emphasize a leadership that enables, empowers, and releases others in their gifts and callings. The problem in many churches is what Boelsterli calls "control flex."[33] In emerging leadership, the young leaders will be passionate and creative, and the youth of the churches will see the success and be excited about ministry. The missional leaders find value in people, develop their potential gifts, allow them to be innovative and creative, and empower others to act. The leaders at Vintage and Brie are flexible and open to fresh ideas. In fact, they encourage it. Furthermore, they practice an approachable leadership. These missional leaders serve as passionate role models for others in their communities.

In the midst of post-Christendom Europe, there are incarnated Christian communities in France and throughout Western Europe where "converts" are living out their faith in fresh expressions. They are emerging, apostolic, organic, and missional. Both Vintage and Brie are examples of such fresh expressions. Their worship is diverse, artistic, and innovative. Their communities are organic and very relational. They do not go to church; they are the church. Life happens in community with others, especially in the home and around the table. Mission is a lifestyle, not an activity. They live out their faith as missional witnesses in their context. They are deliberate in their interactions with others. Discipleship is a lifestyle. They disciple in relationships as life happens in small groups. Leadership at both Vintage and Brie is flat, empowering, organic, relational, and antiauthoritarian. By incarnating the kingdom of God in contemporary culture, these fresh expressions bring hope to a secular, postmodern, and post-Christendom Europe.

32. http://www.briechurch.com/ends.html.
33. Matthew Boelsterli, Pastor ICF Geneva, Switzerland, interview with Blayne Waltrip, June 1, 2008.

7

Emerging Christian Communities in German-Speaking Europe

Peter Aschoff

Culture

The emerging conversation in Germany, Austria, and Switzerland is notably different from emergent streams in North America, and it has to do with the soil where it was planted in post-Christendom Europe. Among European nations, Germany is where different spiritual traditions meet in a unique way. For one, it is the land of the Reformation with a rich theological tradition and a deep Christian cultural heritage, including the nonidentical twins of Pietism and theological liberalism—setting the stage for much of the theological debate during modernity. But parts of Germany (as well as the whole of Austria) are also parts of Catholic Europe. Pope Benedict XVI represents the more conservative stream, while others, like Jesuit and liberation scholar Johann Baptist Metz, represent the progressive voices in Catholicism. Finally, the northeast of Germany, along with the Czech Republic, parts of Scandinavia, and the Baltic states, forms the global epicenter of atheism and secularism in an otherwise very religious world, as sociologists such as Peter L. Berger have observed.

The German population is nominally one-third Protestant, one-third Catholic, and one-third without any ties to organized religion, with less than 5 percent Muslims and people of other faiths. Although the larger church bodies still have some influence on society and politics, they continue to shrink due to demographic change, and about three hundred thousand Germans turn away from the institutional churches every year. Evangelicals have little impact—the Evangelical Alliance claims to represent 1.3 million out of 82 million citizens, and their numbers are not growing. Many evangelicals remain members of the mainline denominations, so most of German evangelicalism can be considered as a Protestant niche phenomenon.

Emerging communities distance themselves from the evangelical subculture as they engage a secular society that considers evangelicalism mostly as an obscure reactionary or even fundamentalist religious movement. While there is fierce criticism from some conservative evangelicals, there is a greater openness with representatives of both the Catholic and the mainline Protestant churches, where theological and cultural diversity is not a new phenomenon and the theme of the *missio Dei* is gradually being rediscovered amid the pressures of dwindling funds and crumbling organizational structures like the fairly rigid parish system.

> The Catholic Church is currently under huge pressure in Germany because there are not enough priests to sustain the parochial structure. This crisis led to a new openness to mission initiatives around the world—especially in Asia, Africa, and South America.
> *Markus Weimer*

Postmodernity has shaped our culture for the last twenty-five years. Theologians Jürgen Moltmann and Michael Welker contributed to the debate, as well as philosopher Jürgen Habermas and sociologist Ulrich Beck, who coined the term "risk society." The modern myth of social and cultural progress leading to a steady increase in prosperity, peace, and well-being collapsed. Making predictions about political and economic developments seems harder than ever. Simple equations that worked a few decades ago fail to do justice to the complexity of this new world. Chaos disrupts our neatly ordered lives at the individual and corporate level. Time and again our wise men, women, and prophets fail to predict our economic or sociopolitical future.

In the midst of the confusion, the pressure is high to create islands of illusionary stability. Traditionalists right and left seek to revive what they consider the golden ages—be it the Pietist revivals of the eighteenth and nineteenth centuries from Zinzendorf to Wilhelm Löhe, or the days of enlightenment philosophy and theological liberalism from Descartes to Bultmann. Others go back to Dietrich Bonhoeffer and discover a more positive view of secularism as a challenge for Christians to embrace new ways of speaking about God and living intentionally on the margins of an increasingly alien, and sometimes even hostile, society. Sixty-five years after his death, Bonhoeffer's thoughts on living together and discipleship are still a great source of inspiration to many young Christians. Bonhoeffer refused to locate God in the gaps of human failure to know or to act rightly.

Many find themselves on a journey into unknown territory. Vaclav Havel said that in the postmodern world everything is possible but nothing is certain. In a world that offers little stability, people seek for new ways of thinking. A few years ago, German comedian Hape Kerkeling embarked on the Way of St. James. When he returned he published a best-selling book sharing his experiences as a pilgrim. He wrote that God is like a stunning award-winning movie playing in a technically ill-equipped village theater—the church. Many people dismiss the show—it is not what they expect to see. But if you swallow your disappointment and take a closer look, Kerkeling says, you catch glimpses of beauty and realize God's world is a masterpiece.

Experiments

Novelty happens on the fringes of institutions and historical movements as Christians engage secular, mostly urban societies in creative ways. Small communities form around an inner-city café; youth workers abandon attractional strategies and explore new practices of being church in a particular place. When people realize they have little to lose but a lot more to gain, and when leaders are not intimidated when they face the confusion that comes naturally in times of rapid change, individuals and groups feel empowered to experiment and discover new ways.

The 1990s saw the rise of the Jesus Freaks in Germany. Originating in Hamburg from an inner-city café and spreading rapidly all over the country, this indigenous movement fused anarchic youth culture with the gospel. Their annual music festival, Freakstock, attracted thousands of young people, both Christians and others, and the Jesus Freaks initiated a debate about contextualization, countercultural living, new forms of church and evangelism, and the use of arts and symbols in Christian formation and communication. Explosive growth was followed by a deep leadership crisis and a process of self-examination and consolidation as well as some clarification regarding theology and structure.

Today, several small networks explore new and experimental ways of being a community of Jesus followers. "Emergent Deutschland" started as a group of bloggers and pioneers in 2006. There is an annual forum and several cohorts (or "initiatives") that meet regionally to discuss issues such as theology, education, gender issues, or new monasticism. The last emergent forum hosted 120 attendees from many streams and denominations. Two book volumes entitled *Zeitgeist* (published by Francke in Marburg) reflect this conversation—their quest for a third way, avoiding the traps of conservatism/fundamentalism and liberalism/syncretism without sacrificing the strengths and partial truths of these movements. The Motoki arts collective in Cologne with their magazine *FROH!* can also be counted as a partner in this conversation.

> The *Zeitgeist* books were published in the "Edition Emergent," in a series that released discourse about topics like the emerging church, but also international books by N. T. Wright or Miroslav Volf. *Tobias Faix*

Kirche 21 works in similar ways within a Baptist context, and across various smaller evangelical denominations is Novavox, which is less theologically diverse, focusing more on the conversation about the missional church as represented by Michael Frost and Alan Hirsch as well as Neil Cole's ideas of organic church. Boundaries between these networks are fluid. Novavox also published a number of books at Neufeld-Verlag. It is probably safe to say that Novavox is more conservative in its beliefs, and its links to mainline denominations and ecumenism are a bit weaker here. Another example is ChurchConvention, which launched in 2006 and is made up of young Lutheran and Reformed pastors who are integrating experiences of the UK-based "fresh expressions" network into their ministry. Finally, there is a group called Emerging Austria, and their project in Vienna is called Seelenstoff. Emergent influences in academic theological reflection and training can be found at the Marburg Bible Seminar (MBS), at some study centers of the Zurich-based IGW school, and at the Academy of Leadership in Ditzingen near Stuttgart.

> ChurchConvention is a network of "loyal radicals" with a threefold vision: (1) connected in friendship, (2) spiritually on the move, (3) passionately involved in life. *Markus Weimer*

In groups like Motoki or Kubik there is a high percentage of artists, educators, and social workers. Perhaps they are more sensitive to what is happening in our society, or perhaps they feel more at ease with change, or perhaps they like the style of worship and the freedom to experiment. Most emergent groups are experiments: two years ago they might have looked very different. They do not consider themselves to be models that others should (or even could) copy. They do not make grand promises about numerical growth and success. They take time to dwell on questions and do not rush to quick solutions.

> In German and Scandinavian countries, with their long history of institutionalized churches (with ties to the state and cultural heritage), the notion of temporary, uncertain groups and forms of church that will not be set in stone (literally) is difficult to grasp let alone incorporate into the existing church paradigm. *Ruth Skree*

Practices

Worship: Places and Practices

Most emerging communities in German-speaking Europe use a wide variety of resources from wildly different traditions in worship. In their own way they follow the lead of the *tuomasmessu* that was initiated by Olli Valtonen, a Lutheran pastor from Helsinki, Finland, who created an ecumenical mass in the late 1980s as a format for people who had lost touch with church and spirituality. Worship can include traditional hymns and new songs—worship choruses or Taizé-style chants. Sermons exist but the heart of the mass is the mystery of Communion. There are different (sometimes even multisensory) stations where people can make a response to God in a meaningful way that they choose. And there are teams preparing these gatherings in which new people can get involved. The Thomasmesse (St. Thomas' Mass) creates many opportunities for participation at different levels. During the 1990s the Thomasmesse has spread all over Germany, especially to inner-city churches that draw people from way beyond their parish boundaries.

Many emerging communities are on a similar journey. Perhaps there are more Macs and video projectors in use, and Communion is not as central in all of these meetings. The meetings might happen in old church buildings, but often people get together in a café or pub or a venue that resembles these places to help nonreligious friends feel more at ease. In the city of Essen, e/motion moved their SONday meeting from a historic industrial site to a Catholic church. Their work recently won the innovation award of the EKD (Evangelical Church in Germany—the association of twenty-two Lutheran, Reformed, and United regional church bodies). Groups and churches like e/motion have an influence that transcends their size or financial possibilities. Kubik in Karlsruhe with their Café NUN pioneered alternative worship and produced great resources that spread to many other churches and groups.

Their monthly public meetings moved to the Lutherkirche. Motoki in Cologne calls itself a "collective." They invite people to monthly living-room concerts and initiate occasional worship events in a nearby Lutheran church building.

> I observed and participated at one of Kubik's monthly gatherings. It was an amazing multisensory experience. There were twenty-seven people that evening ranging between twenty and seventy years old; the majority were young Germans. Mark Reichmann, who organized and led the service, said the goal is to create a spiritual place to connect—"a place where people can encounter God." *Blayne Waltrip*

In the Swiss town of Steffisburg, Sunday Plaza is a monthly meeting of a network of small groups. People come together to share, to engage Scripture, to create and display works of art, to eat together, to meditate, and to pray. The plaza is open for four hours, offering many different opportunities to participate in some form of shared activity. ELIA in Erlangen changed the service on Good Friday from songs, sermon, and Communion to Stations of the Cross using light and candles and material that engages each sense at least once over the course of the fourteen stations. The only visuals were Bible verses and carefully selected objects on which to meditate. Three years ago, this event was moved to a famous local beer cellar several hundred meters deep into the side of a mountain. Outside a famous beer fest is celebrated at Pentecost with more than a million visitors each year. Everybody knows this place and it touches the heart of the community. Last year, eight hundred people came to walk the cellar and meditate on the story of redemptive suffering.

Community/Formation

People who are on a spiritual journey welcome fellow travelers. They enjoy the company and enjoy hearing and telling stories. Often it is the unfamiliar that creates the greatest attraction. Many emerging communities are places of ecumenical learning. People get together to discover the daily office; they start to practice silence and contemplation; and they seek guidance from spiritual directors. In the recent past, contemplation and social action seemed to be opposites. Today, most realize the need to practice both. Walter Faerber is a Lutheran pastor in a rural part of Lower Saxony. A couple of years ago he started learning from Franz Jaliczs, a Jesuit priest who teaches contemplation in the context of everyday life. He describes this as a healthy way to

> The response of a Christian witness to a person enmeshed in postmodern categories must be that of the fellow traveler.
>
> Eddie Gibbs (CN, 29)

create a positive emptiness that allows people to see what is going on beneath the surface of their lives. Interruptions from the unrelenting pressure to be busy and productive are needed if people want to discover their dignity as God's image-bearers. In the midst of our many distractions these desert experiences help to focus our attention on what really matters—the deeper spheres of our relationship with God, others, and ourselves.

> The vision of an ecumenical learning community lives at the heart of many new initiatives. The fresh expressions movement in the UK follows an ecumenical approach.
> *Markus Weimer*

Many are attracted by new monasticism in its various forms. Out of the 24/7 prayer movement emerged Converse, a community near Leipzig where a group of people live, work, and pray together. These new initiatives learn from existing monastic orders but develop their own rule and rhythm. At the core of e/motion is a similar group.

Community is experienced in small groups where people not only share spiritual insight but also eat and have fun together and help one another out in practical ways, says Jens Stangenberg from Bremen. Often small learning communities get together to practice spiritual disciplines, to study Scripture and theological tradition, or to engage in some form of social action.

Mission

For emergent communities, mission describes the life of the church and is not an item on a to-do list. People initiate new projects and use resources differently when they realize that mission is not an extra after everything else (prayer, fellowship, worship). At MBS, students may opt for a master's degree in social transformation, which equips them in both theoretical and practical skills for holistic mission.

Mission, therefore, is understood as integral. The old evangelical/liberal dualism of proclamation of the gospel to save lost souls, on the one hand, and the improvement of social structures through education and humanitarian projects, on the other, is being replaced by a more holistic understanding of the church. It is seen as the first fruit of the coming kingdom that will transform the suffering and destruction of a world that has turned its back on God and his promise of

> The never-churched need to be enveloped by small communities of believers so that they can see the impact of the gospel in their relationships and experience some of the benefits through intentional spillover.
>
> Eddie Gibbs (CN, 197)

the fullness of life in Christ. So witness about our messianic hope in Christ is lived out in word and action. Action includes not just traditional "mercy" ministries but the political responsibility to work for justice and peace and a sustainable way of life.

> A messianic hope in Christ fuses proclamation and social action, redemption and transformation, into one indivisible reality. *Andreas Østerlund Nielsen*

SAM in the town of Sinsheim is an example of this. The group cares for refugees and immigrants. They created a meeting place for intercultural and interreligious dialogue and help newcomers to learn German or deal successfully with the authorities. They inform the public about the stories and needs of those who have come here to survive and to rebuild their lives.

Leadership

In times of confusion, leadership becomes a sensitive issue. Even though it has always been the case that young people leave their parents' institutions to create new wineskins, the current situation does not look like the usual and necessary questioning of authorities during adolescence. True, some have had traumatic experiences and others have seen church leaders fail or collapse. But many have had good guides and wise mentors as they grew up. But they do wonder why others have been crushed—by unrealistic expectations.

Unlike the generation before them, many start to see famous CEO-type pastors from around the globe on big screens in great churches or at popular conferences as part of the problem and not the solution. They respect the experience and wisdom of these leaders but they distrust the culture or system that puts some people into the limelight and leaves others in the shadows. Heroic individualism is a nineteenth-century romantic projection, not a biblical concept. Other unhelpful leadership stereotypes have been the entrepreneur, the therapist, or the scholar. For a long time academic achievement has been a key qualification for pastors. Soft skills and emotional intelligence have rarely been part of the curriculum of church institutions that have traded wisdom for knowledge and techniques. If the key task for emergent leaders in a flexible network of small communities is to encourage participation, different skills and structures are required.

> In a period of confusion and complexity, leadership must not resort to simplistic solutions or rely on borrowed, success-guaranteed formulas. It requires constant course corrections in the midst of opposing currents and prevailing winds.
>
> Eddie Gibbs (LN, 105)

> In redefining church community, we must rethink the practices that limit rather than encourage diversity. *Eileen Suico*

Another important issue is that of women and men in leadership. Here the starting points for discussion and development are diverse. While some regional Lutheran churches have had female bishops for a number of years now and ordain more women than men, some free churches debate whether women can be ordained as pastors or elders. But underneath are deeper questions about the dynamics of the corporate world that make it ever more difficult to have a decent job and to raise children, and about how churches are to respond to that subtle injustice if they want to be alternative societies.

> As with any prevailing intercultural prejudice, it is not only men who indiscriminately disregard women in their new roles in the society, but their own kind, the very women themselves, because of how they are shaped by their culture. *Eileen Suico*

> In a transitional time when women are starting to assume roles from which they were formerly disallowed, men play a crucial role as their voice and sponsor, especially to those who still regard them as unfit. *Eileen Suico*

Practically speaking, many if not all of these communities and churches are led by teams of women and men. If there are clergy on the team, they are expected to support lay leaders carefully. Often there are ongoing debates about how appropriate the structures are and how they need to be improved to allow for more diversity, inclusion, and participation. Sometimes this is implicit, sometimes very explicit, as in the project Volxkirche of St. Paul's Church in Lemgo, where a kind of base community is integrated into traditional parish structures.

> When an accepted and recognized voice speaks in honor of the "once discriminated," people are introduced to an alternative and a contrasting way of being in the society. *Eileen Suico*

At the end of the first decade of the new millennium, new forms of community emerge in diverse places, shapes, and sizes throughout German-speaking Europe. They use existing elements but the inner dynamic is different. Some last just for a while but even they may contain the seeds for a church that is shaped by God's mission to an unpredictable, rapidly changing world.

Part 2
Cultures

8

New Monastic Community in a Time of Environmental Crisis

Ian Mobsby

Culture

For many in the West, cultural and individual identity has been reduced. In a market society, everyone is a consumer but the individual has little or no idea about who he or she is or what it means to be human other than the life strategy of consumptive gratification. "The rich get richer, the poor get poorer, more and more species are driven to extinction, more toxins are released into our water and air and our overall quality of life is eroded."[1]

The Global Economic System

Our global economic system is derived from a notion that is completely unsustainable. Economic growth (the producing of more and more, requiring endless natural resources) is a vital component of capitalism that drives the insatiable need for consumption. This drive now threatens our entire

1. Stephen B. Scharper, *National Catholic Reporter*, September 8, 1995, 24; March 17, 2000, 11.

> The church must stand against the tyranny of materialism by advocating a simpler lifestyle and demonstrating in its corporate life, as well as in the individual lives of its members, an alternative value system in which joy and fulfillment are experienced through interpersonal activities and in bringing joy to others, rather than in the insatiable pursuit of possessions.
>
> Eddie Gibbs (INO, 184)

ecosystem. We are so thoroughly addicted to growth-driven economics that we cannot even conceive of having to think of another way. We need to shift from unsustainable growth to sufficiency, maintaining the world not through competition that dehumanises and enslaves creation, but to cooperation and more life-affirming understandings of social, economic, and ecological well-being. The global economic and climate crises are deeply connected, and it is greed and addiction with a healthy dose of denial that prevent us from taking responsibility for the peril we have created for our planet and all living species.

Since the industrial revolution, which originated in the UK (to the shame of my own country), we have forgotten that life is sacred. We shifted from a society focused on community (common-unity) to one where people became inputs in the capitalist economic steam-driven loom. Society then shifted from a relational community to an impersonal machine. We see this erosion of our personhood continue to the modern day with the millions who died as cannon fodder in World War I and, in the latter part of the twentieth century, the renaming of "personnel management" departments in companies to "human resources." This is the ultimate denigration of a people made in the likeness of God.

> It seems that we are always looking back and seeing how our best efforts to improve our station and conditions have also had unintended and destructive consequences. *Mark Scandrette*

We live in challenging times, and we are faced with a number of crucial questions: What is the good news of Jesus Christ in a context of the twenty-first century, fragmented by war, terrorist violence, ecological catastrophe, and the dehumanising effects of the global market? What is the church called to be when it has colluded with the rich and absorbed the values of competition, oppression, economic injustice, and the unsustainable rape of the world's natural resources? What does it mean for followers of Jesus Christ to live "in" but not "of" the world? And by the same token, how can the church be a life-sustaining and life-giving community in the context of a culture where many have reawakened to the need for spirituality, but where the church has rightly been seen as one of the contributors to all that is wrong?

> I think we are just at the beginning of understanding how to relate our faith in Jesus and our reading of Scripture to this more profound and global understanding of "the fall," "sin," and human brokenness and the opportunity for the Creator's redemption of all things.
> *Mark Scandrette*

New Spirituality in the Midst of Economic Crises

The church prides itself with holding a prophetic role of being countercultural. However, when it comes to the current economic and climate change crises, the church colluded with Western secular capitalist norms that have little or no reference to social, economic, or ecological justice. We, the contemporary church that has emerged in all its diversity out of this cultural mess, begin with the call to repentance for what the church has and has not done. We need to collectively rethink our practices, theology, and ecclesiology to remember our calling as followers of Jesus Christ in the Great Commandment we have not lived up to: a calling to love God, love ourselves, and love others. In addition, we need to learn to love the planet also, and to remember that the Holy Trinity models for us the perfect form of community—love expressed as inclusion, justice, mercy, and stewardship. We remember that the whole of creation is mystically sustained by the Triune God who is Creator, Redeemer, and Sustainer to all created matter. So our repentance begins not only in how we have mistreated people, but also in how we have neglected our love and responsibility for all living things and all matter. This is our greatest calling in the creation story in Genesis and of the Hebrew and Christian covenants. In this understanding, "Thou shalt not kill" refers to biocide and ecocide as well as the killing of humans.

> Protestantism in general and evangelicalism in particular were shaped and stimulated by the spirit of competitive capitalism. They were the religious equivalent of "big business," operating with the same hierarchical structures and controlling leadership style.
>
> Eddie Gibbs (CM, 22)

> [Christians] are to function as the "overwhelming minority." They are to remain vitally involved with the affairs of this world and concerned about every aspect of the well-being of this planet as stewards of God's creation—a solemn responsibility placed upon God's covenant people from before the Fall.
>
> Eddie Gibbs (INO, 107)

Because of the planet's direct effect on the holistic well-being of every human, to love the physical environment is one of the highest forms of neighborly love. *Eileen Suico*

Ian reflects the shift toward an ecological view of consciousness. *Mark Scandrette*

We the church are driven by "the thoughts that distort"—what are traditionally thought of as sin—through greed, pride, anger, selfishness, and fear. We neglect the calling of the Beatitudes to humility, love, sufficiency, generosity, and living peaceably. The world is the way it is, because we the church and children of God neglect our responsibilities, driven by the false self and the ego, perpetuated by the values of capitalism and the global market, which are idolatrous and unsustainable. The human ego is the source for our destructive tendency to need power, to place ourselves "over-and-above" others, or to understand the self as independent:

> Within us there are instincts of violence, desires to dominate, and shadowy archetypes that distance us from benevolence in relation to life and nature. . . . There is no need for anyone to be the ruler and to consider oneself independent, without needing others. Modern cosmology teaches us that everything is related to everything else at all times, in all circumstances. . . . It is important that we recuperate attitudes of respect and adoration for the Earth.[2]

So we start in repentance and the need for a new understanding of the church as the body of Christ based on virtue, generosity, and the inclusion of all created matter as something to be loved and cherished rather than exploited. There is a link between the oppression of the poor and the exploitation of nature. As Leonardo Boff says:

> Instead . . . of globalizing the market and profit mechanisms, we need to globalize other cultural values, such as solidarity, collective compassion for victims, respect for cultures, sharing of goods, effective integration with nature, and feelings of humanity and mercy for the humiliated and offended.[3]

Ian reveals the connection between the heart posture of the individual and the collective systems of "evil" that perpetuate oppression and destruction—or as the apostle Paul said, "the kingdoms of darkness." In contrast to reductionistic theology, we learn to see each dimension of our conscious awareness within the purview of God's redemptive work. *Mark Scandrette*

2. Leonardo Boff; available online at: http://leonardoboff.com/site-eng/eco/eco_ment.htm.
3. Leonardo Boff, *Ecology and Liberation: A New Paradigm* (Maryknoll, NY: Orbis, 1995), 105.

Our journey toward a new understanding of the church needs an affirming language and understanding of "social justice" and "social ecology," or, as Sallie McFague puts it, a shift from an "anthropocentric" to an "ecological" sensibility.[4] "We need to move away from the influence of individualistic, top-down, dualistic and utilitarian ways of thinking and acting."[5] There is a real need for a renewed and integrated Christian "eco-spirituality" as a new understanding of the church, where the connectiveness between nature and humanity is realised. Boff predicted that a new spiritual revolution is needed or the paradigm of connectiveness would be impossible, resulting in further damage to the earth through continued overexploitation.[6]

> **As we see the connectedness of all reality, our compassion for others grows.** *Eileen Suico*

A spiritual reawakening of the Western world may be happening. Many new spiritual questers or seekers appear to be emerging out of a postsecular context. This cultural phenomenon is not coming from any involvement of the church, but as the consequence of global capitalism and social change waking up to the consequences of human impoverishment and global catastrophe.

The theologians who have explored eco-spirituality and eco-theology have been contemplatives, monks, nuns, and friars. Boff is a Franciscan and McFague a contemplative. The monastic model of church, which Avery Dulles calls the "mystical communion" model, was created by monks and nuns in reaction against the totalising power of Christendom when Christianity was made the official religion of the Roman Empire.[7] Its ethos is counter-hierarchical and counter the false self or ego, seeking to be a bottom-up fraternity—a community of those focused on contemplative action and love of people and the world. So the exponents of this model include Antony of Egypt, Benedict, Francis and Clare of Assisi, and Teresa of Avila as well as the lay monastic communities emerging out of the Protestant Reformation that include the Anabaptists and Shakers. We remember that the Protestant Reformation itself was driven by the monastic impulse.[8] All these contributors to the tradition of monks, nuns, friars, and lay fellowships sought to be radical communities but maintained a connection to the wider church. Many changed the wider church by the DNA of their radical desire to follow the

4. Sallie McFague, *Models of God: Theology for an Ecological, Nuclear Age* (Philadelphia: Fortress, 1998), 11.

5. Ibid., 12.

6. Boff, *Ecology and Liberation*, 87.

7. Avery Dulles, *Models of Church* (Garden City, NY: Doubleday, 2002), 44–53.

8. Jonathan Wilson-Hartgrove, "A Vision So Old It Looks New," in "Monasticism Old and New," *Christian Reflection* 36 (2010): 11–18.

Jesus of the Gospels with a high view of the Great Commandment and an expression of church that sought inspiration from the perfect expression of community in the Trinity.

Experiments

It is therefore no coincidence that this church as eco–new monastic community resonates with the aspirations of emerging churches, as articulated by Gibbs and Bolger and in other analyses:[9] participants take the life of Jesus as a model to live, transform the secular realm, live highly communal lives, welcome those who are outsiders, share generously, participate, create, lead without control, and function together in spiritual activities.

> We address our awareness of the individual and collective systems of destruction through the prophetic witness of small communities of resistance. There is historic precedence for the prophetic voice and lived alternatives of relatively small communities and movements that reshape the values and consciousness of the wider church. *Mark Scandrette*

At the heart of this model is a call to shift church from institution to participative community, from selfishness to self-giving, and from exploitation to loving creative stewardship. So many emerging churches have discovered an eco–new monastic basis to these important values.

> In the face of pending ecological apocalypse, the formation of holistic, practical, redemptive communities of Christ is essential. We must come together, empowered by the spirit who is present with us, to confront our own greed, addiction, and denial. We cannot chart a new course on our own. It is only as we face our own illness and dysfunction and begin to live into a new way of being that we can offer a hopeful narrative to the world. *Kelly Bean*

> Our desire to live in the "here and now" of the gospel of the kingdom of love has made us more aware of the extent of devastation into which an apocalyptic solution might be desired. *Mark Scandrette*

Eco–new monastics ask the question, How do we live in contemporary culture but not of it? Or rather, How do we affirm what is good in us, in culture, in the world whilst living a life of praxis to challenge that which takes life away from us, our culture, and our world? Living this way requires a recognition

9. Eddie Gibbs and Ryan Bolger, *Emerging Churches: Creating Christian Community in Postmodern Cultures* (London: SPCK, 2006), 44–45; Ian Mobsby, *The Becoming of G-d* (Lulu Press, 2008), 65–95.

of how the ego leads to sin combined with a call to live counterculturally in love and virtue. Too often, Christians have no idea what the virtues and sins are, and without this understanding, it is impossible to live well toward the earth, God, and neighbor.

> When we live in small intentional communities we discover our own complicity and our stubborn independence. We also discover the need for and possibility for deep redemption. Life in neomonastic community is challenging, hopeful, and transformative. The process of true transformation in community and as a community can be prickly and uncomfortable and slower than molasses. In spite of, or because of, the discomfort, committing to walk with a group of people in shared life and for a common purpose leads us toward the very real possibility of freedom and deep connection with neighbor, self, earth, and God. That is good news. Kelly Bean

Saint Francis of Assisi is a particular inspiration for many new monastics because of his radical understanding of creation and nonhuman species as "brother" and "sister" and his commitment to encounter God through natural revelation. This is not some form of overromanticism (and there is much tosh written about Francis!) but gets to the radical nature of this eco-spirituality that lies at the heart of the monastic and friar tradition. Only by following Christ in the details of life, by facing the distorting effects of the human ego and false self, can we take responsibility for ourselves and our world through an affirmation of earth, God, and neighbor.

> A healthy change is under way as more and more evangelicals are coming to recognize they have more to learn from saints than from celebrities.
>
> Eddie Gibbs (CN, 133)

The problem with many contemporary expressions of church is that at their heart they are consumptive—conforming to the values of business and the global market. Many churches are unaware that this practice colludes with empire, division, privilege, and an oppressive view of the world. This worldview is maintained by simple dualistic thinking that does violence to creation by demeaning it to the status of a commodity.

Practices

Eco-Monastic Worship

Creativity is vital to this form of participative community in its worship, mission, and church life because of the importance of experience as a vehicle for the encounter of God. Worship then becomes an event; in fact the whole of life and its encounters become a transcendent possibility to seek God. In the Moot community we have an artist in residence who has created an icon of the Trinity that we use in most of Moot's worship services. Creativity and the arts in new monastic communities become an opportunity to affirm what is good and also to challenge the more unhelpful elements of culture. For example, Moot adapted a Tenebrae service to use on Good Friday called "God Is Dead." The image used to promote the event on the Moot website was shocking in its implication, unsettling people in order to open up new meaning. The Moot community seeks to establish an Arts Café Church in the city of London, and one of the planned events is to hold art exhibitions reflecting the traditional church calendar—in particular Lent and Advent—which can then soothe and shock people into exploring the faith through self-transcendent experience.

> The arts play a vital role in critiquing the dominant systems and awakening our imaginations for the reign of love that is now possible. *Mark Scandrette*

Eco-Monastic Community Formation and Spirituality

The Moot community, my home emerging and new monastic community, has articulated this as:[10]

Virtues and the Thoughts That Distort Us

We live the rhythm of life by responding to the thoughts that distort by giving attention to the virtues that give us life.

	Virtues	Thoughts That Distort
About the Body	Moderation (Sobriety) Chaste Love (Innocence) Generosity (Non-attachment)	Gluttony (Intemperance) Lust (Shamelessness) Greed (Avarice)
About Heart and Mind	Patience (Serenity) Gladness Courage Spiritual Awareness	Anger (Impatience) Sadness Fear (Anxiety) Spiritual Carelessness
About the Human Spirit	Magnanimity Humility Honesty (Truthfulness)	Vanity Pride Deceit (Untruth)

10. Aaron Kennedy and Ian Mobsby, "The Moot Rhythm of Life: Virtues, Postures and Practices," 2010, http://www.moot.uk.net/community (accessed October 1, 2010).

> Any Christian faith community could explore these two sides of the missional-formation coin as they assess their practice of life together. They form something of a rubric for our life together, inviting us to greater consciousness that we are always being formed. We cannot not be formed by practices and postures; so the Christian community is wise to wonder about possible formative outcomes of all that we do. *Dwight J. Friesen*

Only a life immersed and sustained in the love of God can enable us to be nondualistic and unselfish, and we need spiritual practices and postures to assist in this. Both act as a guidebook: Spiritual practices are about committing to a way of living that brings life to self, others, and the planet. Postures are about dispositions to contemplative living so that life itself becomes an act of worship, catching up with what God is doing. To illustrate what these postures look like I will add what the Moot community seeks to develop:[11]

SPIRITUAL PRACTICES

We seek to live the rhythm of life through the practice of spiritual disciplines:

The practice of prayer and meditation (daily, rhythmic, individual, and in community).

The practice of mercy and justice (personal, local, and global).

The practice and facilitation of communal worship (contemplative, compline, Eucharist, and other forms).

The practice of learning (discussions, biblical reflection, reading, spiritual direction, and retreats).

The practice of presence (making an effort to develop and maintain deep relationships with those in the community and to tithe [regular giving]).

The practice of mission (assisting people to explore and experience Christian spirituality, being a soul friend to those inside and outside the community).

The practice of passionate living (living life to the full, but also with the passion of sharing in God's suffering for the world).

These practices form the core of Christian formation; the great challenge is to embody them as integrated. How might we narrate such practices so that our communities see that the practice of presence informs and transforms the practice of mercy and justice, just as the practice of mercy and justice informs and transforms the practice of prayer and meditation?

11. Ibid. Note that justice is seen in the Moot community as social, economic, and ecological.

In recent history, Westerners have tended to pick and choose practices in pursuit of personal growth, as though the individual has the wisdom and authority to define the good life. One of the beautiful things about what I'm hearing here is that the community, formed by the narrative of God in Scripture, and by the presence of the Spirit of the living Christ, functions with authority to invite life to be formed in the Way of Jesus. *Dwight Friesen*

The pursuit of intentional values and disciplines reveals the level of our vulnerability and fragility—showing us that we are beginners in embracing the Way of Jesus. I think it is important to return to the content of the life and teachings of Jesus as our guide for how to live in the freedom of God's shalom—otherwise we are in danger of replacing the content of the gospel with our idiosyncratic ideals or cultural notions. For those of us who profess to seek an orthopraxy, there is a weight of responsibility to demonstrate visible transformation in our character and social ethics, to live into the question, "Do we bear witness to the transforming power of love?" *Mark Scandrette*

SPIRITUAL POSTURES

Through postures that help us to encounter God in the whole of life, we seek to live out the rhythm of life through dispositions of openness, mindfulness, expectancy, wonder, gratitude, compassion, and obedience. By seeking to go deep with this form of orthopraxis (right living and acting), Christians live out a countercultural calling to self-giving love and economic, social, and ecological justice. Discipleship then becomes a lifelong spiritual path shared with others in community and led by God. So the dehumanizing effects of the market then are challenged, enabling people to shift from being consumptive spiritual tourists to cotraveling Christian pilgrims, where individuals grow in identity and love by interaction with God and the church. These pilgrims then learn how to live in love, stewardship, and community; they practice post-Christendom self-care leading to self-giving but do not embrace the distorting effects of the global market. The faith then is not held captive by consumptive "attractional models of church"; instead it is missional where the faith is not commodified, but lived in radical praxis.

I propose to add to this concluding sentence: ". . . but lived in radical praxis *and proximity*." The global market tends to ignore the reality that human beings are located and particular. While we are more aware of our interconnectedness, the context of post-Christendom may be inviting us to live with even more intentional commitment to our geography. Thus the radical praxis becomes the crucible for transformation as the gospel is embodied as love of neighbor in the most literal sense. Love of neighbor today invites an even deeper curiosity as our neighbors are increasingly diverse, reflecting the deep identity hybridity of today's context. While loving our neighbor has always been challenging, our neighbors do not share the same narrative history. Neighbors are more diverse than ever so loving one's neighbor is both a local and a global act. *Dwight J. Friesen*

Eco-Monastic Mission

In dualistic thinking the stranger, the other, becomes a threat, something to be controlled, excluded, or avoided, which perpetuates division and destruction. To counter this, eco–new monastic communities, contemplatives, and mystics are committed to nondualism and the values of the kingdom of God. They believe that Jesus modeled nondualism in the Gospels by loving everybody and everything. This breaking down of "who is in" and "who is out" is done through a deep commitment to the giving and receiving of love—love to God, to self, and to the other.

I believe it is tempting for those of us who are drawn toward prophetic/neomonastic sensibilities to make the dominant church into a dualistic threatening "other," which can inhibit or block our prophetic witness. Those with eyes to see must relate to the historic institutions of the church with great compassion and humility, appreciating that all of us, to some extent, have been captive to the kingdoms of destruction. *Mark Scandrette*

Such an approach opens up the importance of hospitality—to befriend the other as a gift of God, and to learn from other traditions to enrich one's own walk of faith. In this way we become disciples learning about God and life through direct experience of God through the other. We don't view the other as a threat, and we believe in God's goodness and commit to joining what God is already doing. The world then is not a threatening, godless space, but the opposite—a place of encounter with a God who seeks to reconcile all things into a restored relationship with the divine (2 Cor. 5). The Christian story, our story, becomes one of love, transformative hope, and a gift to the world, rather than what it has often been: just another institutionalized agency of oppression.

The great strength of an eco–new monastic model of church is its commitment to contextual theology. Phyllis Tickle emphasizes that monasticism throughout history has enabled the church to renew and recontextualize from one social epoch into another during times of great sociocultural change.[12] Contextual theology is defined as "a way of doing theology in which one takes into account the spirit and message of the gospel; the tradition of the Christian people; the culture in which one is theologizing; and social change in that culture."[13]

12. Phyllis Tickle, *The Great Emergence* (Grand Rapids: Baker Books, 2008), 19–26.
13. Stephen B. Bevans, *Models of Contextual Theology* (Maryknoll, NY: Orbis, 2002), 1–2.

> This definition reminds me of David Bosch and his book *Transforming Mission*, where he describes contextualization as "doing theology" with "theoria, praxis and poesis."
> *Tobias Faix*

An eco–new monastic model of church uses a transcendent model of contextual theology that assumes a process of questing and questioning of "what is."[14] It starts with one's own religious or spiritual experience of life, recognizing that we are all hybrids (human beings drawing experience from differing cultures, languages, and geography). At the same time this approach affirms our common humanity, as this form of Christian knowing affirms our journey of faith as growing in our "human becoming." The rhythm of spiritual practices lived out in contemplative action within a community of faith that is engaged with the world becomes an environment for the experience and growth of faith that transcends cultural divisions. Exploration and encounter with God helps articulate "who I am" and "who God is" as a product of subjective experience. God's revelation is then transcendent but also revealed in human experience. This is what "transformation" and spiritual awakening are all about. All humanity can experience God through self-transcending contemplative encounters. Revelation then relates to a change of mind or thinking, literally a conversion experience leading to a radical shift in perspective. This is not new; Jesus Christ mastered contextualization in his use of parables. Such an approach "will not appear in books, but in people's minds."[15] Therefore all followers of Christ become contextual theologians. The universal structure of human knowing and consciousness provides a common ground for mutual conversation and interaction.

Possibly the most exciting aspect of this model of church is its strength in mission to the emerging new groups of spiritual questers. Could this resurgence of spirituality in a time of crisis be the spiritual revolution that Boff predicted? Could it be possible that this revolution is led by God the Holy Spirit? Many new monastics believe so. Research suggests that these new spirituality-seeking questers are seeking inner transformation on their own unique spiritual paths.[16] They are not religious followers but spiritual questers yearning for deep spiritual encounters. There is a great difference between questers and followers. Missiologically, most churches in the West are grounded in a culture of modernity and attractional models of church, which are an

14. Ibid., 97–104.
15. Ibid., 100–104.
16. Paul Heelas and Linda Woodhead, *The Spirituality Revolution* (Malden, MA: Blackwell, 2008), 55–60.

ineffective way to engage spiritual questers. However, the combination of a distinctly Christian eco-spirituality with a new monastic missional "whole of life" form of church that utilises a transcendent model of contextual theology can be a potent model for mission to spiritual questers.

While most emerging churches in the United States and United Kingdom seem focused on mission to the de-churched and to an ever-decreasing number of churched people, the importance of mission to the unchurched or never-churched becomes an imperative.

I am excited by a number of new monastic communities that have started contemplative and meditative missional events to seek to engage with spiritual questers. They aim to enable such people to experience the Christian tradition as a focus for transcendent and transformational experience. Many eco–new monastic communities are setting out in this vision. Some have set up radical arts cafés for hospitality and for holding events that promote stewardship of the world and a playful expression of mission as experiencing God through the whole of life.

> Most German churches could learn a good deal from intercultural experiences of mission, but it doesn't seem to be happening. The norms of mission (e.g., contextualization) are rejected as "liberal and dangerous" in many German churches. Sociologically speaking, the emerging church movement could be described as "merely" a contextualization in a (post) modern setting. *Tobias Faix*

Eco-Monastic Leadership

Leadership in new monastic communities becomes a calling to a profoundly loving, contemplative maturity modeled on servanthood, where people are given room to exercise vocations in a flat leadership model. Vocation then is of function and not of hierarchy or privilege, as demonstrated by Franciscan brothers and Benedictine abbots who are elected. Leadership becomes a function of wisdom and inspiration with the right to say no in safekeeping of communities but where governance is consultative and communal as far as this is possible.

> Giving room for each to contribute to God's vision in a community is an essential and timeless leadership quality. It is how Jesus led. *MaryKate Morse*

This is the gift of a distinctively eco–new monastic model of church to the world and to the wider church—seeking to love God, love oneself, love others, and love the planet. In so doing, such mission assists spiritual questers to reach beyond the individualistic human ego and become cotraveling contemplative Christian pilgrims journeying to deep cultural engagement and encounter of the Triune Christian God.

In a time of a renewed spiritual revolution, this form of church just may be able to assist humanity to change gears and nurture creation and take us back from the brink of disaster. By so doing, eco–new monasticism will join a long history of the tradition of monasticism that has brought renewal to the church and new life to the world.

9

Mission within Hybrid Cultures

Transnationality and the Glocal Church

Oscar García-Johnson

The idea that the vitality of Christianity has shifted to the South is a popular missiological understanding by now. I would like to add an epexegetical thought to it: it is also *bouncing back to the North in the vessels of immigrant communities, refreshing and reshaping the fabric of predominant Christianity*. I begin this chapter by providing a practical illustration that situates our theological discourse in today's global context and forces us to produce an understanding of the church and missions that corresponds to such a context.

An Experiment

I recently traveled to Japan to be the keynote speaker of an evangelistic congress organized by an immigrant church in the city of Suzuka. I had been informed, to my surprise, that the hosting church consisted mostly of Sansei and Nisei families who primarily spoke Spanish and Portuguese.[1] Once there, my mis-

1. Usually *Sansei* identifies the third-generation Japanese-born immigrants while *Nisei* identifies the second generation.

sion was twofold: to share the good news and to describe for them how we organize and enable ministry among ethnic churches in Southern California and with their worldwide connections.

The pastor of the church and his wife are among the first, and the few, to have established a Spanish-speaking church in Suzuka and its surroundings, and they have done it without any denominational support. The pastoral couple, Sansei-Peruvians by birth, migrated to Japan with their parents during early adolescence. They met while attending a Brazilian Pentecostal church in Suzuka. As they grew up, they coped with all the demands presented by a polycentric context: the majority (Japanese) society, their Brazilian church, and their Peruvian Spanish-dominant family. This overwhelmingly polycentric and borderline experience enabled them to develop a set of paradigms and skills for coping with life and church ministry that a more monocultural/monolingual individual would find simply unattainable. For instance, they chose to establish a different type of church than the one they grew up in because they acknowledged that a Brazilian-Portuguese speaking base would not sufficiently address their hybrid-borderline existence. So they dared to plant the first immigrant multilingual church in their region as a way to embrace more fully who they are culturally and socially and to provide other immigrants and their children with the same opportunity.

Although Japan is not known as a place where Christian churches grow substantially and promptly, their new church topped long-established churches in a period of five years. Currently, their church houses a number of families that identify as Peruvian-Japanese, Ecuadorian-Japanese, Bolivian-Japanese, Argentinian-Japanese, and Brazilian-Japanese. Interestingly, it is showing notable growth among local (nonimmigrant) Japanese youth due to the networking lifestyles and evangelistic passion of their youth group members, some of whom were born and raised in Japan. Their worship service provides an experience in plurality with its mixing of Spanish-Japanese-Portuguese hymns and songs. Also, the message is translated (from Spanish or Portuguese) into Japanese.

> Even with differences in language and country of origin, immigrants find belongingness among other minorities with whom they find acceptance, empathy, and commonality of experience. *Eileen Suico*

The pastor and his wife are bivocational and have worked as translators for the city hall. That kind of exposure enabled them to seek new ways to seize civic opportunities in order to articulate an ecclesial witness to Jesus Christ in the city.

Moved by all these contextual complexities and ministry urgencies, the pastor began looking for resources and possible mentors to assist them in figuring out viable ways, healthy models, and appropriate partners to exercise a relevant ministry in their context. I quickly learned many of their urgent ministry questions. For instance, how do they understand the emerging generation, while capitalizing on their cultural mixing, crossing, and multiple identities? How can they facilitate ownership by this emerging generation of their experience of worship, discipleship, and witnessing to Jesus? How can they engage in civic life constructively as an immigrant church? These and other concerns typical of hybrid and immigrant communities resonated time after time in our conversations.

> There are resonances with the Sanctuary Fellowship in Birmingham, Britain, and their self-expression as "East and West." *Richard Sudworth*

By the end of my trip, two things became evident: (1) though both doing church ministry in different continents, in truth, we were close in context and mission situation; and (2) we belonged to a common space and were experiencing similar social, cultural, and ministry challenges. This exemplified the ubiquitous nature of globalization and how a place like Suzuka, Japan, is transnationally connected to Los Angeles, USA. Indeed, the pastor from Suzuka and I were doing ministry in the interstices of global society. I was able to facilitate a transnational mission connection with a local church in Los Angeles. Interestingly, it is a Latino church led by a Brazilian pastor who some years ago worked with a Nippon-Brazilian ministry in the vicinity of Sao Pablo, Brazil. Both congregations are now covenanting, networking, and exchanging resources to better accomplish what they believe to be a pertinent mission task in their corresponding global contexts.

> In the United States, Filipino churches find it easier to partner with churches in the Philippines rather than a local church that differs in culture, ethnicity, and language. *Eileen Suico*

Culture: Reframing Mission in Light of Globalization and Transnationality

Christian mission in several global contexts is making a *transnational shift*. Immigrant communities such as those of Latinos/as, Middle Easterners, and Asians are becoming mission-makers and cultural transmitters as they translocate and make new life in their respective contexts. Once they get established in a particular location, their *homes* travel with them, back and forth, thus constructing a transnational route. That is, they carry their *symbolic homeland* (Aztlán) as they acculturate and territorialize in their new location.[2] Many of them can be said to *transmigrate* instead of simply *immigrate*, to make life and ministry in between *Home* and *home*.

> British Asians (those in Britain who trace their ethnic roots to the Asian subcontinent of India, Pakistan, and Bangladesh) experience similar challenges. I wonder whether it is helpful anymore to talk of host and guest communities in a context where younger generations are identifying themselves with multiform cultural patterns. *Richard Sudworth*

These migration movements affect urban environments by reshaping the landscape of city life. As these migrations move forward through global conduits, they affect cities and other geographies, generating great opportunities and great challenges.[3] The migration impact is significant because it mirrors the effects of globalization[4] as do few other phenomena.

> Filipino ministries around the world exist wherever there are Filipino migrant workers in the locality. They hope to provide a community away from home to Filipinos who are separated from their families. *Eileen Suico*

On the one hand, globalization redefined life for everyone, but in particular immigrant communities. Common elements such as speed, space, time, events, sense of territory, and identity can no longer be considered factors of life easily accessible to all, but instead are interactive variables that synergize and flow

2. Aztlán refers here to an "alternative geography," a space of identity-performance of a sojourning community. It can also refer to a space of cultural and social resistance. See Rafael Pérez-Torres, "Alternative Geographies and the Melancholy of Meztisaje," in *Minor Transnationalism*, ed. Françoise Lionnet and Shu-mei Shih (Durham, NC: Duke University Press, 2005), 318–20.

3. Andrew Davey offers an informative discussion on these globalizing challenges and opportunities; see Andrew Davey, *Urban Christianity and Global Order: Theological Resources for an Urban Future* (Peabody, MA: Hendrickson, 2002), 28–55.

4. I acknowledge that views on globalization are controversial. Some, on the one hand, understand globalization as a process of homogenization, relying heavily on modern historical, political, and economic theories. I, on the other hand, hold a contemporary hybrid view of globalization, particularly in reference to cultural processes. Although the definition of globalization is controversial, the general consensus points to globalizing processes in terms of technological change, reconfiguration of states, regionalization, and asymmetry. As such, globalization represents a hermeneutical concept for the understanding of transnational missions and the glocal church. For an understanding of "globalization as hybridity," see Jan Nederveen Pieterse, *Globalization and Culture: Global Mélange* (Lanham, MD: Rowman and Littlefield, 2004); Manuel A. Vásquez and Marie Friedmann Marquardt, *Globalizing the Sacred: Religion across the Americas* (Piscataway, NJ: Rutgers University Press, 2003); Serge Gruzinski, *The Mestizo Mind: The Intellectual Dynamics of Colonization and Globalization*, trans. Deke Dusinberre (New York: Routledge Taylor and Francis Group, 2002).

almost ubiquitously in the global city, particularly among affluent segments of society. Besides, cultural and ethnic regionalization are reengineering and *coloring* cities, barrios, and social and religious structures.[5] Information technology fabricates a new type of social class, or social scale, where the acquisition of wealth, status, and power are based on what Manuel Castells calls "informational capitalism."[6] This globalizing effect, in particular, is modifying the DNA of social life and its political ramifications. In an information-fabricated society, those situated at the top of the informational networks are able to thrive while those placed at the bottom, who find themselves stuck in the continuum of industrial society, are stagnant and socially, economically, and politically invisible. Many immigrants fall in the latter category, but against the odds, they manage to survive even though their sense of *time and employment realization* fades away for lack of the kind of resourcefulness that informational capitalism imposes on the *new* type of worker.

On the other hand, immigrants who fall through the cracks of an informational society do not have it easy, for they are forced to find alternative means for survival and self-deployment. As our case illustrates, a solution points in the direction of enabling them to acquire a set of life paradigms, skills, and networks for managing themselves within a hybrid and global environment. Although many of these "transmigrants" are found in "the back alleys of society," their marginality might represent, in some respect, an advantageous borderline space. In Castells's own words: "It is in these alleys of society, whether in alternative electronic networks or in grassroots networks of communal resistance, that I have sensed the embryos of a new society, labored in the fields of history by a new identity."[7]

Indeed, it is in these "third spaces" or "informal spaces or back alleys of society," where immigrant communities and minorities are plunked down, that we are discerning an *interstitial sacred geography*[8] generated by God's Spirit for the redemption and uplift of immigrant and nonimmigrant communities alike, namely, the glocal church (that is, both global and local at the same time).

So far, we have seen how globalization as transnationality affects immigrant communities in particular. Obviously, the influence is mutual and the

5. See Daniel D. Arreola, *Hispanic Spaces, Latino Places: Community and Cultural Diversity in Contemporary America*, 1st ed. (Austin: University of Texas Press, 2004), 143–291.

6. See Manuel Castells, *The Power of Identity* (Malden, MA: Blackwell, 1997).

7. Ibid., 362.

8. See this idea treated in more detail in Oscar García-Johnson, *The Mestizo/a Community of the Spirit: A Postmodern Latino/a Ecclesiology*, Princeton Theological Monograph Series (Eugene, OR: Pickwick, 2009), 70–96.

interactivity between context and community ongoing. Thus we argue that a new transnational situation unveils a new ecclesial skin, a new type of Christian community, the glocal church. In the following, we will situate the glocal church within the planes of transnationality and the global city, hoping, in this way, to engage some of the ecclesial challenges that our Suzukan pastor presented to us at the beginning of the chapter.

Practices

Transnationality and the Need for a New Organizational Leadership

In our global context, the present circumstances of Christian structures point to certain sociocultural complexities and institutional challenges that can be perceived as riddling. This perplexity is even more acute if one holds the belief that Christianity was once a "simple religious phenomenon" that nowadays has been problematized thanks to the flow of cultures, migration, politics, and so on. However, contrary to this belief, since its origins Christianity has been a complex and diverse sociocultural phenomenon.[9] Today, the relevance and utility of institutional Christianity, in its role as carrier of the Christian heritage, faces a steep hill as Christendom moves against popular religious tendencies that gear toward postinstitutionalization, postrationalization, informal piety, community-based practices, and postmodern views of God, church, and society.[10] Following the logic of Harvey Cox in his book *The Future of Faith*, we could say "belief-based structures" are superseded by "faith-based organizations."[11] According to Cox, Christianity has gone through three quintessential stages: the Age of Faith (pre-Constantinian), the Age of the Belief (Constantinian), and the Age of the Spirit (current post-Constantinian). Cox argues that we are turning a new page in the history of Christianity, for "Christianity is growing faster than it ever has before, but mainly outside the West and in movements that accent spiritual experience, discipleship, and hope; pay scant attention to creeds; and flourish without

9. See James D. G. Dunn, *Unity and Diversity in the New Testament: An Inquiry into the Character of Earliest Christianity*, 2nd ed. (1990; repr., London: SCM, 2002); Alister McGrath, *Christian Spirituality: An Introduction* (Malden, MA: Blackwell, 1999).

10. "Classical church structures" refers here to traditional Christian denominations, churches, and other religious bodies based on creeds and hierarchies. In terms of the tendencies, there are several works that support this perception. See, e.g., Stanley Grenz, *A Primer on Postmodernism* (Grand Rapids: Eerdmans, 1996); McGrath, *Christian Spirituality*; Leonard I. Sweet, *Aquachurch* (Loveland, CO: Group, 1999); Harvey Gallagher Cox, *The Future of Faith*, 1st ed. (New York: HarperOne, 2009).

11. See Cox, *Future of Faith*, chap. 1.

hierarchies. We are now witnessing the beginning of a 'post-Constantinian era'. . . . I would like to suggest we call it the 'Age of the Spirit.'"[12]

> As a counterpoint, many of the growing immigrant churches have a far greater resemblance to a Christendom model of faith than inherited churches. For example, some of the large black Pentecostal churches are creedal and quite hierarchical (e.g., the largest church in London is Nigerian). Richard Sudworth

I argue that the Christian vitality of the Global South is bouncing back to the Global North in the vessels of immigrant communities. Perhaps the big surprise for many classical Christian structures centered on the North is that the immigrant communities are now carriers of the leading energy for missions and religious transformation. Through Christian leadership, immigrant churches are leading change within and beyond classical religious structures. For instance, in global environments such as the United States and Spain, immigrant churches are evangelizing, planting new churches, growing, and even getting involved in foreign missions, while majority culture congregations are declining and struggling to survive. In the same breath, immigrant churches are becoming strategic lead agents in the process of cultural, social, and economic adaptation between immigrants and the majority society. By way of forming the moral character of families and individuals and developing leadership skills among the members of the religious communities, immigrant churches are becoming increasingly strategic partners of societal development. Finally, by way of intercultural networking and civic education, immigrant church leaders are gradually becoming attuned with the judicial system and beginning to lead some of the grassroots movements designed to advocate for social, economic, and cultural justice.

> Denominations that are monochrome in ethos and cookie-cutter in their approach to organizing existing churches and establishing new ones emaciate the gospel. Even within the most monolithic of church structures there is more variety than would appear from official pronouncements or from the ill-informed outsider's perspective. Either this diversity must be celebrated or churches will simply go their own way.
>
> Eddie Gibbs (CN, 67)

> The capacity to adapt distinguishes leadership from management. Management cultures seek to conform. Adaptive cultures are looking for creative ways to engage and change. MaryKate Morse

12. Ibid., 8.

As a church movement, migrant churches bring in their cultural values and translate them into faith practices that become a tangible presence of healing and grace in the cities where they are located. *Eileen Suico*

Transnationality and Worship

Every global city needs a glocal church, and every glocal church is called to articulate a redemptive praxis in correspondence to its global context. The idea of a glocal church represents a way to respond to the challenges of globalization and post-Christendom. Manuel A. Vásquez and Marie Friedmann Marquardt, both social researchers of religion, argue that it is possible for popular religiosity and religious institutions to coexist in a complex and parasitic relationship. In their own words, "Like popular religion, religious institutions are dynamic, polysemic, and open to conflict. In fact . . . popular religion and religious institutions are engaged in a complex, if asymmetrical, interplay that leads to innovation, ambiguity, and heterogeneity."[13]

We can discern here the dialectics required for the sustenance of Christian faith as embodied in two forms of religious life: informal or popular, and formal or institutional. The key dynamic for the continuity of Christian tradition in the *new* religious situation is complex and symbiotic.[14] Christian religiosity cannot succeed without a *form of sociopolitical embodiment*. This, in part, is what made necessary the emergence of denominationalism. What we are learning, however, is that institutional religion is doomed to disappear without a *form of cultural practice* that transcends institutional life. This complex interplay between the institutionalized or territorialized religion and the noninstitutionalized or deterritorialized religion correlates precisely to the phenomenology of globalization. Vásquez and Marquardt's interpretation of globalization and religion here is welcome: "Globalization has precipitated an overabundance of religious meaning that . . . points to the emergence of multiple, overlapping, and heterogeneous religious fields that individuals and institutions must negotiate as they go about practicing religion."[15]

This brings light to one of today's most scandalous issues, namely, that people seem less concerned about maintaining traditional loyalties and affiliations, feeling more empowered to cross over institutional borders. The classic religious institution has ceased to be known as a sacred space.

13. Vásquez and Marquardt, *Globalizing the Sacred*, 10.
14. See this understanding in more detail in García-Johnson, *Mestizo/a Community of the Spirit*, 56–60.
15. Vásquez and Marquardt, *Globalizing the Sacred*, 13.

A way to cope with the challenges presented by today's religious tendencies is to envision the church as a faith community that is able to exercise *local* practices in a *global* way. Vásquez and Marquardt have found such a dynamic in Latino/a churches:

> Why should Latin American [and US Latino/a] cases be of interest to U.S.-based New Paradigm theorists? . . . [T]he rapid circular flow of ideas, people, goods, and capital between Latin America and the United States compels us to go beyond nation-based models of culture and religion and to take into account *regional* (i.e., hemispheric) and global dynamics.[16]

Immigrant communities such as Latinos/as carry within their very lifestyle a model for engaging today's global contexts and the new religious urges: transnationality. But what is it in the concept of transnational religion? How would such an idea guide us toward the reshaping of missions and church life? For one thing, we know that emerging faith communities encompass diversity, transiting among multiple religious matrices, negotiating affiliations and locations, crossing institutional borders, and so on. Besides, we are aware that a significant number of immigrants live in constant flux—in constant "formation of multiple and hybrid identities at 'borderlands,' sites where two or more lifeworlds meet."[17] It is appropriate then to argue that the understanding of *transnational religion* points to a significant way Christianity is being and will continue to be practiced in this new epoch. Vásquez and Marquardt explain:

> In contrast to earlier European immigrants, Latinos in the United States today have the means to carry out "systematic participation in networks that cross borders," such that the fabric of their daily lives becomes *transnational*. Responding to persisting discrimination and segregation, growing nativism, and a subordinate insertion in the new economy, Latinos strategically live *transnationally*. In other words, they "maintain and establish familial, economic, religious, political, or social relations in the state from which they moved, even as they also forge such relations in a new state in which they settle" (Glick Schiller 1999:96).[18]

Following Vásquez and Marquardt's perception, we could say that Christianity is taking on a "transnational character." That is, people are practicing faith and life in transit, maintaining native relationships yet forging new ones

16. Ibid., 28, emphasis added.
17. Ibid., 43.
18. Ibid., 42, emphasis added.

where they choose to settle. In this transit where life is experienced as a constant flux, the need of a localizing force, such as a church, is essential. In this sense, churches and other faith-based networks functioning as local spaces with global character can provide a localizing home to the transmigrant. The relevance of such local/global faith-based organizations or glocal churches consists in their becoming a faith geography where transnational Christians connect—maintaining links with their native location but forging relationships in their new location. As such, the local faith community is to maintain a global character.

> One of the greatest challenges in a post-Christendom, globalized context is the need for being simultaneously rooted (local) and linked (global)—rooted to our personal narrative geography, family of origin, race, ethnicity, faith tradition, while linking with very different narratives, families of origin, races, ethnicities, and faith traditions. We know that diversity and oneness reflect the Triune God yet we struggle to find deep practical resources to guide us into rooting and linking. *Dwight J. Friesen*

The understanding of the glocal church as a faith geography builds on the biblical image of the church as a worshiping community. Our Suzukan church has modeled well some of the dynamics necessary to create an environment fitted for worshiping in the plurality. The Suzukan church has been able to foster an environment of biblical inclusivity, uplifting, and cultural integration by going the extra mile and managing three languages and three cultures (Sansei-Latino/a, Brazilian, Japanese) to accommodate a diverse body of believers. Worship, as it happens with evangelism and preaching, requires multiple levels of cultural sensitivity and theologizing when done in hybrid environments. The goal should not be, for example, to move the first generation of immigrants to the expectations of the majority society in a multicultural setting (assimilationism) or to let them station in their nuclear culture (essentialism), but to enable them to move, along with the other segments, toward a constructive center where Christ is experienced in the plurality.

> The normal struggles in these situations usually go along with the question, Should the church look more like the culture in the homes, or of the larger society? Inevitably, the churches end up representing the in-betweenness culture of the people—yes, a hybrid. *Eileen Suico*

Hybridity as Community Formation

In a transnational situation, as Vásquez and Marquardt notice, "religion plays a major role because, along with ethnicity and nationalism, it is key in the creation and maintenance of the intersubjective world where meaning, identity, and a sense of place and belonging emerge."[19] Transnational Christianity requires a recategorization of significant ecclesiological and missiological concepts. I have argued elsewhere that

> life as experienced by immigrant communities is a flux of realities constantly shaping the social location, cultural consciousness, religious life, political presence, and multicultural practices of these communities. In the same breath, the categories of understanding that so far have been utilized in defining church life in the global contexts where these communities exist must be reconstructed to reflect a more fluid and inclusive understanding of culture and the church.[20]

Transnationality challenges us to go beyond modern anthropological tendencies that seek to universalize and homogenize cultural existence. Modern anthropology offers two dysfunctional extremes for immigrants to construct cultural identity: assimilationism and essentialism. These two models would not make the cut for transnational families and communities. As we saw with our Suzukan pastor, when living in polycentric-hybrid contexts individuals and communities are faced with the need to develop the ability to survive in multiple environments and exercise multiple identities as they go about their everyday life. Theological anthropology, from a transnational perspective, would necessarily have to account for the human subject in fluid and hybrid terms. Thus hybrid cultural categories such as "mestizaje," "mulatez," "criolization," "orientalization," "mélange," and "bricolage"[21] are identity constructs incorporated in the theological process in a way that these cultural realities do not dissociate from the experience of God, being community, and doing missions. For instance, I have suggested that the biblical narrative of Pentecost, as depicted in Acts 2 and embraced in New Testament Christianity, provides us with a paradigmatic approach for understanding and responding to the complexities of Christian experience in hybrid-based communities:

> The Christian community, since its beginnings, represents a cultural space where multiple matrices of identities find commonality and affirmation in the Spirit of Christ, as the transcendent socializing-formative agent. The Spirit acts in both directions simultaneously: it creates a common space for being-in-community and affirms the distinctiveness of each cultural subject within the whole through

19. Ibid., 50.
20. García-Johnson, *Mestizo/a Community of the Spirit*, ix.
21. A basic discussion on the use of these hybrid categories can be obtained in Pieterse, *Globalization and Culture*, 59–83. For the concept of bricolage religion see Vassilis Saroglou, "Religious Bricolage as a Psychological Reality: Limits, Structures and Dynamics," *Social Compass* 53, no. 1 (2006): 109–15.

a polyphonic proclamation of Jesus. . . . Affirmation of diversity means both affirmation of the person *in the diverse body* and affirmation of the *diversity in the person*. These affirmative movements by the Spirit imply a great deal of empathy, relationality, and spirituality. All this is only possible within community.[22]

Informed by this theological rationale, we offer the Suzukan pastor a cultural vision that is rooted in God's vision of his church as mirrored by the Pentecost narrative. Let us begin by affirming that Christian experience, just as cultural hybridity, is polyphonic, diverse, heterogeneous, and intersubjective in nature. In the case of the Christian experience, what makes that experience meaningful and authentic is God himself by means of his own performative self-revealing act in history (i.e., the Pentecost event) and by means of his Spirit, who acts as the intersubjective narrator (a meaning-enabler agent) of God in the community. In the case of our hybridity, it is the act of a complex transcultural performative identity of individuals in the transnational community assisted by a communal sense of self (communal self). In simpler terms, the Christian community is called to be a place where we do not have to give up our cultural complexities to belong but instead are moved toward each other by embracing a *safe center*, a communal space, where affirmation, stabilization, communal crossing and exchange, *convivencia* (life together), and personal deployment are safeguarded and mediated by none other than God himself. The glocal church represents a brand-new Pentecost-church where transnational Christians can say anew with the church of the New Testament: "we hear them declaring the wonders of God in our own tongues!" (Acts 2:11).

> I love the idea of "hybridity as community formation." I would argue that the engagement with the "other" actually helps the church to be truly itself. Is there not a sense in which Christian citizenship is of its very nature a "hybrid community" with consequent overlapping loyalties? Are we not "resident aliens"? Seen in this light, such ecclesial communities are actually a prophetic sign to monocultural, inherited churches. Richard Sudworth

> Churches evolve through everyday relational connections such as crossing cultural barriers in marriages, work, schools, and friendship. Inevitably, the church's local context is transformed by its presence. Eileen Suico

Trans-mission and Evangelism

Transnationality challenges the way church is to do mission and evangelism. If we have followed the transnational logic we will acknowledge that sharing

22. García-Johnson, *Mestizo/a Community of the Spirit*, 109.

Christian faith is not reduced to a task, a duty, a program, and so forth, but it is instead a *domestic performative cultural practice*. This understanding of mission and evangelism flows out of an understanding of the church that uses three interrelated cultural categories: embodiment, relationality, and transmission. In missiological terms, the church is the embodiment of the message of Jesus Christ, made visible in community through the relationality of the Spirit of Christ and the people of God, with the mission of transmitting Christian forms of life within the culture and at large. In a (global) transnational situation, *evangelism* and *mission* are really *trans-mission*.

How is the glocal church, then, to embody and transmit the message of Jesus Christ in a way that corresponds to its polycentric and transnational context? I have suggested three performative cultural practices in this regard: (1) being a eucharistic community, (2) being a proclamation community, and (3) being a pastoral community.[23] The eucharistic practice of the glocal church points to Jesus Christ's table as a space of inclusion: a place where *the other* becomes a "hermano/a" (brother/sister) and the transmigrant can approximate a safe center in search for a common home without losing his/her distinctiveness. The proclamatory practice points to the effort of sharing and exchanging narratives, being a crossroads community where Jesus's story meets the story of the peoples and communities making up the context of the glocal church. Finally, the pastoral practice points to a capacity for seeing people and their stories, embodying a *new social reality*, and becoming a restorative-healing community.

Would it not be an amazing transformation of the global society to see our Suzukan church becoming a glocal embodiment of the message of Jesus Christ that by virtue of its hybridity, communal self, and transnational lifestyle accomplishes the *missio Dei* to evangelize, disciple, and regenerate cultures and global communities and do it all *in apostolic-transnational transit*?

Bibliography

Arreola, Daniel D. *Hispanic Spaces, Latino Places: Community and Cultural Diversity in Contemporary America*. Austin: University of Texas Press, 2004.
Castells, Manuel. *The Power of Identity*. Malden, MA: Blackwell, 1997.
Cox, Harvey. *The Future of Faith*. San Francisco: HarperOne, 2009.

23. See the discussion of these communal practices in ibid., 104–41.

Davey, Andrew. *Urban Christianity and Global Order: Theological Resources for an Urban Future*. Peabody, MA: Hendrickson, 2002.

Dunn, James D. G. *Unity and Diversity in the New Testament: An Inquiry into the Character of Earliest Christianity*. 2nd ed. London: SCM, 2002.

García-Johnson, Oscar. *Mestizo/a Community of the Spirit: A Postmodern Latino/a Ecclesiology*. Princeton Theological Monograph Series. Eugene, OR: Pickwick, 2009.

Glick Schiller, Nina. "Transmigrants and Nation-States: Something Old and Something New in the U.S. Immigrant Experience." Pages 94–119 in *The Handbook of International Migration: The American Experience*, edited by Charles Hirschman, Philip Kasinitz, and Josh DeWind. New York: Russell Sage Foundation, 1999.

Grenz, Stanley. *A Primer on Postmodernism*. Grand Rapids: Eerdmans, 1996.

Gruzinski, Serge. *The Mestizo Mind: The Intellectual Dynamics of Colonization and Globalization*. Translated by Deke Dusinberre. New York: Routledge, 2002.

Held, David, Anthony McGrew, David Goldblatt, and Jonathan Perraton. *Global Transformations: Politics, Economics and Culture*. Stanford, CA: Stanford University Press, 1999.

McGrath, Alister. *Christian Spirituality: An Introduction*. Malden, MA: Blackwell, 1999.

Pérez-Torres, Rafael. "Alternative Geographies and the Melancholy of Mestizaje." Pages 317–38 in *Minor Transnationalism*, edited by Françoise Lionnet and Shu-mei Shih. Durham, NC: Duke University Press, 2005.

Pieterse, Jan Nederveen. *Globalization and Culture: Global Mélange, Globalization*. Lanham, MD: Rowman and Littlefield, 2004.

Saroglou, Vassilis. "Religious Bricolage as a Psychological Reality: Limits, Structures and Dynamics." *Social Compass* 53, no. 1 (2006): 109–15.

Sweet, Leonard I. *Aquachurch*. Loveland, CO: Group, 1999.

Vásquez, Manuel A., and Marie Friedmann Marquardt. *Globalizing the Sacred: Religion across the Americas*. Piscataway, NJ: Rutgers University Press, 2003.

10

Distinctly Welcoming

The Church in a Pluralist Culture

Richard Sudworth

Culture

The great philosophical challenge of our time is epistemology: How do we know what is real to us? The Enlightenment promised a progressively rational world delivering untold benefits from technology. It augured freedom for the individual from the oppressions of tradition and superstition. But all this seems more than a little shop-soiled now. Whether one looks at the scientific efficiency of Nazism or the ever-impending crisis of global warming, the victory of autonomous reason seems hollow. Modernity's foundation that truth can be objectively established and thus be authoritative for what might be termed the "good life" is no longer presumed.[1] If our individual worldview can no longer be verified or tested by rational argument or scientific inquiry, how is judgment or authority to be established?

1. See J. Richard Middleton and Brian J. Walsh, *Truth Is Stranger Than It Used to Be: Biblical Faith in a Postmodern Age* (London: SPCK, 1995), for an excellent Christian overview of this cultural paradigm shift. New Testament scholar N. T. Wright provides a helpful introduction to the implications of the collapse in modernity for the use of Scripture in the church in *The New Testament and the People of God* (London: SPCK, 1992), 31–80.

Rediscovering Public Faith

The presumption of the autonomous individual in modernity has inevitably shaped the church. An emphasis on the rational, independent decision making of the individual, for example, made apologetics a popular component of evangelism. Remembering my own Christian upbringing, the arguments for the resurrection of Jesus figured prominently as part of a number of persuasive encouragements to non-Christians for conversion. I can recall student evangelism campaigns advertising discussions on evolution or sexual ethics. The point was to press for the rational plausibility of the Christian claims and thereby to bring a person to a decision for Christ. Such efforts still exist but they are not as prevalent as they once were; the good news is somehow greater than a message limited to an argument we need to win.

> Previously evangelism training was based on a single approach and a fixed gospel outline. It is questionable whether this strategy was adequate in the past, and increasingly we are finding that one particular approach is not appropriate for many individuals who are open to God.
>
> Eddie Gibbs (CN, 203–4)

The crisis in secular modernity has fueled the rise of new forms of church in the emerging postmodern cultures of the Western world.

The shift that we are witnessing in the emerging church movement involves a recognition that our worldviews are drawn from much more than our independent intellects and indeed that "independence" in such matters is perhaps a fiction. It is not that the apologetic questions no longer matter, but that we are increasingly conscious that we cannot divorce them from the realities of community, practice, and tradition. For the emerging church movement, the mission of the church in the Western world is moving away from the positivism of the apologetic paradigm.

The research in Eddie Gibbs and Ryan Bolger's *Emerging Churches*[2] reflects on church groups in the United States and United Kingdom that are responsive to this new vista we call postmodernity. They emphasize traits such as participation and community, creativity, and generosity. As "authority" is so questionable in this new economy, hierarchies are flattened and there is a peculiarly postmodern blend of the "ancient and the modern"—a practice that the postmodern anthropologist Claude Lévi-Strauss termed "bricolage." Our truth, as Christians, is mediated in corporate rituals, each telling a story about who we are, such that the presentation of the Christian faith is as much about our practice as it is about our words. Being the story

2. Eddie Gibbs and Ryan K. Bolger, *Emerging Churches: Creating Christian Community in Postmodern Cultures* (London: SPCK, 2006).

of the church, it will recall and signal something of that older story, woven into the worship and rituals of contemporary life.

Many of the formative voices for churches engaging in the emerging post-modern cultures draw explicitly from the work of the great British missiologist Lesslie Newbigin (1909–98).[3] Newbigin recognized the barrenness of the Western, secular worldview, and in *The Gospel in a Pluralist Society* grappled with the likes of Michael Polanyi and Alasdair MacIntyre to demonstrate that all our knowledge is situated. We "believe" in community, amongst practices and stories that we learn and mediate. There is no "view from nowhere" that trumps the supposed individual bias of religious experience. For the church to take this account seriously, it could no longer collude with the false secular/sacred divide that has been so characteristic of Western religiosity.

> Credible gospel communication does not *impose* an absolute but *proposes* an alternative.
>
> Eddie Gibbs (LN, 60)

If the Christian faith cannot be reduced to abstracted rational affirmations, then it needed to be demonstrable beyond the boundaries of the church building and Sunday rite.

Newbigin argued for a very public Christian faith and, returning from his many years in India, had come to perceive that the Western world was itself a mission field demanding a public theology and ecclesiology from a church in danger of defaulting to the privatized individualism of its environment. For all the indebtedness to Lesslie Newbigin in the emerging church movement, though, very little is made of the primary causes of his own epiphany and how these continue to resonate today. Newbigin's formative missionary experiences were in India, that melting pot of religions and public faith. He was very conscious that Islam, in particular, with its robust understanding of political faith and corporate identity in the *umma* (community) of believers, challenged the church to have a place in the public square. His return to Britain

---

3. Brian McLaren, *A Generous Orthodoxy* (Grand Rapids: Zondervan, 2006): Brian's outline of why he is proud to call himself a "Missional, Evangelical, Post/Protestant, Liberal/Conservative, Mystical/Poetic, Biblical, Charismatic/Contemplative, Emergent, Unfinished Christian" is essentially a populist application of Lesslie Newbigin's seminal work, *The Gospel in a Pluralist Society* (London: SPCK, 1989). Michael Frost and Alan Hirsch's influential *The Shaping of Things to Come: Innovation and Mission for the 21st-Century Church* (Peabody, MA: Hendrickson, 2003) notes Newbigin's *The Gospel in a Pluralist Society* as a "recommended text." The Church of England's best-selling document, *Mission-Shaped Church: Church Planting and Fresh Expressions of Church in a Changing Context* (London: Church House, 2004), is littered with footnotes to Newbigin's legacy. Andrew Jones, who blogs as "Tall Skinny Kiwi," refers to Lesslie Newbigin almost as a godfather of the emerging church: "much of the wind behind our missional sails was provided by Newbigin": http://tallskinnykiwi.typepad.com/tallskinnykiwi/2010/04/begbie-nt-wright-and-emergent-ecclesiologies.html.

and involvement in pastoral work in multifaith Birmingham made him realise that his robust neighbours in India were also his new neighbours in the home of the now defunct British Empire.[4]

For Newbigin, the crisis of mission in the West was not simply that a privatised, secular individualism was dictating culture and even shaping the church's worldview.[5] A huge part of the trauma he foresaw was that now there were communities of very public faith and corporate strength that saw the poverty of Western culture and would fill the void where the church had vacated. The vestiges of the Christian heritage still available to the churches were insufficient for the burgeoning communities of Sikhs, Hindus, and Muslims to take seriously the Christian presence in society. In many ways, Newbigin was a prophetic voice to some of the most pressing debates of Western society in recent years, anticipating what one title has proclaimed, somewhat mischievously: *God Is Back.*[6]

> There is an urgent need for the churches to equip church members to live out their faith within a pluralist society.
>
> Eddie Gibbs (INO, 200)

> Newbigin's dictum that "the only hermeneutic of the gospel is a congregation of men and women who believe it and live by it" is paradigmatic for my work. Yet, it entails more in terms of a contextually visible communal Christian life than most of us like. Even if individualism is a fiction, it is a story that forms my hybrid life in so many ways. *Andreas Østerlund Nielsen*

The admission that the autonomous, rational individual is a fiction has significant implications for the church's engagement with other faiths. Going

---

4. Newbigin's most thoroughgoing articulation of the challenges of Eastern religions and Islam, in particular, to the church in Britain can be found in Lesslie Newbigin, Lamin Sanneh, and Jenny Taylor, *Faith and Power: Christianity and Islam in "Secular" Britain* (London: SPCK, 1998).

5. In an otherwise excellent summary of Newbigin's "theology of mission to the Western world," Donald Le Roy Stults in *Grasping Truth and Reality: Lesslie Newbigin's Theology of Mission to the Western World* (Cambridge, UK: James Clarke, 2009) exemplifies the common pattern of focusing attention on Newbigin's engagement with secular modernity and the need for the church to recognise its crisis of epistemology, whilst neglecting the significance to Newbigin of other religious traditions to the contemporary context of the Western world.

6. John Micklethwait and Adrian Wooldridge, *God Is Back: How the Global Rise of Faith Is Changing the World* (London: Penguin Books, 2010). This book, by journalists from *The Economist* magazine, follows a piece they wrote for the millennium edition of *The Economist* entitled "God Is Dead." I applaud their willingness to admit an altered scene but wonder, rather, that their original perspective had been very shortsighted and that, in fact, nothing has substantively changed since 2000. Vibrant faith communities have been manifest in London, Marseille, Berlin, and New York, let alone Kampala, Jos, and Hyderabad, long before the headline events of 9/11 and 7/7.

back to my illustration from the world of apologetics, its essential problematic is the assumption that we all share the same mode of discourse. If I can persuade someone about an aspect of the good news of Christ in reasonable terms, then that intellectual "conversion" should shape and define his or her life goal. The trouble is, we may have a convincing argument, but another person's life decisions (in spiritual terms, "who or what is Lord") are made from a whole complex of beliefs, behaviours, and relationships. So, for example, explaining to a Muslim that, in Jesus, she will know the assurance of forgiveness of sins that is unavailable in Islamic observance assumes that forgiveness of sins is a shared ground for religious conviction or even that "salvation" is relevant to Islam. The worldviews between faiths cannot be reduced to a shared checklist of comparatives. Too often our knowledge of other faiths is a travesty of misapprehensions through which we equate, for example, church with mosque, Qur'an with Bible, Jesus with Muhammad. This sort of analysis has presumed an underlying discourse that does not exist. The church has a very different standing for Christians than does the mosque in Muslim communities. It would be most accurate to compare Jesus to the Qur'an in terms of equivalent roles in Christianity and Islam.

> This is an appropriate challenge to understand religions on their own terms rather than forcing the comparative categories of our own faith alongside them. *Darren Cronshaw*

Rethinking Our Theology of Religions

The "theology of religions" pattern of thinking is itself a by-product of secular modernity. It assumes that the individual is the focus for the big questions of transcendence. Secular modernity reduces transcendence to an internalised aspiration or yearning, and, turned inward, religions are thus different answers to the same questions: questions that are atomised and divorced from the messiness of communities, politics, the environment, and social life. Whether we have learned our theology of religions as an "exclusivist," "pluralist," or "inclusivist," this paradigm results in the neutering of public faith. What is known as the "threefold typology of religions," articulated originally by Alan Race, a pluralist Anglican minister,[7] has become the classic delineation of interfaith analysis. According to Lesslie Newbigin, this is a wholly inadequate tool for understanding a missional engagement with other faiths.[8] Each of these three approaches to religions answers a different question; they do not provide a shared framework for defining faiths. Thus I

7. Alan Race, *Christians and Religious Pluralism* (London: SCM, 1983).
8. See *Gospel in a Pluralist Society*, 155–83.

> Humans are both sinners and creatures made in the image of God: thus religions represent both a search for God and a flight from God. The spiritual truths and insights to be found in other religions are derived from general revelation. All empirical religions are, therefore, the "product" of a combination of divine revelation and human sin which obscures and distorts the original revelation.
>
> Eddie Gibbs (INO, 227)

> Leaders need spiritual discernment to distinguish between (1) those elements of a culture that the gospel affirms, (2) aspirations that only the gospel can fulfill and (3) those elements that represent the demonic, which must be challenged.
>
> Eddie Gibbs (LN, 56)

am an exclusivist if asked about the significance of Christ as the hope for the whole of humanity. I am an inclusivist if asked whether I expect to be surprised by some non-Christians sharing in the coming of the new creation. And I am a pluralist if asked about the extent to which I will see God at work in the world.

The inadequacies of a secular modernity model of religions, which effectively puts the position of the bird's-eye view onto humanity, a place that can only be reserved for God, is also apparent in David Bosch's classic *Transforming Mission: Paradigm Shifts in Theology of Mission*.[9] This is why Bosch puts such store by the concept of the *missio Dei*,[10] the mission of God. An appreciation that humanity never has an abstracted, bird's-eye view of truth is a properly humbling preparation for the reality of God at work beyond the confines of the church. We are not the authors of our own destiny, nor do we control or dictate the mission that is properly God's. Hence, in the Church of England's *Mission-Shaped Church* document, there is a proper attention to the mission of God, which is expressed as a foundational theology for the church in this new economy.[11] It surely means, then, that we should expect to encounter God at work amongst people from other faith traditions. This is not to deny the ultimate claims of the Christian gospel, all that we can say about the salvation we have experienced in Christ that is available to the whole world. Thus we are not forced to choose between the poles of exclusivism or pluralism. But an increased understanding of our communal practice and tradition and the place of ritual and relationship for a fuller grasp of what it means to be a follower of Christ sharpens the distinctiveness of who we are as Christians while opening us up to the grace of God in the faith-other.

9. David Bosch, *Transforming Mission: Paradigm Shifts in Theology of Mission* (Maryknoll, NY: Orbis, 1991).
10. Ibid., 10, 370, 389–93.
11. *Mission-Shaped Church*, 85.

This assertion invites us to be curious about where God is at work and to seek to join in with what God is doing. We are, as Rick Richardson suggests, junior detectives working with the Holy Spirit, discovering clues for God being at work, or travel guides on a spiritual journey (rather than salespeople seeking to close a deal), or matchmakers in the dating-and-marriage dance between people and God.[12] This reminds us that God is the primary agent in mission and it is our privilege to cooperate with God. *Darren Cronshaw*

Part of what has been formative for my missionary calling in the UK has been my time working in North Africa. I had the privilege of meeting a Muslim convert who had had a dream about Jesus, signaling to him the direction his life should go. God was evidently already at work in this man prior to meeting any Christian. I had heard too of Muslims, beguiled by the shadowy presence of Jesus in the Qur'an, the healer and miracle worker of the key Islamic text, who were searching out Bibles to read, hungry for an encounter that had somehow been primed from within their own religious tradition. How might the church be open to such stories back in a Western context where Christians meet with Muslims, Sikhs, Hindus, and others daily?

How might we be open to God being at work in our neighbours and friends who are more secular or engaged in alternative spiritualities? How can we learn skills in naming and celebrating and drawing out what is of God in other people who live life outside any religious categories? *Darren Cronshaw*

Practices

Distinctly Welcoming Worship

The phrase that I like to use for this pattern of mission is "distinctly welcoming."[13] I believe this phrase follows something of Newbigin's understanding of our changed situation and reflects the broader pattern of emerging church praxis. An acknowledgment of our situatedness, our rootedness in the communal Christian story, should make us unashamed of the rituals and beliefs that provide our Christian impulse. Thus the centrality of Christ, a trinitarian understanding of God, prayer, and the Bible will all be integral beliefs and practices in our worship. Yet knowing that God can speak to people from within their religious and cultural traditions, our worship could

12. See *Reimagining Evangelism: Inviting Friends on a Spiritual Journey* (Queensway: Scripture Union, 2006).

13. See my book *Distinctly Welcoming: Christian Presence in a Multifaith Society* (Bletchley: Scripture Union, 2007) for a fuller account of distinctly welcoming mission.

be creatively open to encounters and revelations that bring others to know Christ more fully.

> A popular trope in contemporary mission is "belonging before believing." I wonder if serious attention to public faith and the mission of God would permit us to describe a pattern of believing, before belonging, before believing and being baptised. Our other-faith neighbours have no trouble believing that prayer is powerful, that God speaks and heals, and that sacred texts shape powerfully the stories we participate in as communities. The church does not come to a blank page, ready to write the Christian script, but to a story that has already begun, often craving the fulfillment that a true encounter with Jesus can bring.
> *Darren Cronshaw*

Sanctuary fellowship in Birmingham,[14] England's second largest city, has done such work in the shaping of their weekly worship. Led by Pall Singh, who comes from a Sikh background, Sanctuary has noticed that an increasing number of South Asian–background British are a meld of East and West. In Pall's words, they like curry the way their mother makes it, but with pizza on the side! Pall's own journey displays this natural familiarity with the foods, rituals, and clothing of his roots intertwined with all the sensibilities of growing up in a large British city. In many ways, after conversion as a teenager, and feeling that he had to divest himself of much of his "Asianness" to be part of the church, Pall has returned to embrace a more Eastern spirituality, and it has made connections and resonances with younger British Asians around him.

> The world is a riot of colors, forms, shapes and textures. The church, described as the "body of Christ," is an organic miracle of diversity expressed in a unity of purpose.
>
> Eddie Gibbs (CN, 67)

Interestingly, there is much that other emerging church groups would find recognisable in the weekly Sanctuary worship. There is no sung worship but a more contemplative worship style with projected video images, often to sound tracks that fuse Western folk music and Indian spiritual tunes known as *bhajans*. Worship is made participatory by spaces that invite a response by, perhaps, lighting a candle, eating an Asian sweet, or sitting or kneeling by a cross, all as very physical acts of prayer and devotion. Prayer as an active ritual would be familiar to Sikhs, Hindus, and Muslims who come to Sanctuary, often over a period of months and years before making a full commitment to Christ. The worship is Christ-centred, but the cultural expression echoes the sensibilities of British Asians. Food is

14. For information about Sanctuary, go to http://www.eastandwest.co.uk/sanctuary.html.

integral to cultures that would not dream of a communal event without dinner and so, after some readings, meditations, and invited responses, the worship continues as everyone assembles around a large pot of curry.

There is something of home at Sanctuary for British Asians who are searching for more—who have heard something about Jesus and see in this fellowship a community that is familiar and yet new, welcoming and yet distinct. The ethos is one that does not seek to correct or condemn the faith journey that people are already on. Rather, in the language of that great model of mission for Pall, Sadhu Sundar Singh, instead of extinguishing the candle that a person holds in their dark room, the church's role is to open the curtains to the true light.[15]

> M. A. C. Warren appeals for openness to prevenient grace and for discerning where God has already been at work: "Our first task in approaching another people, another culture, another religion is to take off our shoes, for the place we are approaching is holy. Else we may find ourselves treading on [people's] dreams. More serious still, we may forget that God was here before our arrival."[16] *Darren Cronshaw*

Distinctly Welcoming Communities

Pall has a very neat challenge to the church in the West that is worth repeating when one considers the issue of community in relation to our neighbouring Eastern cultures: "People pray for the conversion of Sikhs, Hindus and Muslims. What they don't realise is that, after conversion, they are likely to lose their friends, their family, their marriage prospects and future security. What they get instead is a weekly meeting followed by tea and biscuits." How can the church become family to cultures that may indeed be losing their family for Christ? This encapsulates, for me, the crisis of Western culture that Newbigin foresaw: the isolated individualism and neglect of our corporate faith. Sanctuary has seen that a serious engagement with other faiths demands a level of community life that the customary Western church does not provide. An earlier Christian generation would talk of "no Bible, no breakfast" as they emphasised the need for daily Bible reading. Maybe, for the contemporary scene, we can add, "no food, no church"!

15. Sadhu Sundar Singh (1889–1929) was an Indian Sikh guru who converted to the Christian faith yet continued a life and ministry as a guru traveling throughout India, talking about the Jesus he knew in the culture and tradition of his birth. Sundar Singh has been a longstanding inspiration for Pall, and his teachings and parables can be read about in *Wisdom of the Sadhu: Teachings of Sundar Singh* (Farmington, PA: Plough, 2000).

16. M. A. C. Warren, introduction to *The Primal Vision: Christian Presence Amid African Religion*, by John V. Taylor (London: SCM, 1963), 10–11.

> Love it! "No food, no church."
>
> The narrative of the Bible is not only filled with profound images of community at the table, but many of the pivotal moments are marked by food. From eating the fruit in the garden to the Marriage Supper of the Lamb, and everything in between.
>
> I've always found it fascinating that while table fellowship was central to our Lord's life and ministry, the church has made the Lord's table the most exclusive aspect of our life together.
>
> It may be that the post-Christendom context will invite an evolution of our theology and practice of the table. *Dwight J. Friesen*

> This is an important challenge to hear. Mission is not just about evangelism and helping people understand and accept Jesus, but offering a community of support and shared worship and mission. *Darren Cronshaw*

> Rather than extraction, the church's posture to integrate and be immersed in intercultural and interfaith relations is a vital element in being in community. *Eileen Suico*

> Sudworth highlights a theology of hospitality that has its foundations in the kingdom of God. We are called to welcome unbelievers to experience the local church as the sign and agent of the kingdom. The goal for the church is for unbelievers to be incorporated (i.e., assimilated, resocialized) not into the church, but into the kingdom. *Osías Segura-Guzmán*

Distinctly Welcoming Mission

For many years, I was part of a Church of England–based work in Birmingham, England, where the primary mission engagement was through an integrated family and children's support agency. The Springfield Project[17] provides a shared space for a very mixed community under the aegis of the umbrella of a local parish church. A major provider of children's services in this part of Birmingham, the Springfield Project employs a mixed staff of Christians and people from other faiths who are all familiar with and reminded of the core Christian ethos. The Christian congregation of St. Christopher's provides the bulk of a Christian volunteer base of around forty that ensures that Christians are sharing their working lives with Muslims, Sikhs, and Hindus. The clear Christian ethos, even the very church building with its traditional Anglican symbolism, means that conversations about faith are real and vital. Indeed, the explicitness of the Christian story interwoven in the periodic prayer meetings,

17. For stories of the Springfield Project and its theological rationale, see http://www.communitymission.org.uk/stories/local_stories/children_youth_ministry_stories/the_springfield_childrens_centre.aspx; http://www.communitymission.org.uk/stories/local_stories/children_youth_ministry_stories/the_springfield_centre_where_it_began.aspx; and http://www.sharetheguide.org/examples/faiths.

the lives shared, and the Christian values referred to in working practices all serve to free people to be themselves as people of faith. So Muslim parents will talk of feeling comfortable in the project because it is a house of prayer.

> Sustaining such a bounded-set/centered-set, Christian/multireligious environment is the pivotal challenge of being a missional church—a church that embraces and confronts, as Jesus did. *Andreas Østerlund Nielsen*

The common pattern has been for such community projects to iron out faith distinctives, to attempt to provide a "neutral," secularised service. Apart from this being impossible, as Newbigin would attest, this actually alienates those from other religious traditions who cannot interiorise their religious beliefs. Without exploiting this space, the Springfield Project has become a focus of integral and holistic mission, where the Christian faith is owned and explicit. This has made the church and its associated project buildings a safe space for those of other faiths. Throughout the week, relationships of trust are being built up and friendships developed between Christians and those of other faiths. The St. Christopher's congregation has recognised that any attempts to engage the multifaith parish demand serious attention to relationships over the long term, where the quality of Christian service is made manifest in a context of public faith, distinctly welcoming.

> We need to understand that people of other religions do not want us to water down our religious convictions and practices to meet in a neutral middle. *Darren Cronshaw*

Leadership for a Distinctly Welcoming Church

Graham Cray's booklet *Discerning Leadership: Cooperating with the Go-Between God*[18] summarises much of what I would like to say about church leadership in a plural context. Positing the church's task within the mission of God,[19] Cray argues that a triple listening to God, the church, and the community is required of us.[20] In our plural context, we need to listen to God at work from within the cultural symbols and texts of other faiths, yet utterly shape our communal practices around Christian worship and disciplines. A leadership that will be able to discern God speaking to a Muslim through their Qur'anic readings or through the prayers of a Hindu requires courage and

---

18. Graham Cray, *Discerning Leadership: Cooperating with the Go-Between God*, Grove Leadership series L1 (Cambridge, UK: Grove Books, 2010).
19. Cray quotes Newbigin's dictum that "the Spirit is not the church's auxiliary." Ibid., 7.
20. Ibid., 18–25.

risk. It is ever more important that the leader's personal Christian devotions have integrity because this economy is not about all roads leading to God, nor is it a bland amalgam that produces multifaith worship.

> When God's ability to speak to us falls only within our finite boundaries, we diminish God's immanence. Leaders stay radically connected to the cross and completely open to God's voice in others. *MaryKate Morse*

For me, the emerging church movement at its best is discovering God at work in contemporary postmodern culture and bringing us to discover and rejoice at the prior presence of the Spirit of God. When that impulse propels us into an encounter with other-faith communities, there is a particular responsibility to learn about the texts and practices of our neighbours: to learn about Islamic tradition, the Qur'an, Sikh history, and Hindu rituals. So much of these traditions, we will find, already points to and echoes the story to which Jesus is the fulfillment. Missional leadership will be able to make these connections, weave the stories together around the pivotal significance of the Christ-event, and bless and affirm the journey of faith already begun amongst friends and neighbours.

> God goes before us in the pluralistic religious context we find ourselves in. We will be surprised by how and where God has been weaving his story and bringing the world more in line with God's dream for it. *Darren Cronshaw*

Church in our emerging postmodern culture has drawn from the example and theologies of the likes of Lesslie Newbigin and John V. Taylor, leaders who had a formative experience in the foreign missionary field. That story of foreign missions is now not just "over there" but "over here." I believe that we may find that we come full circle, applying missiological principles not just to the collapsing cultures of secular modernity, but to the vibrant faith communities that are now very much part and parcel of Western plurality.

11

Our P(art) in an Age
of Beauty

Troy Bronsink

The keys to the kingdom got locked inside the kingdom / and the angels fly around in there, but we can't see them.

Josh Ritter, "A Girl in the War"[1]

Culture

Beauty necessitates the beholder. In its generosity, beauty leaves the keys to admission in the door. However, the generous outstretched arms of beauty relinquish artisans and creators from control over the outcome or security against rejection. As such, art's prerequisite lack of control has frequently led religion to trade in the brush and canvas in an attempt to splice beauty from its role in faith formation. This is a story of churches relinquishing that myth of control and relearning how both to follow Jesus *by learning from beauty* and to participate in the mission of God *by becoming art*.

1. Josh Ritter, lyrics to "A Girl in the War," on *Animal Years* (Independent Records, 2006).

Church as Art

My working sketch for the mission of the church is rooted in God's expansive creative character. This God, whom the Christian tradition has come to describe as a mutually serving community of Father, Son, and Spirit, drew out of thin air a formless empty potential and hovered over its waters. The Hebrew Scriptures instruct us through two early narratives that God called all minerals and life forth out of that void, finally breathing life into the dirt until it became a proper noun, Adam, and bringing out of Adam another proper noun, Eve. And after generations, families would also become a proper noun, and beyond families, nations. And at each encounter shared with us through these old stories, God commissioned these individuals, families, and nations to build on that original, mutually serving love.

Finally, God entered into the same dirt, being born of woman as "God with us." And this unique enfleshed God lived a life exhibiting the same expansive characteristics that existed before the beginning. And then God-with-us would breathe on his apprentices the Spirit of God, enabling them to do even greater things than he: healing, demonstrating heaven's news to the ends of the earth, and forgiving and unbinding on earth as it is in heaven. One of Jesus's apprentices would say that walking in that same expansive love toward one another "completes" God's love in us—a love begun in God and demonstrated in the death and resurrection of the enfleshed God.[2] Another apprentice who met Jesus after his ascension said that our lives are "God's handiwork, created in Christ Jesus" for a good-working life, a life dreamt of before any time, space, or matter had existed.[3]

> God's intention for humanity is for us to live with him, to pitch a tent with him, to repent and go back to him. Immanuel, God with us, called us his friends, his church, his body. *Eileen Suico*

Now, this is a broad sketch of the mission of God, and it goes without saying that communities dedicated to that mission have had mixed success in realizing it. And yet a community's calling originates in God's dreams, and the commission's fulfillment calls to the realization of these dreams. The art of the church is much more do-it-yourself than the traditional "intellectual" approach. Therefore, for the purposes of this chapter, I define the church as *the community of commissioned women and men doing and making a way of life that brings more and more time, space, and matter into participation with the expansive love of God in Jesus.* And since the means and the end,

2. See 1 John 4:12.
3. Eph. 2:10.

the cause and the effect are all *love*, all of the church's making and doing both shape and are shaped by God's love.

Why are some churches reintegrating the making and doing of kingdom-of-God things, rather than stagnating in ideological gridlock? Many congregations and emerging communities "open source" their fumbling faith in public, in full view, and freely give away the rights to interpret the experience or enjoy its benefits. These communities pop up in response to an emerging culture.

Our emerging culture is replete with social media and other hi-tech opportunities for *participation* and yet increasingly isolated by competing ubiquitous meaning structures imposed on those experiences. Daniel Pink argues that "we are moving from an economy and a society built on the logical, linear, computer-like capabilities of the Information Age to an economy and a society built on the inventive, empathetic, big-picture capabilities of what's rising in its place, the Conceptual Age."[4] Pink cites gaming expert James Paul Gee, who wrote, "Learning isn't about memorizing isolated facts. It's about connecting and manipulating them."[5] This age is filled with so many new experiences and possibilities that religious experts can no longer stay ahead of them. But adjusting our beliefs by reassessing the facts around us is not new to the church of Jesus Christ. The disciples along the Emmaus way had the facts; they just did not have them woven into stories and rituals to awaken them to the presence of God in those facts.[6] Today, neither discipleship nor evangelism can be about memorizing isolated facts either. All that the church does and equips people to do must model courage and imagination to connect and handle the new information coming at them at epic rates. In culture's return to integrating production and consumption, Christian discipleship (learning and doing) must also become more integrative.

> This is not the time for conformity but rather for creative thinking and innovation organized around an inspiring and innovative vision.
>
> Eddie Gibbs (LN. 167)

> Linear, logical, and even intelligent ideas that remain disconnected are regarded as irrelevant. People's growing realization of their wholeness and their interconnectedness

4. Daniel Pink, *A Whole New Mind: Why Right-Brainers Will Rule the Future* (New York: Riverhead, 2005), 1–2. Pastor and writer Doug Pagitt further explores the church's missional engagement with this shift in his book *The Church in the Inventive Age* (Minneapolis: Sparkhouse, 2010).

5. James Paul Gee, *What Video Games Have to Teach Us about Learning and Literacy* (New York: Palgrave McMillan, 2003), 91.

6. See Luke 24:13–35.

makes them long for something experiential. Truth needs to be sensed, seen, and felt to be understood. *Eileen Suico*

What we would call discipleship, Harvard philosopher Elaine Scarry has assigned to the pedagogical role of *beauty*. Imagine the artist sitting in front of a palm frond for days and days, amazed at the symmetry, the unfolding form that a palm makes with light, scale, and line. Slowly the form influences the creative approach of the artist. In a similar way, Jesus's disciples were reeducated about the realm of God in their willingness to look for God's story in the parables and life of Jesus. Their education was one that engaged their capacity to reimagine over and over again.

I love how Luke begins with Mary's song. A poetic piece of beauty, in which God's kingdom is reimagined. *Steve Taylor*

Jesus continually taught for those with "eyes to see and ears to hear." Their discipleship was a reorientation. The same errors that motivated the church to separate faith and beauty are in fact the unique virtues of beauty's way of teaching. "This willingness to continually revise one's own location in order to place oneself in the path of beauty is the basic impulse of education."[7]

Beauty can be one of discipleship's greatest pedagogical tools. Beauty empowers us with responsibility. It hands the keys of orientation back to us. It puts us in play. It "confronts us with our freedom."[8] Scarry goes on to say that all encounters with beauty (regardless as to whether we name beauty as sacred, unprecedented, or lifesaving) lead to reorientation through honoring the beauty's source or confessing our previous overlooking or rejection of that which we now find beautiful. All art leads toward praise or confession.

When we are surrounded by the ugliness of evil, the sight and sense of beauty brings us back to what we are made of. *Eileen Suico*

A question arises: How well does the church do at handing the keys of the kingdom to the viewers and putting them in play to utter a "new song" of praise or confession? How does the time, space, and matter that we fashion as church help to further this kind of reaction? How does the church embody the mission of God's expansive love in a conceptual age?

7. Elaine Scarry, *On Beauty and Being Just* (Princeton, NJ: Princeton University Press, 1999), 7.
8. A helpful phrase from Peter Block's *Community: The Structure of Belonging* (San Francisco: Berrett-Koehler, 2008).

Jackson Pollock once said, "New needs need new techniques." From church communities embracing this new "conceptual age" new artistic techniques emerge. My colleague Joshua Case and I have identified the following three categories for these emerging church techniques:

1. Open sourcing translation dilemmas
2. Increasing ritual agency
3. Carving open space for listening

The art of translating the story through communal practice and making space to listen for new insights leads the disciple into a life of worship.

Translation Dilemmas

Anyone who preaches Sunday after Sunday realizes the tenuous nature of sermonizing. In postmodern hermeneutics interpreters admit that the choices in translation and in communication of that translation are fraught with pitfalls. The careful preacher always employs conceptual age skills of narratology and pattern recognition. And while such actions are imprecise and culturally nuanced, the preacher knows they are worth the risk. Many preachers deal with this imprecision alone in their study, and then are expected to resolve this into tidy precision each Sunday. Such preaching actually cuts the congregation off from the very learning that Scarry describes.

Biblical theologian Walter Brueggemann proposes, alternatively, that the meeting of liturgy and preaching in postmodernity be "a place where people come to receive new materials, or old materials freshly voiced, which will fund, feed, nurture, nourish, legitimate, and authorize a counter-imagination of the world."[9] In emerging communities the curtain is pulled back on this process. The authority to distill imprecise parables and to make applications is imbued on the whole community; it is viewed as an essential part of discipleship. Emerging communities are discovering that competing narratives can be put in conversation with the bits and pieces of the biblical story to create a communal counter-imagination rooted in the exchange of God's expansive love.

Ritual Agency

Anthropologists and the behavioral sciences teach us that all of life can be understood as ritualization. Everything from shopping at Target to visiting

9. Walter Brueggemann, *Texts under Negotiation* (Minneapolis: Fortress, 1993), 20.

Disney World to updating one's status on Facebook is an engagement with ritual. This raises at least two ethical dilemmas: (1) What are the outcomes of a particular repeated social behavior? and (2) How are people empowered to take responsibility for the rituals that they engage, perpetuate, or design? This same critique is leading emerging faith communities to reevaluate their own rituals. Worship trickster Jonny Baker cites anthropologist Catherine Bell: "The goal of ritualization is the creation of a ritualized agent, an actor with a form of ritual mastery, who embodies flexible sets of cultural schemes and can deploy them effectively in multiple situations so as to restructure those situations in practical ways."[10] As a ritualized agent Jesus took rituals like the Passover and deployed them in ways that would reorient the disciples' categories of the sacred and their calling. Encounters with beauty invoke praise and confession, and in Acts the community of the Way not only sang from Israel's Psalter but also wrote new songs and uttered original confessions.

Open Space to Listen

Beauty simultaneously bids and tenders a glimpse of Itself. On the one hand, Quaker or Zen practices of apophatic spirituality are on the *bidding* side of the gift, clearing the mind of all distractions to receive lifesaving beauty without naming or totalizing the Giver. On the other hand, Ignatian and charismatic practices of kataphatic spirituality are on the *tendering* side, setting the mind on a single image or passage in order to expand upon what we do know of God, willing to be taught more. Both the apophatic and kataphatic are disciplines of releasing one's rationale to be drawn into God's realm. Beauty begs the intentional posture of the perceiver. When approaching beauty, Scarry writes,

> You are about to be in the presence of something life-giving, lifesaving, something that deserves from you the posture of reverence or petition. It is not clear whether you would throw yourself on your knees before it or keep your distance from it, but you had better figure out the right answer because this is not an occasion for carelessness or for leaving your own postures wholly up to chance.[11]

Whether we are admiring effervescent marine life in an aquarium, a dandelion in the hand of a niece, the clever lines in an Aaron Sorkin film, the "time no changes" sound of Miles Davis's second quintet, or the masterful

10. Catherine Bell, *Ritual Theory, Ritual Practice* (New York: Oxford University Press, 1992), 81. Quoted in Baker's dissertation, "The Labyrinth: Ritualisation as Strategic Practice in Postmodern Times" (MA diss., Kings College, University of London, 2000).
11. Scarry, *On Beauty*, 27.

composition of Handel's *Messiah*, beauty cuts to the quick and brings us to our knees in wonder, praise, and humility.

Such postures are located within various forms of art themselves as timing, as white space, as pregnant moments. This open space to listen is being curated in emerging churches through various practices including body prayers, silence, labyrinths, drawing exercises, and meditation. Liturgical open space works—like Advent in a culture that wants quick and simple salvation, and like Lent in a culture that wants quick and simple justice.

Practices

Congregational Worship as Art

For Lent 2010 Neighbors Abbey joined two other congregations in a progressive art installation. For two weeks at a time we would study and then paint one panel of a triptych. With the help of Terry Chapman of Forked River Presbyterian, Derek Koehl at Neighbors Abbey, and Todd Fadel of the Bridge in Portland, Oregon, we designed a reflection on belief as knowing, relating, and trusting. The first two weeks were on *knowing*, and we examined the lectionary passage about the Mount of Transfiguration. As the congregation of the Abbey dwelt with Peter's desire to build tents of worship, we also confessed our desire to pin down God and concretize our habits. We cut collage pieces from magazines. We drew and painted. We built an image that portrayed a prayer for God to give us knowledge that leads us down from the mountain of knowing into the lived life of action. For the next two weeks we reflected on *relating* and read this theme through the lectionary passage of the prodigal son. We drew a large loop, like a cursive lowercase "l," with the long circuitous distance representing the transformational journey of the younger brother and the small distance at the bottom where the loop met representing the fixed place where the older brother remained.

Through painting and designing the collage we discovered that relationships require continual renegotiation, new awareness, and renewed willingness to grow. For the last two weeks of Lent we considered the *trusting* component of knowing. Through the Palm Sunday reading of Jesus's trust of an unridden colt, the disciples' trust of Jesus's errand, and the colt owner's trust, we were struck by the unknown element that they each faced. We drew a large open square and depicted all three characters—Jesus, the disciples, and the colt's owner—walking into the unknown space. Then we added other things including neighbors and family members being pulled into that same space.

The result was an illustration of everything being pulled into a center, a place of promise and possibility. One woman reflected on the fact that what we know is not always defensible, that it does not always belong to the realm of rationale. Some of our knowledge of God is gained only through taking risks. As each week progressed toward Easter, we were visualizing our stories, our neighborhood, our world being joined to this Lenten journey toward the cross and the resurrection. The use of art was not to illustrate, but to move us into deeper embodiment. The exercise helped put us in play as translators, as ritualizers, and it allowed for open space to listen and receive something we had not otherwise planned on.

> I would suggest that most of our knowledge of God is gained only through risk. If we think of knowing in the relational sense, action and risk are required to be in relationship. *Mark Scandrette*

> It is in taking risks in our practice that our understanding of the texts grows, just as our practice is always made more beautiful when we understand the texts, and so it is a never-ending cycle. *Eileen Suico*

Community Formation through the Arts

We are located in a neighborhood known nationally for its participation in the commercial sexual exploitation of children. After raising awareness of our ritualizing agency, one member of the Abbey's order, Anne Chance, organized a daily prayer rite called CU@2. In partnership with other churches and agencies, Anne formed a network of people whose phones and watches go off at 2:00 p.m. and who then take the time to pray a specific five-part prayer: for healing and liberation for the victims of this exploitation; that coalitions and efforts against this would be strengthened; that perpetrators' hearts would be broken and their lives transformed; that politicians and law enforcement officials would support and further the abolition of sex slavery; and that our own neighborhoods and communities would be strengthened to confront and prevent this tragedy. Through Facebook and word of mouth this prayer is now international in scope. Anne's initiative has also been a centralizing force in refining the Abbey's own mission. And it has allowed our other neighbors who do not participate in our worship gatherings or are not affiliated with Christian faith to feel a sense of camaraderie with us in this local issue facing our neighbors and their children.

Another public ritual designed to shape our city was for Ash Wednesday 2008. With the help of the Atlanta Emergent cohort, we organized a flash mob in the busiest station of Atlanta's mass transit system. An artist from our community designed a logo that read "Submit Your Sins Here" to wrap around coffee cans. The cans were distributed to pubs and coffee shops across town with instructions to stay posted for a "flAsh Requiem" on Ash Wednesday. On Fat Tuesday we collected the cans and burned the submissions. We mixed the ashes with oil, and the next day visitors to the website were instructed to join us at 5:00 p.m. at the Five Points MARTA station. Cans of ashes were carried from north, south, east, and west and met at our central train station.

> Creativity in worship arises from the conviction that humans are made in the image of God and are thereby bestowed with a creative capacity to glorify their Creator in worship by offering back to God the fruits of a rich diversity of creative expression.
>
> Eddie Gibbs (CM, 195)

When we arrived Bill, Dan, and Nancy were playing a requiem on cello, classical guitar, and flute. Without any sermon or formal announcement we began marking a cross on one another's foreheads with ashes, saying, "From dust you have come. To dust you shall return. Go with the grace of God." Strangers met up with us and joined in the ritual. Within four minutes the MARTA police had instructed the musicians to stop and we all grabbed our cans and dispersed. We have no idea of the ritual impact this had on strangers. But when we met up later that evening many of us shared the power of sharing an "insider" ritual with "outsiders," and bearing public marks of our mortality with us on the train after leaving the ritual. Blurring contexts pushed participants into a translation dilemma, and reconstructing ancient rituals forced us to reexamine the traditional forms handed down to us.

> It is vital that the church engage in prophetic performance art that arouses response within our post-Christendom contexts. Increasingly, the common assumption is that the church is a known and discarded relic of the past. Actions like CU@2 and flAsh Requiem invite assumptions to be reconsidered. *Dwight J. Friesen*

> Creativity and imagination seem to be somewhat scarce commodities in cultures dominated by mass corporations and conformity. These skills might come quite naturally for those of us who are "artistic types" but are unfamiliar to the majority of people. One challenge and opportunity I see is the need to help people and groups who have not thought of themselves as "creative" or "artistic" to engage in the kinds of reimagining practices that are essential to embracing and embodying the gospel. *Mark Scandrette*

Mission as Art and Art as Mission

There are clear examples where mission work is advanced through this kind of noninstrumental hosting of beauty. Andy Imms is an installation artist in

Atlanta. He heard of a local prayer stations event we were hosting to raise awareness of the sex trafficking issues in our community. Anne Chance (the CU@2 inventor) saw an installation he had built called "System of Chance." He Dumpster-dived for circulars and milk cartons with pictures of missing children, as well as old discarded computers. Then, mixing thousands of tiny pictures with pieces of motherboards and circuitry, Imms built an installation evoking the dis/connection between our heavily networked society and its persistent ignorance of the marginalized and lost people in our midst.

The people who came to see his work were given dilemmas to connect their own participation within the social amnesia about lost community members. This art served to awaken a passion for justice within the participants. Elsewhere in the same event various stations were built for participants to reconnect their senses of taste and smell to their appetite for justice, to move their body into postures of aloneness and foundness, and to use maps to visualize their everyday travel rituals that intersect identified hot spots for sex trafficking. The open spaces and the examination of everyday rituals put participants in play as agents of justice in their life and world.

Leadership as Art

Joseph Myers, in his book *Organic Community*,[12] describes the community of faith in this emerging age as "edit-able, collaborative, and storied." Scott Belsky, founder of the online community *Behance* and author of *Making Things Happen*, suggests that leadership is about moving creatives into action steps. A leader takes many possibilities and, like solving a puzzle, puts them into one coherent story with specific actions. This process lets the participants offer themselves and their ideas but also frees them from staying in the brainstorming phase by moving into actions. This leadership process mirrors the internal process of artisans, who move from idea to artifact. So much religious work is tied to large ideologies keeping communities from ever getting out of the hanger of brainstorming and debate or forcing lone-ranger enterprises. Whether the idea is saving more souls or reversing cycles of injustice, churches are notorious for either waiting for consensus or going it alone.

> Leadership is a physical process involving the engagement of people with the "actioning" of God's movement in a community. *MaryKate Morse*

---

12. Joseph R. Myers, *Organic Community* (Grand Rapids: Baker Books, 2007). Note chart on p. 35.

In our southwest Atlanta community there are endless opportunities for activists and creatives to brainstorm and debate. And there are countless examples of antisocial, passionate people going it alone. The challenge is creating sustainable opportunities for individuals and communities to change together. We have designed "Community Building in Practice" dinners to help with this. About a dozen neighbors from varied race and socioeconomic backgrounds are invited to a potluck where they are given some direction to share their stories and experiences. The facilitator's role is more like that of an artist. She has to play with what folks throw out, decide when one area has been explored enough, and then pull new insights out of the underappreciated voices in the room. After an hour or so the group usually arrives at a place of curiosity where they encounter someone in a new way. While these are not explicitly religious events, I would call this church art because the processes of intentionally examining conversation habits (ritual), reevaluating one's neighborhood's story (translation), and setting aside space to patiently let something emerge that one had not initiated (openness) all take place. The art of leadership in this scenario, as well as in more liturgical spaces, requires an ability to listen for the whole and then move the group to a desired action.

> The "church art" of listening to the whole and creating space for the new is leadership at its best. MaryKate Morse

In keeping with the expansive love of God, the church is always changing. Many are no longer content to separate participation in God's mission from proclamation and demonstration of that mission. Many are no longer afraid of imagination. What these art projects demonstrate is a practice of serving up beauty, freeing the art itself to teach and to serve participants by putting them in play. As followers of God in the Way of Jesus, communities engage people through hosting translation dilemmas, teaching ritual agency, and offering open space. The kingdom of God is a space of emerging transforming beauty, and the art of the church is to join in this beauty. Many more examples of this are yet to be explored as the church emerges into this conceptual age.

12

Mission among Individual Consumers

Stefan Paas

An Experiment

Five years ago we planted a church in Amsterdam called Via Nova, "a new way."[1] We started with mercy ministries, intro courses, and debate nights. After a year we began to gather every Sunday afternoon for worship in a dimly lit neo-Gothic building with vaulted ceilings and stained glass windows. Since then, our meetings contain high-quality jazz and classical music, candles, movie clips, coffee and conversations, and intelligent, timely sermons. If the weather is right we have picnics in the Vondelpark, that once-upon-a-time hippie paradise. Three years ago we launched home groups, which is essential if you want to be church in a city like Amsterdam. They strengthened the community in many respects. Every year we run short courses introducing small groups of people into Christianity.

1. http://www.vianova-amsterdam.nl.

Culture

From Obligation to Consumption

I believe that God works through this small church, and I feel deep gratitude for a wonderful band of brothers and sisters. But two things keep me
wondering. First, only very few people whom we introduce to Christianity
actually connect to our church or to any other church. The large majority will
not become a member of a home group or attend worship services with any
regularity. Second, I spoke with many people who attend our worship services.
Almost without exception they were enthusiastic. They liked the atmosphere
and all the young people; they liked the music and even the sermon (in this
order). Since the Dutch, and especially those from Amsterdam, are not afraid
to be critical to your face, this was more than just being polite. These people
meant what they said. Yet they rarely come back, if at all.

Non-Christians attend almost every worship service. Although we would
like to see more of them, our main problem is not a lack of contact with
non-Christians. Our short introductory courses into Christianity are well
attended, and we offer three consecutive courses. The first always entails the
basics of Christianity, contextualized for highly educated, secular people. The
second class amounts to reading large parts from the Bible, just to "get the
feel of it." In the third course people focus on *lectio divina*, ancient Christian
disciplines of silence, Bible reading, and meditation. In our experience, many
from the young and secular groups in Amsterdam are quite interested in the
Bible (even if only for its cultural value), and some of them are very willing to
be introduced in the spiritual tradition of Christianity. Most of them are not
atheists, and many of them are interested in more than superficial and commercial "spirituality." However, for the majority of them this reconnaissance
of Christianity remains embedded within largely individualized patterns of
life. It is part of their personal self-development, but only very rarely does it
lead to communal worship and service.

Drawing people closer, introducing them into the life of the church, is our
main obstacle. Our core group of regular attenders and home group members
consists of people with a churched background. They have been socialized
in a churchgoing rhythm, even though about one-third of them had not been
active members of a church for some years before Via Nova. Only 10 percent
or so of our members were not raised in a Christian family.

We hear similar stories from other churches in Amsterdam. It seems to be
a very common pattern among the Western white people groups in the city
(immigrant populations from Africa and Asia have a different experience).
We tried several things to change this pattern, but without much success.

Increasingly I have come to believe that it is not a matter of finding a better strategy. What we see in Amsterdam is nothing less than a culture shift, producing new perceptions of "church" in secular Europe. Sociologist Grace Davie has termed this a shift "from obligation to consumption":

> In Europe as well as America, a new pattern is gradually emerging: that is a shift away from an understanding of religion as a form of obligation and towards an increasing emphasis on consumption or choice. What until moderately recently was simply imposed (with all the negative connotations of this word), or inherited (a rather more positive spin) becomes instead a matter of personal inclination. I go to church (or to another religious organization) because I want to so long as it provides what I want, but I have no obligation either to attend in the first place or to continue if I don't want to.[2]

Here, Davie reflects on one of the core elements of secularization, the differentiation of society in reasonably separate domains. In modern societies, especially in northwestern Europe, "religion" or "church" is no longer intimately connected with other domains, like politics, science, or the economy. It has become a separate sector, catering to religious needs only. This means that in the most secular parts of the world there are no pressures left "obliging" people to attend church if they do not want to. They do not need church to get a job, to get a house or a spouse, for social standing, or for political influence. "Equally changed are the internal disciplines—the sense that church-going was the right and proper thing to do, a sentiment enforced by common values or shared beliefs."[3] In other words, people will go to church if and only if they have a need that can be satisfied only by a religious event.

> As far as Germany is concerned, I would only partly agree. On the one hand, the church's societal influence is diminishing. On the other hand, the state church maintains a strongly rooted position in the society as a whole. For this reason, church leaders are board members of television stations and political action committees at the same time the total public influence of the church is shrinking. What we are seeing now is not secularization per se, but a shift in public interest from traditional churches to the spiritual and esoteric. Tobias Faix

> I agree that in countries with strong state-church traditions the situation may be different from the one I describe. However, I would say that Germany will go the same way eventually. Probably, there is less difference between Amsterdam and Berlin than between Berlin and large parts of Germany. Stefan Paas

2. Grace Davie, *The Sociology of Religion* (London: Sage, 2007), 96.
3. Ibid., 144.

This is an important explanation of the different patterns in churchgoing between those raised in Christian families and those who did not inherit this sense that churchgoing is somehow the right thing to do. People with a Christian background have been raised with the idea of the church as a family. Families stick together. People show up at parties and celebrations, even if they don't like them. That's what family members do for one another. They are connected by loyalty, duty, and (hopefully) love. Most other people, at least in Amsterdam, view church as a restaurant. It is a place where you go when you are in the mood—in other words, when you feel a spiritual need. You may like this particular restaurant very much, but this does not imply that you will return next week. There are more good restaurants, sometimes a quick snack is just as good, and often it is easier and cheaper to eat at home. And surely you don't become a *member* of a restaurant. Membership is an idea that just doesn't fit this pattern of consumption. It would be a very peculiar restaurant that invited guests to help in the kitchen or to clean up after they have finished their meals.

To clarify, consumption and consumerism are not the same thing. When a sociologist like Grace Davie uses the word "consumption" she means it descriptively (not ideologically). There is a cloud of words here, roughly referring to what is essentially the same phenomenon: individualization, subjectivization, deinstitutionalization, and the age of authenticity. All these words point to an almost universal experience of late modern people in the West. Our identities are no longer "given," but we must somehow acquire them through the choices we make. That is why modern lives are highly reflexive ("Do I really want this?" "Is this the kind of person I want to be?"), fragile, and biographical (a personal "quest"). Consumption is about choice, about "finding the right path." But this does not mean, per se, that every choice is equally valued. Someone may find his identity in his job and in material possessions, but he may also choose to build an orphanage in Haiti or to join a monastery (but not because he is the third son of the family, or because his grandparents expect him to).

"Consumerism," however, is an ideological perversion of consumption. On a philosophical level it may betray itself in slogans like "whatever you choose is good, as long as you choose for yourself." On the more popular level consumerism tells us that our identities can be acquired simply by piling up material goods and experiences: iPhones, cars, sex, spirituality, and so forth. Consumerism therefore trivializes the morality of choices we make, and thus undermines our humanity. It tells us that the world (including God) revolves around our individual wants, which is usually not a good way to start if we want to live a life that matters.

In our Western context many people are sick of consumerism and try to find ways (inevitably, in a highly "consumptive" way) to live more fulfilled, more profound lives. This "postmaterialistic" trend can be found especially among young, white, highly educated urbanites. But *consumption* is not something we can just leave behind. This would mean that we return to a traditional society, where others (tribe, party, family, church) decide what is right for a person. I do not see how this can be a realistic desire; besides, there is a lot in an age of consumption (or authenticity) that we must strongly affirm from a gospel perspective. Consumption, in the sociological meaning of the word, is nothing but "living by choice." It cannot be equated to "materialism," "shallow consumerism," and the like.

The Search for the Self

The shift from obligation to consumption reflects a wider cultural development in the West. Canadian philosopher Charles Taylor calls this "the subjective turn." It entails that people no longer receive their identities from the outside (parents, family, church, nation), but rather construct them by looking inside, at their "true selves."[4] Our age is an age of authenticity, of trying to find out "who you really are." In this context people tend to see religion as an instrument of personal development and no longer as something one belongs to. They go to church like they go to a restaurant. Their quest can be very serious and deeply personal, but they will feel trapped and "inauthentic" whenever they are expected to submit their own desires and values to external authorities and moral expectations. There is a very deeply felt conviction in all this, that a person is the only one who can find out his or her identity. No one can do this for someone else, nor should anyone try.

> People search for who they are and what it means to be truly human. However, they make the mistake of questing through consumption, which can only lead to materialism if it does not draw on a real or deeper understanding of spirituality. *Ian Mobsby*

Indeed, this can happen and it happens a lot. But I would call this "consumerist" religion. To identify consumption with consumerism is not helpful, since it tends to create general negative (moralistic) evaluations of the culture that we are living in and that we are part of.

4. Cf. Paul Heelas and Linda Woodhead, *The Spiritual Revolution: Why Religion Is Giving Way to Spirituality* (Malden, MA: Blackwell, 2005), 2: "It is a turn away from life lived in terms of external or 'objective' roles, duties and obligations, and a turn towards life lived by reference to one's own subjective experiences (relational as much as individualistic)."

> We cannot escape consumption; it's as simple as that. To deny this means that we lack the tools for credible contextualization. *Stefan Paas*

As missionaries to Western culture we need to know the driving power behind this quest for authenticity. I think it is triggered by some existential polarities embedded in our culture. For example:[5]

- *Freedom vs. choice*: We *can* choose a lot more than our ancestors, but we also *have* to choose all day. Free choice is not just a lifestyle we have accepted; it is a fate we are unable to escape. We cannot but choose. This paradox creates a search for true freedom. What does it mean to be really free?
- *Fragmentation vs. wholeness*: Modern societies are characterized by differentiation. Unlike our parents and grandparents we are no longer able to live our lives in one piece and under the same moral conditions. We must occupy different roles throughout the day: tender father, aggressive salesman, funny friend, and warm lover. Often, the expectations implied in our different roles are contradictory. We learn to play them, and to negotiate them, to such an extent that we find it difficult to say who we "really" are. This role differentiation creates a search for wholeness, something that connects our life and keeps it together.
- *Uprooting vs. connecting*: We have been cut loose from ancient cultural and religious traditions. Many late modern people enjoy the liberty implied in this, but they also feel the loneliness. Somehow we want to "belong," but without being absorbed again by external rules and expectations that suffocate our internal spaces. This creates the question of new connections with old traditions, often resulting in "bricolage"—individual patchworks from different spiritual sources, giving us a sense of connectedness with the past without being ruled by it (like, for example, in pilgrimages or cathedral events).

> Concerning those three points, wouldn't it have to be "as well as" instead of "versus"? *Tobias Faix*

> By using "versus" I want to express that these terms are polarities: they create tensions that cannot be solved easily. It's exactly these tensions (or paradoxes) that make human beings religious creatures. *Stefan Paas*

---

5. I borrow this from the Dutch authors Erik Borgman, Marjolein de Vos, and Anton van Harskamp, *Hunkering naar heelheid: Over nieuwe religiositeit in Nederland* (Budel: Damon, 2003).

People look for true freedom, wholeness, and roots, but the point is: they can no longer find these outside themselves, because of the collapse of hierarchies and traditions. So we look for answers inside: somewhere deep inside of us must be a "true" self of freedom, wholeness, and connection with deeper grounds of meaning.

In sermons and courses my colleagues and I often use this ontology, and people (in our case mostly young career people) invariably respond with recognition. I connect this with a fair dose of creation theology, since I believe that God works through these turbulences of the soul. Here, I find theological resources in Augustine. If we feel agitation in our hearts, a nagging unrest, where does it come from? Augustine's profound answer was that the One we look for, without knowing him yet, is the same who stirs our deepest being. The way to God outside us may be the way inside our soul. As a Protestant I have been taught that we should mistrust our feelings and longings, since they are sinful. I still believe that (I even believe that our rational thinking is sinful too!), but I think it is not enough to say this and leave it there. I believe in God, the Creator of all that is good, who answers the desire of the nations. So I invite people to take their deep longings seriously and to consider that God is there, urging them to become pilgrims.

A critical point, of course, is whether we identify God with our deepest self (in my opinion not a Christian view) or whether we see our quest for our deepest self as an opportunity to be surprised by God who is "under" and "outside" our deepest self. I connect this with the postmodern notion that people do not have immediate access to their deepest self and can seek it only by exploring it in a narrative way. Quoting a British artist who once said that all great art is "images looking for a story," I would say that our lives consist of experiences, feelings, longings, and thoughts, looking for a Story.

Practices

Worship à la Carte

If church is a restaurant, this means at least three things for worship. First, people usually do not go to restaurants because they must. Late modern people who explore Christianity are intrinsically motivated. Of course, this motivation may not be more than casual curiosity, but even that is better than dutiful boredom. Often it is much more. People who attend church today expect religion and spirituality. They want the real thing, and they want it done well.

Second, in an age of individual journeys it is important for the church to accept to some extent that it needs to facilitate this quest. This means, among other things, that we have to be careful to find a balance between collective and individual moments during the worship service. In Amsterdam, for example, we have found that people without a churched background generally do not mind listening to sermons, as long as the speaker is courteous, vulnerable, and capable of laughing about himself. However, they feel very uncomfortable when we arrange "collective rituals," such as singing together or saying the Lord's Prayer, even if we assure them that they do not have to participate. They will value moments of silence and meditation, since these moments offer room for a personal interpretation. But everything that narrows down this private space of reflection can be experienced as an obstacle for personal development. Developing worship in a late modern culture is like designing a dance: if I take a step toward you, you step back; but if I step back, you may decide to come forward. Virtually all people who have joined our church told us what they valued most: that they had been allowed to doubt, to ask critical questions, to say that they just couldn't believe everything in Christianity. When they saw that this did not offend us, exactly this gave them room to trust God.

Third, all good restaurants have a sense of honor. They will not just serve anything. Although they want to serve their customers, they do cherish some ideas about what is good and wholesome food. Although they do not want to follow their culinary traditions without imagination, they are proud to present their French, Italian, or Russian kitchen. They offer a menu with many options, but hamburgers are not on it. So the restaurant church, although eager to serve and help people in their personal quests, will offer the wealth of the Christian tradition creatively and lovingly. It will not settle for anything less.

I agree that consumption is just part of our Western culture, no way to avoid it, too stupid to fight it. If we should use it to "attract" people to our church-restaurant, I believe we should find ways to change our "customers" into participants. Particularly in worship, performance should lead to interaction. We would start with some well-prepared dishes, then invite our guests into an open kitchen to have fun preparing themselves, corporately, the main course. Participation opens up the (only) way from consuming to belonging. *Eric Zander*

I make a distinction between worship as formational practice and worship as attractional show. Worship is more than just showing up. It implies a formative commitment beyond one's self: a liberation from the tyranny of the need to have one's own desires and wants met by some kind of religious service arrangement. *Paul Roberts*

We do want a formative commitment. But are there really only two options for worship: either "formational practice" or an "attractional show"? If we want worship to be a formational practice we need to attract people first. In any worship service there must be elements that attract people (friendship, good food, charisma, music, the sense of higher ideals, finding a safe haven, their "inquisitive interest," whatever). We better take that seriously and wonder what attracts them, and why others are not attracted (without trying to be too judgmental, it's always easy to say that people do not come because they commit "consumerism"). So, I would say: almost every worship service is a mixture of attractional and formative elements. Of course, we always need to be self-critical and ask whether the mix is right. But I see no specific holiness in putting off people. So what I describe here is precisely this self-critical process: accepting that we live in a culture of consumption (for better and for worse), accepting and lovingly affirming that this is what people bring to our church (again, for better and for worse), and finding out how people can become disciples, not by turning them into traditional people again, but from within their own culture.

There is an assumption that anything that is formative cannot be attractive, and vice versa. I sometimes call it the "Christianity-is-medicine" approach: "Yes, it tastes awful, but it's good for you, so drink it!" Again, I think that this is a false dilemma. As a Reformed Christian I believe that the gospel "is not after man" (Gal. 1:11 KJV), and that it therefore offends us once we really understand it (unfortunately, most people do not reach that point due to the Christianity-is-medicine approach). But if there is indeed sweetness in the service of the Lord, I cannot present it as something unattractive. There is something within the gospel that appeals to "the desire of the nations." At least that is what I have often found when people enter our church. I could put this differently: I deeply believe that the Holy Spirit has written his story in the lives of people when I meet them. The sheer fact that highly secular, late modern people darken the door of a church in today's Amsterdam may be just a pointer to the Spirit working in their inquisitive interest. At least, that is how I approach them, and that is why I want to tell them: "You may hear a lot here that sounds pretty strange, but I really want to 'seduce' you to see that this is what you have always really wanted, that this is the kind of person you always wanted to be." We may need a dose of Hosea's "alluring" God here (Hosea 2:14). *Stefan Paas*

Community as Gift

If the church has become a restaurant where people drop by occasionally, how is it possible to build a life-changing community where people will be turned to the kingdom of God?

To some extent, an emphasis on a communal lifestyle, as in emerging church ecclesiology, goes against the tide of our culture. The main reason for this, I think, is the differentiation of society that is a consequence of modernity. We

live our lives in constantly changing environments and roles, while our ancestors lived a much more integrated life. What is often viewed as an *ideological*
attempt to split our lives in public and private sectors ("liberalism" being the .
evil force) may be caused more by the complexities of modern life, forcing us to
obey different expectations and regimes during the day. I am afraid there is more
than a little romanticism involved in current pleas for disciplined Christian
communities, showing a communal kingdom ethic. How many modern Christians would be prepared to submit themselves so completely to a communal
lifestyle? "Community" is an ambiguous word for most modern people. They
desire it and fear it at the same time. This is an age of "light communities,"
temporary and with many exit options. The most popular communal form
today is the retreat, enjoying one another's fellowship for some days, without
the pressing social controls involved in "heavier" traditional communities.

Yet community is the specialty of the house in the restaurant church. People
can decide not to eat it (there is a kids' menu), but our chef thinks that it is
important for people to be in community. He does not force them to eat what
they cannot digest yet, but he keeps inviting them to connect with others, to
love them as we love ourselves. After all, a restaurant church does have some
ideas about what is our deepest self, and what is merely a travesty of it. In an
individualistic age people have learned to protect their privacy. In the restaurant church they may learn that faith is very personal but never private. In
our culture it may be the best mark of maturity and leadership when one is
prepared to lower the walls of privacy and give others access to one's life. It
is a sign of grace when we do not fear the judgment of others.

> We all live in multiple community networks, but we keep considering church to be a
> single local network. We are open to diversify the menu but still consider that the whole meal
> should be offered at a single table. I am exploring multiple expressions of church, offering
> not only diverse tastes (cultural identities), but accepting to limit that to only some aspects of
> church life, counting on other expressions to develop the others. I wonder if the future of our
> Western church should move from the local church idea to a network of limited expressions,
> "light Christian communities" interacting with one another. Eric Zander

So we unashamedly invite people to Communion. This means, of course,
that we organize all kinds of social events. Without pressing them too much,
we explain to people that it is hard to be a functional part of this church
without being in a home group and without being involved in mission. At
the same time we accept that people make their own choices and that some
keep their distance. Time and again we emphasize: what we do is a gift to
you. Feel free to be selective; take all the time you need. We are delighted when

you show up, regardless of whether you attend every week or have been away for a year. We are quite relaxed with irregular guests. Amsterdam is a culture of consumption. If you are not prepared to start where people are, this is not your mission field.

> Arguably the church exists with one primary mission, to form disciples of Jesus Christ (in the most holistic sense of that phrase). So it seems more than a little odd that the church has been complicit in adopting a volunteer mind-set, so that little is expected of us. It's as though we see ourselves in competition with the entertainment industry; as though the church could possibly be content with a small piece of the market share. Dwight J. Friesen

Some may take issue with the mere fact that we give people space to decide if and when they are ready to commit themselves on a deeper level (i.e., take a culture of consumption seriously). But what is the alternative? Manipulating them, even if they don't want to? Denying them access if they have not decided within, say, six months?

Well, the only thing we do is to create an environment as "seductive" as possible (and therefore also a bit chaotic), to give people all the possibilities to be in touch with Christians and a Christian community, but within a culture of choice and authenticity. And we hope (and have seen) that this (and only this) will move them toward more commitment.

Another issue here is that churches often tend to confuse discipleship with "being as busy as possible in the work of the church." It means making the church the centerpiece of individual lives. It's not something to discuss here, but I would ask two questions concerning this: (1) Is there not a very subtle temptation of idolatry here—meaning: putting the life, organization, and well-being of the local church in the place of God's kingdom? and (2) To what extent does discipleship mean that one is as committed as possible to the life of the local church? I don't see how someone can be a disciple without any meaningful communion (accountability, etc.) with other Christians, but I can see how someone leads the life of a disciple, without being in church every Sunday. Stefan Paas

Mission in a Restaurant Culture

A church is no church if it teaches people to form warm huddles with their backs turned to God's world. We believe that it is essential for us to help people in our church to connect with others in our city. Volunteer work in the city has been a core activity of our church right from the start. There was a mercy ministry before we had worship services! Instead of starting "missions" *for* the city, set up by churches in suburbia, we want to be a church serving God's mission *from within* the city, by turning city people to one another. A small part of the vitality, wealth, time, and gifts of young urbanites flows to the elderly, lonely, and poor people in Amsterdam through the mediation of our church.

We do this in a contextual way. In a church where almost everyone is young, pressed by demanding jobs, and in the first stage of family formation, we cannot expect people to have all the time in the world. We have found that the main obstacle for people to become active in diaconal ministries is lack of time. So we help people by contacting social service agencies, selecting addresses of people who need help, and arranging materials and equipment. We invite people who attend the church to apply individually or in small groups, and these groups are deployed to the selected addresses.

Interestingly, almost everyone—occasional attenders and our "restaurant staff"—likes this part of our church. Many people want to be involved in mercy ministries, even if they hardly ever show up in a worship service. It is a mistake to think that individualization must lead to egoism. If people want more room for their own experiences and desires, and are less inclined to listen to external authorities, it does not imply that they think only of themselves. It just means that they will only be committed to goals and projects on the basis of approval. Individualization changes the reasons why people do things; it does not necessarily change the things people do. Many people, Christians and non-Christians, share a desire for justice. Many city dwellers want a better city, with less poverty and loneliness. Many of the young career people who are the bulk of our attenders and participants feel guilty about being so absorbed by their jobs. So they appreciate it if a church helps them to serve others.

> I am struck by the resonances in this chapter with such expressions of the religious life as Franciscan and Benedictine models of church. Refectories were the restaurants of their day—practicing radical hospitality. Makes me think that the emerging church finds its roots in more ancient expressions of the church sharing the same sensibilities. *Ian Mobsby*

We are inspired by ancient combinations of liturgy and service. I believe that contextualization of the church in Europe always needs this combination. Europeans generally are not prone to attend church services often, but there is usually much sympathy for what we might call "spirituality and diacony." For example, the Aegidius-project in Italy and Belgium seems to touch exactly this string, and with success. In our own context we find that people, even very secularized people, can see why the church creates worship services ("sacred spaces") and why it wants to serve the poor. It's the communal aspect (together with regular attendance, moral obligations, and the like) that they understand least. This may mean that formation in my part of Europe (at least among post-Christians) will take this bipolar shape of "spiritual experience" (usually in the setting of a worship service) and "helping someone." Community may grow out of these experiences (by sharing them, narrating stories, reflecting on them), but usually it is not seen as a condition for them, or as something worth achieving on its own (of course, some core community, or "restaurant staff," is needed to organize worship services and mission). On the contrary, "religious communities" that do not show themselves as "spiritual" and "diaconal" will usually be looked at with some suspicion (sources of intoleration, division, superiority, etc.). Community in the United States is usually something positive, whereas in Europe it is associated with conformity, tribalism, or worse. "Community" is not a sacred word where I live. Stefan Paas

At Your Service: Leadership in a Restaurant Culture

In a more traditional age, the pastor had a position of authority. He (almost never a "she") was one of the very few with some higher education. Social life in Europe consisted of natural hierarchies in which church leadership had a revered status. Now this has changed almost completely. This may help us to understand what the apostle Paul said when he called himself "weak." In a consumerist culture church leaders are indeed weak people: there is nothing that requires people to listen to them. There is a bright side to this, however. In our time there is less distance between the pastor and the congregation.[6] Today, people will be less inclined to keep up appearances, because they are generally less prone to give answers that are socially desirable. This allows church leaders to develop relationships of greater honesty and freedom.

Leadership in a restaurant church is not about telling people what to do. Our role is that of servants, waiters at the table. The question we ask most frequently is, How can we help you to take the next step in your life? For me, a lead text from the Bible is something that Paul wrote to the Corinthians: "Not that we lord it over your faith, but we work with you for your joy, because it is by faith you stand firm" (2 Cor. 1:24).

Leading in an age of individualization implies taking seriously that people want to take responsibility for their own lives. I believe that this enables us to grow more mature relationships in church. In the restaurant church, leaders refuse to be treated as parents, and they reject infantile attitudes in "their" congregations. Children expect their parents to tend to all their needs, and rightly so, but adults cannot expect their leaders to fill every wish or answer every request. If people want to go their own way, leaders will respect this, even if they think it is the wrong way. But it would be childish indeed if people would become angry when the pastor subsequently would kindly refuse to bless their choice. As an adult the leader is responsible for his or her own choices too. Leaders are *not* responsible for the spiritual progress and ethical behavior of

---

6. Charles Gerkin, *Widening the Horizons: Pastoral Responses to a Fragmented Society* (Philadelphia: Westminster John Knox, 1986).

people in church. They can only be responsible for themselves and show how that can be done. And, conversely, the leader may expect that people respect his or her responsibility as a fellow traveler, when he or she draws a line. In a restaurant culture, leaders must be very open about what they believe to be the way of the kingdom, but they must withstand the urge to drag people into it or to be manipulated into the position of a substitute parent.

In cities like Amsterdam we see that we are on the brink of a new era, one of consumption instead of obligation. This will change our church life considerably. We cannot claim to have found the answers yet, but we have found that it is helpful to accept to some extent that the church for many people has become a restaurant. Like any metaphor this one must be applied critically, but it may be fruitful to think through worship, community, mission, and leadership from this perspective.

13

Mission in a New Spirituality Culture

Steve Hollinghurst

Culture

The early years of the twenty-first century have seen much talk of a "new atheism," particularly represented by works such as *The God Delusion* by Richard Dawkins,[1] *God Is Not Great: How Religion Poisons Everything* by Christopher Hitchens,[2] and *The End of Faith: Religion, Terror and the Future of Reason* by Sam Harris.[3] The titles speak for themselves; these negative assessments of religion view it not only as a delusion but also as a dangerous one that is a menace to society, leads to fanaticism and violence, and threatens the march of scientific progress and reason. Such ideas are not of course "new" in themselves; rather it is the reappearance of this approach that makes it new. In Europe sociologists of religion had begun to view the decline and eventual death of religion, by which they primarily meant Christianity, as an inevitable consequence of modernity and scientific progress. If the situation in the United States was different at least in part due to the separation of church and state, perhaps removing some of the pressure associated with European efforts to

1. Bantam, 2006.
2. Atlantic Books, 2008.
3. Free Press, 2006.

curb the power of state churches, it is clear from thinkers like Thomas Paine onward that there was a move by some in the United States to see reason and religion as incompatible, and this voice gained momentum particularly from the 1960s onward.

Postmodernity and the Reenchantment of the West

At the start of the twenty-first century, not only has the religiously inspired terrorism of Al Qaeda and the rise of the Christian Right in the United States put religion back on the political agenda, but also the secularization process itself looks far less certain. Sociologists like Britons Steve Bruce[4] and David Voas, who continue to argue for a secularization thesis, now have to account not only for the persistence of religion but also, crucially, for the rise of new nontraditional spiritualities. Others like Grace Davie are suggesting that secularization is in fact a strange European phenomenon in a world that remains otherwise religious.[5] American sociologist of religion Peter Berger put it like this in a 1997 interview:

> The process of secularization is not irreversible. It does not bring about the demise of religion, but rather becomes ultimately self-defeating by generating a hunger for that transcendent dimension of life which it has worked so persistently to deny.
>
> Eddie Gibbs (INO, 197)

I think what I and most other sociologists of religion wrote in the 1960s about secularization was a mistake. Our underlying argument was that secularization and modernity go hand in hand. With more modernization comes more secularization. It wasn't a crazy theory. There was some evidence for it. But I think it's basically wrong. Most of the world today is certainly not secular. It's very religious. So is the United States. The one exception to this is Western Europe. One of the most interesting questions in the sociology of religion today is not, How do you explain fundamentalism in Iran? but, Why is Western Europe different?[6]

In the same interview Berger refers to "the existence around the world of a thin layer of humanistically educated people—a cultural elite."[7] It is within this group that the new atheism has emerged with the realization that religion

4. For instance *God Is Dead: Secularization in the West* (Malden, MA: Blackwell, 2002).
5. Grace Davie, *Europe, the Exceptional Case: Parameters of Faith in the Modern World* (London: Darton, Longman and Todd, 2002).
6. "Epistemological Modesty: An Interview with Peter Berger," Christian Century, October 29, 1997, 972–78, accessed online at http://www.religion-online.org/showarticle.asp?title=240.
7. Ibid.

has not been banished as they thought. But is it simply that the secularization thesis was wrong, or just a European phenomenon? If this is the case then Christian mission and apologetics can remain in the familiar territory in which secular humanism is its main opponent and with a renewed confidence address the issues it raises.

However, I do not think this is the correct picture. Clearly most people are not becoming secular atheists. Berger is right that this remains largely the preserve of a small cultural elite; but if belief remains high, people in the West are not remaining Christian in their beliefs. I discussed secularization and changing beliefs in Britain, Europe, the United States, and some parts of Africa in far more depth in *Mission-Shaped Evangelism*[8] and so wish to build on that here. To illustrate the point, however, one can look at changing beliefs about God in the UK from 1947 to 2000.[9]

There has been a small decline in overall belief in God or a life force from 84 percent to 70 percent over that period of time. However, there has been a substantial shift within as to what kind of God is believed in. Belief in a personal God, expressed by 45 percent of people in 1947, was expressed only by 26 percent in 2000, whereas belief in a spirit or life force has risen from 39 percent to 44 percent over the same period. When people say they believe in God they increasingly imagine something more like the force in Star Wars than the God of the Bible. This shift has been accompanied by an increasing distance first from personal church attendance, then from raising children in church, and lastly from Christian affiliation. So for the builder generation in the UK, roughly those born in the 1920s and '30s, 65 percent were raised in church or Sunday school, though only 12 percent now attend regularly. Eighty-two percent, however, would call themselves Christians, and 84 percent think children should be raised with a belief in God. Seventy-eight percent believe in a God or spirit-of-life force, with 50 percent believing in a personal God. For Gen X in the UK, roughly those born in the 1960s and '70s, the picture is very different. Only 35 percent had a church background, and only 7 percent now attend regularly. Christian affiliation has fallen to 59 percent, and even fewer, 51 percent, think children should be raised with a belief in God. Sixty-nine percent of them believe in a God, spirit, or life force, but 60 percent, that is, almost all of those believers, see God as a spirit-of-life force.[10]

8. Steve Hollinghurst, *Mission-Shaped Evangelism* (Norwich, UK: Canterbury Press, 2010), see especially chapters 2–5.

9. The figures come from the Soul of Britain report, April 25–May 7, 2000, drawing on the European and World Values Survey.

10. Past and present attendance are based on headcount surveys, partly past surveys in 1905 and 1950 and more recent data from Christian Research from 1978 to 2005. Questions on religious

> Any engagement with the work of Callum Brown, who argues that gender plays a crucial role in the change in British religious identity? *Steve Taylor*

> I engage Callum Brown in my book, mentioned earlier, but to add a brief comment: I think Brown is right to cite gender as a factor in that women played a key role in the socialization of children into faith. Women leaving church means children are no longer raised in the faith. He rightly notes the effect of '60s culture on women's roles as a factor in declining Christian influence since then. However, he puts far too much emphasis on this: the statistics show that childhood connection with church was declining long before the '60s. *Steve Hollinghurst*

Even though some European countries have a much higher connection to Christianity, nearly all follow these trends. The differences reflect a combination of three factors in the countries' histories: (1) the economic development of the country (the trends were most marked in the most developed countries); (2) the major Christian expression in the country (on the whole the trends were more marked in Protestant countries); and (3) whether the country had been part of the Communist Bloc (the trends were most marked in those countries that had been). So in highly developed, former Communist, traditionally Protestant countries like East Germany, such trends were more obvious, whereas in Catholic countries with less economic development in the West, like Malta, they were less so. Significantly, many Catholic countries that showed little sign of such trends in 1980 had seen the most rapid movement toward them by the year 2000. Good examples would be the Republic of Ireland and Spain.

There were, however, a few exceptions, but all had one thing in common: the significance of religion in political conflict. In the countries of the former Yugoslavia and Northern Ireland this meant interreligious violence. This is why one of the consequences of peace in Northern Ireland has been falling church attendance amongst the young. More positively, the part the church played in opposing Communism in Poland is the reason it has resisted this trend. However, this is threatened by Polish migration; Poles moving to more secular countries often adopt the pattern of the host nation and don't return to church if they return to Poland.[11] David Voas draws very similar conclusions from the European Social Survey, fitting them into a traditional secularization thesis by viewing changing patterns of belief as a stage toward secular atheism,

---

affiliation and raising children with belief come from a 2006 survey on religion by Populus. The figures on belief in God come from the age-related figures from the World Values Survey 1999, at time of writing the most recent UK figures prior to the 2008 data released in November 2010 (available online at http://www.worldvaluessurvey.org/index_surveys).

11. The analysis referred to here comes from that published in *Mission-Shaped Evangelism* and is based on the European Values Survey 1980–2000.

what he calls a "fuzzy fidelity."[12] This, I believe, fails to take account of the nature of these emerging beliefs. They are not a diluted Christianity but a different approach to belief and spirituality.

One of the reasons some observers failed to appreciate the significance of what I refer to as the "new spiritualities" is that these new forms of faith do not operate like traditional Western religions in which people belong and are supported by some kind of leadership or priestly group. Instead, new spiritualities are client-based religions like those of the Far East, in which the majority of people are clients of a smaller group of practitioners and teachers who act as the new priests.[13] For example, in Japan about half as many people say they belong to a religion than in Britain, but twice as many attend religious ceremonies and events. Furthermore, they attend the shrines of different religions for different festivals according to personal tastes. The great power of this approach for the new spiritualities in the West is that it makes it the perfect form of spirituality in a consumer society. As Paul Heelas and Benjamin Seel comment:

> Whereas until the "60s" it was "natural" for people to turn to Christianity, it is becoming "natural" for increasing numbers to turn to alternative spiritualities of life. So long as great value is attached to the development, cultivation and exploration of subjective-life, so long as we live in a subjectivized consumer culture propounding expectations of well-being, there is no reason to suppose that the future of New Age spiritualities is anything but promising.[14]

This changing pattern of belief represents not only a growing consumerism but also postmodernism. Postmodernity challenges the division between objective and subjective that led modern secular thinking to exalt science and reason as objective and dismiss religion as subjective. For the postmodern person everything is subjective and truth is measured at the bar of personal experience. Such a world welcomes the religious back to the public sphere, but any and every form of religion, naturally favoring a multifaith mix-and-match approach in which all religions are seen as containing truths and useful

12. David Voas, "The Rise and Fall of Fuzzy Fidelity in Europe," *European Sociological Review* 25, no. 2 (2009): 155–68.

13. See, e.g., Rodney Stark, Eva Hamberg, and Alan S. Miller, "Exploring Spirituality and Unchurched Religions in America, Sweden, and Japan," *Journal of Contemporary Religion* 20, no. 1 (2005): 3–23; Raymond L. M. Lee, "The Re-enchantment of the Self: Western Spirituality, Asian Materialism," *Journal of Contemporary Religion* 18, no. 3 (2003): 351–67; and Xinzhong Yao, "Religious Belief and Practice in Urban China 1995–2005," *Journal of Contemporary Religion* 22, no. 2 (2007): 169–86.

14. Paul Heelas and Benjamin Seel, "An Ageing New Age?," in *Predicting Religion*, ed. Grace Davie, Linda Woodhead, and Paul Heelas (Burlington, VT: Ashgate, 2003), 242–43.

practices that can be combined to make a package of faith to suit each person. This preference explains why people still are turning away from commitment to traditional religions whilst at the same time turning toward the spiritual as a part of their lives.

If this is true for Europe, and indeed Australasia, what of America? The United States is clearly consumer oriented and in many ways postmodern, yet it appears to have a much higher adherence to Christianity. The nature of American religion is, however, more complex than it might appear. Attendance figures are deeply uneven from state to state, as they are between countries in Europe, and many share European levels. In the latter part of the twentieth century, the start of a decline in church attendance by young people may be the first sign of the pattern of decline that began in Europe fifty or so years earlier. This is reinforced by the Barna observation that adult churchgoing in the United States is largely predicted by childhood attendance, which is based on whether one's parents attended themselves as children.[15] Perhaps most significant, the incidence of new spirituality beliefs in the United States as shown by various surveys, most notably the Baylor Survey 2006,[16] is the same as in Europe. The difference, however, is that church attendees in the United States are twice as likely to hold such beliefs as in Britain.[17] In Europe new spiritualities have occurred primarily as an alternative to church, whereas in the United States for many they have occurred as an addition to church, with the two not seen as incompatible. The comment of Christian Schwartz is telling:

> The more American people and institutions are redefined by mass-consumer capitalism's moral order, the more American religion is also remade in its image. Religion becomes one product among many others existing to satisfy people's subjectively defined needs, tastes, and wants. Religious adherents thus become spiritual consumers uniquely authorized as autonomous individuals to pick and choose in the religious market whatever products they may find satisfying or fulfilling at the moment.[18]

The cultural elite still clinging to an increasingly outdated secular humanism ensure that the voices of the "new atheists" are loudly broadcast and

---

15. See http://www.barna.org/barna-update/article/5-barna-update/62-adults-who-attended-church-as-children-show-lifelong-effects?q=child+church+attendance.

16. "American Piety in the 21st Century," Baylor Institute for Studies of Religion, September 2006.

17. Based on comparable data for questions asked in both countries in the World Values Survey 1999/2000.

18. "The National Study of Youth and Religion," quoted in C. Smith with M. Denton, *Soul Searching* (New York: Oxford University Press, 2005), 176–77.

therefore need to be addressed. However, they are not the main issue facing churches struggling to communicate faith in a Western, postmodern, consumer world. If for some consumerism itself is their "religion," for many others the new spiritualities are an expression of religion naturally at home within this culture and far more attractive than traditional religions. Not only does this mean we need to understand these spiritualities to engage in mission, but they may actually teach us lessons about how to create an incarnational Christianity within the newly emerging Western culture and warn us of the pitfalls to avoid.

Practices

Worship in a New Spirituality Approach

In cross-cultural church planting, worship is not where one begins but something for later on in the process. This is because it needs to emerge from the spiritual journeys of those who have come to faith from the culture, rather than be something the missionaries think will work for them. Church plants that begin with worship tend to attract those with church backgrounds; indeed, these can often be people already attending other churches.

In many ways it is still too early in this mission to be sure of the way worship will be expressed; there are currently very few communities of people from new spirituality backgrounds. So it is a case of cautiously spotting trends. However, some new spirituality groups already have ritual elements, and a mixture of these and often more ancient forms of Christian worship, especially those with a mystical element, seem to be the likely pattern. For some the concept of worship will need exploring as a new thing. Ritual will be familiar but often it can be focused on personal experience rather than relating to God. Many from a Pagan background would be familiar with the concept of a celebration of life and the seasons, and this is likely to be the starting point from which an indigenous Christian worship develops. There is also a strong element of personal meditation and of spiritual practice that informs personal devotions for Christians in this culture.

Is gathering in community even important to new spirituality? *Steve Taylor*

For many the answer is no, which is why I say corporate worship would be a totally new thing. For Pagans it is normal to gather, and some form of using their approach is a potential starting point. This would probably not be a weekly gathering. *Steve Hollinghurst*

Place is important, and often special places in nature are favored. Worship is often in the round, and contributions by all are encouraged, with little being led by a designated worship leader. Elements of worship associated with recent interest in Celtic Christianity, readings from Christian mystics, and times for meditation are likely. There might also be use of dance, drawing on folk tradition and music. Drumming and drum circles have also been used. Others might go for a more ambient electronic style. What is certainly unlikely are styles of worship common to many churches that work through a leader up front with people seated or standing in rows before them. This feels too much like a power play to many in the new spiritualities.

> Our post-Christian, neopagan, pluralistic North American context presents crosscultural missionary challenges every bit as daunting as those we would face on any other continent. Unfortunately most pastors and church leaders have had no missiological training.
>
> Eddie Gibbs (CN, 36)

Community in a New Spirituality Approach

One of the issues a postmodern society raises is, how can we celebrate difference yet live well in community? The increasing fragmentation of society into tribal groupings and tension between them as well as the growing numbers of those living in isolation is a consequence of this. Both New Age and Pagan spirituality provide answers to fragmentation and isolation. At one end Eastern religious ideas state that ultimately everything is part of the same divine spirit; and at the other end the ecosystem is looked to as a model of interdependence of life. This invites a Christian response that asks questions of these approaches but also needs to model its own understanding of the body of Christ as a community that centers life on the presence of Christ and welcomes diversity. This is easier to say than to do; Paul wrote what he did because the Corinthians wanted to exclude people who were different, and we are prone to the same.

A key issue in helping new spirituality adherents to become disciples of Christ is to recognize that people are on journeys of faith and may travel slowly. We need a model that, rather than getting people to cross barriers, encourages changes of direction, sometimes dramatic and sometimes subtle, as part of becoming more and more like Christ. This is true of most groups that don't have a church background, and when successful it tends to create different levels of community. At the first level, Christians become part of non-Christian communities where they build relationships and seek to be a blessing. This may be done in this culture by involvement in fairs, festivals, online forums, and meeting groups. At the next level, Christians create neutral groups in which relationships are deepened and issues of faith and life explored. One example is a weekly pub meeting organized by a Christian in which those of all backgrounds exploring spirituality and the supernatural come to share stories and explore one another's experiences and beliefs. Other examples include storytelling circles, meditation groups, craft and spirituality groups, or groups involved in nature conservation. The third level requires specific places for those seeking to follow Christ. Leaders must allow people to find their own current level but not lose sight of Christ. All groups must maintain their identity if they are to remain as stages on a journey of faith.

> You raise an important point about the developmental nature of spirituality and forma-
> tion in the Way of Jesus. Many streams of Christianity have rites and rituals marking being
> "in," but few of our traditions have helped people mark the multitude of important events,
> decisions, and experiences that compose the journey. The exception would be ordained
> ministers, who often have a number of journey markers.
>
> The three kinds of groups (non-Christian, neutral, Christian) appear to be a useful step
> toward helping people mark movement. My concern is that it sounds a bit like the central
> moment in this model is the conversion event. Certainly conversion is an important part
> of evangelism yet it may not be the most helpful way to imagine the work of evangelism.
> Evangelism may be better thought of as recruiting participants in God's redemptive mission
> for the person, community, and creation. As such evangelism is about involving people
> in the good news of God's dream for all of creation. I wonder what sign posts along that
> journey the church could identify and celebrate as we journey together with God in mission.
> *Dwight J. Friesen*

> I agree. I like to talk about conversion to Christ as a lifelong process, not an event of
> becoming a Christian. I also talk about evangelism as a process of discipleship with those
> who do not yet see themselves as followers of Christ. *Steve Hollinghurst*

Mission in a New Spirituality Approach

The declining numbers of children being raised in the Christian faith, which has been particularly marked in Europe and is now showing signs of deepening in the United States, has big implications for mission. As David Bosch points out, the distinction between foreign mission to those who have never been Christian and evangelism at home to the no-longer Christian is breaking down.[19] We are increasingly foreign missionaries in our own countries. We would

19. David Bosch, *Transforming Mission: Paradigm Shifts in Theology of Mission* (Maryknoll, NY: Orbis, 1991), 410.

not expect to be effective missionaries in a foreign culture without learning its language and understanding how that culture worked. Further, research on adults who came to faith in the UK showed that 76 percent had a church upbringing. The 24 percent who came to faith as adults but did not have a church upbringing rarely responded to evangelistic events but instead came to faith over a long period through personal relationships with Christians.[20] If we do not change how we do evangclism and mission, we are likely to end up like the foreign tourists who, having failed to learn the language, speak in their own increasingly loudly and slowly in the vain hope of being understood.

This has led to the pioneering of an incarnational approach in a number of Western nations among those exploring spirituality outside of traditional religions, in both New Age and Pagan forms of spirituality. First, this involved a shift away from viewing the new spiritualities as something to warn Christians to stay clear of, and toward building relationships with their practitioners, seeing them as people loved by God and seeking to understand them and their beliefs.

This approach in Australian, in European, and increasingly in American groups has worked in contexts like New Age fairs, alternative festivals, and ancient spiritual sites. Approaches have been tailored to each context but have often involved use of spiritual gifts like prayer for healing, prophecy, and dream interpretation. The realization is that spiritual experience is a gateway to a fresh look at Christianity, which is often viewed by those in this culture as unspiritual. This has also led to a rediscovery of Christian mysticism as part of the kind of Christian tradition that can impact today's spiritual people. Presence at such events has enabled further exploration of spiritual experience and understanding, both at the time and through internet forums. Often those we encounter have experiences of God but interpret them differently. We find ourselves, like Paul, seeking to make known the unknown God. Like all cross-cultural mission this is a long-term ministry, but people are coming to faith and others are significantly changing their attitude to Christianity.

Leadership in a New Spirituality Approach

In common with most postmodern groups, those in the new spiritualities are suspicious of power and favour very flat organisational structures. While charismatic spiritual individuals can wield considerable influence, the more client-based approach to spirituality means that people do not expect the people they admire to also be in authority over them but instead to offer them

---

20. See John Finney, *Finding Faith Today* (British and Foreign Bible Society, 1992).

guidance that can be followed or not. People look for a guru but expect him or her to be generous in teaching others to operate with their own wisdom. At a Mind/Body/Spirit fair one meets many people trained as Reiki masters, but far fewer who are full-time practitioners and teachers of this healing method. The same is true for other paths and therapies. In such a world traditional church leadership structures seem very rigid and hierarchical and pose a barrier to the Christian message.

In the history of cross-cultural mission, missionaries adopted the style of the indigenous priesthood as a way of aiding the sharing of the Christian faith. The Celtic monks adopted much of the appearance of the druids and spent time at their holy sites. In a similar way, Jesuits adopted the style of Confucian scholars as part of their mission in China. More recently the Norwegian mission to the Buddhist world run by Areopagus constructed places like the Christ Temple in Hong Kong, embodying Christian faith in a Buddhist cultural style. This approach must avoid compromising Christian values and beliefs, but I think it is needed in the new spirituality context; we need holy men and women working in culture who can inspire and draw respect.

> For indigenous peoples, the freedom presented by an "incarnational Christianity" is urgent, just, and long overdue. The implications of a more incarnational and contextual mission—and, with it, a more comprehensive, biblical, and global awareness of God's presence in creation—are central to the revelation and embodiment of an indigenous church. Mark MacDonald

Christ's model of servant leadership is important in this context. It subverts the power games that are so mistrusted and enables the Christian guru to be the one who refuses power and serves others. Inspired by this model, foot washing and foot massage have often become part of the ministry Christians offer at festivals and Mind/Body/Spirit fairs.

> Jesus was a servant leader who used his power and influence to extend status and grace to those judged "unworthy," the ones "outside religious norms." MaryKate Morse

While church attendance has declined in western Europe, the United States, and other Western nations, this has not led to a rise in secular atheism but instead to new spiritualities naturally suited to a postmodern consumer society. These new practices challenge the church to discover new approaches to mission, community, leadership, and worship. New missional approaches may appear similar to strategies adopted in foreign mission within pre-Christian societies, and in fact they are also much like approaches adopted by the early church as it moved beyond the familiar territory of Judaism out into the alien Greek pagan culture. Like Paul in Athens or the Celtic church, such an approach will expect to find God already at work in the people's spiritual journeys and use that as the way for Christ to become fully alive within their culture. The communities formed will need to rediscover much that was valued by the early church. For example, diversity can be celebrated within the body of Christ, just as Paul had to remind the Corinthians. Leadership will need to surrender power and adopt a servant role, and worship will need to reflect local culture and not be imposed in a one-size-fits-all approach. These discoveries will be challenging; they run counter to many cultural pressures and the increasing diversity of a globalised culture. But they are also in the church's DNA, waiting for the missionary Spirit to bring them to life.

For Further Exploration

Books

Clifford, Ross, and Philip Johnson. *Jesus and the Gods of the New Age*. Oxford: Lion Hudson, 2001.

Drane, John. *Do Christians Know How to Be Spiritual? The Rise of New Spirituality and the Mission of the Church*. London: Darton, Longman and Todd, 2005.

Hollinghurst, Steve. *New Age, Paganism and Christian Mission*. Cambridge: Grove, 2003.

Websites

Communities of the Mystic Christ: http://www.mysticchrist.co.uk
Eden People: http://www.edenpeople.webeden.co.uk
In the Master's Light: http://www.inthemasterslight.net
Journey into Wholeness: http://www.journeyintowholeness.net
Sacred Tribes Journal: http://www.sacredtribesjournal.org
Soul Clinics: http://www.soulclinics.com
Western Institute for Intercultural Studies: http://www.wiics.org

Part 3

Practices

14

Rethinking Worship as an Emerging Christian Practice

Paul Roberts

Practices

Worship is essential to the life of the church. Indeed, worship sits alongside mission as one of the two core practices that constitute the purpose of the church. Christians have a double calling: to be agents of God's transformation within the world through mission and to anticipate the consummation of the kingdom through worship. The book of Revelation contrasts the picture of suffering witness, which was the experience of the churches to which it was written, with a vision of the final consummation of God's new creation marked by praise and fellowship with the divine. So when Christians worship, they are anticipating through their practice the kingdom that their mission proclaims and works toward.

> I struggle with the dichotomy you seem to be setting up. Does mission only reach the door of the kingdom, never entering into God's active, present-tense promises, and does worship only "rehearse" a future reality? *Troy Bronsink*

From the point of view of worship. I think it's important that we keep the future focus strongly before us, whilst bringing from the present a sense of celebration from creation. Without a focus on the joys and pains of the present, our worship risks losing connection with the present experience of being human. Yet unless we look to our worship to transfigure the present with the hoped-for future, there is a danger that we "settle for the now," which, as history has shown, can mean affirming things that are the product of human projects and structures, rather than the kingdom of God. Worship must always have an element of both/and, dissociation from and integration with, carefully negotiating the relationship between what we are and celebrate now, and the future that God has stored up for us in Christ. *Paul Roberts*

The church of Christendom presented worship as a public event that was deeply embedded within the practices of Christian societies. Very soon after the conversion of Constantine, Christians either took over old civic buildings for their liturgies or emulated the civic court architecture with their first purpose-built churches. Their liturgical[1] theology changed from one founded upon hopeful anticipation of glory amidst present suffering[2] to one of public celebration by a social institution, from subversive gatherings of refusal in the pagan state to the triumphant normalisation of the Christian state. Given this shift in social identity, it is no surprise that when, many centuries later, Christendom sought to expand itself through global mission, its liturgical practices were those of the colonising state powers. Christian worship only slowly learned to reinculturate itself in the forms of the subjugated peoples.[3]

> Mission is the result of God's initiative, rooted in God's purposes to restore and heal creation.
>
> Eddie Gibbs (CN, 51)

If we are now witnessing a global emergence of genuinely post-Christendom forms of Christian community, then we can expect worship to be the place where we see new understandings of theology, "church," and mission expressed, celebrated, and explored. Liturgical practice can be the most authentic expression of the underlying theology of the Christian community, because the practice of worship has to "feel right" in regards to God and in regards to oneself. This is particularly the case where worship has been set free to adapt itself to meet new needs and circumstances. Nevertheless, "reading" worship

---

1. In this chapter, I will use "liturgy"/"liturgical" and "worship" synonymously, without implying the use, or otherwise, of written liturgical texts.

2. Rom. 8:18.

3. Even now, "reading" the liturgical theology of newer churches in the postcolonial South is a complex exercise of differentiating between liturgical visions of the kingdom and competing models of Christendom, old and new.

in this way requires caution, since even within the most self-consciously radical groups previous baggage carries over in the form of overreactions to past practice alongside other assumptions about worship that have carried over without criticism.

Is Worship the Servant of Mission?

One of the most important of these items of previous baggage is the view that worship is there to serve the missional function of the church. This notion was entirely unknown in the pre-Constantinian church: nonbelievers were forbidden from entering gatherings for worship. Even catechumens could only join in the first part of the liturgy and probably did not even witness the Holy Communion until after their baptism.[4] The church of pre-Christendom simply did not use access to its worship as a missional tool.

> Worship at best is accessible to de-churched people and completely alien to unchurched people. Christendom as an attractional model of church overplays worship as formational because it assumes that the culture is predominantly Christian. *Ian Mobsby*

> Part of Christian mission is to progressively induct people who are "on the way" to belief into worship practices, since it is in the worship encounter that we get a glimpse of the thing the gospel talks about. The gospel isn't simply a "message" conceived of cognitively; it's something lived and experienced, so a gradual engagement with liturgy has a role in mission. I think this "gradual engagement" is an area where we all need to do some missional and pastoral exploration. *Paul Roberts*

The contemporary notion of using worship services as an agency of mission, therefore, should be recognized as a distinctly modern practice. Worship-as-mission happens when the churches of Christendom try to use liturgy as

---

4. Restriction of access to the Eucharist ("closed table") can be dated as early as the late first or early second century AD. See *Didache* 9.5, text in M. Johnson, ed., *Documents of the Baptismal Liturgy*, 3rd ed. (London: SPCK, 2003); Justin Martyr, *First Apology* 65.1, text in C. C. Richardson et al., *Early Christian Fathers*, Library of Christian Classics, vol. 1 (London: SPCK, 1953); Hippolytus, *Apostolic Tradition* 18, text in E. C. Whitaker, *Documents of the Baptismal Liturgy* (Collegeville, MN: Liturgical Press, 2003). The secrecy of Christian liturgical gatherings was one accusation made against Christianity by Celsus, where the practice was affirmed and defended by Origen (*Against Celsus*, 1.1). The practice developed from the late third century onward to a fully developed culture of secrecy regarding baptism and the Eucharist, which peaked in liturgies and texts from the later part of the fourth century. Thereafter, the increasingly normative practice of infant baptism would have reduced its secret, inaccessible nature, although this was offset, to some extent, by the separation of the "sanctuary" from the main body of the church in developments in Christian architecture.

bait to re-attract the wider populace back to a practice that had once been normative. In Britain, many mainstream churches celebrate an annual Back-to-Church Sunday while, in America, the seeker-sensitive approach is well documented. In both cases, the church is attempting to "up its game" in the liturgical domain by providing forms of worship-like activity aimed at enticing nonattenders to join, or rejoin, the liturgical community. In these examples, the most important missional influence acting upon worship is whether it is sufficiently culturally appealing to reestablish its social role as a public event. So the Constantinian assumptions underlying such "shop window" worship should be obvious: Christian worship is seen as a socially *normal* activity, in a state where Christian social hegemony is also normal. The role of "the unchurched" in seeker-friendly and "back to church" approaches is that of the deviant, rather than the norm.[5] In these missiologies that use worship as a point of attraction, adapted liturgies are being used as a therapy for socioreligious deviance. In post-Christendom, however, *worship itself is a form of social deviance.* This changed circumstance should cause us to rethink and reconfigure the relationship between a church's mission and its liturgical practices.

What you describe resembles some expressions of liturgical renewal where the exiled church pines to re-create the original countercultural practice, even though the counterpoint (current culture) has changed. And so the point is always reactionary rather than appreciative. Using liturgy to attach people to something is placing the tool of ritual in the hands of so-called enlightened authorities. As a result churches close off the possibility of true transformation or re-creation. *Troy Bronsink*

I think you are right in recognizing a kind of nostalgia in some critics of the seeker-friendly approach and advocates of a new pre-Constantinianism. However, I think we do have something to learn from the way the pre-Constantinian church operated as we learn to live as Christian communities in post-Christendom cultures. I also believe that residual Constantinianism is doing immense damage to the authenticity of the Christian faith in the West. *Paul Roberts*

Alternative Worship as an Emerging Church Practice

"Alternative worship" has proven to be a useful gathering term to name the distinct liturgical approach of some emerging churches. Although in the UK, New Zealand, and Australia alternative worship preceded the "emerging"

---

5. There is even a linguistic sense in the use of the prefix "un-," which implies a deviation from the norm of "churched."

title by a decade or more, those church groups that had first self-identified as alternative worship communities were generally content to be called emerging as the term gained currency. Given the closeness of this relationship, some specific analysis of alternative worship can be instructive in understanding the various liturgical influences acting within emerging churches more generally.

Alternative worship began with the rise of the Nine O'Clock Service (or NOS) at St. Thomas' Church, Crookes, in Sheffield, UK, in the second half of the 1980s.[6] NOS's appeal was twofold: (1) its astonishingly creative and innovative approach to worship and (2) the vision it held out of a church and faith that was fully contextualised in the culture of urban young adults. This shows that alternative worship initially grew out of an attractional model that recognised the church's need to address cultural diversity. Originally, NOS was a way of providing worship services to which its members could bring friends from the nightclub culture of Sheffield without the need to cross a cultural divide into mainstream church. Only after changing the culture of the liturgy was it clear that all other aspects of church life would need to make a similar transition. Between 1987 and 1994, NOS expanded its ecclesial agenda to include the eco-theology of Matthew Fox, a conscious engagement with postmodernism, and the reinterpretation of traditional Christian liturgical and symbolic practices, such as the labyrinth. It was only when the system of unaccountable, personality-driven leadership was challenged by this new theological framework that the cultic and abusive elements within NOS were exposed, leading to its collapse.

Most alternative worship groups that began in imitation of NOS started with a similar approach of adapting worship into new subcultural domains in order to provide a basis for outreach. Again, like NOS, most of these groups discovered fairly early on that it was about much more than worship, that to be truly contextualised would require a new engagement with ecclesiology, theology, and mission. Often just at an intuitive level, they realised that there was something wrong with the assumptions about the relationship between mission and worship that they had inherited. This transition away from running a worship service merely as an agent of local church mission explains some of the tensions and opportunities that have arisen during the story of alternative worship and some other emerging churches.

> From my experience alternative worship communities realised that worship was only part of what church was about, and they were challenged by the need for community and for

---

6. R. Howard, *The Rise and Fall of the Nine O'Clock Service: A Cult within the Church?* (London: Continuum, 1996).

nonattractional forms of mission, which helped some groups to shift from being alternative worship groups to emerging churches. *Ian Mobsby*

In retrospect, however, I wonder whether this was an entirely good thing. The shift away from the "doing" of worship to "missiology with Macs," with some fairly heavy self-promoting agendas in the mix, has not led to healthy church life or to a grounded mission. One implication of my argument is that our recognition of the limits of "alt worship" as an attractional model of mission then led to a "baby/bathwater" rejection of something that is vital to Christian community health. New monasticism, with its interest in community liturgies, is one reappropriation of the liturgical dimension of healthy church life. I think we need to recognize and foster this among missional communities who do not necessarily engage with a monastic self-identification. *Paul Roberts*

Whose Church Is It?

Those groups that had been set up under the aegis of parent churches often struggled to maintain a link to their parent bodies, especially when the "parent" saw the group chiefly as a way to extend its own mission. Theological experimentation bred suspicions, which were compounded when shifts in spirituality followed. When their missiology moved beyond just being an outreach congregation, a breach occurred.[7] The ecclesiology of parent churches has proved determinative of whether a full post-Christendom contextualization of liturgy can expand to include theology, spirituality, and missiology. Alternative worship groups founded by Anglican, Lutheran, and Methodist churches have tended to fare better than those founded by churches having a more congregationalist ecclesiology. Parent churches that are part of large denominations have greater resources that enable them to accept diversity within their planted offspring. Despite having structures of liturgical governance, most Protestant denominations tend to tolerate and even encourage liturgical diversity and innovation.

Power Relationships within Liturgy

There are two ways of interpreting the challenge to inherited power structures that has taken place within alternative worship. One way is to see the challenge as an effect of postmodernist critiques of structure and control, reflecting a scepticism of power structures in general. Another way is to see it

7. There are echoes here of the story of many "Gen-X ministries" that were instituted by American churches in the late 1990s.

as a breakdown of the social structures of ecclesial power that were endemic within the Constantinian settlement, which reflected Christianity's role as the state religion. It is possible to combine both of these interpretations when looking at the liturgical developments of alternative worship. In emerging church practice, the liturgy ceases to reflect the social expressions of power associated with residual Christendom in both its composition and its performance. One such abandoned expression is the professional "worship ministry" of musicians, supported by kilowatts of amplification with a lucrative marketing operation running in the background. Another is restricting liturgical roles and tasks to those who are officially empowered and qualified to do them. Alternative worship replaces these restrictive expressions with communal and every-member approaches to liturgical creativity and leadership.

What about the residual power of ritual in post-Christendom culture? So even if the "users" leave behind the superstar leader or sacerdotal shaman, those who are new to such an emergent community need clues and education in the new power-divesting approach being taken. Otherwise you end up with a group of people who enjoy the irony of historical role-playing without the shared intent of following or remaining teachable. My early steps of forming Neighbors Abbey with de-churched and unchurched neighbors amounted to this in some ways, half the group wanting the ease of religion that worked everything out for them, and the other half resenting any form of organization. I think we moved past that but some of it came when we started giving clues to how a power-divesting approach could work. *Troy Bronsink*

I have had similar experiences, but I still believe that it is possible, indeed essential, that we take these steps. *Paul Roberts*

Rejecting the Expressions of Cultural Triumphalism

The rejection of expressions of cultural triumphalism accounts for a number of features in alternative worship. One is the typically small size of groups and their reluctance to adopt strategies aimed purely at congregational growth. Another is the struggle to find a distinct doxology that stands apart from the triumphalistic tones endemic in the contemporary Christian music industry. Whilst there is a certain amount of overreaction going on, alternative worship seems to be embarking upon a long-term project of replacing the doxology of the triumphant church of Christendom, with all its questionable allegiances. To do this, emerging worship practices need to find words of praise that eschew aspiration for a kingdom of human worldly power, by discovering again the exuberant and heavenly praise of the deviants and those whom the world has marginalised (see Rev. 5:9–10).

> Emerging churches have discovered the contemplative Christian tradition that integrates life and prayer as worship. New monastics take this further when they talk about "contemplative action." *Ian Mobsby*

Having made the transition away from the conventional church of modernity and late-Christendom, emerging communities now face the task of integrating and evolving a distinct liturgical praxis across a range of cultures. A new set of challenges is presently establishing itself as an agenda for how mission and worship relate to one another. It is to this that we now turn.

Culture

Worship as an Engagement with Life in the Real World: Worship within Creation

To be missional involves the church in a complex engagement with the issues of life on earth today. It means avoiding the old liberal/evangelical dualism of either "letting the world set the agenda" or inventing a parallel "niche theocracy" that exists in the language of Sunday worship, but then breaks down on Monday morning. The words and thoughts of authentic Christian worship are unashamedly doxological—proclaiming God's glory—but the context must remain the real world. The Scriptures, which we hear read in worship, speak from and address this real world in which the Word was made flesh. The sacraments, through which God covenants to meet us, use ordinary water, wine, and bread. Issues such as sustainability and the environment are not only things that perplex and concern us as beings-in-the-world today; they are also central to the missional sending of the Son into the real world and the outpouring of the Spirit on God's enfleshed holy people right now. Worship is the glue that holds together our everyday experiences and the faith that we proclaim and live out in mission. If worship fails to engage with life in the world, then it is not remotely missional in the New Testament sense (1 John 1:1–4), but merely the last nostalgic sigh for a past Constantinianism.

> Worship must not be used for other means that result in it becoming both subverted and diverted. Worship is not entertainment. It is not an expression of cultural elitism. It is not religious education. It is not emotional self-indulgence, or a vehicle for evangelism. Worship does not produce a quick fix but flows out into the whole of life, and the whole of life is then drawn into worship.
>
> Eddie Gibbs (CN, 156)

> Worship that is in touch with socioeconomic injustice invites people to participate with God in his mission to heal and reconcile all things. *Eileen Suico*

Worship as an Engagement with Personal and Cultural Embodiment: Worship within a Culture of Hybridity

A wonderful thing about Christian worship is that it forces an engagement with the diversity that so often divides people. We are forced to be "present" to one another, and this involves negotiating the foibles and eccentricities of our coworshipers. For this reason, missional worship needs to be suspicious of approaches that seek to sidestep or make optional the messiness of human encounter by either turning liturgy into a platform for the young and pretty, or by using disembodied technologies that mask the truth of our embodied imperfection. True mission works through *embodied practices*, as Jamie Smith has powerfully reminded us.[8] Embodied worship tells the truth about ourselves to ourselves, and, through that truth, applies the real gospel, exposing our idolatries (images) and facing us with the difficult challenge of being transformed, through our rich diversity, into the image of Christ. This is a deeply *humanising* experience, as Ian Mobsby has already noted (chap. 8). Also, as Oscar García-Johnson indicates (chap. 9), with increasing hybridity our rich and diverse identities can either be celebrated and transfigured by the experience of worship, or worship itself can become a force for dehybridization. True missional worship is the ultimate example of what García-Johnson calls a "borderland," a place where, in Christ, difference is essential in order for the church to be a sign of the reconciliation of God's created diversity that is proclaimed in the gospel. By contrast, where worship clings to the values of Constantinianism, the liturgy merely genericizes the worshipers, dissolving diversity into a gray goo of "Christian" ("Western") conformity.

> I like this image of borderlands of reconciliation. Have you seen forgiveness ritualized in communities in ways that walk that borderline between the lands of reconciliation and nonconfrontationalism? How? *Troy Bronsink*

> I find hints of this in Oscar García-Johnson's chapter. Personally, my mind goes back to multichurch gatherings in Manchester in the wake of the 1980s riots we had there. *Paul Roberts*

---

8. James K. A. Smith, *Desiring the Kingdom: Worship, Worldview, and Cultural Formation* (Grand Rapids: Baker Academic, 2009).

Worship, to be missional, must be aware of the fallacies of idealization and colonization; a missional worshiper overcomes these foes by centering on the polyphonic, polyglot, humanizing Spirit of the resurrected Christ of the Pentecost. *Oscar García-Johnson*

The Renewal of Worship Practices as Part of a Missional Hermeneutic: Worship within a Pluralistic Culture

Since we cannot draw a sharp distinction between "world" and "worship," it is perhaps inevitable that the struggle to be true to context and to faith tradition becomes focused at the point where God is specifically named and addressed. Richard Sudworth's account of the experiences of Sanctuary fellowship (chap. 10) highlights the importance of worship practices as a critical learning space for the church and its mission. Part of the challenge, where Christianity is neither culturally nor religiously dominant, is to rediscover "who we are" when we cannot easily say whether we are Asian or European, and see how that reflects on what it means to be Christian—"who we are in Christ." The lost heritage of a comfortable Constantinian identity leaves a creative, though perplexing, liturgical vacuum to be filled. Such missional approaches to the liturgy tread a difficult line between retaining those traditional practices that are central to Christian identity (sharing in Communion, daily prayer, reading Scripture together, baptism) and discarding those that, in all probability, are not (certain styles of singing, music, and preaching, architecture, roles, vesture, hierarchies). Part of the missional hermeneutic of liturgy is to discover what is "ever new" in liturgical tradition, to discard that which is unhelpful (or, in Sudworth's terminology, unwelcoming), and also to recover lost practices that have a strangeness to them within which something strangely familiar can be rediscovered. It is this commitment to the "deep traditions" of Christian liturgical practice that will ensure that Christian communities, and their leadership, have sufficient resources drawn from within their own faith's tradition to engage constructively and discerningly with their neighbours of other faith traditions.

I especially like this attention to the "recovery of lost practices." There seems to be a common thread within many emerging church communities to embrace a tradition that may have been strange but that recalls something "strangely familiar." It is a reminder that an authentic creativity in our liturgy is never about mere iconoclasm but will have resonances within a communal identity that is inherently catholic. *Richard Sudworth*

Am I reading you to say that Christian liturgy's identity is basically historical? How does this jibe with liturgy as a world-based event? Does liturgical boundedness really equip us to be this-worldly in our interfaith friendships? In my experience, the varied liturgies, old and new, of other faiths are helpful inroads to discussing the narratives that we live by. But many other traditions struggle as much as Christianity to differentiate their daily lives and the power of precedence in liturgy. In my chapter I discuss ritual agency as one key in shaping disciples with vision and skills to engage their culture critically. Do you think liturgical renewal addresses this? How have you seen the "strangeness" of "deep traditions" empower congregations to take responsibility for their actions? Have you ever seen ancient liturgies shape congregants into noncritical passive recipients? *Troy Bronsink*

We should be careful that we don't assume "historical" is somehow disconnected with "world." The world today is deeply connected with the historical practices of past times, which, for me, argues for acknowledging the historical dimension of all worship. The church is part of the story of the world. I'm not advocating "liturgical boundedness"—on the contrary, I am arguing for the presence of the church as a liturgical creation within the world. To recognize one's historical position arguably frees one up to engage critically and creatively with one's experience of the world now. Liturgical practices help reset one's bearings, but only when closely correlated with the way things are beyond and after the liturgical event. *Paul Roberts*

Worship as Joy and the Encounter with Beauty

The axiom "worship the Lord in the beauty of holiness" (Ps. 29:2; Ps. 96:9 KJV), referring originally to the beauty of the temple, has influenced Christian worship throughout its history. Throughout the twists and turns of Christian history, there is a recurrent sense that God's creative beauty inevitably finds echoes within the worship of God's people. Anyone who has taken time to listen to spiritual searchers today will hear, again and again, a witness to God through natural beauty and its reflection in the arts and music: "they have neither speech nor language and their voices are not heard, yet their sound has gone out into all lands and their words to the ends of the world" (Ps. 19:3–4).[9]

> In a postmodern world, diversity is celebrated. This should not come as a threat to biblically informed Christians because creativity and variety are characteristics of the world that God created and that he saw was very good.
>
> Eddie Gibbs (CN, 67)

The echoes of God's revelation through the beauty of the natural world, and its responsive expression in human art, is an integral part of God's mission that we discover within the Scriptures. The church's role in mission should reflect the joy of belonging to God's beautiful world; so worship space is art space.

9. From *Common Worship: Services and Prayers for the Church of England* (London: Church House Publishing, 2000).

There are two influences that have sought to frustrate this. The first is a rejection of art out of fear of idolatry—a response that confuses a joyful, doxological reception of creative beauty with human sinful responses to it (which are indeed idolatrous). The second is the professionalization of art by church authorities in the interest of using "high" art to boost the church's reputation, an aesthetic of cultural power, rather than an aesthetic of joy. Among emerging churches, alternative worship has sought to return art to the hands of worshipers as an integral part of the corporate act of creating worship together. This contrasts with the attempts of some churches to use art in the service of mission by using big budgets and professional artists and musicians. This reduces worshipers to the role of mere consumers. Within emerging churches, there is a democratisation of liturgical aesthetics that seeks to reconnect the response of the worshiping body to the universal experience of joy in the midst of creation. Such worship reconnects the missional body to the joyful mission of the Word within the whole created order.

> I have always liked to address the fear of idolatry through the imagery of the church as a part of God's work of art. Our art, then, is as commissioned artisans, apprentices of God's creative dreams and practices. *Troy Bronsink*

> Mark Pierson and Jonny Baker expound an alternative in which the practice of church is more akin to curation than marketing or propaganda to consumers. *Troy Bronsink*

Liturgical Hospitality, Differentiation, and Communal Identity in the Cultures of Post-Christendom: Worship in the Context of the Individual Pursuit of Spirituality

The differences between the missional context of North America and that of Europe have already been discussed by Stefan Paas and Steve Hollinghurst (chaps. 12 and 13). Their conclusions, however, raise further questions from the perspective of worship. It is clear that some commentators on the Western church and its mission have an understanding of affiliation (and therefore mission) that is probably "over-creedal"—that is, it focuses on believing and the articulation of belief, whilst ignoring the missional significance of practices. If this is so, Hollinghurst's observation that new spiritualities are client-based serves to highlight *practice* as distinct from *belief*. When we speak of practices, we are in the realm of the liturgical. This echoes Jamie Smith's anthropological assertion, drawn from Augustine, that humanity is fundamentally a desiring species before it is a thinking species.[10] To recognise this distinction does

---

10. Smith, *Desiring the Kingdom*, chap. 1.

not yield a straightforward missiological paradigm, however—at least not in the context of Christianity's decline in Europe. There is a danger of merely adapting our practices (and, in their wake, all other aspects of faith) to a missional "marketplace" with a disordered and distorted set of desires. This would accord comfortably with consumerism, but at a very high cost and for a most questionable benefit. There are elements of alternative worship that have toyed with this approach, using the analyses of anthropologists to create metarituals, which have a somewhat arcane relationship to the Christian gospel and whose main aim is to function therapeutically for the "clients." Yet the ritual analysis that undergirds such approaches has not been without its critics, most notably Talal Asad, who argues that the interpretation of ritual practices into abstracted "meanings" by Western anthropologists is merely an Enlightenment construct.[11]

Why the pre-Constantinian church practised restrictions of entry into its liturgical gatherings remains a matter of historical conjecture. One possible reason is that it was in order to preserve Christian communal identity from dominant social identities and values that were starkly different from the kingdom values of the gospel. Another reason, however, may have been persecution, or at least the threat of it. Indeed, it could have been a mixture of both reasons, purity and danger, that led to the practice of liturgical restriction.

With the establishment of Christianity as the religion of empire, these liturgical restrictions were, paradoxically, not removed. Instead, the bulk of the society was itself brought within these boundaries, leaving only deviants outside.[12] The boundaries that had once reinforced the deviancy of the Christian community of faith against conformity with pagan society now reinforced the deviancy of a different set of minorities (residual pagans and Jews). In this new situation, liturgical restriction had the effect of containing the body politic *inside* the liturgical space (which had become the same as public space), whilst highlighting the deviancy of the minority. In post-Christendom, the evacuation of this bounded liturgical space sets the scene for a new relationship between liturgy, mission, and the environment.

11. T. Asad, *Genealogies of Religion: Discipline and Reasons of Power in Christianity and Islam* (Baltimore: Johns Hopkins University Press, 1993), chap. 2. I am grateful to Professor Graham Ward of Manchester University for alerting me to the significance of Asad's work.

12. The practice of delaying baptism to the deathbed (to avoid incurring postbaptismal sin), the slow decline of the catechumenate, Augustine's doctrine of original sin, and the making normative of infant baptism all witness to the gradual move by the wider population across the boundary of liturgical restriction to operate within it.

> [Alternative Worship's focus on transcendence] challenges the modernist notion that we humans can renew the church through our own strategic thinking and technical expertise. And its stress on creative participation challenges the twin heresies of consumerism and individualism.
>
> Eddie Gibbs (CM, 181)

By contrast, radical hospitality is a defining feature of emerging churches, and this includes the liturgical domain. Liturgical hospitality is, in turn, indicative of ecclesiology and church identity. But, again, it is important to examine *why* the hospitality is being extended. If it is merely to give putative church members a sense of welcome in order to attract them into deeper involvement, then all we have is another example of the attractional model of worship-as-mission. But it can equally arise from an unbounded church identity, of which open liturgical hospitality is a natural corollary. This raises further questions. If the Eucharist is an open table, what is its meaning, and what does it mean to participate? If baptism does not initiate through death into life, what does it signify? If emerging liturgical practice does not recognise and foster differentiated levels of participation, what does it mean to participate in the church and to participate in Christ?[13]

> This question is crucial if we are to allow for a liturgical hospitality and follow through Pascal's suggestion that the sacraments have mission impact, because it is encounter, not argument, that is truly apologetic. This, I think, requires us, as Roberts recognises, to have a centered understanding of practice, not to offer sacraments as some form of reader response, but then also to recognise that God works beyond our intentions. This is a centered-set rather than an open-set approach: we make it clear what the sacrament means and then make it open to those who will receive it. But this also means there will need to be liturgical practice not just at the center but further out where others can share in an experience of God that is not so clearly focused on a centrality of the death and resurrection of Christ that many may not yet be ready to participate in. *Steve Hollinghurst*

> Perhaps we should be thinking of a "graduated liturgical missiology," at least in part. *Paul Roberts*

> I like your suggestion of hospitality. To that I would add that appreciation (as an organizing tool) can teach emergents how to move beyond being or making deviants, by instead "listening" with "openness" for the gift that the other brings to any group. *Troy Bronsink*

13. So 1 Cor. 10:16–17 ESV, "The cup of blessing that we bless, is it not a participation in the blood of Christ? The bread that we break, is it not a participation in the body of Christ? Because there is one bread, we who are many are one body, for we all partake of the one bread."

Ritual studies[14] show us how boundaries within liturgical practice are key to determining identity. So an important missiological question facing emerging communities is one of liturgical identity: how boundaries are established, fostered, and understood in the midst of a new commitment to contextual engagement. The issue of liturgical boundaries and hospitality indicates the stark difference between attractional models of church, which invite the post-Christendom world to cross back over the long-established liturgical boundary,[15] and emerging models, which cross the boundary themselves and seek to live beyond it, where everyone else is, albeit as deviants. Given all that has already been said, it would seem that, even if we embrace the need to be liminal in the landscape of post-Christendom, identity in Christ has to be preserved or reconstructed for there to be any sense of mission. To be truly "deviant," some boundaries will need to be retained, reevaluated, or even reconstituted.

I recognize the challenge of opening up our liturgical space, without throwing everything for grabs. Especially in a post-Christendom context there is a widespread feeling that "religion" must be accessible and available for everyone, even if one will never make use of it. Many post-Christendom Dutchmen consider the church as a hospital: it is a place where you hopefully will never come, but it should be available just in case. A hospital is a public service: it will never refuse people (at least not in a society like ours), because health care is a right. A church that does refuse people or that holds some "services" back from them will encounter misunderstanding or even outright anger (it denies people their rights). Or, take the restaurant metaphor I explore: a restaurant should not expect people to be loyal to it, but it should never refuse customers. So, pointing out that Holy Supper (for example) is not for everyone, is something that will not be understood. However, we do think that the Lord's Supper is not for everyone. We have therefore adopted a practice of "differentiated invitation": we never say "X and Y should not come to the table" (do not use the word "not"!). We say something like this: "There are different ways to be involved in the Supper. If you love Jesus and want to follow him, please take bread and wine. If you do not know what to believe, or if you need more time, please come forward and receive a blessing. If you want to participate while you remain sitting, you could silently pray the prayer in your bulletin." In our practice this works very well. We succeed to convey something of the meaning and seriousness of the Lord's Supper, but we do this in a late modern setting of "choice." In this case we also take seriously that some people do not want to be considered as (anonymous)

14. Particularly those associated with the foundational work of Arnold Van Gennep and Victor Turner. For an introduction, see V. Turner, *The Ritual Process: Structure and Anti-structure* (Chicago: Aldine, 1969), chap. 3.

15. Or, in some cases, drill some holes in it—hence the practice of liberal mainstream churches locally or temporarily abolishing eucharistic or baptismal discipline as a way of getting some to return.

Christians. I feel that this is an implicit danger of complete inclusivism: it does not respect the feelings/self-understanding of unbelievers who do not consider themselves as part of the group (regardless how much we do consider them as such). *Stefan Paas*

Stefan's point illustrates well how complex the relationships between inclusion and differentiation can become when there is still a residual institutional role for the church in society. *Paul Roberts*

Alternative worship provides a considerable range of examples of how emerging liturgical practice can situate itself as a missional and communal response to post-Christendom. If "worship-as-mission" approaches retain the assumption of nonbelief as deviance, alternative worship explores the contrasting alternative of the post-Christendom landscape: that belief is deviance. When emerging churches try to occupy the liminal space of faith in their liturgies, the paradoxes and tensions of the project crystallise. Questions of corporate and personal faith identity, modes of engaging public space, and their relationship to past Christian hegemony permeate the core of acts of emerging liturgy. In a sense, emerging worship (as exemplified by alternative worship) is doubly liminal: with respect to the historic church it has mostly stepped out of the boundaries of liturgical and sacramental conformity; with respect to the societies of post-Christendom, its stubborn conformity to Christian faith is a new deviance, which is paradoxically hospitable rather than sectarian. Whether this double liminality is sustainable, only time will tell.

The "deviance of hospitality" is another great turn of phrase. In my experience the "crystallization of paradox," when faith reenters the deviant space, is spot on. But I'm not sure that the crystallization has to be a permanent thing, or has to compete with the construct of historical precedence. I wonder, here, if the various integrative spiritualities like Quakerism, Eastern Orthodoxy, Celtic Christianity, or Pentecostalism aren't already examples of ways past the need for justified liturgical bounds? Perhaps emergent alt worship is more akin to these than the invisible church arguments of reformed and liturgical renewal communities. *Troy Bronsink*

15

Formation in the Post-Christendom Era

Exilic Practices and Missional Identity

Dwight J. Friesen

The post-Christendom[1] shift can, if we are wise, usher the church into a season of refocusing our energies on the primary mission that Jesus gave his followers: to form disciples of Christ. It is toward that end that this chapter will focus on what I believe is the most pressing issue for the Western church, missional[2] Christian identity formation.[3] First I will offer a brief account of how Christian

---

1. I am using "post-Christendom" to refer to a cultural context in which the role and the authority of the church in the public sphere are increasingly being obsolesced. Or as Stuart Murray has written, "Post-Christendom is the culture that emerges as the Christian faith loses coherence within a society that has been definitively shaped by the Christian story and as the institutions that have been developed to express Christian convictions decline in influence." Stuart Murray, *Post-Christendom: Church and Mission in a Strange New World* (Bletchley, UK: Paternoster, 2004), 19.

2. I use "missional" to describe life lived in the sent Christian community, embodying the kingdom of God through action, proclamation, community, disciple making, service, creation care, and justice. Further, "missional" communicates the inseparable linking of the being of the church with the doing of the church. The church is missional because God shows Godself to be missional. Missional is simultaneously a hermeneutic and a way of being present, indigenously inviting fullness of life in Christ.

3. "Formation is about learning to live the alternative reality of the kingdom of God within the present world order faithfully." James Davison Hunter, *To Change the World: The Irony,*

identity formation evolved within the Christendom context, which over time reduced holistic life formation to "spiritual formation." Second, as a means of sparking our formational imaginations, I will highlight five formative practices local churches can intentionally engage to form missional identity.

Culture

Christendom Formation: From Life in the Way of Jesus to Spiritual Formation

Just a few years following the Edict of Milan (AD 313),[4] which declared religious tolerance in Rome, Christianity became the state religion (AD 380) and all other religious practice within the empire was banned. Christendom was in its infancy. In relatively short order the hierarchical church[5] began to shape and dominate nearly all aspects of public life in the empire.

Christendom provided the church with significant influence in shaping public institutions. The Christendom era was a lot like an American football game, church versus the world. In this "winner takes all" football game, the institutional church played both quarterback and middle linebacker, meaning that the hierarchical church called both the offensive and defensive plays.

Recognizing the holistic nature of Christian identity formation, the hierarchical church enlisted other players onto its team. Other players included governments, legal systems, penal systems, health care, education, military, the arts, and other social or public institutions that shaped identity. Having all these team players on board with the hierarchical church freed the local church to locate its primary formative activity on cultic practices, Word and Sacrament. The hierarchical church trusted that other partnering institutions would play their role in the formational mission of the church, and the hierarchical

---

Tragedy, and Possibility of Christianity in the Late Modern World (Oxford, UK: Oxford University Press, 2010), 236.

4. The Edict of Milan declared Rome to be religiously tolerant, thus Christianity was no longer outlawed, but it wasn't until the Edict of Thessalonica, also known as *Cunctos populous*, that Christianity was made the official religion of Rome. Nonetheless, I follow John H. Yoder in recognizing what he termed as the "Constantinian shift." Yoder writes, "The most impressive transitory change underlying our common experience, one that some thought was a permanent lunge forward in salvation history, was the so-called Constantinian shift." John H. Yoder, "Is There Such a Thing as Being Ready for Another Millennium?," in *The Future of Theology: Essays in Honor of Jürgen Moltmann*, ed. Miroslav Volf, Carmen Krieg, and Thomas Kucharz (Grand Rapids: Eerdmans, 1996), 65.

5. I am using the term "hierarchical church" to refer to the leadership of bishops and the papacy who served as architects of Christendom.

church had the power to force compliance in cases of rogue players. So while the popes, cardinals, and bishops designed and called the plays, the local churches pastorally cared for parishioners and the spiritual life of the people. The hierarchical church called the shots and the other institutions more or less fell in line, ran the routes, blocked advances from the opponents, and arguably scored a few touchdowns. And for quite a few centuries this game plan seemed to work.

> Under Christendom, the church was granted a privileged position as an agent of the state. It provided the moral and ideological bulwark of society.
>
> Eddie Gibbs (CM, 25)

It must be stated that the "church versus the world" premise that seemed to drive Christendom was flawed from the beginning. I say this with deep respect for the church leaders who were for the most part seeking to faithfully serve God, the church, and the world; nonetheless, God's calling to the church is not to conquer and rule the world but to live as a testament to God and God's reign. The people of God are called to demonstrate in action, community, service, humility, and proclamation that God is; that communion with God, one another, and creation is available in and through Jesus Christ; and that life lived in the Way of Jesus is the best of all possible lives. Thus the Christendom game plan of the church versus the world set up a false opposition, with winners and losers. Christ is the conquering king, yet Christ "conquers" as a servant who lives, proclaims, and acts out of love, as seen in his life and ultimately in the cross: this was and is to be the church's game plan.

In part this flaw in the Christendom game plan set the scene for growing strife within "team church." The question of who had the proper authority to call plays was at least part of what fueled the Great Schism between the Eastern and Western churches. Later as the Renaissance, Protestant Reformation, and Enlightenment swept through the West and the players (public institutions) on the church team came into their own, they increasingly looked within themselves and not to the hierarchical church for the authority to call their plays. Yet the quarterback didn't seem to notice the shift.

Thus the church was left holding the formation ball and didn't seem to notice that those to whom we were handing off were no longer committed to forming Christlike identity in the individuals and communities within their care. This is the crisis of formation for church within post-Christendom cultures. The church within post-Christendom contexts has just begun to notice that it has few, if any, secular teammates committed to forming Christian missional identity, which means that the church must reimagine how to fulfill its God-given mission to form holistic Christian identity without the aid of public institutions.

St. Tom's Church in Sheffield, England, discovered that forming holistic Christian identity was something even the Vineyard movement, which had a profound effect on St. Tom's, had moved away from embracing. While the Vineyard movement gave St. Tom's an emphasis on small groups, it was St. Tom's innovation that came out of their loss of their mega-venue that made them eventually create over forty more self-reliant, contextualized, and multifaceted "clusters" (each composed of three to seven small groups). These clusters were viewed by St. Tom's leadership as "midsized missional communities," for it was in these venues, reminiscent of an extended family, that most conversion growth took place. *Bob Whitesel*

One of the great ironies is that Christian identity formation within Christendom was far more holistic than it is today, in the sense that nearly all aspects of life were being intentionally and theologically constructed so as to weave a tapestry of Christian belief in the hearts, minds, and actions of individual persons within the Christendom nations. Do not hear me suggesting that we must return to Christendom; we must not (even if we could), for life in the way of Christ cannot and should not be legislated. But living in the Way of Jesus is to be a holistic way of being in which the persons and the community of faith live into and out of the gospel story, as active participants with God in God's great story of redemption. This is why I believe that missional identity formation is the greatest challenge facing churches within post-Christendom contexts. Today the weight of Christian missional formation rests squarely on the shoulders of the local church.

Practices

How can today's church holistically form Christlike identity in individuals and faith communities in cultures increasingly marked by a post-Christendom sensibility? Since formation requires narration and practice over time, it seems wise to address these kinds of questions by briefly considering a few of the practices local churches are engaging in light of the post-Christendom formation challenge.[6]

Welcoming the Stranger: Hospitality and Serving within God's Created Order

To be in a position of power is to demand service; to be stripped of power is to be made a servant. This axiom may capture one of the unexpected gifts

6. I commend James K. A. Smith, *Desiring the Kingdom: Worship, Worldview, and Cultural Formation* (Grand Rapids: Baker Academic, 2009), as a clear and useful text demonstrating the centrality of formation.

the post-Christendom shift seems to be offering the church: an opportunity to return to our servant role. Of course we may reject this gift, choosing instead to fight for power in a struggle to maintain the comfort of church as we have known it. It is love that compels Christian hospitality and service: love of God manifesting itself in love of neighbor, love of God displayed in stewardship of God's created order, love of God made evident in the welcome of the stranger, and love of God made real by serving the least.

Harvey Drake is the pastor of Emerald City Bible Fellowship[7] in one of the most diverse neighborhoods in Washington state. A few years back Harvey learned that the people living in the church's zip code also had the highest rate of obesity in the state. Knowing his neighborhood well, he could think of many fried-foods establishments but he couldn't remember seeing a single fitness center. Looking into the matter further he discovered that there was a ten-mile radius around his church without a health club, and the nearest one was priced out of reach for most people in his community. He and the church took this matter to prayer and planning. As a practical way of serving their community they eventually built and opened a fitness center right next to the church. They set up the fitness center under the direction of a community-based nonprofit that the church helped

> As Christendom gave
> way to a secular and
> religiously pluralistic
> society, so the ministry
> sphere of priests and
> pastors began to shrink.
>
> Eddie Gibbs (CM, 25)

create so that the church wasn't in charge of the fitness center. They even created a sliding-scale fee structure so that anyone who wants to get healthy isn't excluded by the cost. And to make it personal, Harvey and the director of the nonprofit began to work out together, and last I heard they have lost more than a hundred pounds between the two of them.

Harvey and the folks at Emerald City Bible Fellowship believe that in the kingdom of God, people who want to improve their health will have afford-able access to fitness centers—a simple yet profound example of followers of Christ forming life through humble hosting and serving, and a creative form of welcoming the stranger.

Word and Sacrament: Reorienting Identity in a World of Hybridity

Today most of us know what it is to be a hybrid. When asked who I am, I often describe myself as a Canadian from the prairies living in America's

---

7. To learn more about Emerald City Bible Fellowship, visit http://www.emeraldcitybible .org, or to learn more about their nonprofit that manages the fitness center and does so much more, visit http://www.urbanimpactseattle.org.

Pacific Northwest; I'm an emerging, Anabaptist evangelical; I am a pastor, academic, entrepreneur; in short, I'm something of a hybrid. In a world marked by increased hybrid identities we would be wise to begin by emphasizing the formational importance of opening Scripture, the rite of baptism, and gathering around the Lord's table. I'll say just a little about each of these.

As "people of the book," most Christian traditions have long histories of reading, studying, teaching, memorizing, and preaching from Scripture. Our varied historic practices will be no less important in our emerging post-Christendom context. Yet our new context will invite us to become even more skilled at telling the whole story of God such that our churches see themselves as the continuation of God's capacious story. This is more than learning Bible stories or being able to recite creeds, as important as these things may be; we will need to help our churches live the narrative of the gospel. This means that in the post-Christendom context it will no longer be sufficient to apply Scripture; we must be shaped by God's narrative. Think of the difference between a girdle and being physically fit. A girdle gives the appearance of fitness while forming people around the value that how one looks is what matters. Fitness, on the contrary, forms a person by holistically altering patterns of life from eating to rest, from exercise to use of time. The life, death, resurrection, and ascension of Christ must become the lens through which we see all of life.

> In Christendom, society itself was shaped by the Christian narrative. Where that narrative has become unrecognisable or laden with extra baggage that is somehow counter-gospel, church communities need to be involved in an act of "re-narration" as described. One of the challenges of working with other faith communities is that their perception of European and North American cultures is that they are still very Christian in character. It means, I think, that there is a more nuanced task for the church to own and name the positive effect of the Christian inheritance on a culture and to be appropriately humble about the errors of that history. Richard Sudworth

Baptism is the church's initiation rite by which the community acknowledges God's adoption of an individual into God's family. The post-Christendom era underscores the importance of the initiation ritual in the process of missional identity formation. Baptism is the new identity event where a person identifies with the life, death, and resurrection of Christ, and this is witnessed by the local community. It is essential for us to search our respective traditions with respect to baptism and creatively wonder how we might strengthen our practices, so that new Jesus followers and the community are reminded of who they truly are in Christ.

> Though an Anglican church, St. Tom's in Sheffield, England, embraced Wesley-inspired initiation rituals by requiring small group participation by all members (similar to Wesley's requirement of attendance at class and/or band meetings). The rationale at St. Tom's was not historical fidelity, but what they observed as the small group's effectiveness for holistic formation. *Bob Whitesel*

I won't say much about Holy Communion, as most Christian traditions engage this practice in some way, except to say that it provides the local church with a tangible practice that puts in action the narrative of Christ's life, death, resurrection, and ascension. As such the table affords the church a regular way for our communities to enact the life of Christ as they are nourished, body and soul, within the context of the family of God.

> The role of worship as it breaks through into a post-Christendom context seems to suggest two approaches: one is "worship as expression" (whereby what we say and do in worship expresses what we want to say about ourselves or about God) and "worship as formative practice" (whereby worship is seen as a transcendent encounter with God mediated through a practical pedagogy of Word and Sacrament). Many church approaches take the first of these to an extreme whereby they become little more than a narcissistic show for postmodern consumers. I therefore welcome Friesen's focus here on the formative practice of Word and Sacrament as righting the balance which, as his chapter goes on to show, leads further into a holistic missional way of being. *Paul Roberts*

> At the core of hybridity rests the issue of identity: identity crisis, identity exchange, identity politics, and so on. Thus the need for powerful and unifying narratives that ground us in the reality of Jesus Christ—such as the Lord's baptism and Holy Communion—as Friesen points out, is of huge significance in our time. *Oscar García-Johnson*

Contextualizing Rites and Rituals through the Creative Arts

The church has historically understood that moments of transition are vital marking points toward the formation of Christian identity. We mark births, deaths, and marriages; depending on transitions we mark conversations, confirmations, and ordinations. We know that seasons of transition are the times when people are most likely to drift away from the church.

Not long ago I took a group of divinity students on a field trip to a church in the heart of Seattle's trafficked and prostituted population. Pastor Ben Katt told us about the way his church developed a deeply contextual ritual rooted in historic Christian practice and contextualized for its neighborhood as an art installation. During Holy Week their church commemorates the Passion of the Christ by inviting the community to take a prayerful pilgrimage through the Stations of the Cross. Rather than engage the stations in a church sanctuary, they create stations on the street, using mostly found art objects that are already present on the street, crafting a liturgy that people engage as they walk through their neighborhood. It is streetwalking redeemed in a powerful way by a church seeking to embody the way of Christ in their neighborhood. The creation of artifacts, including both art and liturgy, forms persons and culture. Identity formation in post-Christendom contexts is an invitation for the people of God to create art that forms our collective imagination around the reign of God. What if every church in every neighborhood sought to contextualize rites and rituals for their respective places, such that the good news really seemed like good news?

> With a band of songwriters, we've been asking just this question. "How does this song shape our imaginations as practitioners of justice and mercy in our particular part of the city?" *Troy Bronsink*

Rooting and Linking: A Christian Response to Individualism, Consumerism, and Environmental Crises

Paul pastors a church in Tacoma that has what may sound like an odd membership requirement. To be a member, one must live and work within a fifteen-block area of the city. They do this because they believe that God is calling them to take full responsibility for the people in their neighborhood, the land they occupy, and the local businesses that are operated there, and to actively participate in civic life so as to make their neighborhood a more humanizing and livable place. This kind of commitment may sound extreme to some but it takes creation care very seriously and invites people to consider their use of fossil fuels, built environment, neighborliness, and location as formational.

When I first met Paul, he guided me through his parish, sharing some of the stories of his city and neighborhood. As we walked we encountered people on the street and in shops, and it became abundantly clear that he was deeply rooted in that place. Although the church membership requirement places a limit on how large his church can grow, they have also found that living, working, and worshiping in close proximity strengthens Christians' missional identity formation because the people who are part of the church see one another and are seen by one another in multiple settings every week, rather than driving a distance and only seeing one another one or two hours a week. They are finding that proximity is a crucible for formation. With increased proximity, conflicts increase, which in turn invites discipleship. Repentance and forgiveness are moved out of theology books and lived into as a functional necessity. What they've also found is that being rooted seems to invite linking beyond themselves. The practice of embodying the gospel in local settings and linking to others will become even more important in the post-Christendom era.

While they seek to be rooted in place so as to be formed by the limitations of human particularity, they also seek to link with other groups beyond themselves. Linking is a vital formative practice that challenges the impulse toward both individualism and consumerism. Linking confronts the lie of individualism that can cause a person or a church to deny their needfulness; furthermore, linking is an assault to consumerism's commodification of the other for one's own ends. For them the practice of linking means participation with diverse others seeking the common good. They link with city leaders to bring in speakers who help the city think about public life, with local farmers through managing the local farmers' market, and with other communities of faith through what has become known as the Parish Collective.[8] Together rooting and linking invite a kind of reciprocity for the common good of their neighborhood.

> At the ground level, ministry needs to be based on a block-by-block approach. A number of North American churches have initiated an "adopt-a-block strategy," in which they pray for individuals, develop relationships, and help them in practical ways, such as painting a fence, shoveling snow, babysitting their children, and taking food over when sickness strikes. Such a strategy must be an expression of genuine love for the other person, with no strings attached.
>
> Eddie Gibbs (CM, 110)

Creating a New Missional Spirituality and Prophetic Art

In order for our local churches to be forming missional identity in an increasingly exilic era, we will need to create new worship and prophetic art. While many of our hymns are useful theological teaching tools, and many of our choruses reflect a personal relationship with God, there are surprisingly few (though more are being created every day) worship resources for forming missional identity. We would be wise to reframe our corporate worship such that we move beyond passive cultic practices that often fail to connect our worship of God with our everyday lives.

8. To learn more about the Parish Collective, visit http://www.parishcollective.com.

The dispersed mode of St. Tom's Church, where they scattered into seven different celebrations across Sheffield, England, created indigenous worship expressions such as the techno-pop music of the Club Scene celebration, the U2-inspired music of the young professionals' celebration, and the neo-Pentecostal worship in the mother church. Because these multiple venues required more musicians and additional songs, seven indigenized music scenes emerged with a much more introspective and heartfelt yearning than its generic record-label counterparts. *Bob Whitesel*

Recently I was visiting a multilanguage church in Burlington, Washington, called Tierra Nueva.[9] The church began almost twenty years ago with a focus on serving the Spanish-speaking migrant population in that region; it has since expanded into the local prisons where they host seminary classes, serve people in gangs, support families of inmates, and so much more. One of the first things I noticed as I entered their gathering was the racial and ethnic diversity of the people. The service was effortlessly conducted in Spanish and English with translation into two other languages in different corners of the room. But what captured my imagination was the creative and formative missional emphasis of the music, readings, prayers, Communion, and sermon. Let me give you one example of this church's missional adaption of the beautiful chorus by Paul Baloche, "Open the Eyes of My Heart."[10] Excerpt from the original version:

> Open the eyes of my heart, Lord,
> I want to see You.
> To see you high and lifted up,
> Shining in the light of your glory,
> Lord, pour out your power and love,
> As we sing Holy, Holy, Holy.
> Higher, Higher, Higher,
> I want to see you.

Missional adaption by Tierra Nueva:

> Open the eyes of our hearts, Lord,
> We want to see you.
> To see you lying in the street,
> Lonely or imprisoned or hungry,
> Jesus as you wash our feet,

9. To learn more about Tierra Nueva, visit http://www.tierra-nueva.org.
10. Paul Baloche, "Open the Eyes of My Heart" (Integrity's Hosanna!, 1997).

Invite us lower, lower, lower,
Lower, lower, lower,
We want to see you.

Some very intentional missional changes by Tierra Nueva transformed this song. For starters, it shifts the pronoun from first person singular to first person plural, better positioning the individual persons within the context of the people of God. Even more profound, the adapted version reflects the scandal of God's incarnation in that Christ enters humanity not as the powerful but as the weak. Going still further, the adaption of the song reinforces to the community that serving the least is serving Christ, and in fact that Christ is present in our encounter with the other. This missionally forms the expectation that loving and serving Christ looks like being present to those we meet in the everyday stuff of life. It is true that God is holy, yet if worship celebrates only God's transcendence without also speaking to God's immanence, our worship can form the church in ways that separate us from the world we are called to serve. This kind of creative work reframes missional identity formation.

These five practices signal the kinds of formative reimagining our local churches must engage if we are to faithfully form Christian missional identity with diminishing aid of public institutions. So while "team church" may have lost its players, our mission to form disciples who faithfully embody life in the Way of Jesus remains. Christ is the *telos* of formation for both the individual person and the community. It is Christ who gives form to his body, the church. The post-Christendom shift is an invitation for our churches to recover our missional formation calling. We are a sent people—sent not to conquer in a winner-takes-all, us-versus-them way, but sent in a way that reflects the "sentness" of Jesus: present, kingdom proclaiming, disciple making, serving, healing, striving for abundant life for all.

16

Toward a Holistic Process of Transformational Mission

Tobias Faix

What reconciliation and redemption, what regeneration and Holy Spirit, what love of enemies, cross and resurrection, what life in Christ and discipleship means . . . is all so difficult and so remote that we hardly dare to speak of it. In the words and actions that have been handed down we anticipate something completely new and groundbreaking without being able to comprehend and articulate it.

Dietrich Bonhoeffer[1]

Practices

The Biblical Commission: Holistic Salvation

Holistic transformation begins with the idea that God created the entire person in his image (*imago Dei*), as a spirit-soul-body unit (Gen. 1:27). The whole person (after the fall) needs redemption and healing. Even if our body

1. Dietrich Bonhoeffer, *Widerstand und Ergebung: Briefe und Aufzeichnungen aus der Haft* [Letters and papers from prison], ed. Eberhard Bethge (Munich: Kaiser Verlag, 1956), 206.

never becomes completely healed here on earth, the longing, nevertheless, is there in the human being as well as in the whole of creation (Rom. 8:19). The human being wants and needs healthy relationships, but even our relationships need redemption. I want to briefly explain holistic transformation using two central terms from the Old and New Testaments.

The Hebrew term *shalom* is not only a devout greeting with which someone wishes his or her contemporary "peace,"[2] but also, in the Old Testament, shalom comprises all human relations: human–God (love of God), human–self (love of self), human–human (love of neighbor), human–nature (love of creation). Through sin these relations were violated, and yet the longing of the human and of nature to thrive in these relationships, to develop them until the final redemption comes and everything is made "perfect" again, remains (Rom. 8:18–25).

The human longing for redemption becomes clear in the New Testament term "salvation." Salvation (*soteria*) encompasses the same categories as those of the Old Testament term *shalom*: human–God (John 3:16), human–self (Matt. 22:36–40), human–human (Matt. 5:38–48), and human–nature (John 3:17; 12:47). This holistic understanding of *shalom* and salvation demonstrates God's relation to the whole of creation. We cannot and should not neglect any one of these relationships. Transformation speaks into these different relationships and promotes a holistic, mission-oriented process. Holistic transformation therefore has to do with offering practical help such as taking care of socially disadvantaged people (Deut. 10:18; Acts 6:1–6) or taking on a politically unjust system (Isa. 1:23; Jer. 5:28; Mal. 3:5; Mark 12:40). As Christians we cannot withdraw from this commission.[3] The Bible does not distinguish between individual and social processes of change, since both belong together. Historically, this has not always been the case, especially within the evangelical theological tradition.

> Our commitment to a holistic gospel is not merely one that includes the healing of our relations to God but is enabled by God: a holistic manifestation of all that arises from God's rule (much as the original Jubilee discharge of debts in Lev. 25 occurred when the atonement of the people was declared). That is, the kingdom of God shows us what the arena of Jesus's lordship looks like. The ever-present challenge of holistic mission is how we participate in

---

2. The term *shalom* has here been chosen as an example; other central terms such as the exodus (Christopher Wright, *The Mission of God: Unlocking the Bible's Grand Narrative* [Downers Grove, IL: InterVarsity, 2006], 265), the Jubilee (John Howard Yoder, *Die Politik Jesu* [The politics of Jesus] [Maxdorf: Agape Verlag, 1981], 67), or the prophets could have been used.

3. Jürgen Moltmann, *Theologie der Hoffnung* [Theology of hope] (Munich: Kaiser Verlag, 1984), 123.

> such a holistic gospel while naming the source of the good news we offer in ways that are not colonizing or abrasive. *Richard Sudworth*

The Nature of Transformation

The versatile descriptions of the term "transformation" in the different disciplines (sociology, political science, social work) show that the topic not only gained importance in the past years but also has been accepted by the different disciplines regarding its subject matter.[4] Transformation is used to describe the changes not only of whole communities, but also of parts of towns, villages, districts, and even big cities. The changes take place according to the values of the kingdom of God and the "better righteousness" of Jesus (Matt. 5:17–20). There is no area of life that would not be a priority for transformation, because the kingship of Jesus applies in the same way to all economic, religious, personal, and political aspects of life. Hence, a contextually appropriate interpretation of the gospel is an evangelistic testimony regarding all areas of life. When we enter into this holistic process of transformation we honor God and worship him, for his longing for restoration is a central motif throughout the whole Bible, and it gives us hope and strength today to live the "better righteousness" in the midst of this world.

> Christian transformation, on all levels, is a painful and hopeful process of death and resurrection. In our eagerness to create open and welcoming communities, we must remember to tell people that this is what church is about, that this is how God works. *Andreas Østerlund Nielsen*

The missiologist Vinay Samuel illustrates this well when he writes:

> Transformation is to enable God's vision of society to be actualized in all relationships, social, economic, and spiritual, so that God's will may be reflected in human society and his love be experienced by all communities, especially the poor.[5]

From Samuel a few distinguishing features of the process of holistic transformation can be deduced. Transformation has an individual character that focuses on relational change, as well as a structural/collective character that

---

4. Urs Fuhrer and Aristi Born, "Wie steht es um die persönliche Identität Ostdeutscher acht Jahre nach dem Fall der Mauer?" [What about the personal identity of East Germans eight years after the fall of the Berlin Wall?], in *Postsozialistische Transformationsforschung*, ed. R. Kollmorgen and H. Schrader (Münster: Ergon, 2003), 263–84.

5. Vinay Samuel and Chris Sugden, eds., *Mission as Transformation: A Theology of the Whole Gospel* (Oxford: Regnum, 2003), 227–28.

moves to change social structures. Both influence the other directly, and the social structures as such are not sinful, but the people who, through their immoral actions, build these structures that facilitate this immorality and consequently let it spread definitely are sinful. The sociologist Elias points out that there is no "individual," or any "individualistic action," but that every human being and every action is woven into a collective and is therefore part of the society.[6] Social injustice can be found in both kinds of dependencies, the personal and the social.

> In living as community, all our actions or inactions, what we say or do not say, what we think or do not think, what we care or do not care about will inevitably affect the culture around us. *Eileen Suico*

Transformation is liberation and the experience of new power. The liberating power of the gospel applies to all, poor or rich; however, in many places in the Bible God sides particularly with the poor and the disadvantaged. Whenever the gospel is lived and preached concerning the social environment, communion and reconciliation take center stage.[7] Neither evangelization nor social action exist on their own. Both are inseparably linked. Mission as transformation always means mission in context. A critically contextual theology always merges revelation and context in an interdependent tension.[8]

> Our reading of the text enhances our practices, and our practices enhance our reading of the text, and so it goes on. It is this that forms us, and it is also this that shapes our contexts. *Eileen Suico*

> The Church of England's holistic approach can be summarized in three words: change through mission. *Markus Weimer*

Transformation starts in the local church, and theory and practice join together in processes of transformation. The Spirit of God links together faith, hope, and love as they can be experienced in the church through mutual contact. Mission as transformation also means that the church is a community of change and of hope for its immediate surroundings. Christians must be involved in different places in their social setting to be able to advocate a change leading to a fulfilled life and a change according to the principles of love.

6. Norbert Elias, *Was ist Soziologie?* [What is sociology?] (Munich: Juventa, 2009).
7. Miroslav Volf, *Exclusion and Embrace: A Theological Exploration of Identity, Otherness, and Reconciliation* (Nashville: Abingdon, 1996).
8. Paul Hiebert, *Transforming Worldviews: An Anthropological Understanding of How People Change* (Grand Rapids: Baker Academic, 2008).

> What would happen if transformation started at both ends? On the grassroots level as
> well as on the senior leadership level of the church? *Markus Weimer*

This change can only become possible if all the church's members stand together and if it is supported by an intense communion (*koinonia*). Christian life as lived transformation of society implies simultaneously to live one's faith and the gospel more intensely and consistently. This happens in everyday life, within the church and through overlapping networking of Christian organizations and associations (for instance, the Micah network). Only in such a way will we meet the requirements of the challenges that are coming toward us.

Culture

Transformation and Creation: The Divine Commission for the Preservation of the Environment

Within ourselves we notice that it is much easier for human beings to subdue the earth than to be able to control themselves. This becomes more than apparent regarding our consumer behavior. Closely related to this pattern of behavior is our understanding of the creation commission in Genesis 1:26 and 28, or as the psalmist says: "You made them rulers over the works of your hands; you put everything under their feet" (Ps. 8:6). An ethic that is based on the Creator and the world as creation cannot avoid the realization that the human being as "crown of creation" is at the same time its greatest risk factor. As already mentioned, due to being made in the image of God, humans need to bring all their actions and deeds in alignment with the example set by God; accordingly, the fulfillment of the imperative to subdue the earth is subject to the consistent divine mandate to enable existence and life. The human being, as part of creation, is consistently dependent on the same and has the task to cultivate and preserve it (Gen. 2:15; Matt. 20:25–28).

> Transformation, which includes both spiritual renewal and organizational restructuring, need not, in most circumstances, be conceived in revolutionary terms. Transformation implies changing of vital elements of the organization's value system which have been forged during its long history.
>
> Eddie Gibbs (INO, 105)

Concerning the ecological commission, there is an eschatological tension between actively pursuing it here on earth, on the one hand, and yet knowing, on the other hand, that the whole cosmos is yearning for redemption and that this will indeed find its fulfillment in the second coming of Jesus. Until then it is a privilege to support the preservation of the environment and to oppose destructive structures such as deforestation of rain forests, the depleting of fish stock in the seas, or contamination through nuclear waste.

> In our congregation we try to raise levels of consciousness regarding environmental and social issues. This fits very well with Amsterdam culture. However, I also meet with much uncertainty in this respect. Many young urbanites I meet in Amsterdam do have an ecological awareness, but they lack the certainty that radiates from Tobias's article. How do we know exactly how the world hangs together and how my consumption relates to other people's poverty? Here I see the problem of living in an information society. Day after day we are overloaded with a wealth of (often contradictory) information. I meet people who are confused: the "left" will tell them that we are consuming the wealth of the South, whereas the "right" will tell them that our consumption brings wealth to the South. Sometimes it seems as if today's wisdom is tomorrow's stupidity. So, to motivate people for an eco-friendly lifestyle, how do you approach the problem of complexity and uncertainty? We may "unmask" social reality as a mechanism of self-defense, and there is truth in this. But I believe that this is not the only thing here. There is honest confusion, and confused people are usually not prepared to make radical lifestyle choices. Instead they opt for small adaptations, at best. As a pastor I am looking for an honest way to be a prophet: giving people a clear vision in a world saturated with information. How to approach this? Stefan Paas

Transformation and Creation II: The Social Power of Transformation (God Enters the Neighborhood)

Jesus devoted himself to the outcasts and the socially ostracized; he not only healed them physically, but also reintegrated them into society. Healing was a precondition to function in life again and to be integrated into the people of God and into salvation. This holistic form of salvation demonstrates the new righteousness, which constitutes the kingdom of God, then and now, and distinguishes it from a secular social background.

With reintegration into social life the restoration of the person begins. Hence, it is not surprising that Jesus, for instance, commands the man healed of leprosy: "Go, show yourself to the priest and offer the gift Moses commanded, as a testimony to them" (Matt. 8:4). In Judaism the priest was responsible for reintegration into society. Only if he consented was the person deemed healed and allowed to leave the leper colony outside the city and enter into the city.

> The church's message of reconciliation is directed toward itself with a view to bringing about a transformation which is evident both in the church's internal life and in its engagement with the world.
>
> Eddie Gibbs (INO, 107)

The Protestant theologian Ulrich Luz correctly points out that the social help Jesus offered was rarely taken seriously.

Many churches have created their own middle-class culture in which the "ostracized and sick" of our society can hardly find any space. Of course, everyone is allowed to come, but between a heartfelt reception and integration on the one hand, and a toleration on the other hand, lies the "heart of God," which beats exactly for people such as these. We do, indeed, pray in the Lord's prayer, "your kingdom come . . . on earth as it is in heaven," but we often focus on heaven and forget that the kingdom of God starts here on earth, starts now, with me. We often define too quickly what a "normal Christian" is and what is spiritually good and right.

> Jesus's salvation has been viewed for its postmortem implications. However, as we start to experience wholeness, Jesus's salvation is not divided or separate, which makes the question "is it for the dead or the living" irrelevant because it is bigger than life or death.
>
> All of Jesus's ways save. In death, his resurrection comforts us. In living, his ways at a party, at a table, on the streets, in the garden, or with friends save us from ways that steal, kill, and destroy. His death on the cross shows us that this is what cultures will continue to do to people. His death on the cross says, "Repent and live the kingdom of love that is now at hand." *Eileen Suico*

Granted, our society deeply affects our focus on health and fitness, to the point of obsession. The "health cult" influenced by the West sees healing as individual power, but healing as holistic encounter is understood by Jesus as a sign of faith of the coming kingdom of God revealing itself in different areas such as physical, spiritual, and social. Healing, for Jesus, is always also a sign of the restoration of different types of relationships: God, neighbor, and self. One of our problems is the fear that we might miss out in our own church, that we might not receive enough spiritual nourishment, enough attention, that we might lose the place of tranquility and strength for our own life. This concern is justified. It is also one-sided and shows an unhealthy view of the kingdom of God.

Transformation Creates an Opportunity for Hybridity: Breaking the White Middle-Class Exclusive Church

Many churches in Germany retreated to the realm of the middle class in society and settled into its social background, remaining among their own peers. Consequently, the main focus of middle-class churches turned inward, toward worship, counseling, mentoring, and small groups. In and of themselves these are good things, but they entail the danger that church becomes one-sided. The outward dynamic gets short shrift as churches in villages and cities cease to play a social or cultural role. To the contrary, many free churches have ensconced themselves outside the cities in inexpensive industrial parks where socially weak people, children, and elderly people are unable to attend. Hence, the majority of churches rarely come into contact with fringe groups, minorities, and the lower class.

During the time of a mounting recession, dwindling middle class, and growing poverty, completely new, practical questions need to be asked of the church. Suddenly these problems are forcing themselves onto the church, and theological questions are being asked: Do we have a white middle-class gospel? Have we been deeply shaped by the modern culture of the last thirty years? What does the Bible say to poverty? to politics? to ethical questions that until now seem to have had an obvious answer (children, homosexuals, foreigners, people with disabilities)? These questions will arise on a massive scale and will pull us out of our "church comfort zone." The mistaken understanding of pluralism (everything is on a par with everything else and therefore we can simply remain as we are, while putting on a facade) bounces back to us like a boomerang and reinforces the questions that face Christians, bringing great uncertainty.

At the same time, many have the feeling that they will lose their spiritual foundation. This feeling is not entirely wrong since every social change also entails a theological change whose implementation has painful side effects. Here are two examples of forced theological change from the Bible: (1) the Babylonian exile and captivity caused the people to rethink their understandings of God (Jer. 29); and (2) the contextualization of faith into a Greek context challenged the first Christians, shaped by Judaism, to rethink their understanding of God as well (1 Cor. 8; 10; Acts 17). Hence, it is not enough to appear postmodern in our changed church practices; instead, we need our transformation to be thoroughly theological and thereby to create a deeper spiritual foundation for ourselves.

> Perhaps the best way to a new theology, to the new and necessary subject matter, is a new way of life. As we embody new praxis in small neighborhood-based communities and in the messy realities of day-to-day life, a compelling theology that speaks to the real needs of that community will naturally take shape. Holistic transformation must be lived into. *Kelly Bean*

Transformation and Dialogue in a Pluralistic World

Pluralism has become a catchphrase suggesting that somehow everything can coexist together. This opens up a multitude of opportunities, especially in the market of religious possibilities. In a pluralistic context a new facade is not enough, however. Truly viable religious options are matters of substance, but our Christian "substance" tends to be framed within a modern theology that is unable to enter into dialogue with other traditions because it is based on an outdated idea of truth. In addition, people can become insecure due to the many possible beliefs they can choose from, and they congregate at the edges. This is valid for the "left fringe" that wants to change the world in an idealistic manner and is thereby made more radical again, as well as for the "right fringe" that, in a time that has become insecure, desperately clings to the "old truth" and leans toward fundamentalism.

Even in the midst of a society that lives in a pluralistic way, the fringes harden, which surprises Christians even more, since this appears to contradict our understandings of postmodernity and pluralism. This becomes apparent when looking at the subject matter of "mission." It is true that the term "missional" has gained acceptance in recent years, but it is difficult to discern what this means for a life consisting of family, job, and church. One attempts to increase the value of the "action" in contrast to the "word" and to overcome the barriers between "church and world"; but when direct inquiries are made one falls far too easily back on the "old apologetics." Another example of resorting to older, Christendom strategies of mission is interreligious dialogue. Other religions are often seen by many Christians to provoke anxiety and are therefore declared to be an "enemy" (e.g., Islam). Having defined the subject matter in this way a dialogue is hardly possible. In contrast, a dialogue can succeed only on the basis of respect and esteem for the other and within a democratic context. We do have the latter in Germany; however, the former is scarce, although dialogue and mission are not at all mutually exclusive—as David Bosch proved in an impressive way twenty years ago.[9] Here the opportunity arises to communicate and convey the good news in a manner that reaches people in a way that they can understand. Bishop Klaus Hemmerle got to the heart of the new culture of dialogue when he said, "Let me learn you, your thinking and speaking, your questioning and being, so that I can learn anew the message that I need to pass on to you."[10] By being capable of self-reflection, critical, and willing to learn, Christians in Germany can meet the desires of people who long for spirituality[11] but who are hardly able to find it when turning to the evangelicals, who often stand in their own way.

9. David Bosch, *Transforming Mission: Paradigm Shifts in Theology of Mission* (Maryknoll, NY: Orbis, 1991), 483.

10. Quoted online at http://www.klaus-hemmerle.de/cms-joomla/index.php?option=com _content&view=article&id=446&Itemid=33.

11. Thus, religiosity increases significantly in young people who do not belong to any of the two big confessions (Protestant and Catholic). See Mathias Albert, Klaus Hurrelmann,

How Transformation Breaks the Monoculture of the Church: The Beautiful New Faces of Faith

Through the Holy Spirit this kingdom of God transforms our thoughts and our consciousness (Rom. 12:2), and therefore our actions. The reconnection of humans to the God of creation and the recollection that every human being, despite all estrangement through sin, carries the image of God (*imago Dei*) in himself or herself, release new hope in us. Humankind as the "crown of creation" carries a creative potential of intelligence, creativity, and the capacity for community in itself. Where is this reflected in our churches? our services? our home groups?

Instead of honoring God through his creational diversity, we often capitulate to a monocultural service, which we have spread throughout the whole world. Worship in its diversity is more than music, prayer, or sermon. Worship of God shows itself in art, creativity, dance, architecture, literature, and many other gifts, which glorify God through their presentation. Transformation reflects the colorful faces of God here on earth and encourages us to live. To see it realized, we will need the assistance of the Holy Spirit as well as the help of many Christians in the world. Some people God might simply bring to us; we in Germany are blessed with 15.6 million migrants. Among them are many Christians from whom we can learn how the diversity of God looks in his great family. Unfortunately we overlook this sometimes in our monocultural churches or, even worse, we do not feel enriched but rather irritated. Instead we might learn a lot about the diverse faces of God from different cultures.

> Diverse relationships expand, broaden, and enlarge our limited self, experiences, points of views, and even our framework of how we see God, ourselves, and the whole creation. *Eileen Suico*

> We must overcome the morphological fundamentalism within our churches. We need many new different styles and rhythms that are driven by a holistic approach. As Bishop Lesslie Newbigin put it: The church is the translator of the gospel. *Markus Weimer*

> I like what you seem to be suggesting. A friend recently helped me draw a comparison between my pastoral and community development work with the ephemeral art of folks like Andrew Goldsworthy, who stacks stones and sows leaves. Ecclesiology as an ephemeral art can celebrate our glory when it does emerge and can pick up the work again tomorrow after the

---

and Gudrun Quenzel, "Shell Jugendstudie 2010" (Frankfurt: Fischer Verlag, 2010). Cf. Stephan Kulle, *Warum wir wieder Glauben wollen* [Why we want to believe again] (Frankfurt am Main: Scherz Verlag, 2006); Wolfram Weimer, *Credo: Warum die Rückkehr der Religion gut ist* [Why the return to religion is good] (Munich: Deutsche Verlags-Anstalt, 2006).

winds of change have again scattered the beauty asunder. Diversity is like mixed media, it is never comprehensive: there are always more possible collection-types of people. *Troy Bronsink*

How Transformation Changes Our Consumer Behavior: "Our Daily Bread . . ."

When we speak of the dawning of the kingdom of God, we do not mean a program or a goal that has to be reached but a lifestyle that is reflected in daily life. It is a matter of living a life in contrast to society in the midst of a consumer society. It is a matter of simple and complex questions. Where do I buy what? At whose cost do I live my daily life? Who in the third world pays for my standard of living? These questions seem to bring even the "neighbor" in China very near in a globalized world.

The kingdom of God confronts social standards, which are increasingly focused on consumerist behavior, with a prophetic lifestyle consisting of love, holiness, and suffering, which manifests itself in the relational levels of daily life. The renewed create a new fellowship through which the kingdom of God becomes discernible and visible (John 13:34). The churches as the body of Christ in the world are the basis of the dawning kingdom of God and therefore also a countermodel to the hegemonic power structures of the world with their economic, political, and social injustices (Mark 10:42–44).

This can be deduced from the new behavior of the first Christians. For example, they shared everything with one another, not only their spiritual life, but also money, possessions, and property. Churches that were well-off materially bore responsibility for those that were in need (Acts 2:42–47). In the new churches collections were frequently made for the church in Jerusalem, which was facing financial hardship. God is the giver of all gifts and we are the economic stewards on earth (1 Cor. 3:7). The first Christians wanted to live the kingdom of God in their sphere of influence; they understood themselves as a contrast society to the world. We continue in this tradition today, and through us God's kingdom becomes visible in the world.

Living in community is not about shunning the individuality of a person. Rather, it is about broadening one's awareness and concern toward everyone's well-being in the choices and decisions one makes. *Eileen Suico*

Transforming Spirituality: Singing Together the Tune of Heaven

The diverse changes in our lives, our churches, and our society cause a new search for God. This spiritual search is not only for a self but for a community as well. With recourse to the Bible, a rich Christian tradition, and our cultural possibilities, we can encounter God together in various ways and let his kingdom shine through us on earth. The kingdom of God shows itself in the social shape of the disciples of Christ and is the visible hope of the now and not yet, revealing itself in the holistic saving ministry of Christ. We are not yet in heaven, but together we can already sing the tune of heaven!

> Much of this search is happening outside the church and is an opportunity for mission but also a challenge to our assumptions of what this search is like. *Steve Hollinghurst*

> An important issue here lies with our understanding of the kingdom. Is it about God's governance over human society or is it a vision for the new creation? If the latter, as I believe, one of the challenges the new spiritualities present is for the church to be good news for all creation and a sign of its liberation as pointed to by Paul in Romans 8. *Steve Hollinghurst*

The church is the visible sign of the kingdom of God; it reflects this kingdom in the "now and not yet." As N. T. Wright says: "Through the church God wants to announce to the world that he really is the wise, loving and just creator, that through Jesus he has defeated the powers which corrupted and enslaved the world and that through his Spirit he is healing and renewing the world."[12] Church as the healing dimension of the gospel exists for the world, to bring hope to the people around us. In the kingdom of God, liberation on individual and structural levels becomes visible, which, through the cross and resurrection, sends a ray of hope right into the middle of the world.

Bibliography

Albert, Mathias, Klaus Hurrellmann, and Gudrun Quenzel. "Shell Jugendstudie 2010." Frankfurt: Fischer Verlag, 2010.

Bosch, David. *Transforming Mission: Paradigm Shifts in Theology of Mission*. Maryknoll, NY: Orbis, 1991.

Elias, Norbert. *Was ist Soziologie?* [What is sociology?]. Munich: Juventa, 2009.

Hiebert, Paul. *Transforming Worldviews: An Anthropological Understanding of How People Change*. Grand Rapids: Baker Academic, 2008.

Kusch, Andreas, ed. *Transformierender Glaube*. Entwicklungspraxis. Nürnberg: VTR, 2007.

12. N. T. Wright, *Surprised by Hope: Rethinking Heaven, the Resurrection, and the Mission of the Church* (San Francisco: HarperOne, 2008), 127.

Moltmann, Jürgen. *Theologie der Hoffnung* [Theology of hope]. Munich: Kaiser Verlag, 1984.

Samuel, Vinay, and Chris Sugden, eds. *Mission as Transformation: A Theology of the Whole Gospel*. Oxford: Regnum, 2003.

Volf, Miroslav. *Exclusion and Embrace: A Theological Exploration of Identity, Otherness, and Reconciliation*. Nashville: Abingdon, 1996.

Wright, N. T. *Surprised by Hope: Rethinking Heaven, the Resurrection, and the Mission of the Church*. San Francisco: HarperOne, 2008.

17

Leadership as Body and Environment

The Rider and the Horse

MaryKate Morse

Practices

Leadership is hard. Leading like Christ is even harder. Some fail. Many burn out. Most struggle with the people they are called to serve and lead. I myself feel that I make mistakes more often than I "get it right." I want to be humble and lead well, but at times I feel threatened and frustrated. Sometimes the preaching is good and sometimes not so good. Sometimes people respond and lives are changed, but not as much as one would think, given all the resources, time, and talent poured out. Something crucial is missing from our understanding of servant leadership. I believe it is an awareness of where our leadership really gets shaped.

As leaders we struggle because we focus more on the rider and less on the horse. The rider represents the intentional part of our leadership, the conscious part. The horse represents the unconscious part, and it is powerful. The unconscious is interested in safety and well-being. It is constantly sniffing the air and watching for clues that things are stable and that survival is assured. When there is any type of threat the horse is alert and ready to run or stomp.

We often underestimate the power of the unconscious body to influence our thoughts and behavior when it has picked up a scent of danger or distress.[1]

A body is interconnected in all of its systems with a primary goal of keeping itself alive and healthy. The brain receives information from the central and peripheral nervous systems, and then governs the body's actions and reactions.[2] The information gathered is both conscious (the rider) and unconscious (the horse) data. The unconscious information includes the body's response to anxiety or stress as well as regulatory functions such as sleep and digestion. The body is constantly adjusting and fine-tuning as it adapts to the environment, and this is all done without our thinking or deciding. We don't have to tell the body to act or react; it will decide on its own. This fundamentally shapes our leadership, and we don't even know it.

We assume that the cognitive functioning of the brain is under our complete control. However, the brain is much more than the sum of our thoughts. The brain is as influenced by the body as the body is influenced by the brain. The body absorbs all the messages it receives from the environment, the physical and emotional, and sends powerful unconscious messages to the brain, which can trump rational thought processes. These messages come in on a sensory train full of impulses for how the body should react to protect and thrive.

If I am leading a meeting and a person walks in late, I see the person and am aware that I am already moving through the agenda. My conscious mind registers the arrival and my subconscious brain begins adjusting. Will I say something? Will I nod and continue? Will I experience frustration or anger or concern? A lot will depend on my threat sensors, the type of relationship I have with the person, the nature of the meeting, and the persons involved in the meeting. Does the room feel tense, relaxed, or ambivalent? The brain, in a matter of nanoseconds, will have formulated a response, and the response will be partially overt and partially unconscious. Leadership is not simply what I do and who I think I am. It is how I manage the billions of neurons firing in my brain, some of it known to me and much of it unknown.

The environment plays a major role in the messages the horse sends to the rider. As long as the environment is normal and anticipated, the horse is fine. If the environment changes and the horse gets spooked or upset, off it goes. Only the most experienced riders can stay on the horse and bring it under control. As leaders we need to be aware of the environment and how it influences the horse; otherwise the body will be leading us.

1. The image of the horse and rider is from Laurence Gonzales, *Deep Survival: Who Lives, Who Dies, and Why* (New York: Norton, 2003).
2. A good resource is Antonio Demasio, *The Feeling of What Happens: Body and Emotions in the Making of Consciousness* (San Diego: Harcourt, 1999).

This is especially hard today when our environment is polarized and stressed. We live in a culture full of fear, which is heightened by a poor economy and ongoing wars. Church members often have unrealistic expectations for what a pastor should or could do. In a connected world concerns like terrorism, environmental disasters, natural disasters, poverty, and crime are on our doorsteps 24/7. All these environmental factors add a physiological burden to the horse. The environment creates a constant underlying anxiety in the horse. Leaders have the responsibility of motivating and guiding people toward purposefully following Christ. This is not normal to the human species in a stressed environment. Our basic motivation is stability and safety. So stepping into the unknown can have its perks, but the body resists the change. It is a journey that does not feel very safe.

The bottom line for leadership is this: There is much more going on inside us and shaping our leadership than simply our ideas about what leaders do and how they act. The good news is that the brain is plastic, so it can change.[3] When Jesus promised to set us free, it was not an empty promise for some mythical future kingdom. We can be transformed as leaders, and our transformation then impacts our environment and those we lead. I offer two suggestions to help the rider become more aware of the horse and the environment.

Emotional/Physical Reflection: The Connection between Horse and Rider

The more threatened a person feels, the more the unconscious takes control of the emotions. The threat can be minor, such as a disagreement with another person, or major, such as an accusation of failure. The threat can be real or imagined. The cognitive part of the mind can make very fine distinctions and quick decisions, but the emotional part of the mind is always a part of the process. Being human means experiencing the environment with emotional antennae. The entire Emotional Intelligence movement is directed toward exactly this awareness.[4] Managing our emotions requires active reflection that gets alerted as soon as we recognize anxiety in ourselves. If you are reacting with rebellion, blame, inner frustration, addiction, or disengagement, your body is protecting itself from threat. Even if you maintain a smooth professional facade, the roiling emotions will not be denied their day. After a while the horse gets bigger and wilder, and the rider is less and less in control.

3. Norman Doidge, *The Brain That Changes Itself* (New York: Penguin Books, 2007); Barbara Strauch, *The Secret Life of the Grown-Up Brain* (New York: Viking, 2010).
4. Daniel Goleman, *Emotional Intelligence: Why It Can Matter More Than IQ*, 10th anniversary ed. (New York: Bantam, 2006).

I suggest three helpful steps to managing the horse. First, name the threat. Instead of the "dismiss, deny, or dunk it down deep" tendencies (which don't help and waste time in the long run), name the threat. Second, reflect on its origin. The majority of our intense reactions toward a person or event in our environment are really a reflection of what is going on internally in our unconscious world. It is almost always about you. Become skilled in figuring out the source of the reaction. Third, pray. To keep the horse controlled, deal with it each and every time through prayer. Create a prayer to soothe the beast and draw attention to the bigger leadership picture, following Christ. "Jesus, I see you. I follow you. Give me grace." No matter how many times you have to repeat it, say the prayer. Such repetition of prayer compels the body to come in alignment with its primary purpose: not survival, but following the Lord.

Environmental Attention: The Connection between Rider/Horse and the Environment

Paying attention to the environment is also major, because we do it so poorly. For several years researchers have studied the phenomena of "inattentional blindness," the reality that we perceive only what we pay attention to. This means that a gorilla can be walking through a room and we would probably miss it, if we were busy enough paying attention to something else.[5] Leaders have a lot to think about and do; they are on deck all the time. That is exactly why Sabbath and prayer practices are absolutely essential for those who want to lead like Christ. A leader creates space for paying attention to something other than what he or she is doing or thinking. Without this we develop an inattentional blindness to Christ. We do not mean to, but we do. This is why we need spiritual disciplines.

To pay attention to the environment requires taking mini spiritual-discipline breaks. We were taught as kids to "stop, drop, and roll" if our clothes caught on fire. Ministry is fire. It is meant to light up and warm, but if we are not careful it can burn up and destroy. The Holy Spirit came as fire. As Christ's leaders we require the Holy Spirit perspective on the broader picture. Therefore, tuning into the Spirit matters throughout the day. We need regularly to stop, drop,

> Biblical spirituality . . . is concerned with bringing our body and soul into an intimate relationship with the heart of God. It is concerned with holiness, which means that it is related to every aspect of life, as lived from day to day, rather than focusing attention on transient experiences.
>
> Eddie Gibbs (CN, 142)

5. Arien Mack and Irvin Rock, *Inattentional Blindness* (Cambridge, MA: MIT Press, 1998).

and roll. For leaders, stop the clock, drop to the floor, and reflect. Create a rhythm for stopping the clock every few hours. Change your position. Either lay down on the floor or stand up and look out a window or kneel, whatever, but change your body to reflect your attention to the Holy Spirit. Then for five to ten minutes simply be still with the Holy Spirit and listen—not to figure something out or plan the next words, but to bring your attention back to Christ, to have the Holy Spirit's perspective.

Culture

The Horse and Rider in Creation

Since our bodies are influenced by our environment, it is easy to see that the health of our environment is directly related to our own well-being. The first directive from God was to steward the earth. This entails its care, and its care is directly related to our survival. God created an interdependence between human beings and God's beloved earth. God sees creation as good; therefore, it is good for us to pay attention to it. It will change us and change our neighborhoods. Being involved with the care of the earth builds community and grounds our being as leaders. It brings the rider, horse, and environment together.

> This resonates deeply with what I have written in my chapter. *Ian Mobsby*

For example, a church planter in a blue-collar neighborhood close to a major city decided that he and his community would turn a vacant lot into a neighborhood garden. The lot was full of concrete, broken bottles, needles, and weeds. As they began working on the lot, slowly people in the neighboring homes wanted to know what was going on. They got involved in different ways: picking up the trash, pulling weeds, creating the beds for flowers and vegetables, watching over it, and watering. One neighborhood alcoholic in particular took a deep fondness to the garden. He started talking to the faith community people. He would come by often to help out and then spend a lot of the day sitting in the garden on a bench. When asked why, he said, "It is so beautiful, and I am helping my neighbors. I am not just a drunk."

The Horse and Rider and Hybridity

Hybridity is taking two different things and making a new thing, such as a hybrid vehicle, which uses two different fuel sources to propel it. In a similar way male and female leadership are two different fuel sources to propel our kingdom work. Men and women bring different perspectives to ministry. The biological natures of maleness and of femaleness are distinctive enough that harnessing the horse takes different sets of skills for each, as well as the ability to notice different stimuli in an environment. On the *Mad Men* television show, Don Draper asks several men and women, "What do women want?" Yet he does not hear it when women give him the answer, and the men do not know. Seeing effective leadership from a male *and* female perspective would greatly increase the leadership capacity of the church worldwide.

God's kingdom is best represented by both sexes. The concerns, experiences, and insights of males and females bring a more complete understanding of the environment—allowing for better decision making and better service. For the best results, the executive or top levels of leadership should consist of at least 30 percent female leaders.[6] Tokenism, a commitment to a woman on a leadership team, gives the appearance but not the experience of the female rider on her horse. We would be a stronger team if the various experiences were all valued. We would be a stronger church if we rode together. I also believe there would be fewer problems with inappropriate sexual behavior by male pastors if female leaders were valued partners and not sexualized enigmas.

The Horse and Rider and Pluralism

Pluralism has a wide variety of meanings. Here I define it as a creative engagement with differences—which is not easy, especially for leaders. Leaders help motivate and guide a group to becoming more Christlike in character and mission. Christ is truth (John 14:6), and often by engaging creatively with differences we grow beyond our finite and sometimes limited understandings of that truth. Because we prefer control and safety at a fundamental level, anything different from us will be a visceral, deeply felt threat. It is the leader's job to help people see a bigger kingdom than their corner church on 5th and Main. If the leader cannot rise above the perceived threat, it is extra difficult for the people he or she serves. Therefore, it is crucial that we keep our eyes on Jesus and relinquish control to him. From the beginning of his ministry when he was tempted in the desert, to the end when he prayed in the garden, Jesus gave control to God. By doing so, Jesus was able to love and serve on a plane that seems impossible.

What do we do with something like the proposed mosque and community center two blocks from Ground Zero? This proposal was incredibly divisive in a country founded on the fundamental right to religious freedom. The horse is

---

6. "Mapping the Maze: Getting More Women to the Top in Research," http://ec.europa .eu/research/science-society/document_library/pdf_06/mapping-the-maze-getting-more-women -to-the-top-in-research_en.pdf.

running wild in an environment that fears for its very existence. The problem is not whether the mosque should be there; the problem is an inability to work through this highly sensitive issue. Therefore, leaders must go to the garden with Christ and relinquish control (of the wild horse running amok in our souls) to God. Then we are able to listen to the heart of Christ on the matter and respond as he would. Pluralism becomes less a threat and more an opportunity.

The Horse and Rider and Creativity

Creativity is a physical experience that shapes the horse and rider and engages the environment. Creating involves all the senses. The body sees, smells, remembers, touches, and connects with beauty in a way that draws us to God's sovereignty and glory. Therefore, the leader can use imaginative creation to engage the community with God.

The challenge is to encourage creativity and not reproduction. For example, early Sunday school classes were much the same: Little chairs faced a larger chair for the teacher. On the wall would be pictures of Jesus with children or Jesus carrying a lamb. The children needed to have their minds and behaviors shaped. The teacher taught. Crafts involved reproducing the Bible story with colors, glue, and glitter.

Godly Play is a different experience based on two fundamental ideas.[7] First, children have their own leadership engine, and, second, the best way to tame the horse is to give the children space to know the rider and the environment for themselves through the imagination. The teacher is a "storyteller." Children step into "sacred space." They participate as the story is reenacted with figures and lots of imagination and questions. The children are then given a wide range of possibilities for reflecting the story as they heard it. Godly Play is a different way to lead others, and its principles work for adults too. Using creativity rather than telling empowers persons to independence and interdependence with God, rather than codependency on a leader.

> This dichotomy of creation versus reproduction is one I have thought about a lot. On one hand, the mastery of a classic can shape the skills of the artisan or musician. On the other hand, the freedom to reinterpret that classic after having mastered it is the power of the greatest of artists.
>
> In worship music leadership circles it is similar to the idea that people worship best "with the familiar," and innovation is seen as aberration. Like many renewal movements that want to "get back to the biblical practices," creatives struggle to get audiences to leave behind old hardened metaphors, worn-out songs, and predictable allusions. For me the key has been

7. Jerome Berryman, *Godly Play: An Imaginative Approach to Religious Education* (Minneapolis: Augsburg, 1995).

asking about the values we place on precedence. Instead of biblical imagery being evocative of deeper and deeper stories, we fall into the rut of domesticating stories, be they biblical, historical, even our own faith stories, to serve a single meaning. When we do this we miss the very function of beauty's un-precedence to bring awe and wonder. Storytelling is a subversive approach to all our media as churches. *Troy Bronsink*

The Horse and Rider and Consumerism

Consumerism is simply horses running amok. Horses cannot get enough to assure their feeling of safety and well-being. Whether their method of consumption is overeating, overrunning, or overstimulating their senses, it becomes all about the horse and less and less about the kingdom. They run wild and free with little regard for the devastation of the environment. To counter these powerful tendencies requires leadership that is in control of the horse, a rider who understands the pull of its surrounding culture and offers alternative perspectives and options.

> Creativity blossoms in an atmosphere of flexibility and freedom. It requires an environment where precedents and assumptions can be set aside and where there is a willingness to allow fresh thoughts.
>
> Eddie Gibbs (LN, 140)

The church from its inception understood the importance of simplicity. Christian leaders today can renew this call to a simpler, less distracted lifestyle. They begin with their own lives and then help their faith communities become places of simplicity, with regard to both the stuff the community owns and the things it calls its people to do. Dave Bruno is an example. He wrote *The 100 Thing Challenge*, describing how he simplified his life and ended up regaining his soul. He wanted "to free up physical, mental, and spiritual space" in order to live a more thoughtful life.[8] The church is exactly the place where the discipline of simplicity can be a powerful antidote to the addiction to consumerism. And the Christian leader is exactly the person who can prophetically live and call others to a countercultural lifestyle of simplicity.

The Horse and Rider and Spirituality and Culture

Today's faith seeker is hungry to connect the fragmented self into one whole self. Who one is, what one feels and knows, where one lives, and what

---

8. See http://www.guynameddave.com/ and David Michael Bruno, *The 100 Thing Challenge: How I Got Rid of Almost Everything, Remade My Life, and Regained My Soul* (New York: Harper, 2010).

one does is integrated in Christ. There is not a church life, a spiritual life, a work life, a broken life, a community life, and a relational life. All is one in Christ. The horse and rider look to Christ for companionship and direction and healing. Leaders then create environments where horses and riders engage their desire to be conformed to the image of Christ for the sake of others in the real world in which they live.

> The vision of the body of Christ is central to this and a gift for a world that often tends toward an edgy tribalism. New Age and pagan spiritualities are also seeking this holistic approach and whilst for some this proves illusory others seem to demontrate it better than we do in the churches. How we live as a diverse body of Christ and are whole in the way Morse rightly stresses is a major mission challenge. Will people look at us and believe we have reconciliation to bring to all humanity and creation? They will judge us by what they see of it in our lives. *Steve Hollinghurst*

This requires accountability and authentic community, which leaders help create. For instance, many young people are seeking monastic-type faith communities. This is not a Catholic movement. This is a Pentecostal, mainline, fundamental, liberal, evangelical movement. Faith seekers are less interested in big church success and more in transformed lives and communities. They seek authenticity, which happens best when culture is engaged and where spiritual disciplines help shape the horse and equip the rider. New monastic movements are the desire to experience spirituality physically together and in community. The fundamentals are contemplation and community with a theology and practice of hospitality and serving the poor.[9] There are other possibilities, but all integrate spirituality with the whole person in local and global cultures.

Leaders mess up not because we love Jesus less or are full of ourselves (though sometimes that is true), but because sometimes we don't pay attention to what really shapes us. Leadership is defined as much by our bodies and the environments in which we live as by our actions and thoughts. This is one of the reasons why Jesus came in a physical body and to a specific time and place, to model for us our capacity for authentic spiritual leadership. This leadership thinks carefully about how the rider and horse interact with each other and is attentive to the larger environment of God's world and purposes.

9. Jonathan Wilson in his book *Living Faithfully in a Fragmented World* (Norcross, GA: Trinity, 1998) coined the term "new monasticism" and is thought to be one of the primary leaders.

Part 4

Experiments

18

The Underground

The Living Mural of a Hip-Hop Church

Ralph Watkins

What is hip-hop, and how is it informing what it means to be the church? Let us be clear: hip-hop is bigger than music, bigger than rap. It is bigger than what we see in the story of this worship experience at The Underground Church, even though it informs what we see there. Hip-hop is a break from the traditional. Hip-hop takes what was meant to be used one way and uses it another way. Records were not meant to be touched, but hip-hop took records, touched them, remixed them, and extended the break beat. What we see in The Underground or BASIC Ministries or any other hip-hop church is a break from the past. As I lay out the story of The Underground versus my home church, FAME, the distinctions are obvious. The hip-hop church is not the old church we were raised in. It is a church that embraces the basic tenets of hip-hop culture as they are baptized in the Word of God to serve as the key building blocks for their quest for an authentic Christian community.

Culture

Hip-hop is a culture. It involves morals, values, ideas, ideals, ideology, and a way of life. It is a product of the African American youth culture that was birthed out of the sociopolitical context of the late 1970s. The sociopolitical-economic timing of its coming out is important. Hip-hop was born at the end of the civil rights period. While the middle class, both black and white, were running for the suburbs, hip-hoppers were left in the inner cities with a crumbling economy. Within this inner-city milieu there was a cross-fertilization of minority groups coming together to bring to maturity what African Americans had birthed. From its early years hip-hop was multicultural. What is seen in hip-hop today, and especially in the hip-hop church, is this multicultural reality. Hip-hop churches are multicultural churches.

According to KRS-One, the teacher of hip-hop, hip-hop culture is composed of nine elements:

> True Hiphop is a term that describes the independent collective consciousness of a specific group of inner-city people. Ever growing, it is commonly expressed through such elements as: 1 Breakin' (Breakdancing), 2 Emceein' (Rap), 3 Graffiti art (aerosol art), 4 Dejayin', 5 Beatboxin', 6 Street Fashion, 7 Street Language, 8 Street Knowledge, and 9 Street Enterpreneurialism. Hiphop is not just music and dance, nor is Hiphop a product to be bought and sold. Discovered by Kool DJ Herc in the Bronx, New York, around 1972, and established as a community of peace, love, unity and having fun by Afrika Bambaataa through the Zulu Nation in 1974, Hiphop is an independent and unique community, an empowering behavior, and an international culture.[1]

KRS-One defines hip-hop culture in its broadest and purest from. Hip-hop is an international culture, born in the Bronx, New York, and has extended its influence throughout the world. The nine elements form the base of the culture, and in the Christian context these nine elements sit on the foundation, which is Christ.

Hip-hop is a culture that informs the lives of those who consider themselves hip-hop and provides the framework and ethos of the hip-hop church. When you look at hip-hop culture and allow it to be a lens for looking at the hip-hop church, what you see is a church that will not be mainline. It will develop its own line. An example of the hip-hop church's move away from the mainline is found in Tommy Kyllonen at Crossover Church in Tampa, Florida, who is developing a network of hip-hop pastors who are mentoring one another. They aren't trying to break into mainline denominations; they have felt that rejection and moved on. The entrepreneurial spirit in hip-hop is to develop, to literally start from scratch (pun intended). Tommy is the mentor of Pastor Tymme, and it was Tommy who hooked me up with Tymme. This is an

---

1. KRS-One, *Ruminations* (New York: Welcome Rain, 2003), 179–80.

informal network that goes around the system to create its own system. This is hip-hop. We will make our own beats, perform on the street, sell our own mixtapes. We do not need the system.

The hip-hop generation, according to Bakari Kitwana, are those born between 1965 and 1986.[2] When we accept Bakari's generational time frame for the hip-hop generation we have to understand that we are not talking about teenagers. We are talking about young adults. The hip-hop church is a church that by definition is to comprise young adults and those who love them.

An Experiment

My Journey to The Underground

On October 24, 2010, my wife and I went through our regular Sunday morning routine. We got dressed and made our way over to our home church, First African Methodist Episcopal Church (FAME), in Los Angeles, California. Today was not a normal day, however, because as we were preparing to go to our church, we were looking forward to what would come later that day. After the first of our three worship services, Vanessa and I would leave our church to go celebrate with The Underground Church as they marked the grand opening of their full-time ministry. At FAME we went through our normal, predicable worship experience. Even though it was Women's Day, there was nothing new in the routine. Given the predictability of the method in which we do what we do, I could not wait to go to The Underground. I knew The Underground would be stimulating.

> Hip-hop churches are emerging to engage young people who are not attracted to the traditional form of service.
>
> Eddie Gibbs (CM, 128)

I dressed for The Underground, not for FAME, even knowing that I would be considered nontraditional by many of my FAME church family. As one who does both youth and young adult ministry, one would think I could be who I am, but in my church I occasionally get comments about the way I dress. As a man in his mid-forties who is an old hip-hop head, I must admit that I dress a bit casual. My casual dress is in line with what young adults and the youth might consider cool for an old man. But my peers tend to make fun of or at a minimum chide me for my style. On this Sunday I wore a pair of jeans, hard shoes, and a collared shirt with cuff links. I thought I was pretty dressed up,

---

2. Bakari Kitwana, *The Hip Hop Generation: Young Blacks and the Crisis in African-American Culture* (New York: Basic Civitas Books, 2002), 7.

considering, but sure enough I got comments and looks. As I was pricked by what members of the congregation said to me, I could not help but project what my reception would be at The Underground. Being a frequent visitor to churches that embrace hip-hop culture, I could predict how The Underground family would receive the old hip-hop head. I am always amazed at how unyielding and unwelcoming traditional churches can be when it comes to anything that might be considered hip-hop, new, or different. The acceptance and willingness to create the new is one of the things that distinguishes churches that embrace hip-hop from traditional mainline churches. I knew The Underground would receive me in my new shirt with a warm welcome and no chiding comments.

Vanessa and I made our way from FAME to The Underground. The drive was only about thirty minutes, but the difference in distance was literally from the past to the future. As we pulled into the hotel parking lot, I saw "me." I saw young adults who were dressed like me, and I saw a few adults my age who looked at me as if we were looking in the mirror. I felt good about this place right away. Whenever I walk into a worshiping community that embraces hip-hop, I am always touched by how they embrace me as an elder who loves them. The emerging community of the hip-hop generation is in search of elders who embrace them and their culture. They are quick to return the love in a look, a nod, a hello, and a genuine welcome. The community in hip-hop is by definition welcoming of diversity in age, dress, and ethnic background. They tend to be younger congregations, and their youth is a factor in the older generation's preference for traditional church and/or rejection of hip-hop culture.

No one frowned on my dress at The Underground. The greeters welcomed Vanessa and me as we walked up to the hotel. With a smile and the opening of the door they said, "Welcome to The Underground." As we approached the building we saw a white female and male; they smiled at us, and we of course smiled back.

The Underground

Tymme and Aury Reitz were professional dancers who were called to serve God in early 2000 and in 2001; they committed their gifts as dancers to the kingdom of God. After working with such artists as Madonna, Will Smith, Missy Elliott, Backstreet Boys, Dru Hill, and Shanice, Tymme and Aury co-founded the dance ministry at In His Presence Church and soon thereafter founded Word in Motion Dance Company to present the gospel while developing a nation of dancers for Christ. In the hip-hop church, professionalism and high standards are the norm. People do not expect to come to worship and get a warmed-over sermon or see praise dancers who are not gifted and a worship service that is not tight.

Tymme and Aury started The Underground as a monthly service "utilizing relevant biblical teaching and worshiping through original rap, R&B, and dance genres."[3] This monthly service morphed into a weekly meeting that, as of October 24, 2010, became its own freestanding church with the blessings of In His Presence Church. The first meeting of this new church was held at the Burbank Marriot Hotel in the San Fernando Valley, just north of Los Angeles.

Practices

Worship

As I entered the ballroom-turned-sanctuary I did not see a lectern but instead saw a stage—a stage with black curtains behind it, and in the center a purple banner that read, "The Underground: Not Your Typical Church." The Underground makes it clear that their call, like all hip-hop churches, is not to be like your typical church. This is a statement about who they are and how they understand the "typical church."

Worship at FAME is a mix between old-school, traditional African American worship and more contemporary gospel flavor. It has a congregation of over six thousand, mostly in their fifties and sixties, with a minority of young adults and young families. That night, we saw the young adults who weren't at FAME because they were worshiping at The Underground. Where FAME starts with the traditional call to worship, The Underground starts with prayer and spoken word: from spoken word to praise and worship. Praise and worship is backed up not by a band or a choir, but by a DJ who is spinning on his Mac computer using Searato (a digital DJ software package). The DJ appears to be in his mid-twenties, white, with the flavor of an old-school DJ like Grandmaster Flash. Behind the praise team is a young white male playing the guitar. The praise team is a mix of African Americans, Latinos, and whites, both male and female, but all young adults. The lead

> Many . . . urban churches . . . represent indigenous expressions of church. They are faith communities that have been *birthed* within their neighborhoods and are therefore culturally appropriate to their contexts; they do not represent preconceived church models that are *planted* by outside agencies and groups. Urban contexts are so diverse that faith communities will have to discover what "church" will look like for them, enabling them to express worship, embody fellowship, and engage in ongoing mission to their wider community.
>
> Eddie Gibbs (CM, 136)

---

3. See http://theunderground.la/about-us/our-story.

singers are two African American females who would fit perfectly at my home church. They sing praise songs, and then the group is joined by four young men who have microphones in their hands. As the young men merge into the praise team, they rush up front and the mood changes from melodic praise songs to holy hip-hop rap as the rappers begin to rap to the glory of God.

The lights are turned down low. The room feels intimate as we are led through worship with a remix of praise songs and rap. You can feel the power in the room. Eyes are closed, hands are being waved in the air, worshipers are in the front of the church coming out of their seats and breaking into dance. The praise team continues to sing, the rappers continue to rap, the DJ continues to mix it up as the screens on the side of the stage are flashing the words to each song so the audience can rap and sing along. I am feeling this! The room is filled with call and response as we are all singing and rapping together.

From all four corners of the stage enter the praise dancers. As they take the stage the praise team simultaneously exits. In a seamless transition, our praise breaks out into a dance. These praise dancers are not like the praise dancers at FAME who wear long flowing garments, as the audience watches and claps. These praise dancers make you get up and move, and the audience moves with them while watching them. The beat drops, and the choreography is totally professional. A mix of breaking, popping, and smooth hip-hop moves graces the stage. The praise dancers are dressed in normal street clothes that I would not see any of my young adults wearing at FAME on Thursday night for our weekly gathering. They are hip, cool, and in style.

The professionalism and spirit of excellence in the worship service at The Underground typifies what the hip-hop generation expects. They have heard the best rappers and seen the freshest dancers, and they expect worship to be on point. As the praise dancers finish, the pastors take the stage.

In the hip-hop church the embrace and lifting up of the Bible is something I have always been enamored of. There is an embrace of Scripture as a text for life. In the sermon the pastor referenced seven extensive passages of Scripture, in contrast to FAME, where the pastor takes a single text and preaches for twenty to thirty minutes. In the hip-hop church multiple texts tend to be sourced as a conversation piece for the teaching. It is a teaching church where members want to get more into the Word of God.

It seems that in the United States the reinvention of church is a different one than in Europe. The United States seems to reinvent toward a society that is still deeply culturally Christian. The Christian narrative is still there, but the culture may have perverted it into something un-Christian. In Europe, the culture already erased the Christian narrative, requiring a different reinvention of church altogether. *Nico-Dirk van Loo*

Community

Prior to the dancers taking the stage you would have thought they were regular members of the congregation. Part of the hip-hop ethos is that those up front do not stand out but rather fit into a community. This community does not worship them or set them apart but worships *together* while recognizing the gifts in the community as they manifest themselves from the audience through the stage. These dancers did not have special seating or special dress, but they did have a special gift to dance. These were professional dancers who were gifted and well trained.

After the chatter between the pastors, they excused the kids for children's church. The emphasis on kids and young families is a central component of the church's identity. Pastor Tymme announced that they were only having one worship service this week at 10:30 a.m., but starting next week they would move to their normal format of having a worship service at 10:30 a.m. and at 1:00 p.m. As he shared about the format and why they started this way, he explained that he wanted the parents who volunteer in the children's ministry to hear the message and to have an opportunity to worship.

Hip-hop culture is a participatory culture in which the audience members are cocreators—not sing-along muses. Community in hip-hop culture invites people to come in as equals, and community forms in the process of our creative communal experience. As the worship service progresses we move from the praise team to the praise dancers.

The hip-hop church looks hip-hop from dress to mission. It strives to be an oversized church by loving those who haven't been loved by the larger church or society. Those who are looking for real community in a world that has gone digital will find it in the hip-hop church, where real touch makes a real difference. These are small communities where everybody knows your name. The hip-hop church is akin to that old house church that we see reflected in the New Testament. Ironically enough, that is the model of church that is lifted up in the hip-hop church's ecclesiology. It is a church that goes back to its roots. The hip-hop church moves forward by looking backward at the biblical standard for church that many of its mainline seniors have forgotten or dismissed.

As the children at The Underground were being dismissed, the pastors welcomed the visitors, who were not asked to stand but simply to wave their hands in the air. The pastors made the visitors feel welcome and told them that there was a free gift waiting for them after worship. All people were then asked to stand and "love on somebody next to them." The church exploded into a hug fest as members went around and hugged one another—including the visitors. They introduced themselves, and the party was on. We felt genuinely welcomed. After the welcome, the pastors lifted the offering, being very clear on where the money was going.

Mission

When we first stepped into the building a young African American woman handed us a beautifully printed brochure. It was not a church bulletin, or an outline of the service, or a list of the sick and shut-in; it wasn't a list of weekly activities either, and it made no mention of the pastor and his or her spouse. This beautifully printed, slick document was entitled "The Scoop," which was The Underground's bimonthly newsletter–type thing. I have to say "type thing" because it was not a typical newsletter or bulletin. It explained that parking was free, talked about their commitment to the kids and childcare, their vision of the ministry, and what was coming up—like Partnership Classes, The Underground Live talent showcase in February 2011, Word in Motion Dance Conference in July, and the Men's and Women's Ministry sometime in 2011. What stood out was the church's outreach to Mexico; "The Scoop" shared how the church would partner with their sister church and supply needs to eighty-seven families in Tecate, Mexico. On the back of "The Scoop" was a list of twelve additional ministries to which The Underground had given financial support over the previous two months.

None of these types of things were in my FAME church bulletin. At FAME we had an outline of the worship service, which is the same every week, a list of weekly activities, a picture of the pastor and his wife (which is there every week), and our core beliefs, but no list of ministries we had helped, churches we had partnered with, or families to whom we had given direct assistance. Churches that embrace the ethos of hip-hop, which comes out of inner-city poverty, are poised theologically to give back. It is a movement that looks outward at those the society has forgotten, because the forgotten are the ones who birthed hip-hop in the first place.

At first take I could see that The Underground was an active ministry that was not simply about in-reach or growing a big church. It was clear from reviewing "The Scoop" that this church saw Matthew 25:31–46 as central to its understanding of the gospel. They were about feeding the hungry, clothing the naked, and visiting those in need. When the pastor broke this down in his sermon and was very clear that this was the type of church that The Underground would be, I was not surprised. While the appeal for the offering was given, clear, plain envelopes were handed out. Giving is black-and-white in the hip-hop church. The pastors shared their commitment to helping others and gave specific examples of who the church was helping.

The hip-hop church has inner-city cultural roots, so by definition it feels the pain of the poor. Its mission comes out of the mission of the poor who created the culture. The average hip-hop pastor links back to the golden years of hip-hop and has a sense of the activist beginnings of hip-hop when groups like Public Enemy were calling for social justice. These leaders are young visionaries who want to see a church that is vibrant, relevant, and making a difference. Hip-hop's street knowledge puts them in touch with the pain of the poor, and they are committed to doing something about it.

Leadership

One thing hip-hop expects is transparency and authenticity. The hip-hop generation doesn't want leaders who pretend to be perfect or superhuman; rather, it wants leaders who are real, who struggle, who are honest about it and walk with one another through life. There is a transparency in the leadership when it comes to giving and supporting the ministry. The next fund-raising goal of the church is to move to a permanent location. The members can see where the money is going and understand the reason behind the financial appeal.

> An essential characteristic of spiritual leadership is *authenticity*. Church leaders must embody what they teach.
>
> Eddie Gibbs (INO, 109)

Pastors Tymme and Aury serve as a team. The challenge of sexism in ministry and in the larger hip-hop culture is present in hip-hop churches as they seek to be inclusive. Pastor Tymme and Aury engaged in banter as they prepared for the preaching moment. They both shared how blessed they were on this day. It was a few minutes of obviously unscripted dialogue as they shared with each other. The dialogue was loving and transparent. They were just being honest about how thankful and overwhelming this moment was for them. The church affirmed this transparency, honesty, and authenticity.

There is a sense in the hip-hop church, and especially in churches like The Underground, of wanting to get back to the core of ministry. This church saw something awry in the mainline churches and wants to be part of something new. There is a sense, in the hip-hop church, that it is trying to rediscover the faith in its purest form.

19

Bykirken (The City-Church)

Pray and Eat

Andreas Østerlund Nielsen

This is the story of Bykirken (The City-Church) in Aarhus, Denmark, a church plant that existed from 2002 to 2009, a time of excitement and struggle in which God let a group of Christians gain experience, learn, and grow. Most important, for several people, Bykirken was their first Christian community.

An Experiment

A "Congregation of Choice" in a Country of Parishes

In March 2001, a group of young Danish theology students began meeting to talk about forming a local church in mission. Some of us had recently attended a church leader conference and had gained renewed excitement for mission and a first sense of leadership. At that point, we were eager to utilize this inspiration. For a year and a half, we read books, prayed, visited churches, had a lot of discussions, and formulated a bunch of statements. My mentor advised us to create a common vision and only thereafter settle the question of organization. Our vision was to create a Christian community that could "communicate the gospel to a certain group of people in Aarhus and thereby serve God's mission in the world." We made drawings of our ideal "target group," and to our own surprise they were all mirrors of ourselves. "Students and young professionals, age twenty-five to thirty-five, on their way in life and hence open for new things, desiring to make a difference."

> Emergent movements always start from the network of the initiators and mirror their own cultural identity. The challenge is to expand the target to include other networks. *Eric Zander*

Having the vision written down, we went on to decide the structural frame. A SWOT-analysis[1] convinced us to start from scratch, yet stay within the Evangelical Lutheran Church of Denmark, the state church of which 83 percent of the population are members. The Evangelical Lutheran Church is made up of parishes, but an old church law allows a group of people to establish a "congregation of choice" and hire (and pay for) their own pastor. We decided to do that. However, because of the parish system, church planting is very unusual in Denmark. We found it difficult to convince anybody that it was really necessary to establish a new congregation. Constantly having to defend our work was exhausting, and as a result the core group shrunk to two people: the later chair of the church board and me. Nevertheless, other people began to show interest.

> In the Netherlands the parish system is often a hindrance too. Especially more traditional people use it as a way to say, "There is already a church here: they should come in here." *Nico-Dirk van Loo*

Sunday Service at The Swineness

In August 2002, after eighteen months of thinking, talking, and writing, we launched three small groups. We had finally taken a first step from ideas and vision to real community. Various motivations lay behind the decisions of the fifteen people who joined these groups, but we tried as best as we could to get the vision growing in each of them. By December, twenty-five people had joined us, and we began meeting on Sundays in private homes. Now the application process of becoming authorized as a "congregation of choice" began, which implied finding facilities for public Sunday services.

One of us was reminded of a restaurant called Svineriet (The Swineness), located in a downtown courtyard. We set up a meeting with the owner and

---

1. SWOT stands for strengths, weaknesses, opportunities, threats.

his right-hand person, who were both *bon viveurs*, creative entrepreneurs, and absolutely unchurched people. They had been dreaming of sweaty, Harlem-like gospel services in their restaurant! We had to explain that we were neither black nor by any sense musical. It turned out, besides being lovely people, they needed to attract activities in order to convince the public authorities to grant them license to sell alcohol. Hence, we were allowed to rent the place for a symbolic amount. Svineriet was thereafter the main identity-forming meeting place during Bykirken's entire lifespan. I was installed as pastor at Svineriet in September 2003. A Sunday service held at a restaurant called The Swineness was without precedent and sounded sufficiently spectacular to attract the national television. Two representatives from the local parish church also showed up, much to our delight. We wanted to have a positive agenda; thus we needed to underline that we were not protesting against, but supplementing, the work of the other churches in downtown Aarhus.

> Both traditional and emergent churches should understand and accept the complementarities of the different expressions of the church of Christ. Unfortunately, such a respectful attitude is not obvious. Traditional churches, even more in a parish structure, fear for their hunting area, considering the missed attendees as a shortfall in their development. Emergent initiatives, convinced that they are the future expression of church, forget that the future is still to come, and that many still carry a modern worldview satisfied with the traditional church approach. *Eric Zander*

Mission Round-Trip

During the first years, we prioritized and succeeded in attracting attention from both local media and national church media. The formula seemed simple: connect "church" or "pastor" with something not usually related to Christianity, and have some architect students make some great graphics. I spent my Sunday evenings for one year as a "café pastor," installing myself at a table at a local café called Smagløs (literally, "Tasteless"), inviting others to conversation and debate. Even though only a few people came to converse with me, many were occasioned to debate faith, and I became part of a video art installation combining my story with the story of a German who ate his best friend! Inspired by the Danish filmmaker Lars von Trier's *The Five Obstructions*, I asked five people to set up "obstructions" for five sermons. I prepared one sermon in a mall, preached to music and a drinking bear, without saying "God" or "Jesus," and so forth. The media coverage we had did not in itself attract anybody to the church, but it did give the members a healthy self-confidence, and I hope that it made people revise their opinion on God. In church contexts our work was regarded as pioneering, and it inspired many.

Mission was a focal point for Bykirken. Our formulated purpose was to "make people authentic disciples of Jesus Christ," and the vision for three years was to be "a Bible-based and innovative community that is the first Christian community for at least one in five within the church community." I'm not sure if we ever succeeded in that regard, but out of forty adults, more than a handful had not been part of a Christian community before. People attending Bykirken corresponded to our initial "target group" (people like us), and we were aware of the challenges in being a rather homogenous congregation. Thus we connected to the larger body of Christ by being part of the Lutheran Church of Denmark, a national charismatic network, and Evangelical Alliance. Our target group in fact turned out to be too broad and abstract; it was more of a mental picture, and not real human beings whom we personally knew and cared for. For instance, we never tried to contextualize to the experimental, postmodern school located next to Svineriet, The Chaos Pilots, or to the middle-aged, middle-class people dining at the restaurant. As a result, we tended to become a small, inward-looking group of people doing church in a way we really liked. Later on we struggled tremendously to resolve that problem. First, Bykirken had to handle an embarrassing result of our missionality.

> Many church plants I know are indeed just Christians playing church the way they always wanted, while denominational leadership pat themselves on the shoulder for allowing a church plant. *Nico-Dirk van Loo*

> Emergent initiatives always start with disillusioned and eager Christians wanting to live church more genuinely and in sync with their culture. So from the start, there is a danger of producing a Christian club, like many traditional churches are accused of doing, but simply of a postmodern variety. The challenge is to integrate into the DNA of the project, from the very beginning, the outward dimension, both individually and corporately. The church must interact with the world, both individually and corporately, letting the world affect the church, and at the same time making an impact on the world. That is true incarnation. Easy to say, but so hard to do. *Eric Zander*

> They do not *always* start with disillusioned people; at least we were not "disillusioned Christians," even if we were reasonably disillusioned concerning the future possibilities of establishing a missional community in the context of our parish church. *Andreas Østerlund Nielsen*

An Open Community "With an Edge"

Bykirken was an open and welcoming community. We proclaimed the church to be "on its way" and wanted to create a safe zone to grow as human beings and in our relationships to God. We did not try to hide that our work was based on the Bible, and for insiders our church background betrayed evangelical conservatism. We wanted to be a community that could help all of us to grow in authentic discipleship of Jesus Christ. However, we did not want to scare anybody away for undue reasons. Therefore, that we had ethical demands for membership and "unpopular" points of view was not presented until our membership course. In one case, when a person who had been an engaged part of our community for a year wanted to attend the membership course, she found out that she could not become a member. It took a lot of mutual love, prayer, and discussion to sort out how Bykirken could reflect both the embracing and the confronting ways in which Jesus met people. Finally, we decided on fully opening up membership, but keeping requirements for leaders and actively turning our politically incorrect kingdom values into a positive brand. We did so, believing that the difference would be attractive. We wanted to be an open community "with an edge." Easier said than done. However, the decision made us more comfortable with being who and what we were.

> Turning politically incorrect kingdom values into a positive brand is a crucial, self-conscious way to be a contrasting community. *Nico-Dirk van Loo*

Disastrous Missional Reinvention

Before we knew it, we had gone from the first uncertain beginnings to a more stationary phase. After three years, we were about fifty people, what must be seen as a success in the highly secularized Danish context. But we seemed to have come to a standstill at that point. The pioneers moved away to other parts of the country. Instead, more settled people came, attracted by the small and cozy community with the reputed creative Sunday services. Babies also showed up and made their demands. It became a huge challenge for us to contain the initial missional vision and transform it into a more sustainable form. So, as the entrepreneurial founding pastor, I strived for what I was best at and set out to reinvent the church. Maybe that wasn't the wisest thing to do.

> Recycled Christians is a key factor in destroying a church plant. *Nico-Dirk van Loo*

Backed up by the church board, I gathered a process team of three people. We initiated a process of coming back to the roots, labeled "Nearby-Church"—a changing from a "come to us" church to a "go out" church. We planned a period of two years for this transformation to take place; we included the whole church in discussion nights and dedicated several Sundays to preaching and talking about Nearby-Church. Still, many were unsure about how to engage themselves in the process, and I wasn't satisfied with the results. Our identity as a church did not turn missional; rather, it was centered on the Sunday services' edification of Christians' individual relations to God. Leaning on the recommendation to "maximize discontinuity," I insisted on the church meeting less frequently on Sundays, thereby threatening what had initially attracted people to our church and what they found most fulfilling. In the end, even the church board found themselves set apart from the process. Being too idealistic and stubborn to soften my eagerness for change for the sake of the flock, I concluded that since I was followed only by a few, I could no longer lead the church. Therefore, in good standing with the church board, I quit. They advertised for a new pastor, but no one applied, and the congregation decided to close down. Bykirken had had its time. Thanks to the accountability and great effort of the church board, I am comforted to know that everybody from the church is still today partaking in a Christian community. The story of Bykirken ended, but the experience and skills acquired live on. Let us now dive into some of these.

> Several church plants in the Netherlands suffered the same struggles and fate. *Nico-Dirk van Loo*

> Many emergent initiatives, if they do not fall into a success-consumerist megachurch model, seem to last from five to seven years. I wonder if that temporality is part of the characteristics of a postmodern response. Is it because of the inherent refusal of entering a maintenance mode? *Eric Zander*

Practices

Tasty Worship

Bykirken over time had different kinds of Sunday services in various localities. They differed significantly from the traditional, strictly regulated parish church morning services in old church buildings all over the country. The most exceptional was the monthly prayer and brunch service. Tables lined with white tablecloths filled the cozy gourmet restaurant Svineriet, and there was a welcoming atmosphere; people hugged one another good-heartedly, but also made sure to talk to newcomers. A welcomer broke the small talk, and a delicious homemade brunch buffet was served. Easy jazz and small talk filled the air until the host broke in, introducing the forty to fifty persons present to the theme of the day.

After a hymn, the pastor led the gathering in a confession of sins. Then came a creative introduction: a film clip, a surreal drama, or perhaps free lottery tickets for everybody. Occasionally, there was a baptism (infant). A Bible text was read aloud or recited by somebody from the church. The sermon reflected actual or existential experiences of the audience. Firmly rooted in the gospel of grace, the pastor explained how God makes a difference and suggested new ways of conduct or new life possibilities. The sermon was followed by two minutes of individual reflection, often supplemented with group discussions. One person stood up and asked for intercession requests, then led the assembly in prayer. Contemporary worship followed. Some did stand, but most stayed seated at the tables. The worship culminated in Communion before a prayer and a blessing ended the service.

> Hospitality entails not only a seat in the church, but a place at the table.
>
> Eddie Gibbs (CM, 47)

All services were prepared by teams, and everyone in the church was engaged in preparing food, preaching, doing practical work, and welcoming. Eating was an intrinsic part of all services, and beginning with brunch was a brilliant way of establishing a good sense of fellowship.

> Andreas's mentor who emphasized the importance of sharing meals together gave brilliant advice. Feminist theologian Letty Russell calls this kind of organic, human community formation "church in the round." Her image of the church as a hospitable round table with room for all is powerful and transformative. The ordinary act of gathering around a table to share food, and the natural distribution of power when all hands and all gifts are needed to create community together, combined with the practice of radical hospitality, has the power to at once draw us close together and open us to making room for others in a new way. *Kelly Bean*

We encouraged interaction and a range of individual options, which, together with the presence of toddlers, made space an ongoing issue. All along the way, we discussed whether our aim was to make the service easily understandable or to provide new expressions of faith for those attending. The Sunday service never really succeeded as an evangelism project, but it worked tremendously well as familiarization and formation of those who had already been introduced to faith and to Bykirken.

> In the Netherlands, social engagement with the local neighborhood is the key success factor. It is one thing to do the same thing in a new way, and it is another to reinvent church as a social network of the kingdom incarnated in a particular time and place. *Nico-Dirk van Loo*

Formation by Communities

Bykirken consisted of forty to fifty committed people. Thus everyone knew everyone else. Many were good friends, and some were relatives. This was valued, and our relationships were a way of experiencing God's nearness in situations of sickness, disease, and unemployment. The cofounding chairman and his wife were unique role models of hospitality and warmhearted friendliness. Their virtues permeated the whole church. My mentor insisted on the need for sharing meals together if we wanted to plant a church, so we shared innumerable meals. The basic unit of community was small groups called "City-communities." Five to eight people met every other week to share a meal, read from the Bible or another text, discuss, and pray. Some of the City-communities had diaconal purposes, such as homework help for immigrants or doing acts of love in the inner-city shopping area. Some went for retreats.

> We also discovered the natural validity of a multidimensional church, with a convivial central gathering meeting in a socially central place (with purposely a maximum of fifty participants) and several intimate groups gathering in homes. *Eric Zander*

Several people established "cowalking" groups of two to four people who were to be mutually accountable for their spiritual and personal formations. They met regularly to talk, ask personal questions, read the Bible, and pray. Once we introduced a two-week lifestyle traineeship. The concept was to let a person take part in another person's life for one week and then vice versa the next week. The purpose was to present the Christian life, not just spoken words, in a dialogical way. Bykirken also arranged various training courses, such as a course on spiritual gifts, a group studying a self-help book, and a couples' course.

There was a tendency to develop a flurry of new ideas and concepts but not always find enough people or time to let things mature or become rooted. Nevertheless, the experience of starting Bykirken from scratch and depending totally on God in very practical ways was formational. Because it was a small church, everybody was committed and engaged; many had the opportunity to test their personal gifts in a safe context and learned and grew extensively. Last but not least, the unceasing insistence on mission had a lasting impact on everyone.

> Do what is doable. Be patient. Doing what is real takes time. *Kelly Bean*

Intersections with the Mission of God

Bykirken was established so that more people in Aarhus could become disciples of Jesus Christ and committed to a Christian community. "Church is mission!" we insisted; but if everything is mission, then nothing is mission. Mission must be practiced. We did so in several ways, discovering that God worked across our plans.

We wanted the worship service to be the flagship of our evangelism. Hence, we promoted it as a welcoming and relevant place with the opportunity of a meeting with God. But no one walked in "straight from the street" as we had expected. A small team started to canvass people, referring to it as "provoked occasions." They met a young man whom God had been calling for two weeks. He started attending services, searching for God. Over time he realized that it was God who had been seeking him. On Easter morning the next year, at sunrise, he was baptized. We set up Alpha courses that made unchurched people more conscious of their faith and led some of them into our community. Less evangelistic confronting activities, such as a self-help group, a couples' course, and various diaconal projects, were all important ways of manifesting a holistic gospel. However, they did not create lasting relationships, and the visible impact was negligible.

> In a post-Christendom era can a Sunday service be the flagship of evangelism? I doubt it seriously. It is by definition a holy place, a holy moment, a holy gathering. Probably too holy for post-Christians (seeker-sensitive works only for culturally prepared non-Christians).
> Nico-Dirk van Loo

Nearby-Church was our most radical mission initiative. Inspired by the Church of England's "fresh expressions" initiative, a process group worked enthusiastically. We wanted to see small missional church communities planted in delimited contexts in which these communities shared with people who were not yet disciples of Jesus. Our ambition was to defy the hybridity of modern life and place the Christian community, ideally even sharing the Eucharist, where people actually lived their lives, so that it could be seen, smelled, and experienced. Two families moved to a troubled neighborhood, a prayer group met in another neighborhood, and a group started meeting frequently at the university bar. But, as described, the idea didn't catch on and the project was never accomplished.

Our understanding was, first and foremost, that it was God's mission. It was also an affirmation of the central importance of relationship in the process of authentic discipleship. We had to realize that contextualization is highly complicated in cultural contexts of individualism and hybridity. Furthermore, creating a missional identity in a Danish Lutheran congregation surely presents a challenging mix of paradigms, mentally and theologically.

Learning Leadership

Change requires leadership skills that Danish theology graduates have not even heard of. Thus we had to learn from failure along the way. We gained knowledge in leadership from reading, leadership courses, and by practical experience. Leading is organic; it is leading people. We led by vision and example (but evaded conflict). It is high responsibility, low control; requires entrepreneurship rather than maintenance; demands an awareness of individual gifts and personalities; and happens in teams, whenever possible. These are buzzwords, yes, but they created a positive atmosphere of freedom and engagement for leadership.

> Andreas's story is such a great example of the realities in Scandinavia, where the seminaries are just about to wake up to what the post-Christendom reality requires for leadership skills. Andreas and his friends tried to do something utterly different from the present model. The story of Bykirken brings hope that the traditional denominations will be able to experiment with new expressions of church. *Ruth Skree*

It was required that Bykirken, as a "congregation of choice," be organized as a democratic association with an annual general meeting and an elected board. However, we never had to vote. Since Bykirken was a church plant with no sending mother-church or initiating network, it was essential for us to have wise mentors on whom we could rely. Still, a formal relation to a mother-church or a church-planting network would have been healthier, and could have spared us much trouble.

The church board initially functioned as the daily leadership team; I served, as pastor, as the main leader in fruitful cooperation with the cofounding chairman. Later the board held a more big-picture position and I became the daily leader of a small pastoral team. This required bringing new personalities onboard and was in fact overkill for such a small organization. I coached all the team leaders and small-group leaders once or twice a year. The most committed leaders were assembled in my mentoring group, which was dedicated to leadership training.

Perhaps insufficient leadership skills were the most important factor for Bykirken's inability to reach beyond fifty in attendance and for its closing down. Insisting to lead the whole church into the radical decentralization process of Nearby-Church overwhelmed the community. If we had encouraged just a few first movers to pioneer the process, either the rest of the church would have followed later, or maybe they'd have convinced us of doing otherwise. Who knows? Anyway, shifting from the demands of visionary entrepreneurship to the demands of sustainability is always difficult and may require a change of person in charge in due time. Yet, God is merciful and allows us to learn from our failures!

> Let us give ourselves permission to fail. Andreas Nielsen's honest and humble telling of the story of Bykirken and his thoughtful analysis of its strengths and weaknesses help us all. Let us hold our dreams and efforts loosely even as we tend them with care. Let us lean forward to learn, and let us be willing, as Andreas has, to look back with grace. *Kelly Bean*

The first value of Bykirken was "To the honor of God!" I hope that God was and is honored by the story of what he did in and through Bykirken. I pray and hope that the story will inspire and encourage others who explore new territory in carrying on God's great mission.

20

House for All Sinners and Saints

Nadia Bolz-Weber

House for All Sinners and Saints started with eight people in my living room. It feels weird to say this since in our culture we are awash in origin myths of great giants of industry, technology, and manufacturing, all having suspiciously humble beginnings in mythical garages—as if Microsoft and REI and Facebook all started with nothing more than bailing wire, duct tape, a one-car garage, and "a dream." Wanting to believe our American notion that anything is possible if you dream big enough, we cling to these stories of big, impressive enterprises starting from nothing. Living rooms, then, are the garages of start-up churches—as if Willow Creek, Quest, and Mars Hill all started with nothing more than bailing wire, a Bible, a living room, and "a dream." So I'd love to say that (1) HFASS started some other, more interesting way and that (2) we too have become a big, impressive, successful church from humble origins. But if I did so I would be lying.

Having said all of that, I'll just say: House for All Sinners and Saints started with eight people in my living room. It was the fall of 2007 and I was still in seminary, but I knew exactly what I was going to do when I graduated, so I figured, why not do it before I graduated?

Story: Not Pastor Material

I did not actually go to seminary to be a pastor. It is a longer story than can be told here, but suffice it to say, I did not go to seminary to become a pastor because, simply put, I am a lousy choice to be a pastor. Not once has anyone met me and thought, "I bet she's a pastor." Maybe it's the sleeve tattoos. Maybe it's the fact that I swear like a truck driver. But I'm not pastor material. So I went to seminary hoping to just stay forever in the academy since academics was the only thing I was ever very good at. But about two months in, when I was studying website content for several emerging churches, I read something that made me start thinking in a way I never had before. Church of the Apostles (a Lutheran-Episcopal emerging church in Seattle) featured a statement on their website that said something like, "No need to check your culture at the door. So sport your tats, carry your java, wear your jeans and join us for Eucharist." I reread it like five times. Was there a Lutheran church out there that was asking me to show up? Me?

> Many of our churches seem to be exclusive and separative. *Markus Weimer*

Here's a bit more background. I was raised in the Church of Christ. Not the gay-friendly liberal United Church of Christ. The Church of Christ, which is like Baptist-plus. The church I attended three times a week for sixteen years was sectarian and fundamentalist; women were not even permitted to pray aloud in front of men. Suffice it to say, I left that church when I was sixteen and was happily "de-churched" for ten years until I met my husband, who was then a Lutheran seminary student. I had at this point in time been clean and sober for four years. Four years prior to meeting my now-husband, God had suddenly and somewhat rudely interrupted my life, picked me up off my path of self-destruction, and said, "That's adorable, but I have something else in mind," and plunked me down onto another path entirely—a path that eventually led of all places to the Evangelical Lutheran Church in America.

During Matthew's final year of seminary I began attending St. Paul Lutheran church in Oakland, California, where I was exposed to the Lutheran theology of grace, a teaching I immediately recognized as true, not because I was choosing to adopt some foreign ideology as my own, but because I had actually experienced it to be true. I had undeniably experienced God's grace in getting clean and sober, and now I was hearing a historically rooted, beautiful articulation of what I had already experienced in my life, but in the form of Lutheran theology. It changed everything. I was in the adult confirmation class at St. Paul, and I was also attending liturgy every week—equally as unexplainable. I had never in my life experienced liturgy, and it felt like a mysterious and ancient gift handed down from generations of the faithful. It washed over me. I thought, "I want to go back and do those things and say those things again," and I had no idea why. That's how I fell in love with Lutheranism.

Honestly, I would sit in the pew and look around and think, "No one here looks like me." My friends were not going to ELCA churches, and not because the Lutheran Church is doing something wrong. It's just that in order for my friends to go to a Lutheran church, they have to culturally commute from who they are to who the church is, and they just are not going to make the trip. I happen to be native to a very particular cultural context: I'm an urban young(ish) adult who is heavily tattooed, a bit cynical, overeducated, kind of artsy-fartsy, and socially progressive. My friends aren't going to show up to a nicey-nice Lutheran church with the friendly chit-chat and the pews in a row and the organ music and the awkward formality. Again, there is nothing wrong with traditional church. It's often a faithful and genuine expression of living out the gospel; it's just not an expression that is native to or conversant with my context.

> The appreciation of the traditional church is rare among pioneers, but much needed unless we want to create short-lived new traditions that the next generation will then discard likewise. Peter Aschoff

Community: The Beginnings of HFASS

So there I was in seminary studying the website content of churches when I realized that maybe I was called to be a pastor to my people. Maybe I was supposed to share what I had discovered with people in my own cultural context. That's how HFASS started. In late 2005 I started a monthly "theology pub" at the Mercury Café in downtown Denver—an artsy hangout and about the last place in the city you'd expect anything vaguely Christian to take place.

In the fall of 2007 I began to meet monthly in my fabled living room with seven others who were compelled by the idea of starting a church. We prayed together and ate together, and that was really about it. The following spring we went on a retreat over Holy Week in which we celebrated a condensed Triduum (Maundy Thursday, Good Friday, and Easter vigil); we gathered in a room with the Stations of the Cross and silently, meditatively walked around writing questions and statements on pieces of paper at each station. I feel as though it was in those moments and in those actions that we became church. Later the next day we sat around with big sheets of paper trying to discern how

God might be moving in and through us. Convinced that God had created us to be who we are and where we are, we tried to really get down to describing what characterizes us and the others in our context.

> Church happens when people encounter the risen Christ (Mark 3:14). Suddenly you realize that there is plenty of room for diversity in rhythm and style. *Markus Weimer*

Here is what we came up with: We are people who went to church once and are now evangelical refugees. We are people who never stopped going to church, yet are seeking a community that provides a different level of engagement. We are youngish and adultish. We resonate more with the mystical and contemplative than the obvious and simplistic. We work in nonprofits (and with nonprophets); we are graduate students, social workers, and young professionals. We participate in virtual culture and are tech savvy enough to realize that we are not actually tech savvy. We are artists who mediate progressive culture outside the mainstream. We are postmodern urban dwellers who are delighted to not live close to such things as Applebee's. We are terminally ironic, white, and educated. We are the injured who are striving to be self-aware; struggle is an almost constant. Our cynicism can sometimes just be masking our confusion and vulnerability. Our idealism is based in the trust that transformation is possible in the individual, the church, and the whole world. We are queer. Some have children, some live alone, some are alone, some are partnered. We tend to overthink things because we're geeky and analytical. Some of us are rooted here, but most are somewhat transient. We are friends and allies of all the above.

And here is why we decided it was needed: House for All is important because it is experimenting with new ways to do church that make sense to urban postmodern young people. It is a place where the gospel matters; liturgy is recontextualized; we reclaim the word "Christian"; Scripture is honored enough to be faithfully questioned and struggled with; we welcome those wounded by the church; we address issues that the wider church has often forgotten or ignored; we no longer have to culturally commute or bracket out parts of ourselves to be in Christian community. Instead of complaining or criticizing we are empowered to be creative; we are cocreators of worship and community, rather than just passive participants; aesthetics and theology both matter. The community is both intellectually and spiritually stimulating; we provide a connection or a bridge to the mainline and to the traditions of the church.

> Brilliant description that reflects the genuine Lutheran pattern of both freedom and being bound. *Peter Aschoff*

> That kind of close association to the established church is a very important sign of hope.
> The DNA of a mixed economy seems to be central to the young church for sinners and saints.
> *Markus Weimer*

House is important because it takes community and relationships seriously. It is a place where there is authentic space and accountability; people can land, and they can call this community home. We are on a shared journey; there is vulnerability, challenge, and growth. The work of the Spirit is witnessed to through challenging and nurturing relationships; our deepest longings can be expressed and heard. True community is offered, and people belong to one another. We offer intimacy, not megachurch anonymity. We can really share joys and sorrows, and where do urban young people get to do that? We can help one another live out our shared values. We connect the margins and the mainstream.

Our little group of eight decided to finally have a public liturgy, so in April 2008 we clumsily and excitedly hosted a liturgy called the Stations of the Resurrection wherein we each took one of the resurrection accounts and created a way for folks to experience that text. One station featured the text of John 20 in which Mary Magdalene mistakes Jesus for the gardener (a mix-up I'm certain her friends never let her live down). She then, of course, does not recognize Christ until he speaks her name. This text was printed out on either side of an icon of Mary Magdalene. Under her picture was printed one verse from the middle of the story, "Jesus said to her, 'Mary,'" and under the "Mary" was a long set of empty quotes ("_____") where people were invited to write their own names.

Our community continued to offer liturgy once a month for the next eight months until my ordination, after which we worshiped weekly. The past two and a half years have been unforeseeably fun and frustrating. We have grown into a real church and have done so in what feels like the most clunky and beautiful way possible.

> Being myself an indistinguishable introvert, average and ordinary, and a Dane, it is surprising how many traits of the genesis of House for All Sinners and Saints resemble those of Bykirken, which I coplanted in Denmark. *Andreas Østerlund Nielsen*

Practices

Worship

Worship at House for All is pretty much just like a Rolling Stones concert—uh, I mean, nothing at all like a Rolling Stones concert. We follow the ancient liturgy of the church (chanting the Kyrie, reading from Scripture, chanting the psalm, sermon, prayers of the people, Eucharist, and benediction). We also sing the old hymns of the church. So there is lots of ancient tradition at HFASS, but there is also some innovation. We always include poetry and a time called "Open Space," in which we slow down for prayer and other opportunities to actively engage the gospel, writing in the community's Book of Thanks or writing prayers or making art or assembling bleach kits for the needle exchange in Denver.

During Advent one year, over the span of four weeks of liturgies, we created an Advent icon (classic image of Mary with the Christ child still within her). The final piece was beautiful: four feet tall, three feet wide, and made entirely out of torn-up bits of Christmas advertising. As a community we took what society said Christmas is about (J. Crew sweaters, new electronics, and red and green candy) and did a little death and resurrection on it. On some level, that is what this Christian faith is about. Finally there is nothing that God is not making new.

We like to say that we are "anti-excellence/pro-participation," meaning that the liturgy is led by the people who show up. The pastor offers the eucharistic prayer and the sermon; all the other parts of the liturgy are led by people from where they are sitting. As a matter of fact, even the music is made by the community. With the exception of the four or five times a year when we have a bluegrass service, the liturgy is a capella. So all the music you hear in liturgy comes from the bodies of those who show up. Our worship is deeply liturgical and sacramental; for us it is entering a flowing stream of generations of the faithful using the same actions and words of those who have come before us. We gather to be reminded of, and indeed swim in, God's promises.

> Nadia's approach is completely unapologetic about the traditional components of liturgical formation. HFASS reflects a creative ease which is simultaneously rooted in the tradition, yet free to recontextualise it so that its full missional potential becomes apparent. A number of writers have indicated how using the Stations of the Cross has permitted a reengagement with public space with strong missional potential. Is such an approach to public ritual merely trading on a residual memory of Christendom, or is there something lasting in liturgical tradition that will hold good in contexts and times when public "Christian" memory has completely faded? Will the future use of Christian liturgical formative tradition be restricted to within the Christian community, or will it remain a useful tool for engagement beyond the church's bounds? *Paul Roberts*

Community

The HFASS community is one that is always in flux. When we were just starting out someone asked me what my five- and ten-year plans were. I answered,

"To be an adaptive, responsive leader, and who and what I am adapting and responding to changes with everyone who joins us and everyone who leaves us." This has proved to be truer than I imagined. The vast majority of the church is single folks ages twenty-two to forty-two, a population that is transient, without a lot of resources, and more than a little commitment-phobic, but it's also a population that is found the least in the pews of Lutheran churches. Young adults seem eager for community, comforted by mystery, and their engagement with the world is in itself their spiritual practice. So church becomes not another product in a marketplace of lifestyles but an antidote to the messages received about self and other in this deeply consumeristic society. Finding meaning in the beautiful and heartbreaking reality we live in, and doing that in community while tethered to a rich theological and liturgical tradition, is what we do.

> I believe Nadia's ten-year plan is truer and wiser than the most elaborate church leadership strategy you can find. If church is all about relationships, and the people are continually moving due to the high mobility in our globalized society, church is about responding to change and continuously reshaping itself. *Ruth Skree*

On a Sunday last June I got a call at 11:00 a.m. It was Rachel calling from her hometown church. It took several minutes before she could form a proper sentence through her sobs. Finally, in a shaky voice, this came out: "I'm at my parents' church . . . they are doing Communion . . . and I'm not allowed to take it." Having spent the last year in such a deeply sacramental community where all freely receive the gifts of God, Rachel was devastated at being kept from the table. I texted her later to ask if I could share this story with some of the other HFASSers and she agreed. "Rachel called me sobbing," I told them, "because she wasn't allowed to take Communion at her parents' church this morning." Stuart immediately responded, "Well then we'll have to take her the Eucharist at the airport when she gets home." Of course.

When Rachel got off the escalator she saw a sign reading "Rachel" on one side and "Child of God" on the other. I then lied just a tiny bit and asked if she wouldn't mind if we popped upstairs because someone had asked me about the chapel and I wanted to make sure I knew where it was. So at 10:00 p.m. on a Wednesday night, eight people were waiting in the aesthetically questionable "interfaith prayer chapel" at Denver International Airport to give our sister in Christ the gifts of God that are truly for her and for all. "This is how they will know that you are my disciples": that you take my body and blood to the airport.

Mission

If you have never shoved a bunch of people into the basement of a bar from which you belt out old hymns at the top of your lungs while drinking a pint of beer, then, well, you should. Our Beer and Hymns event, held every few months, is "outreach." Or maybe it's "evangelism." Or is it "mission"? Whatever it is, it's fun and quirky and we love it. What's even better is that people in the broader community join us for our "signature events": Beer and Hymns, the Blessing of the Bicycles, Operation Turkey Sandwich, Fat Tuesday at the Thin Man Bar. At first I saw these events as a way of getting people to know who we are and what we are about so that then they would come and join our church (I mean, come on . . . a church that blesses bicycles? Who wouldn't want to join that!). After a year of putting on really wonderful, dynamic, fun events that were all well attended, we realized not one person joined as a result. Not one. For a minute I felt the events were a failure until I realized that maybe these things we do (which we love) are a beautiful way of being the church in Denver and therefore are an end in themselves and not simply a means to an end. So in liturgy, when we assemble bleach kits for the underground needle exchange (for IV drug users) in Denver; or hand out fresh roasted turkey sandwiches, pumpkin pie bars, and stuffing muffins in sack lunches closed with a sticker that says "It sucks you have to work on Thanksgiving. Operation Turkey Sandwich, brought to you by House for All Sinners and Saints"; or bring a monthly home-cooked meal to Rainbow Alley (a drop-in center for queer youth), we do so because that is authentically how we are church. It's not recruitment.

> The attempt to draw people out of the pub and into the HFASS community could be described as a typical "bridge-trap." Instead HFASS realized that they *are* church in their context. *Markus Weimer*

Leadership

I know it's not very cool, but I'm the pastor of HFASS. It's not a house church. It's not an autonomous collective. A couple years ago I was on a panel at Greenbelt (a faith-based justice, music, and arts festival in the UK) about authority and leadership in the emerging church. After others had shared about their communities being flat and there being no formal authority given to any one person, I finally realized what it felt like to be the pastor at HFASS, so I spoke up, saying, "Being the pastor at House doesn't mean I'm the one who is ontologically more special and more Christian than everyone else; it just means that I am the one who is set apart to not have the same freedom as everyone else in the community."

I am not free to have private conversations and talk about them with others. I'm not free to flirt with people in the community or get my emotional needs met through them. I'm not free to point to anything but Christ and him crucified. I am set apart for Word and Sacrament and take the office of preaching seriously. Knowing the community, I take them with me into what feels like a wrestling match with the text, and I don't walk away before demanding a blessing from that text for my community; and when I walk away, I walk away limping. So that's what being the pastor means. It also means having a really clear understanding of my limits.

> Even in postmodernity, there can be no leadership without an appropriate exercise of authority. Such authority does not arise from a leader's position or title but originates in the trust built up on the basis of character, competence, respect, and consistency.
>
> Eddie Gibbs (LN, 66)

While this church was started from my vision and passion and, perhaps, idiocy, the only way for the community to have its own life and identity is for me to not be at the center of everything. The leadership of others is what will continue to make House for All Sinners and Saints a viable and vibrant church. We are at a place now where things happen at church that have nothing to do with me. Which is beautiful and, for me, a little terrifying, as it means letting go and allowing for the possibility that maybe God is acting upon us in ways I never thought of.

21

L'Autre Rive
(The Other Bank or Shore)

Eric Zander

Story

It all started with a deep personal crisis. As director of the Belgian Evangelical Mission, the main church-planting mission in Belgium, I had fallen in despair in response to the irrelevance of the current church model that we kept duplicating as if it was the only available one. According to common wisdom, its lack of success was due to poor engagement of the Christians (inwardly) and the hardness of the harvest soil (outwardly).

Need for a New Model?

Obviously, the model we pursued does not work in Belgium. Inside the church walls, most local churches cannot afford to pay their pastor's salary but still expect him to be available full-time. They struggle to even find the required number of elders. They allocate the largest part of their budget to maintaining a hardly used building. They put the pressure on a minority to serve a majority, and they produce consumers living on assistance. Outside the church walls, the church developed its own culture apart from, and often against, the surrounding culture, requesting from outsiders a difficult integration and initiation process. In this scenario, conversion to church precedes conversion to Christ.

Cosmetic adaptations to church will not fix the problem; the church model itself needs to be reconsidered. The only hope for the future of church planting is through a fresh vision of church, an eradication of an irrelevant church culture, and a reimagination of a new model. Only these changes would address the deep fight within me between my frustration of existing church reality and my aspiration for a living church against whom even the gates of hell would not prevail.

I realized it would mean leaving the boat, the boat of my leadership position, the boat of my strategy expertise, the boat of confidence in my own skills and experience, to jump into the depths of a journey to the unknown. The whole strategic process had to be reversed; instead of the typical "Z-thinking" defining

> The problem with the image of planting is that it suggests a predetermined model that will be inserted into a host culture, without regard for its relevance. In order to avoid this impression, I personally prefer the language of birthing, which emphasizes that a new church is not simply the latest model of an already-existing church, but rather represents a newly created church that is birthed within specific cultural contexts.
>
> Eddie Gibbs (CM, 67–68)

the way, new intuition must lead to experimentation, and constant evaluation would show just the next step of our way. Frustration and aspiration were replaced by anguish and passion—anguish of the unknown and passion for a new hope for me and for church planting.

That reminds me of Alan Roxburgh's Missional Change Model. *Peter Aschoff*

But where to start? Intuition had to be fed, not by existing surrounding models, but in three different ways: by reflection, observation, and experimentation. So with the blessing of our mission agency, we set a year apart for that crucial process.

The motivations are strikingly similar between Zander's experience and the emerging groups in Latin America, and the temptation remains the same! The idea of avoiding doing church in the old way, and seeking a new way for doing church, can lead any group onto an empty path going nowhere. My point is this: we must avoid the temptation of finding creative ways for doing church. Instead, we must seek new ways for the Spirit to develop within us a faithful contextual way of being the church. If doing church is about better strategies, then being church is about discovering the purpose for the community, as agent of the reign of God, in the immediate world that surrounds us. *Osías Segura-Guzmán*

Doing church is merely a manifestation of being church. First, doing church expresses concretely our vision about being church. The goal is not to look any different but to consciously reflect our understanding of what a Christian community is to be. Second, the ways of "practicing church" educate both believers and outsiders about the meaning of a Christian community, inwards and outwards. *Eric Zander*

Reflection

Through the start of a new degree in applied theology with a focus on ministry in contemporary society at Spurgeon's College (London), I received the opportunity for theological reflection, acquired skills in research methods, and read a wide variety of content that opened my eyes to alternative ways of conceiving the church. In addition, a series of visits to ecclesiology professors at different European Bible schools allowed me to confront some of these strange ideas.

Theological preparation is crucial indeed. In the Netherlands the more theologically trained the church planters, the more they engage in contextualization. *Nico-Dirk van Loo*

Observation

Theological reflection led me to visit some twenty-five alternative expressions of church around Europe (France, Switzerland, the Netherlands, the UK) and the United States. Confronted with the same questions, they offered concrete answers, some proposing a real alternative model, and others just cosmetic adaptations.

> The primary task of the leader is to reconnect ecclesiology and missiology in order that the church be defined first and foremost by its God-given mission.
>
> Eddie Gibbs (LN. 38)

An Experiment

Experimentation

Through a combination of reflection and observation, the original intuitions turned into concrete ideas ready for experimentation. A network of about fifteen young adults agreed to gather once a month and allowed me to try out some "new ways" of doing church. Of course that closed experiment would never correspond to a real church community, but it offered a useful context to discern some dynamics of a renewed church model. It also showed the great worth of liturgy as a tool for enculturation and participation.

During a season, from September to June, we learned so much and felt we were ready for an open experiment. We took the summer to define and visit our own family social network. We chose two interrelated levels of engagement and development within a defined network context: (1) inside the church—an intranetwork enculturated Christian community with a series of monthly church gatherings with open experimentation; and (2) outside the church—incarnation within the social context.

The Network Context

Traditionally, a target group for a new church plant is strategically established according to the geographical spiritual distribution of the population, with typical strategic goals (e.g., one church for every ten thousand people). Our approach focused on our relationship network and the observation of the absence of a Christian impact within that specific network. As we dreamed of an incarnated Christian community, it had to take flesh within an existing social network and through its codes and culture.

> This is key to being church in mission. Not just to target, but to exist as a Christian community in a certain, delimited context, so that God's redemption can be smelled, seen, and tasted through the body of Christ present in this social network, neighborhood, workplace. *Andreas Østerlund Nielsen*

> Eric is working on new ground. The main emphasis in France is now on "one church for every ten thousand people." Eric's emphasis is relational, not statistical, and that is courageous indeed. It is not just "one church with every ten people" who then reproduce the mother church, but "one culturally adapted church with every ten culturally aware Christians." *Matthias Radloff*

The Social Incarnation

Listing all the different organizations serving in our social networks, including public and religious authorities, allowed us to meet personally with the people already involved in the community. We shared with each of them a triple message: (1) the willingness to listen and understand their part in the service of the community and their most pressing needs; (2) the thankfulness for their service, underlining the failure of many Christians in the responsibility they are carrying; and (3) the question about what priorities and format a new Christian community should have if it has the desire to integrate the social network, and what synergies could be foreseen. We then could define a "church strategy" integrating their remarks and serving the community. I could also personally evaluate and engage with some concrete needs. I chose two different organizations with pressing needs that I could handle. Since then, I serve the community every week, and along the way I develop and strengthen our social network, and I gain a social identity and credibility as well.

> Before L'Autre Rive ever launched their first gathering, Zander was very active in social programs for the city. Because of his social participation and networking in Gembloux, the city workers perceive him as a colleague. Considering that many evangelical churches are perceived as sects, L'Autre Rive's role and perception in the community is a role model for emerging churches in Europe. *Blayne Waltrip*

> Starting your own social network in the Netherlands is a key factor for success. In the Netherlands, *only* the socially incarnated projects are successful in the long run. *Nico-Dirk van Loo*

The Enculturated Community

Before starting any specific activity, we visited all the friends of our family network, believers or not, sharing our dream of an alternative Christian community that would be not exclusive and separated from "real life," but open to everybody and enculturated in our society. We mentioned our desire to try to experiment with another way of being church, asking them for advice on the how, where, when, who, and so on of this crazy project. We insisted on the need for their evaluation of our attempt to integrate our culture into a new community.

So even before the start, the evaluative dynamic of the project underlined the experiment. But at some point we needed to actually start the project. Based on the different inputs, the lessons of our previous "closed" experiment, and the ideas taken from other alternative projects, we set a series of ten gatherings. We directly chose a seasonal structuring, mirrored on school and television calendars: once a month for ten months, ten episodes, one big narrative story, adult and children programs in parallel. But only the first gathering was prepared, pending the reactions and evaluation. We had to reformat our vision of a Christian gathering and reexpress the fundamentals of the gospel with contemporary cultural tools.

> Interesting to see that the initial things the community does are "events" in a totally different format than expected. In the Netherlands, "events" are of less and less importance in successful Dutch projects. *Nico-Dirk van Loo*

The location was also a serious issue. If we wanted the new expression of church to emerge from the culture, it had to happen within the cultural frame, not only in behavior but also in the physical setting. God opened the way for us to use a community hall, commonly dedicated to public social care. Our initiative was eventually considered as one other social service to the population.

The Gatherings Begin

The first season helped shape a new open format and dynamic. Although the priority in the first season was the conceptualization of the gatherings, the people attended regularly and community ownership developed. The second season added a second monthly gathering, but focused more on building the community, with additional "family activities": meals, parties, a first family weekend away. As we are now halfway through the third season, we have seen the need to deepen relationships and spiritual rooting. We stayed with two monthly open gatherings, but alternatively added "church at home," with smaller groups gathering on weekends in homes for a more intimate time of sharing and meditating.

But the evaluation process is still going on, and we see now the need for an exaltation dimension to our gatherings, less often and confidential, but with a bigger crowd and a more celebrative program. We also want to invest in the networks of the people of our Christian community, encouraging and helping them in their own context. And what's next? We remain sensitive to the intuitions generated by our current experience, lighting up the next steps: church at home, social expressions of church, a new exaltation dimension. But the final model is not clear, and actually should it ever be?

> Your intuition certainly seems to be well founded. This is the story of well-planned, strategic straightforwardness. Potential missional-emergent church planters should notice this exemplary approach. *Andreas Østerlund Nielsen*

Practices

The Missional Gathering

Developing an enculturated, missional Christian gathering was one of the two dimensions of our original endeavor. The open Christian gathering expresses the essence of the Christian community and, even more in our post-Catholic context, the public identity for the society. This regular event also presents a typical entry point for people on a spiritual search. For Christian

> Within an eastern culture, table-fellowship and the sharing of a meal is regarded as a particularly intimate form of association. The fact that Jesus was prepared to act in such a fashion, and to be *seen* doing it, communicated as powerfully as any pronouncement, both to his friends at the table and his enemies at the window. . . . His actions were deliberately intended to demonstrate the present reality and radical nature of the Kingdom.
>
> Eddie Gibbs (IBCG, 73)

believers, it carries a pedagogic dimension and a stimulation for their spiritual walk and their engagement in the world. For spiritual seekers, it offers an opportunity to taste the fellowship of the Christian community and to journey communally with Jesus. Two principles would guarantee the "missionality": enculturation and participation, underlining the physical setup and the format of the gathering.

The chance to use a socially identified location offered an ideal frame, but still needed to be optimized by a setup that would culturally express fellowship, authenticity, and spirituality. This social environment had to become a "contemporary sanctuary": both a friendly and a sacred place. In Belgian culture, fellowship requires table and food. So there needed to be a meal (we chose breakfast) with decorated tables, and people seated face-to-face, and good food. But at the center of this family restaurant setting, the "table of the Lord" stands with a big cross, candles, and other typical "religious" symbols, to remind us of the sacredness of this privileged time and space. More specific decorative elements can also add beauty and the arts, as well as creative illustrations of the topic of the current day. Avoiding a stage or up-front presentation, but positioning the speakers and musicians all around, and even walking among the tables, breaks down the spectator-consumer mentality and makes everybody an active participant.

> The liturgy at L'Autre Rive is something that contemporary people can appreciate because of how mystical it is. It is a place where the ancient meets the contemporary. They may use ancient texts and ancient songs, but with contemporary arrangements or melody. At L'Autre Rive, liturgy flows from one end to the other. *Blayne Waltrip*

We rediscovered liturgy as a wonderful missional tool for enculturation and participation in the unfolding of the service. The liturgical reflection forces intentional content and opens a frame for creative and coherent participation. The whole gathering becomes a journey, the leader a guide, and the disciples travelers on a cooperative exploration. Starting with the meal, we travel through the different elements expressed through contemporary culture, encouraging creative inspiration and making room for holistic involvement. Preaching becomes collective discovery, proposed theoretical applications are replaced by shared self-questioning and personal engagement. There is often an opportunity for physical gestures, during the exploration process or in response to the encounter with God and his Word. Every aspect is colored by our culture: it could be religious, like the chant of the "Kyrie Eleison" or some profession of faith proclamations; it could be contemporary media, like movie trailers or pop music; it could be our French culture, like French poets or drama, but also our Protestant-evangelical background in our worship and individual prayers. It is all like surfing on constant ambiguity, between the tradition and the contemporary, between the sacred and the secular, between the individual and the collective, between reflection and active participation, between noise and silence; it is all like life! Hopefully this is our goal: that entering the Christian fellowship would not mean leaving real life for an artificial religious event, but opening another dimension, maybe a little strange and unusual, to our authentic life.

> Great preaching and high-quality music may be able to draw a crowd, but they do not build an *organism* in which all have a functional role.
>
> Eddie Gibbs (CN, 199)

> L'Autre Rive's goal is to have a flexible, conscious, and fluid liturgy. It is flexible in that the liturgy is organized in interchangeable blocks. The blocks of liturgy are removable and replaceable. The conscious liturgy is something that a person from a Catholic background can hold on to because it is part of his or her tradition. Yet, their liturgy is fluid compared to the Catholic Church. *Blayne Waltrip*

The Community Development

From the start, we avoided, as much as possible, identifying with the common understanding of church, but insisted on the "alternative Christian community" character of our project. This rather countercultural choice regularly required some explanation. Actually, our first location plan was canceled a few weeks before our first gathering, and we were left in uncertainty until just a few days before holding our first service. But although it was not our first choice, it revealed a strategic start underlining the primacy of the community experience over the meeting place. Of course, the emphasis on the existing relationship network also contributed.

The request we made to people, even nonbelievers, to help in evaluating our endeavor opened a danger zone for genuine participation and community development: they would come with an expectant and maybe even a consumer attitude. There is a very thin line between the attraction of a quality performance feeding consumerism, and the personal and communal transformation produced by a creative journey stimulating ownership. So we had to intentionally engage people in conviviality through the participative service, but also in adding other community development actions (e.g., meals, parties, a weekend out).

> Nominal and non-Christians feel comfortable at L'Autre Rive gatherings. *Blayne Waltrip*

Our original and creative new way of "doing church" presented an even greater threat in attracting "Christian tourists" zapping from church to church, searching for the new trend. We chose to confront this typical behavior by welcoming those strangers for a one-time visit and asking them not to come back for a while.

> Great! How can you do that in a good, respectful way? And how did you know who was a "tourist"? *Peter Aschoff*

> These "tourists" usually come from outside our social network. They have a church history, often unstable. We explain that our vision is that a community emerges through our local social network, and that natural relationships are foundational to our community. Visitors from outside this natural network just cannot integrate and belong. We now have friends who visit us once in a while, to be encouraged and to encourage us, but remain occasional outside visitors. *Eric Zander*

The open character of our gathering encourages genuine community. Everybody is welcome to journey at his own pace, but also together as a community. Allowing each participant to walk at his own rhythm actually stimulated the sense of ownership. The encouragement and openness for every traveler, professing Christian or not, to engage in some concrete contribution, in preparation or during the gatherings, also contributed to the ownership feeling. Not only could the people get involved in the community, but the community got involved in the people's lives, encouraging their personal dreams of engagement for the world. We are collecting clothes for the homeless through an organization where one of us is engaged, selling Indian spices to support a project in India engaged by another one, collecting food, selling waffles, praying, and caring. Less structure (no membership), combined with more openness and involvement, brought less church and more community.

Finally, this current season adds a "church at home" dimension to our gatherings. This intimate approach is not publicized, but limited to the regular travelers. The time and location are communicated to the participants only, protecting the privacy of the gathering within a "home" setup. This "exclusive" development obviously contributes to shaping the community ownership.

The Missionary Impact

Of course, the outward dimension has to be intentionally emphasized to avoid a "ghettoization" of the community. From the start of the reflection process, the wider social community actors were consulted to help draw the outlines of the community yet to come. This consultation led me, the initiator of the project, to engage concretely in two different local social care projects, as a model for the community and as a direct link. Being actively involved in numerous workshops, advisory groups, and consultations outside the Christian community allowed a double identity for the community I am representing, both religious and social. My personal contributions opened the way for greater community involvement, both within our gatherings and out in the world.

Our liturgical gatherings include a missionary section, presenting a specific project to support and, when possible, proposing a concrete action. We have even welcomed some secular social organizations to present their work within our service. Using a public building as our gathering place within the wider social network contributes to the social identity of our community. This social identity is recognized by the public authorities inviting our representatives to the secular network consultations. We are now asked to hold liturgical gatherings, both occasionally and regularly, in other social contexts—for example, a gospel celebration during a country music festival, and a monthly liturgical service in a retirement home.

By our connections and involvement we generate synergies between different social actors, acting ourselves as network facilitators. We feel strongly that we exist in our social context and that we impact our world with the values of the kingdom, but it requires repeated efforts of integration, a permanent attitude of service, and a constant awareness and availability.

This community social mind-set has a direct influence on our participants' own social involvement, through our community projects, but also on their own. Our role is to stimulate, encourage, follow up, and help when needed, but also to leave room for people to serve the outside community in their own way. We have purposely chosen not to propose any activity during the weekdays, no Bible studies or prayer meetings. Limiting our church programs will leave people more available for their neighborhood and for a potential social engagement. Less church for more mission!

> Very good to see that there are no "during the week" church things; this forces the church to limit its consumption of resources and frees its members to live lives engaged with neighbors. *Nico-Dirk van Loo*

The Leadership

It all started with a very personal initiative, almost private, as our family was actually carrying every aspect of the new endeavor. The typical original church-planting leadership dynamic placed the church planter as the initiator and leader. But we soon involved another couple in sharing the direction of the project. Beginning with the second season, two couples joined us for an "educative team," leading the intuition-evaluation-reaction process. The original dream of building a realistic enculturated church model has to include a vision of a local nonprofessional team leadership. We are still experimenting and it sometimes seems utopian, but our intuition is leading us toward an episcopal format, with local lay leaders teaming up as educators, translating the vision in local terms, and regional supervisors setting the vision, overseeing a network of communities, and being available for training. But our vision is still unclear, and we move on one step at a time as God lights our path.

After having lost courage and every hope for an authentic church expression for our post-Christendom culture, we now have a deep sense of a new opening, not the final strategy, but the beginning of a renewed journey of the church of Jesus for our contemporary world. Is it a success story? I don't know. But whatever happens, even if it stops tomorrow, we would have been alive in this exciting journey. But for now we walk on, with passion and anguish, realizing that many surprises are waiting. What an adventure, the church!

22

With

An Experimental Church

Eileen Suico

An Experiment

"With" is an experimental church exploring what it means to live in community with God and with people. It is an ethnically diverse community in Federal Way, Washington (twenty miles south of Seattle). Most of the people grew up in multilingual homes, and the largest group, ethnically, is Filipino. It is composed of a few families and mostly students with ages ranging from sixteen to twenty-three. With started as a small group of tweens in our living room in 2003.

The importance of knowing that we are on a journey is that we are aware that we have not arrived yet. We know that we are in the midst of a shift from how we were raised into how God intended us to become. We are aware that during a shift, we constantly make choices. We confront difficult questions. What do we do with meetings that have become stale? Do we get rid of them or do we find their essence? What were their purposes? What good comes out of meetings? Do we meet only for the sake of fulfilling an obligation? We are aware that the moment we stop asking these honest questions, we cease to be true to the journey on which we have embarked. Moreover, in the midst of questioning, we realize the need to redeem rather than eliminate practices. Through this process, we find ourselves in good company with a God who is in a mission of redeeming rather than eliminating.

> Great questions. A Pentecostal church in Melbourne, Urban Life, asked why they sing and preach to one another in their midweek small group meetings. No one was enjoying it much, so they ditched the singing and intense Bible study and set only two rules for small groups, which became known as "Get-Togethers" or "GTs": (1) a big table to share a meal, and (2) no Bible study. Participation from people in and outside the church increased dramatically.
> Darren Cronshaw

Our Story

With was once a youth ministry called BASIC (Brothers and Sisters in Christ), named after an older group of youth from a church who used to hold Sunday services twenty-five miles north of where we live. Being so far from the rest of the people we see on Sundays, my daughter wanted a church group for her friends from school and for our neighbors for the rest of the week.

We started with three kids and met at our house. Looking back, we attempted various church growth strategies we could think of to invite people. We called friends the night before, which almost felt like cold calls, to make sure we had lots of people coming the next day. We held events and programs to draw students in. We hosted summer carnivals, Valentine's Day parties, graduation celebration, harvest festivals, and so on to attract students and make them come to church. We measured our success by the number of people who came and stayed.

Disconnected

Since we shared a gospel that guarantees forgiveness of sins and a place in heaven through Jesus's death, our concern was getting people to hear the only way toward eternal life. We spoke a message that we are saved by grace and not by works, and we put more emphasis on the life after than the one now. The temporal implication of this current life and the permanence of the one later seemed to stir indifference to matters of the present. It somehow lessened any sense of urgency to act on issues like poverty, AIDS, malaria, and especially environmental concerns. Since heaven awaits for those who have accepted the gift, this life and this world are regarded as mere temporal holding ground while waiting for heaven. Our heavenly focus was strongly represented in our lifestyle as a church. In our camps and picnics, we filled the trash bin with plastic cups, spoons, forks, disposable trays, plastic wrap, Styrofoam, unsorted recyclables, and so forth. School programs (e.g., Key Clubs, food drives, and food awareness) promoted better well-being and care than we did.

Churches need environmental checklists and carbon checks. *Darren Cronshaw*

We taught about a God who is compassionate, gracious, and other-centered. However, our preoccupation with meetings, discipleship programs, event planning, and other attractional events gave us little time to associate with people outside the church. We treated our work and people at school with less importance than the work we did within ministries. We were indifferent to anyone or anything outside of church-related relationships and activities. Our isolation from everything else outside church made us unaware of the issues people confronted. We noticed a widening gap growing between us, the church, and the unchurched.

The good news we shared sounded sensible to us yet was disconnected from our visitors' situations—for example, evictions from apartments, a mom diagnosed with cancer, a brother's beatings when high on drugs, a father's absence and unfulfilled promise to reunite, and pressures regarding parties, sex, alcohol, and drugs at school. Our program-oriented youth could not connect with the real issues kids have "outside" the church. We were exhausted and burned out with organizing, planning, meeting, and hyping programs, which left us no time to visit or live with people outside the church. Our fund-raising efforts were directed to church programs rather than to transforming society's pressing problems. Somehow, our lack of participation and awareness of these issues made us appear uninterested and uncaring, and thus irrelevant. The message we preached about a God who cares seemed to be contradicted by the things we spent all our time worrying about.

> Churches which are prepared to take seriously the cultural shift from being a predominantly church society to one which is unchurched must recognize their need to turn inside out! In other words, the focus of attention will not be on running programs in order to gather the congregation together, but on equipping the people of God to exercise its God-entrusted mission to the world.
>
> Eddie Gibbs (INO, 248)

Leadership Mess

The way we raised up leaders was disastrous. I discipled as I was discipled, failing to realize the cultural shift between generations. It seemed like our leadership formation was a big back door that led people out faster than we got them in. In raising up leaders, we emphasized responsibility, religious discipline, goal setting, and number-related goals in discipleship. The students felt like they signed up for grace, but ended up being controlled and controlling others. They felt pressured to keep up and felt like failures when they did not. They were inspired to follow the footsteps of Jesus, but were burned out by the requirements of leadership. They felt their everyday life scrutinized and harshly judged. To be a good Christian leader, they had to be at a certain time and place, and they had to make themselves available at all times and felt guilty if they had other commitments. They felt inauthentic as they hid their flaws in secret. It did not take long before they gave up. The grace, transparency, and unconditional love that drew them to Christ did not line up with the pressures placed on them in leadership formation.

Redefining Church

We knew something was wrong, and we needed to rethink our ways as a church. Inspired by the image of a communal God who cares and loves endlessly, With started to explore what it means to be a community, which has brought us to where we are now. We began letting the ancient Scriptures question the way we interrelated with one another and our lack of frequency in engaging with the larger society. We chose grace in our relationships and took small steps by joining already rooted organizations to participate in global concerns, watching and learning from them. The exploration broke our hearts, and we developed a sensitivity toward others' situations, needs, and struggles. We became aware how much people needed our connection, but we also realized our own deep-seated need to connect. By joining people in endeavors to bring social justice, we encountered God, who is already at work for the cause of the oppressed.

With's humble beginnings in 2003 from a small living room developed into a ministry for tweens called Jr. BASIC. It later evolved into a youth ministry when we joined together with our church's new church plant in Federal Way in 2007. In 2010, With formed as a church. Our vision is to cultivate community living in an individualized society by promoting a life of generosity, compassion, kindness, social justice, and appreciation of diversity, as characterized by our trinitarian God.

> With seems to mirror the dissatisfaction with inefficient, complex, and self-centered forms of church that caused an Anglican church in Sheffield, England, (St. Tom's) to reject the megachurch they had become and instead emerge as a dispersed church of various

neighborhood celebrations and discipleship clusters. Though St. Tom's, like With, grew upon a foundation of traditional church actions and structures, a growing dissatisfaction with these trajectories eventually led St. Tom's into bold experimentation with innovative and dispersed forms of structure. *Bob Whitesel*

Our Local Culture

We took steps to understand why people do not trust churches, do not believe in God, think of church as irrelevant, and have very little interest in Christianity. We realized that instead of taking offense, we needed to develop empathy toward what the unchurched think and feel. To do this, we shifted away from our fragmented thinking of "us" and "them" or the sacred/secular divide. We saw ourselves as one people created by God. We were reminded that God made everything, and thus all things are sacred.

We looked into the issues confronting our locality. It was difficult to miss problems concerning loneliness and depression. Seattle has one of the highest suicide rates in the nation. We listened to issues related to the growing drug and alcohol dependence among families in schools and homes. We sat with people and heard their relational dilemmas—for example, divorce, separation, broken families, and runaway kids. Through this process, we realized how deeply the Western culture of individualism permeated the lives of the people in the Puget Sound area.

People craved community but were not willing to invest what it takes to be part of one.[1] As much as people value privacy, being alone is a common source of loneliness, which leads to substance abuse in order to cope. Families are often torn apart due to frustrations related to "unmet needs." Churches split up and dwindle in numbers whenever members think their consumerist needs are not satisfied. In the recent economic downturn, companies laid off people not because companies were bankrupt but to protect their own wealth. The self-centered consumerist characteristic of an individualistic society hurts the society. We realized that both churched and unchurched suffer the same consequences of their everyday choices born out of individualistic tendencies, such as consumerism (what's in it for me?), capitalism (how much can I get from what I put in?), and fragmented thinking (neglect to see the effects of one's action or inaction on others, whether now or in the future). Sadly, even we, as a church, fostered these cultural tendencies rather than subverting them through an alternative way of life. We read Scriptures with eyes focused on

1. Eddie Gibbs and Ryan K. Bolger, *Emerging Churches: Creating Christian Community in Postmodern Cultures* (Grand Rapids: Baker Academic, 2005), 97.

our personal individual needs rather than the transformation of society. Individualism shaped the way we think and operate and has kept us in an endless cycle of desiring its advantages, and yet continuing to suffer from its ill effects.[2]

More important, we saw the need to understand God all over again, to know the characteristics of his image in which we are created. Since God is the Father, the Son, and the Holy Spirit, who are in an endless-loop relationship of giving and receiving, it is difficult to miss the implications for how we Christians are to live. The kind of communal relationship God has is a forceful energy of reciprocity where there is regard for the other as each one is mindful of oneself.[3] We realized that instead of thinking of God as a separate community, it is our community, the community in which we are all intended to belong.[4]

In contrast to what an individualistic culture tells us, we are not meant to be alone. Nor are we created to be individually centered. Instead, we are to be relational and community-oriented. Reciprocity of love, compassion, and honor are evident in the trinitarian relationship. The same is made possible among us with God. In a time, place, and culture that suffers from thinking "It is what it is," the message of community can be the good news people long to hear.

Practices

Worship

At With, we explore various ways of worship that allow us to express God's unspeakable worth and, at the same time, to reflect on how he allows us to identify with him as his people. We integrate elements that are naturally part of an unchurched person's lifestyle as worship expressions to avoid requiring people to cross cultures in order to worship God. Worship should not alienate but should energize toward mission.[5] Our worship includes songs, drawings, poems, storytelling, and social service. We pray communally: we pray for our individual needs on the first round, pray for the person next to us on the second, and pray for a global concern on the third. This experience affirms our relevance as individuals, but at the same time makes us realize that we are part of a global community, a divine kingdom.

A few months ago, we held a Sunday service by helping a friend move into her new apartment. That felt very good. At the end of the day, we knew our

2. Eddie Gibbs, *LeadershipNext: Changing Leaders in a Changing Culture* (Downers Grove, IL: InterVarsity, 2005), 24, 58.

3. Darrell W. Johnson, *Experiencing the Trinity* (Vancouver, BC: Regent College, 2002), 51–52.

4. Gibbs, *LeadershipNext*, 118.

5. Ibid., 86.

beautiful worship honored God and brought joy, relief, blessing, and good-ness to someone's life. Our newfound friend experienced the unconditional generosity of the good news.

> St. Tom's Church in Sheffield, England, regularly holds a "Cluster Sunday" where all of their clusters (a cluster is a missional combination of three to seven small groups) meet in lieu of going to church. This is analogous to the Sunday service that With held by helping a friend move into an apartment. Emerging churches are discovering the benefit of exploring new forms of connecting with God. It may be through service, meditation, or song, but it is diverse. This forces participants to see God in the everyday tedium as well as in the triumphs of life. *Bob Whitesel*

On some Sundays, we attend old car shows. We go to where people already are. We join them to appreciate their creativity and hobby. As exhibitors tell their stories about how their cars came to be through creativity and commu-nity, we realize that hobbyists do not own cars for the sake of possessing but in order to create and restore, just like our God. In addition, these events remind us of the delight we bring to people when we appreciate what's close to their hearts, such as hobbies, projects, and interests. We watch people's faces light up with pride and joy as they talk about their ingenuities. We see how each one takes interest in others' cars, and instead of competition, we see support and camaraderie. Most of all, they appreciate our interest and thank us that we care.

I admit my fear in trekking a path outside of the conventional examples set before me, not to mention leading a group of people with me. I came from traditions where faithfulness is determined by one's availability to be present in church services and events. But I have also seen the limitations of this practice, and how it can lead to complacency in being missional. These fears can divert us toward guarding one's practice rather than being good news of love, grace, and hope to the world around us. We have become so afraid to deviate from our scheduled meetings, and we are often inflicted with guilt whenever we do. Worship happens anywhere and everywhere as people intentionally join God in what he values and finds worthy. Worship draws our attention to God, and at the same time, enables God to be encountered in the world.[6]

Community Members

People see themselves as members through their participation and pursuit of Jesus's alternative lifestyle. We gained better understanding of belong-ingness through the trinitarian relationship, wherein commitment is a given rather than an option, and where participation is born out of compassion

6. Gibbs and Bolger, *Emerging Churches*, 75.

and generosity rather than obligation. We can identify with this relationship through families or friendships.[7]

Participation happens in various ways. Rather than limiting membership to all or nothing, every engagement is considered participatory and an opportunity for community formation. Groups are organically formed depending on people's interest, passion, and/or work- or school-related availability. The nature of groups varies: they can be action related, social justice oriented, work initiated, study inclined, a social/family gathering, prayer and worship focused, or social media centered. Not everyone is involved in all groups or activities, but people tend to cross groups eventually. Through this participation, webs of relationships form naturally. We do not find any need to classify their level of involvement or to label their type of membership. Somehow, without our intention, Facebook, Twitter, and other forms of social media became our hub where everyone communicates, touches base, posts encouragements, shares life experiences, pictures, announcements, and prayers. The entirety of what With does and pursues can be seen through social media. Through this virtual phenomenon, we realized that participation is not limited to physical attendance.

Social media has become an intuitive way for people to connect, and virtually connected friends outside Seattle—for example, friends and relatives from the Philippines—are participating in the same journey With is pursuing. This new way of connecting as church has served as With's hub anytime and anywhere because it is already integrated with people's everyday lives.

> The communities of the future will be far more complex than those that existed prior to the knowledge revolution. They will incorporate a variety of expressions and will reflect both the mobile nature of our society as well as the complexity of our communication networks. They will not be made up of friends and neighbors who live and work in the same community.
>
> Eddie Gibbs (LN, 103)

Mission

With fear and awe, we decided to embrace our call to be a church who would be salt and light in this world. We believe this is our calling as an ethnically diverse community in Puget Sound. We follow Jesus and consider the alternative life he taught in the Gospels. We consider ourselves recovering addicts, who were once addicted to the endeavor of self-satisfaction. God met us at our moment of poverty and invited us to pursue a lifestyle of loving God and loving our neighbor. We are learning how to be gracious, to listen, and to be

7. Johnson, *Experiencing the Trinity*, 76–77.

empathic toward one another. In giving and in forgiving others, we experience our own forgiveness. With joins God by participating in his work toward social justice and peace to humankind—the shalom of God—where his blessings and goodness are seen and experienced by everyone. We believe that God is in the business of putting this world into right.[8] Mission is no longer one of the things we do as a church; rather, it is the very essence of why we exist as a church.[9] This is our journey.

Leadership

At present, leadership is vague and our structure is flat. In comparison to how we were in the past, our current structure may seem chaotic, but it is not disorganized. I, as a pastor, serve a particular function according to my passions and strengths. Another leader, who is gifted in organizing, facilitates our operations. Leaders who found themselves angered by modern slavery led our campaigns against human trafficking. Environmental cleanliness and green initiatives are led by those who felt a sense of compassion to generations after ours; with some urgency, they demand that change should happen now. People rise to leadership according to community need and what one can do rather than through assignments.

> St. Tom's Church in Sheffield keeps processes and procedures from driving their leadership by placing their main emphasis on local-level leaders, such as small-group leaders and cluster leaders. This diversification of St. Tom's leadership flattened the typical hierarchal structure of an Anglican church, giving way to more freedom in decision making at the local small-group level. As a result, local small groups and their clusters could choose what goals, missional activities, and events worked for them. This created higher satisfaction among emerging leaders because they felt they were in charge of their direction and goals. Emerging leaders also gained more direct and candid feedback from their small group and cluster constituents. *Bob Whitesel*

Currently, we are exploring a type of leadership based not on power but on service.[10] We studied how Jesus incarnated the trinitarian essence. In the Gospels, Jesus, as part of the rabbinical tradition, affirmed its ethical practices while subverting unjust positional expectations of such an office. This type of leadership does not require titles, office, and position; rather, leadership forms through one's relationships within a community. Jesus subverted oppressive

8. Ibid., 51–52.
9. Gibbs, *LeadershipNext*, 77.
10. Ibid., 179–80.

social practices through meals. The sick, the poor, and the needy were attended to not in the temple or an office, but in the most mundane situations, such as in the streets and at the market. Through Jesus's example, we realize the power and influence resident in everyone. It is not a question of who the leaders are, but more of, do we recognize leadership within each one of us, and for whom do we use it? As a community, we try to listen to the Holy Spirit and to one another carefully to incarnate his leadership paradigm.

> South Yarra Community Baptist Church has done away with a formally elected leadership team and asked people to self-nominate as visiting guests, regular participants, bring-a-plate people (who want to contribute but not take responsibility), or hosts (who take responsibility for leading and ensuring church flows for everyone else). The existing team of "hosts" considers the appropriateness of new hosts, but is generally happy to invite anyone who wants to make a contribution to name what contribution they want to make. Leadership as "hosting" the party is a wonderful image. *Darren Cronshaw*

With this view of leadership, we regard anyone a leader according to his or her unique qualities. A person leads every time they take courage to initiate change, subvert harmful ways, or teach life-giving ways consistent with the mission of God. This way, we also promote the diversity of the community in terms of talents, personality, age, ethnicity, and cultural background.

> Yes, leadership is action, not position. Let's encourage everyone to lead in their spheres of interest. *Darren Cronshaw*

My leadership as a woman became an advantage in exploring this paradigm shift. Instead of trying to lead like other male pastors, this paradigm continues to press me to lead with integrity as to how God created me. I finally realized that if God wanted a man to lead With during this time, he would have made me a man, or had a male leader step in, but it has been eight years since we started. With this understanding, I realized my purpose, which allowed With to understand diversity in leadership embodied in a style that is organic and may seem messy, but is truly essential.

> I long for the day when the church is much more blind to gender differences and celebrates the contributions of everyone, women as well as men, children as well as adults. *Darren Cronshaw*

As an experimental community, we realize endless possibilities on how a church can be enriched by tradition, relevant to the present, and reconstructive toward the future. We are moving away from being a church isolated from the society into becoming more involved in the spaces where we live and breathe. We shift our energy away from maintaining ministries within the church and direct them to issues that concern the broader community. We move away from attractional ways focused on bringing people in and instead go into the spaces where people already are, and we do this by getting our hands and feet dirty as we live out Jesus's resurrected being. We move beyond celebrating love inside buildings and enter the larger culture to give to those who desperately need to know that love still exists in our world. The desperate may be those unjustly abducted into human trafficking, the generationally impoverished, the innocent victims affected by AIDS, undocumented aliens fearful in hiding, or low-income single parents. We move away from avoiding those who are different from us by entering into dialogue and suspending our judgments, which somehow broadens understanding and heals us from becoming insular.

> Leadership is about connecting, not controlling. It is about bringing people together for creative synergy.
>
> Eddie Gibbs (LN, 106)

With is still at an early stage of exploring what it means to be a community of God in our society. Our hope as a community is to be a fresh word of good news to the people confronting issues in the localities of Puget Sound, and, at the same time, to actively participate in what God is doing globally, be aware of what he has done throughout history, and be concerned with his plans toward the future.

> Stories like this one leave me without words and with tears. This seems to be the road all church planters of new expressions of church have to travel. It is a dirt road; and it appears that walking through the dirt is the only way toward the kingdom. *Nico-Dirk van Loo*

Bibliography

Gibbs, Eddie. *LeadershipNext: Changing Leaders in a Changing Culture.* Downers Grove, IL: InterVarsity, 2005.

Gibbs, Eddie, and Ryan K. Bolger. *Emerging Churches: Creating Christian Community in Postmodern Cultures.* Grand Rapids: Baker Academic, 2005.

Johnson, Darrell W. *Experiencing the Trinity.* Vancouver, BC: Regent College, 2002.

Wright, Christopher J. H. *The Mission of God: Unlocking the Bible's Grand Narrative.* Downers Grove, IL: IVP Academic, 2006.

23

The Jesus Dojo

Mark Scandrette

While I was working as a youth pastor in the mid-1990s, I began to notice an alarming pattern: although many of the students I worked with wanted to follow Jesus, few if any were interested in participating in "church" as they knew it. They were more likely to show up to jam sessions at my house or volunteer with me at a soup kitchen than to attend our formal youth programs, church services, or the "big" trips to concerts or amusement parks that I was obliged to organize. They told me they wanted to be part of something "real" where their voice and participation mattered and to have a place where they could bring their friends who weren't familiar with Christianity. I began helping them organize "do-it-yourself" home-based groups where they could lead and care for one another and explore what it might mean to be what we perhaps naively described as "a New Testament community." In retrospect, I was seeing glimpses of the participatory impulse that emerged as a characteristic of Generation Y.

In seminary I discovered that what I had experienced with these students was part of a larger societal change that, at the time, was being described as a postmodern cultural shift. In 1997 I participated in the first of many forums and conferences where my colleagues and I discussed how to "reach" a new generation that was less inclined toward organized religion. There was a palpable hunger for what my friend Dieter Zander at the time described as the "real, relational, and raw." It wasn't long before I realized that, personally, I had many of the same struggles and longings for a more holistic faith and life that my students expressed. I reasoned that I could either continue to support the religious tradition I was part of (and be part of slow incremental changes), or set out on an adventure to explore what faithfulness to the Way of Jesus might look like in the future.

> Maintenance-minded churches need to be transformed into missional communities, which will entail decentralizing their operations. Church leaders will need to facilitate this transition by giving higher priority to working outside the institution, functioning as teams of believers located in a highly polarized and pluralistic world.
>
> Eddie Gibbs (CN, 218)

In 1998 my wife and I and our three young children moved from an iron mining town in northern Minnesota to an urban neighborhood in San Francisco. For us San Francisco represented the post-Christendom edge of America: ethnically and religiously diverse, culturally creative, and socially progressive—an ideal place to experiment with how the Way of Jesus might be practiced in the emerging world. We bought and renovated an old crack house in a historically Latin arts district, and then went to work meeting neighbors, forming a core community, and learning to engage cultures that were largely unfamiliar to us. We formed "house" churches, lived in intentional community, volunteered in the neighborhood, organized community mural projects, and shared meals with homeless friends. Yet our efforts didn't have the immediate results that we, or our funding partners, anticipated.

An Experiment

Beginning to ReIMAGINE

Ten years ago I began inviting friends into experiments in which we could explore the life and teachings of Jesus through specific shared actions and practices. Instead of just talking about things like social justice or poverty, we organized groups to build intentional friendships with homeless neighbors, do violence prevention in our community, or advocate for victims of human trafficking. We've made the streets, alleys, brothels, and galleries of our city the pulpit and sanctuary where we learn to live as followers of Jesus. When we wanted to wrestle with what Jesus taught about money and our stuff, we challenged one another to sell or give away our possessions, to share how much we earned and spent, and to help one another take specific steps to choose simplicity and generosity. To learn to pray, we practiced contemplative prayer together or took forty-eight-hour silent retreats. To explore how the gospel of Jesus touches the messiness of our lives we wrote poetry and screenplays, threw paint, and learned to tell our stories as God-bathed narratives of hope and redemption—sharing these discoveries through public art shows and open-mic events.

With other families who had relocated to the city and had similar disappointments, we formed a missional think tank of sorts where we asked, "What is the essential message of Jesus—and how does that message connect with the needs and longings of the people and place where we live?" It took us a while to transition away from pragmatic and strategic questions like, "How do we start a culturally relevant church here?" to more basic questions about the nature of the gospel and the purpose of the church.

During our "think tank" era we spent time with philosopher and theologian Dallas Willard, who often and memorably told us that to experience the kingdom of God, "a group of people should get together and simply try to do the things that Jesus instructed his disciples to do." We do not enter the kingdom of God merely by thinking about it or listening to one another talk about it. We have to experiment together with how to apply the teachings of Jesus to the details of our lives—within our particular social context. This is when, in discussions with friends, I began to say, "What we need is a Jesus dojo—a place where we can experiment and work out the teachings of Jesus in our everyday lives."

For the early church, the Way of Jesus was a revolutionary and countercultural force that offered an alternative to the power structures of the Roman Empire. After Christianity was legalized under Constantine, prophetic/monastic movements formed that continued to present the Way of Jesus as a compelling alternative. When Christianity becomes the "folk religion" of a society that supports the establishment, fringe movements arise that call people toward more authentic discipleship to Jesus. Through the actions of smaller, more radical communities (like the desert fathers and mothers, the early Franciscans, or the Wesleyan class meetings), the church as a whole is renewed and called forward into the kingdom purposes of God.

It is interesting that many of the Anglican leaders at St. Tom's Church in Sheffield, England, spoke very favorably about the radical small group strategies of Anglican pastor John Wesley. While I found other Anglicans misinformed or at best indifferent to Wesley, St. Tom's embraced him as their innovator (after all, he never left the Anglican Church). Some of St. Tom's small groups use variations of Wesley's small group questions, including the famous "What sin besets thee?," to foster an open and authentic dialogue similar to that in the Jesus Dojo. *Bob Whitesel*

Over the past decade we pioneered a local, communal, and improvisational expression of discipleship to Jesus that is our best attempt to integrate the gospel of Jesus with the stories of our lives in the time and place where we live. ReIMAGINE, our organization, comprises an expanding network of people who experiment together with how we might seek the Way of Jesus as residents of the San Francisco Bay Area and beyond. Our various efforts attract three kinds of people: (1) post-congregational Jesus seekers who are skeptical about organized religion but wish to do something constructive with their discontent; (2) seekers, primarily from Eastern spiritual paths, who have been drawn toward exploring Jesus and his message; and (3) self-identified Christians who long to deepen their practice of faith.

Entering the Jesus Dojo

So many of us want to live in the Way of Jesus—pursuing a life that is deeply soulful, connected to our real needs, and good news to our world. Yet too often our methods of Christian community and spiritual formation are individualistic, information driven, or disconnected from everyday life. We are simply not experiencing the kind of transformation that is the historically expected result of the Christ phenomenon. Perhaps what we need is a path for transformation, community, and mission that is more like a karate studio than a college lecture hall.

We like to describe what we do as a "Jesus Dojo." "Dojo" is a Japanese term meaning "place where you learn the way," commonly associated with a practice space for martial arts, meditation, or prayer. We are fond of the term "dojo" because it invokes an active learning environment where participation is invited and expected. Jesus referred to himself as "The way" (John 14:6) and invited his followers to enter his way of life based on the reality and power of God's eternal reign. The earliest disciples of Jesus called themselves "follower[s] of the Way" (Acts 24:14). For us, a Jesus Dojo is (1) an experiment (2) inspired by the life and teachings of Jesus (3) in which a group of people commit time and energy to a set of practices (4) in conversation with real needs in society and within themselves and (5) reflect on how these experiences can shape their ongoing rhythms of life.

How do we do this? Through friendship and online social networks we invite people into one-time and longer-term experiments based on the specific instructions and example of Jesus. Each year we host a nine-month series of four- to six-week projects and learning labs based on themes we've identified in the Gospels. We invite people who have participated in our learning labs into yearlong neighborhood Tribe communities.

Practices

The Art of Worship and Tangible Obedience

In the book of Romans, the apostle Paul defines the act of worship as the surrender of the body to the will of its Maker (Rom. 12:1). So, in the most basic sense, true worship is the act of tangible obedience. Many of our post-congregational participants, through overfamiliarity, have an aversion to the kind of group singing associated with ritualized "worship" that feels foreign to our local context. Over the years we've looked for ways for the community to express gratitude, praise, and longing to God through various art forms that have included spoken-word poetry, painting, and songs written and performed by community members. Group singing and extended teaching hasn't been part of our regular practice, though we recognize the need for more of these in the future. We have wanted to put our primary energy into what we feel is our most distinctive contribution to the body of Christ: contexts of action and practice.

Formation and the Holistic Nature of the Gospel

At one time many of us thought of the postmodern shift as a deconstructive reaction to enlightenment assumptions. What has become evident over the past decade is that the critique of scientific rationality has given birth to a more ecological lens of perception. By "ecological" I mean not only awareness of our interdependence with the natural world but also a more basic way of seeing that appreciates and searches for the connections between all aspects and levels of existence. We are becoming increasingly aware of how the body, mind, and spirit are interrelated and that our individual choices contribute to the health or suffering of others—of future generations and the earth itself. This "emerging ecological consciousness" is evident in many aspects of our society, from the rise of social networking to increasing awareness and activism about issues of global justice. The irony is that as we have become more mobile, globally connected, and aware, we have also experienced increasing levels of social fragmentation, loneliness, and existential alienation.

This is where the gospel of the kingdom (or to use the more ancient language of the Shema, God's "oneness" or *shalom*) provides hope to a generation that deeply longs for wholeness and integration. The life and teachings of Jesus offer a path and power to experience true and lasting integration of the whole person. How can we access the healing and redemptive reality of the kingdom of God? The ancient and enduring path of transformation is whole life surrender to the authority and power of Jesus—recognizing Jesus as our savior *and* teacher for how to live in God's reality in God's world.

A ReIMAGINE Tribe is an experimental group practice in following the Way of Jesus. Tribes are made up of people who commit to shared vows and rhythms, practiced in community, to facilitate spiritual formation and transformation. Our Tribe season begins in September and concludes in May (though people may join at any point in the year). Tribes are led by two collaborative leaders who receive training and coaching from ReIMAGINE. Many, but not necessarily all, Tribe participants have undertaken to live by a set of seven vows inspired by the life and teachings of Jesus: love, obedience, prayer, simplicity, creativity, service, and community. The Tribe rhythm of the year rotates around paying attention to these seven themes from the life of Jesus.

Tribes meet weekly to remember and practice the teachings of Jesus. Each week we are either taking part in a project or learning lab or spending time together sharing a meal and the Lord's table, praying, applying Scripture, caring for one another, and identifying and planning actions to serve and transform our neighborhoods. There are also two to three overnight retreats per year that Tribe members are encouraged to participate in. Each Tribe member contributes to a Tribe "pot" from which the Tribe pays for things that fall under three basic categories: community, benevolence, and missional activity. Vowed members commit to giving 5 percent of their income to the Tribe fund and 5 percent to the charities of their choice. Tribe members make decisions about how to spend their Tribe "pot," according to guidelines that include prayer, discussion, and voting on spending proposals.

> St. Thomas' Church creates a similar type of Jesus Dojo by combining three to seven small groups into what the Sheffield church calls "missional clusters." These missional clusters fulfill many of the communal aspects of the ReIMAGINE Dojo, but the clusters operate year-round. The clusters, which can range in size from 25 to 175, create a type of extended family characteristic of a "Dunbar group." Sociologist Robin Dunbar found that tribal people groups often hover at about 150 because this is the largest size where everyone feels a sense of community and purpose. Oxford professor Dunbar has cited this effect in hundreds of social networks.[1] *Bob Whitesel*

1. Robin Dunbar, *How Many Friends Does One Person Need? Dunbar's Number and Other Evolutionary Quirks* (Cambridge, MA: Harvard University Press, 2010).

Mission

SUSPICION AND HOSTILITY—CHALLENGES TO MISSION

We once had an intern who was turned down for an apartment because he revealed he was a Christian. The landlord said, "I just couldn't have someone like you as my tenant." As outsiders to faith, many people have formed their assumptions about Christians from what they have seen on television, or, more sadly, by the hurtful ways they have been treated by religious people in the past. Local news outlets thrive on reporting clashes between residents and religious crusaders who visit the city to demonstrate with signs reading "God hates fags" or worse. When we identified ourselves as "Christian" during our first years in San Francisco, what we encountered, almost universally, was suspicion or hostility—accompanied by uninvited history lessons about Christian involvement in the Inquisition, Crusades, slavery, homophobia, and preemptive foreign policies. In the words of one of my early acquaintances, "Jesus is cool, it's just that Christianity has [expletive deleted] with Jesus."

> Mark is touching a nerve here by focusing on the practicality of the faith. In the Scandinavian culture, the suspicion and hostility are similar to the San Francisco context, only nationwide and sometimes systemic. People are looking for actions, both people of the faith and people without, which is displayed by people's goodwill toward the Salvation Army. *Ruth Skree*

> An incarnated Christian community in a post-Christendom culture will always have to surf on constant ambiguity . . . being genuine community but not irrelevant church, authentic followers of Jesus but not suspicious Christians, loving missionally but not being manipulative proselytizers. *Eric Zander*

When people have found out about our faith they are often wary of our motives for friendship and have even asked, "Are you spending time with me because you hope to convert me?" or "Do you think my family is going to hell?—Because if you do, I don't think we can be friends." In our experience, the greatest apologetic question of our time isn't, "Is Christian faith intellectually tenable?" but, "Does your faith in Jesus make a positive difference in how you show up on the planet?" Through these experiences we recognized: (1) that our work needs to demonstrate the transformational potential of the gospel in an embodied community; and (2) that our motivation for action and engagement must come from a pure and genuine desire to love rather than ambition toward predetermined results.

In a society where words are empty, promises are easily broken, and to be held by one's word is no longer a value of commitment, people no longer see good news in words, especially when ill-represented by arrogance and judgmental legalism. *Eileen Suico*

St. Thomas' Church experienced the same disappointment with an attractional model of ministry, when St. Tom's became the largest Anglican church in the UK, meeting in Sheffield's largest indoor auditorium. In a matter of weeks they lost this city's only sizable venue, but because of a premonition by Rector Mike Breen that this might happen, the church immediately dispersed into a network of "clusters" (networks of three to seven small groups). Like Scandrette they found that they could much better demonstrate the transformational potential of the gospel in this smaller, less attractional missional community. Most of St. Tom's conversion growth took place in the cluster groups, probably because these Anglican "dojos" could indigenize ministry while creating a sense of community. *Bob Whitesel*

THE QUEST FOR INTEGRATIVE SPIRITUALITY

We began by asking, "How are the people we live among expressing their longing for God, spirituality, and meaning?" We listened to what people said and noticed the signs of spiritual hunger around us: holistic health centers, psychic readings, yoga studios, book clubs, classes on meditation, books and workshops by well-known new-thought practitioners, and retreats offered by yogis and gurus. Many of the people we live among are self-motivated spiritual seekers searching for wisdom and embodied practices of spirituality that connect mind, body, and spirit. The low-level intensity of a congregational meeting with a single dominant (usually male) figure would not be an appropriate or likely venue for people in our culture to explore the reality of life in the kingdom of God. We would need to provide interactive spaces for conversation and an opportunity to practice the topic being explored.

> From a strategy of *invitation* the churches must move to one of *infiltration*, to being the subversive and transforming presence of Jesus.
>
> Eddie Gibbs (CN, 218)

Leader as Rabbi

In the early days of our experiments, we identified ourselves as a church community and then quickly realized that using that term to describe what we were doing attracted people who expected a meeting with group singing and a speaker—something very different from what we hoped to offer.

As we reread the New Testament we quickly recognized that our understanding of the gospel had largely been shaped and limited by cultural concerns about personal piety and hope for the afterlife. What we discovered in those pages was a rabbi-messiah who spoke constantly of the present *and* coming reality of "the kingdom of God" and a new way to be human—available by receiving his grace, following his example and teachings, and sourcing energy from the power of his resurrection. The goal of the church, in light of God's eternal reign, is to help one another have a transforming encounter with the reality of God and God's kingdom that results in an empowered life and a growing community of love.

We realized that to do something new we would need to renegotiate the typical contracts between leader and participant toward a more rabbi/apprentice model. We make our expectations for participation clear, require people to pay a nominal amount for our learning labs, and ask them to make a formal commitment to complete exercises and projects.

I realized that I would need to rethink my role as a pastor-leader, which up to that time had largely been based on my ability to communicate ideas and organize programs and social activities for an already captive audience. In the culture I was now a part of, my credibility would have to come more from my embodied presence and my skill at helping people experience the Way of Jesus for themselves. I would need to understand and tap into the ancient model of the rabbi, who taught as much by what he did as what he said.

Twenty percent of San Francisco residents move away each year. This means that we have a brief window of opportunity to impact people who will most likely relocate to another city. To address this we orient our activities around a series of short-term projects and practices that have easy on and off points. Participants in ReIMAGINE Tribes have migrated across the globe and started their own experiments inspired by their experience in the Jesus Dojo. Due to our location and calling, our primary goal isn't increasing group size and retention, but inspiring and equipping a contagious movement. The vision of ReIMAGINE is to be revolutionized by the life, power, and teachings of Jesus and to empower new leaders who can revolutionize their communities.

> Rather than accumulating members for retention and future extraction, discipling toward a contagious movement places church participation in light of the *missio Dei* once again.
> Eileen Suico

24

St. Tom's

From Gathered to Scattered

Bob Whitesel

An Experiment

St. Thomas' Anglican Church (Sheffield, England)[1] underwent rapid change when the leaders had only five weeks to vacate their church facility due to asbestos. As England's largest Anglican church, with a congregation of two thousand meeting weekly in Sheffield's largest indoor arena, simply moving to a bigger locale was not feasible. The rapidity of the move would not allow a new facility to be constructed or converted. The result was that a congregation where 85 percent of the attendees were under the age of forty had only a matter of days to inaugurate a strategy, implement change, and maintain ministry effectiveness while holding true to their theology and values. Not only did St. Thomas' expand its cultural pluralism through a creative dispersed model, but it also created unity amid hybridity. Yet the seed for this change was planted many years earlier.

1. Dr. Eddie Gibbs has been involved as a member and board member of St. Thomas' for over two decades. As a PhD student under Eddie Gibbs, I researched the recent history of this church.

> Other churches could use this as a case study. What if the same situation faced us? What would we do? *Darren Cronshaw*

I have seen few churches embrace a scattered model without being forced to do so. *Bob Whitesel*

Beginnings[2]

In 1978 renovations at St. Thomas' forced it to share facilities with Crookes Baptist Church. In 1982 the two churches became a yoked Anglican and Baptist congregation and were designated a Local Ecumenical Project (LEP).[3] In 1983 Robert Warren became rector of St. Thomas' Church. Two years later John Wimber, leader of the network of Vineyard churches, conducted a series of renewal meetings at Warren's request. Soon after, Robert Warren invited a local charismatic community, the Nairn Street Community, to conduct a 9:00 p.m. alternative worship celebration on Sundays.[4] This became known as the Nine O'Clock Service (NOS), which has been called the "birth of a postmodern worshipping community" in the UK.[5]

Mike Breen

In October 1993 Warren resigned to work with the Anglican denomination and Paddy Mallon became the Baptist minister of the LEP.[6] Soon after, Mike Breen accepted the call to St. Thomas' and sensed the Lord underscoring the word "Ephesus" in his prayer life. Breen emphasized to the congregation that in Acts 19 Ephesus had several unique characteristics:[7] it was the principal city of the region, Paul trained local leaders in a rented building, leaders went out from Ephesus to plant churches in neighboring areas, and from there "the word of the Lord spread widely and grew in power" (Acts 19:20). Breen concluded that "the church of St. Thomas' was to function as a resource to its city and region. It was to be a base for church planting and mission and a centre for teaching and training."[8]

2. This history was created from personal interviews and visits by Bob Whitesel (see the books listed in the bibliography) as well as books written by leaders of St. Thomas' (Mike Breen, Paddy Mallon, Bob Hopkins).

3. Paddy Mallon, *Calling a City Back to God* (Eastbourne, UK: Kingsway, 2003), 20.

4. Robert Warren, *In the Crucible* (Surrey, UK: Highland Books, 1989).

5. Eddie Gibbs and Ryan K. Bolger, *Emerging Churches: Creating Christian Community in Postmodern Cultures* (Grand Rapids: Baker Academic, 2005), 82.

6. Mallon, *Calling a City*, 25–26.

7. Ibid., 26.

8. Mike Breen, *The Body Beautiful* (West Sussex, UK: Monarch Books, 1997), 25.

In March 1994 Breen introduced an icon-based training program based on biblical principles, eventually calling it Lifeshapes.[9] The six icons of the training tool were readily adopted by the expanding base of small "cell" groups. Mallon credits Lifeshapes as "the most fundamental change in this period . . . an easily transferable method of planned, disciplined and structured membership activity, at a personal as well as a corporate level."[10] Small group participation was also expected. "In the UK it is different," stated Joannah Saxton, one of the early leaders. "It is not popular to be part of a church in the post-Christendom culture of the UK. So if you are going to get involved, you tend to get involved all the way and you attend a small group."[11]

Lifeshapes helps make missional principles concrete and transferable. Darren Cronshaw

The Evolving Structure of Small Groups and Clusters

In the mid-1990s the leaders combined groups of three or more small groups into what they called "clusters" to better manage the burgeoning small group network.[12] Clusters gave the small groups an "extended family" feel, providing a social gathering larger than a small group, but still smaller than the churchwide meetings.[13] To the surprise of St. Tom's leaders, most evangelism now took place through the semiautonomous environment of the clusters.[14] Another factor contributing to the growth was Breen's consensus-building style of leadership.

An Anglican Megachurch

In September 1998 leaders began to sense that the size of the parish facilities was "restricting growth."[15] To alleviate this problem, the congregation held services one Sunday each month in a community center.[16] Because the venue was more accessible for unchurched people than the parish facility, growth among unchurched attendees increased. The temporary nature of the facility

9. Mallon, *Calling a City*, 18, 25.

10. Ibid., 18.

11. Joannah Saxton, personal interview by Bob Whitesel, Los Angeles, June 1, 2011.

12. Saxton, interview.

13. Mallon, *Calling a City*, 37–43.

14. Bob Hopkins and Mike Breen, *Clusters: Creative Mid-sized Missional Communities* (Sheffield, UK: 3D Ministries, 2007), 38–39.

15. Paddy Mallon, personal interview by Bob Whitesel, Phoenix, Arizona, June 8, 2007. Mallon was the associate team leader of St. Thomas' who, though retired, still advises churches on missional strategies.

16. Ibid.

was fostered in part because the facility was only available thirty-five Sundays a year, it was expensive to rent, and much labor and time were spent in setup and teardown.[17]

In January 2000, The Roxy nightclub became available for lease and appeared to overcome the sociological strangulation of the community center. The Roxy garnered media attention because it had been a bawdy concert venue. In one month four hundred people joined the church.[18] "I think what we saw was every time we created space people joined us," Mallon recalled. "Some of that was transfer growth, but a lot of it was conversion growth."[19]

Three different worship expressions drew three different audiences. Sunday mornings at The Roxy mainly attracted baby boomers, while Sunday evenings attracted Generation X. Services also continued at the parish church in Crookes and were attended by approximately three hundred people committed to the local Crookes parish.[20] Almost without strategic intent, St. Thomas' had evolved into multiple subcongregations.[21] They designated these subcongregations "celebrations" after a term used by C. Peter Wagner.[22]

From Megachurch to Dispersed Church

In January 2001 Mike Breen sensed God saying to him, "What would you do if I took away The Roxy?"[23] "I was in a bit of a panic about that," recalled Breen,

> because we had just been surveyed with the rest of the churches in Great Britain . . . as being the largest church in Great Britain at that time. So most certainly we were a megachurch. And, it felt like God was giving me the option of really going in the megachurch direction or really embracing this thing he had been developing in us the last few years.[24]

In December 2001 an attendee who had concerns about the safety of the "torpedo-style heaters" used to heat The Roxy contacted the local authorities

17. Mallon, *Calling a City*, 36.
18. Ibid., 36–37.
19. Mallon, interview.
20. Mallon, *Calling a City*, 36–37.
21. George G. Hunter III, *The Contagious Congregation: Frontiers in Evangelism and Church Growth* (Nashville: Abingdon, 1979), 63; Bob Whitesel and Kent R. Hunter, *A House Divided: Bridging the Generation Gaps in Your Church* (Nashville: Abingdon, 2001), 26–27.
22. C. Peter Wagner, *Your Church Can Grow: Seven Vital Signs of a Healthy Church* (Glendale, CA: Regal, 1976), 101–2.
23. Mallon, *Calling a City*, 38; Mike Breen, personal interview by Bob Whitesel, June 7, 2007.
24. Breen, interview.

requesting a safety inspection.[25] A subsequent inspection revealed that asbestos rendered The Roxy an immediate health hazard.[26] "If we were going to do the work on the building that we wanted to, we would have had to put a bubble over the building and put people in space suits," remembered Mal Calladine. "It would have cost around $7 million to renovate. . . . We could've come up with $60,000, but it's $60,000 into a money pit."[27]

"One minute we were in the building, and basically several weeks later we were out because we had to close immediately due to the health and safety issues," remembers Mick Woodhead.[28] Though this event occurred just before Christmas 2001, the leaders were able to negotiate a five-week grace period before they were forced to leave.[29] Paul Maconochie recounts the spiritual preparation for this change, stating, "We'd been talking about it for nearly a year and so we just said to the guys, 'Well the Lord said it was going to happen and it has happened and there you go.'"[30] Woodhead adds, "So he'd [Breen] already shared that with the staff team. The senior staff and then the staff team and some of the cluster leaders were aware of this word. But was it going to happen? We don't know because we've got this building and then that was it . . . it was taken away so they [the leaders] were ready to go."[31]

On January 27, 2002, the last celebration was held in The Roxy, with seventeen clusters commissioned to begin meeting the following week to replace the two Sunday gatherings.[32] The diffusion from two weekly Roxy events to seventeen weekly cluster meetings democratized the process, according to Woodhead, for "people had to really begin to sort things out for themselves. They couldn't depend on the center for everything. So leadership took on much more of a dynamic, much more of a community, [that] 'we're in this together' for each cluster. 'We've got to go out and find the venues. And, we're looking to

25. Mallon, *Calling a City*, 39; Mal Calladine, personal interview by Bob Whitesel, June 6, 2007.

26. Calladine, interview.

27. Ibid.

28. Mick Woodhead, personal interview by Bob Whitesel, Sheffield, England, June 14, 2007. Woodhead is the former associate team leader of St. Thomas' who now serves as its Anglican rector.

29. Mallon, interview. Communicating the venue change to a large congregation flowed through the cell-cluster-celebration structure. "The most effective way of communication was . . . through four phone calls," recalls Calladine (Calladine, interview). The rector would (1) call the celebration leaders, who would (2) call the cluster leaders, who would then (3) call the small group leaders, who would then (4) call the small group attendees.

30. Paul Maconochie, personal interview by Bob Whitesel, Sheffield, England, June 14, 2007. Maconochie is the pastor of the Baptist segment of the church and currently leads the Philadelphia Campus.

31. Woodhead, interview.

32. Mallon, *Calling a City*, 39; Calladine, interview.

see what God's heart is for this particular area.' So there was a whole different dynamic, it seemed to me, when guys were reporting back."[33] Joannah Saxton recalls, "The story we shared had a huge role in what we did . . . so even if we were reaching outside of our culture, we had the shared story of being part of a church that was 'calling a city back to God.' The shared vocabulary helped too because we all used terms like clusters, celebrations, etc."[34]

Growth as a Dispersed Church

On February 3, 2002, seventeen clusters, meeting weekly, were planted throughout Sheffield as St. Thomas' took on a "dispersed church" mode.[35] The bishop gave permission for clusters to meet within the boundaries of other Anglican parishes.[36] That same year, the Diocesan Handbook indicated the average Anglican parish in Sheffield had twenty-five worshipers.[37] One year later St. Thomas' Church had thirty-four to thirty-five clusters[38] comprising 2,500 members, with 85 percent under the age of forty.[39]

In one year the church had morphed into a network of small churches meeting across Sheffield. Mallon believes this one year period was

> the greatest growth we saw as a church. It showed us that we were not going to go down the megachurch road, which was an option. And when we had The Roxy, a plan was to make it a large worship complex that would have been glass and chrome and glitter. And now, we were spared all of that.[40]

This growth surprised the leaders. Mallon recalls, "Even developing the resources for the clustering for the six months beforehand, we had no idea we would double in size in terms of cluster leaders in the subsequent twelve months that we were in a dispersed mode. It's a bit like the Acts of the Apostles: the idea of expansion, contraction, consolidation, and then you grow again."[41]

By 2005, the church comprised a network of clusters, which in turn were joined together into seven "celebrations," including Connect (ministry to young adults), Encompass (ministry to specific neighborhoods), Mother Church (the original church in the Crookes area), Community Church at Crookes (an urban

33. Woodhead, interview.
34. Saxton, interview.
35. Mallon, interview.
36. Ibid.
37. Mallon, *Calling a City*, 36.
38. Mallon, interview; Breen, interview.
39. Mallon, *Calling a City*, 36.
40. Mallon, interview.
41. Mallon, interview.

outreach based in Crookes), Expression (outreach to college students led by Joannah Saxton), Radiate (ministry to young professionals in the workplace), and The Forge (inner-city ministry). The diversity of celebrations allowed the church to reach out to Sheffield's diverse population. The dispersed model created a multicultural church by emphasizing culturally and aesthetically different celebrations united within one church organization.

A Rhythm from Dispersed to Gathered to the Present

In 2006, sensing that unity was needed among the seven culturally diverse celebrations, the leaders created a Sunday evening "uniting" worship service. Leadership and worship teams from the different celebrations were rotated each week, allowing attendees from other celebrations to hear testimonies, music, and preaching from the culturally distinct celebrations.

In 2009 the availability of a large warehouse provided an alternative to the often-packed Sunday evening "unity" gatherings. This space also compelled the leaders to combine celebrations on Sunday morning. Soon, the church no longer had more than seven Sunday morning celebrations but only two: the warehouse celebration (increasingly identified as the "Philadelphia Campus," to which the Baptist leaders and congregants were attracted) and the "Crookes Campus" (i.e., the Mother Church). In this way the church contracted into fewer culturally distinct celebrations.

Recently, the church has functionally returned, if not officially, into two, possibly three congregations: the Anglican St. Thomas' Church (at the Mother Church venue) and the Philadelphia Church (at the Philadelphia warehouse), along with a new experiment called "city:base," an emerging urban congregation. Though attempts have been made to maintain a degree of unity—for instance, with the commissioning of Anglican Vicar Anne MacLaurin as a leader with Baptist Paul Maconochie at the Philadelphia

> The Order of Mission [as rooted in St. Tom's] stands in the stream of movements in past centuries that responded to the spiritual needs of their day, such as the Celtic monks and nuns who first evangelized Ireland, Scotland, northern England, Scandinavia, and northern Germany. They did this by organizing themselves into itinerant bands that settled and formed communities alongside pagan settlements. By so doing, they were able to demonstrate the impact of the gospel in their own personal and corporate lives. In more modern times, the Methodists in eighteenth-century England and the Salvation Army in the nineteenth century also stepped outside the structures of the established churches, reaching out to the segments of the populations that they were failing to influence for the gospel.
>
> Eddie Gibbs (CM, 149–50)

Church—the church is moving back toward two to three distinct megacongregations. Overall, the church continues to grow, and the youth continue to flourish.[42]

Practices

Worship in Dispersion

The organizational complexity of the big move from The Roxy forced the church to link culturally similar clusters together into what they called "celebrations." These then created a multicultural church with nine different worship expressions. By linking together two to eight clusters into "celebrations" the church was able to offer nine culturally distinct styles of worship. This connected the church to more cultures within the Sheffield community. The Sunday uniting service exposed the burgeoning congregation to its various cultural counterparts.

When the Philadelphia warehouse became available, a push to fully utilize this facility steered the church toward fewer worship celebrations. This is not dissimilar to churches across England and North America that build a bigger facility and then combine multiple worship expressions into fewer options with fewer cultural styles. The "uniting service" at St. Thomas' was more animated than the other celebrations. This could have to do with the pan-cultural feel of this Sunday evening event. Subsequently, the nine distinct cultural celebrations received less attention, and eventually two larger gatherings (Sunday mornings at the Philadelphia campus and at the Crookes Mother Church campus) replaced the nine culturally distinct celebrations.

> This story is both very cool and very alien, and it underlines, for better or worse, the importance of buildings. There are some wise lessons and remarks on church services held in dispersion or more centrally. *Nico-Dirk van Loo*

> The struggle of large churches to remain missional when facilities and organizational concerns steal energy and focus is understudied. *Bob Whitesel*

Spiritual Formation in Dispersion

Leaders at St. Thomas' built a foundational structure of small "cell" groups, eventually requiring participation in these groups as a condition of membership. Since the clusters were focused more on their extended family feel, the intimacy of small groups became the main teaching and discipling venue of

42. Saxton, interview.

the church. Small group leaders would meet with their cluster leader to go over that week's small group lesson.

The cluster leaders had already received this lesson in their weekly meeting with their celebration leader. The result was that the teaching became a unifying connection among the expanding cell-cluster-celebration network. Clusters created an extended family community, which is something many young people miss because their family is far away. According to former rector Mike Breen, clusters "create an extended family feel, like the movie *My Big Fat Greek Wedding.*"[43]

Spiritual formation in small groups created a flexible, indigenous discipleship environment. A small group leader meets with people of a similar culture and often in a nearby locale, and may adapt the church's lesson plans for the small group attendees. If the message is not getting across or if accountability is needed, a resident small group leader can more quickly and locally meet that need.

Mission in Dispersion

Not surprisingly, the greatest periods of growth occurred in the dispersed church mode after The Roxy venue was lost and seventeen clusters indigenized mission across the city.[44] As St. Thomas' went down the road toward becoming a megachurch, it mainly adopted churchwide, one-size-fits-all programs. As Joannah Saxton recalls,

> The default position was to do something throughout the whole church. If we did an outreach, the whole church did an outreach. If we did Alpha small groups, the whole church did them, and if we did nights of prayer, the whole church did it. But when we lost The Roxy we really had to disperse, and this required us to culturally diversify to reach the city in an entirely new and more tangible way.[45]

Though it was the diverse "celebrations" that connected the church's message to varying cultures in Sheffield, it was in the extended family feel of the clusters where commitments to Christ most often took place. Yet clusters were initially organized to give small groups enough person-power to undertake community service. Breen reflects,

> If you say you are going to help someone in need—say, paint their house—and a small group of twelve to sixteen people plans to do this, you only get three

43. Breen, interview.
44. Mallon, interview.
45. Saxton, interview.

to four people showing up. It's a disaster. But, if you cluster together three to
seven small groups to do this, you get a couple dozen showing up. Then you
get something done![46]

A church with multiple cultural bridges can connect with a larger segment
of a community. At St. Thomas' the clusters and celebrations had culturally distinct behaviors and ideas.[47] Diverse cultural options connected the
church to more segments of the Sheffield population.[48] Clusters provided a
suitable mixture of intimacy and anonymity to foster conversion. It came
as a surprise to the leaders that many people came to Christ in the cluster
environment.[49] The cluster's mix of accountability and anonymity provided
the right environment for new Christians to focus on their commitment and
their witness.

Leadership in Dispersion

Breen's Ephesus vision united the congregation through calamity and disper-
sion. Breen's forthright yet not-too-hasty vision gave the leaders a chance to
absorb the significance of the word. The loss of The Roxy created a dispersed
church. Multiple centers of the church ensued, and small groups increased
in importance.

Small groups provided an incubator for emerging leadership. Because membership in a small group is required of all members, at St. Thomas' there was
an upsurge in the number of small group leaders needed. This shortage not
only resulted in greater emphasis on leadership development but also created
easier routes into leadership. Because there are three to seven small groups
in a cluster, the cluster leader does not have an unwieldy number of trainees
to oversee.

Celebration leaders enjoy similar ratios. A cell-cluster-celebration model
created a leadership relationship based on history, culture, and proximity.
Because an effective small group leader could be promoted to a cluster leader
(while still remaining within the same cultural celebration), a leader did not
need to leave his or her culture to move up the leadership ladder.

46. Breen, interview.
47. For more on cultures as "integrated system of learned patterns of behavior, ideas and
products characteristic of a society," see Paul Hiebert, *Cultural Anthropology* (Grand Rapids:
Baker, 1976), 25.
48. Saxton, interview.
49. Hopkins and Breen, *Clusters*, 36–37.

From their history and innovations, St. Thomas' Church and its partner, the Philadelphia Church, have emerged as flexible congregations not afraid to be, in the words of Paddy Mallon, "a bit like the Acts of the Apostles: [embracing] the idea of expansion, contraction, consolidation and then you grow again."[50] These churches continue to grow,[51] and the fact that they embrace an elastic model of church growth indicates they are not outcome driven but process focused. It is their cultural flexibility, wed with a focus on making disciples in a cell-cluster-celebration structure, that has allowed this unlikely Sheffield church to emerge as one of the United Kingdom's most innovative congregations.[52]

Bibliography

Breen, Mike. *The Body Beautiful*. West Sussex, UK: Monarch Books, 1997.

———. *The Passionate Church*. Colorado Springs: Cook, 2004.

———. *A Passionate Life*. Colorado Springs: Cook, 2005.

Gibbs, Eddie. "From Crossing Bridges to Building Pontoons: Regaining Lost Ground and Crossing Cultural Frontiers." Paper read at the Annual Meeting of the American Society of Church Growth, November 12, 2005, at Fuller Theological Seminary, Pasadena, CA.

———. *LeadershipNext: Changing Leaders in a Changing Culture*. Downers Grove, IL: InterVarsity, 2005.

Gibbs, Eddie, and Ryan K. Bolger. *Emerging Churches: Creating Christian Community in Postmodern Cultures*. Grand Rapids: Baker Academic, 2005.

Hiebert, Paul. *Cultural Anthropology*. Grand Rapids: Baker, 1976.

Hopkins, Bob, and Mike Breen. *Clusters: Creative Mid-sized Missional Communities*. Sheffield, UK: 3D Ministries, 2007.

Hunter, George G., III. *The Contagious Congregation: Frontiers in Evangelism and Church Growth*. Nashville: Abingdon, 1979.

Mallon, Paddy. *Calling a City Back to God*. Eastbourne, UK: Kingsway, 2003.

Wagner, C. Peter. *Your Church Can Grow: Seven Vital Signs of a Healthy Church*. Glendale, CA: Regal, 1976.

Warren, Robert. *In the Crucible*. Surrey, UK: Highland Books, 1989.

Whitesel, Bob. "The Perfect Cluster: For Young Adults, St. Tom's, Sheffield Creates Extended Families, and Everyone Knows Where They Fit." *Outreach Magazine* (May/June 2005): 112–14.

50. Mallon, interview.
51. Saxton, interview.
52. Each year the church hosts a visitors' week they call Pilgrimage, where attendees from around the world experience firsthand the principles of this innovative congregation. See http://www.stthomascrookes.org/?attachment_id=392.

———. *Inside the Organic Church: Learning from 12 Emerging Congregations*. Nashville: Abingdon, 2006.

———. "Organic Change: 12 Emerging Communities of Missional Theologians." *Journal of the American Society for Church Growth* 18 (2007): 3–16.

Whitesel, Bob, and Kent R. Hunter. *A House Divided: Bridging the Generation Gaps in Your Church*. Nashville: Abingdon, 2001.

25

Urban Abbey

The Power of Small, Sustainable, Nimble Micro-Communities of Jesus

Kelly Bean

Story

Once upon a time, a long, long time ago (the 1970s) in the small suburban burg of West Linn, Oregon, there was a dreamer. This dreamer imagined communities and housing where the old and the young, the brown and the white, the lonely and the overworked found a home together. While some spent time going to homecoming dances, painting their nails, and sharing schoolgirl gossip, she sketched out designs for residential complexes where people would share gardens, kitchens, pets, and day-to-day life.

But the dreamer grew up and bought into a new dream: "The American Dream." She married and had children. She, with her husband, started a good business, joined a church, built a big house in the suburbs, worked hard to get more and better stuff and to make sure that her children had every opportunity to learn.

Even though she loved Jesus, served lunches to street people, and had thirty-four different people live with her family at one time or another, the dreamer began to feel hollow. She tried moving to the country. She built a bigger house and filled it with friends and family. But that bigger house was expensive, and instead of living a relaxing country life she and her husband found they were working harder than ever. They both knew they were going the wrong way, so they made the tough decision to let go of the beautiful home with the trout-filled creek and the stand of old-growth trees. They moved back to the suburbs into a much smaller house on a postage-stamp-sized piece of land to reassess life.

Over the course of these two decades of pursuing the American Dream, the dreamer had also been leading and pastoring a small Christian community in her living room. By the time she sold her country home, the larger church that this small house gathering was part of closed its doors, but the little community, Third Saturday, continued on. It was in that incubator of growing community that her long-lost dreams began to resurface.

She began to think thoughts like: How do large church buildings help the neighborhood they are in? Who is served by our gathering? Why is it that when I want to gather with my Third Saturday community friends, we must schedule far in advance and people must get into cars and drive far from their homes to get together? Why is it that I am too busy to sit and have tea with a good friend on short notice? Why am I so tired? Why is it so hard to befriend the poor and "the other"? How can we make do with less, drive less, and give more? And as she thought, some in that little community began to wonder with her as well.

One day the dreamer had a cup of coffee with a good friend and mentor. The mentor had been asking himself some questions too: In what ways have I become culturally captive to a Western, middle-class, consumer understanding of Christianity? How can I begin to break free from this to begin to live out the holistic gospel? They both agreed that such a reorientation must be done with the support of a community of Christ-followers who were also willing to take such a journey. What if they were to uproot from the comfort and isolation of their suburban neighborhoods and gather others to form a transformative community?

An Experiment

The Journey to New Church

But what would it take to leave the suburbs and become rooted in a more economically and ethnically diverse urban neighborhood where households could be in close proximity? Would doing so help challenge them to look beyond their white middle-class view of the world? Would they learn from the neighborhood, and could they then give something back to the neighborhood? Could they model a healthy egalitarian community where women and men lived and worked together? Could they open themselves to being transformed and in the process make a difference in the world?

The important first step was to share this spark of an idea with their spouses. The wife of the mentor was hesitant. Letting go of what she knew sounded very scary. But she also knew that she was not content with her isolated suburban life. Her children had grown and moved out, and she wanted something more. The husband of the dreamer was not at all excited. He had grown up the son of a poor single mom in the very neighborhoods that were up for consideration. He had worked his entire life to get away from those neighborhoods, and now that he was away, to consider going back with purpose was hard to fathom. However, he loved the dreamer, and he knew that look in her eye when God planted an idea. The bottom line, as he liked to put it, was: "I will follow the redhead anywhere." And so the spark became a flame.

> The church in the postmodern era must be prepared to witness with vulnerability and humility from the margins of society, much as it did in the first two centuries of its existence.
>
> Eddie Gibbs (CN, 30)

Starting Small

Such a big step becomes more reasonable when it is taken a little bit at a time. The dreamer had learned that "doing what is doable"[1] is better than biting off more than you can chew. So this is how they began. First this foursome began to imagine together. At times the dreamer and the mentor were prone to charge ahead, but the more hesitant two kept them in check. Together they committed to a path: starting small, taking one step at a time, taking a risk to be real, be known, and be authentic, taking time to be formed and transformed together, learning from the neighborhood, serving in doable ways, and staying small but multiplying.

> This is one of the tough lessons of mission in our innovative grassroots age. We read of dreamers who drive toward a project lassoed to nothing short of the kingdom of God, and in doing so burn out. I experienced that in the past eight years of my work at Neighbors Abbey.

1. Jim Henderson shared with me the wise practice of doing what is doable and has reassured me that ordinary attempts count: http://offthemap.com/about-page.

The patience required to innovate is a lesson in meekness, being content with who I am, no more, no less. These meek folks give up on visions of good careers. Such meek folks have nothing to lose. They end up inheriting the earth! *Troy Bronsink*

Then they began to pray together. They read books, traded ideas, and shared the struggles and joys of life. They walked through personal crisis together, and they walked through neighborhoods. They did not rush. They studied demographics, met local leaders, and cooked meals. In time others were intrigued and joined in, bringing their hopes and dreams, their favorite recipes, and their longing for a new way to live out their life as followers of Jesus. They named their newborn community Urban Abbey.

I wonder why the name was intentionally new monastic? What is it that is bubbling up? There are deep resonances here with what I have written. *Ian Mobsby*

Together they asked: What if we were just one of many micro-communities planted in neighborhoods, meeting in homes, led by lay leaders, women and men with hearts to serve and to empower others to do the same? What if these communities were places where authentic relationships were nurtured, where people were truly known, where pain could be acknowledged and embraced, where resources and strengths were pooled, and where weakness was where Christ showed up? What if it was possible to gather without first getting into a car, and just putting on a pair of sneakers or jumping on a bicycle would get people where they needed to go?

Wow! As the little abbey began to form it became clear that these dreams were best fulfilled in ordinary ways, by doing what was doable and by helping one another along the way. They were all ordinary people living out day-to-day life, interacting enough to get on one another's nerves, helping one another to remember to drink a little less wine, walk a little more, think twice before going on an IKEA shopping spree, befriend neighbors, make handmade gifts together, take Sabbath time, play with children, clean up messes, and make efforts to learn from the neighborhood. A savvy young leader of another micro-community told the dreamer, "After three years in community I can tell you that becoming part of the neighborhood is not as sexy as it might seem. The best way to get to know your neighbors is to plant some broccoli in your front yard and then hang out to talk as people pass by."[2]

Ordinary doable efforts actually count!

2. Brandon Rhodes, the wise broccoli planter at Springwater Community, http://springwater community.org.

As the excitement began to build, the dreamer began to fret: What if we end up inadvertently contributing to gentrification and oppression of the poor by moving into this neighborhood? That was an unsettling feeling. One day she was invited to a lunch meeting and found herself seated right next to a delightful older gentleman by the name of Dr. John Perkins. She happened to know that Dr. Perkins was someone who could address her concern wisely.

She told him the story of the little community being birthed in the northerly neighborhood of Portland, Oregon. And she shared her fears. He took her hand and patted it in a grandfatherly way. He told her something like this: "My dear, someone is going to buy those houses. What I want to know is who that will be and why they are moving into the neighborhood. You go right ahead and buy those houses and you learn the history of the neighborhood. You find the indigenous leaders of the neighborhood. You become friends, you get behind them and support them in leading the way."

> When I first moved into urban community as a middle-class white male, I thought, like a good liberal, that I should divest myself of responsibility. Then I realized that was a form of victimization: reinforcing my inaction with the myth that I might look like the gentry. A mentor of mine, Bob Lupton, challenged me that I was gentry and that I could not change that if I was going to stay. Neighbors Abbey formed about five years later with the assumption that gentrification is not something to pretend we are exempt from if we live in the community. Instead, we took the virtue of the Good Samaritan as a signifier that nonprivileged voices could be saints, examples to gentry life in the kingdom of God. That is why we called it "Neighbors" Abbey, a place where those who have gone before us are the saint and the guide. *Troy Bronsink*

Connections with the Larger Community

As they went forward they wondered how their little abbey and other microcommunities for Jesus could best be part of the larger church. They didn't have to look too far for inspiration. The dreamer had a good friend in Seattle, Washington, named Pastor Rose.[3] Pastor Rose had begun to imagine what would happen if church buildings were given over to job training, twelve-step groups, childcare, and after-school tutoring, to regular rhythms of prayer through the week, to parenting and marriage classes and even block parties. Pastor Rose did more than imagine. She led her church forward and made it so. The church became known to the broader community as a light and an agent of loving transformation to the neighborhood and even to the county that church congregation was located in.

3. Dr. Rose Madrid-Swetman can be found at http://vineyard-cc.org.

> The church began as a movement driven by a vision. It consisted of small groups of people who believed that Jesus was the Son of God and who had committed themselves totally and unreservedly to him as Lord and Savior. These groups replicated themselves throughout the Mediterranean world and beyond. They had no real estate. Their leaders were, for the most part, local people whom the apostles appointed and empowered. The movement had no social prestige or influential patrons. It operated from the margins and succeeded in infiltrating every level of society and department of life. The church of the twenty-first century must recapture this same dynamism and must not fight to try to regain the prestige it enjoyed in past days. It can assume no special rights or privileges but exists and thrives only through the grace of God.
>
> Eddie Gibbs (CN, 234)

The Urban Abbeyites wondered what would happen if many micro-communities joined hands with church leaders who were willing to freely share their buildings and resources with their neighborhoods. What if people saw a church and immediately knew they could go in the doors and find real hope and help? What if congregation members formed into micro-communities themselves? What if instead of funding programs to serve church members they met their own needs by living out real life in small communities that equipped them to give their resources and time to make the love of Jesus visible to their entire neighborhood?

Culture

Living Well toward Earth, God, and Neighbor

The possibilities seemed promising, maybe even mind-boggling. The dreamer began to meet with neighborhood leaders and pastors and to consider the gifts and talents of those who had been drawn to the abbey. The circle and the dreams continued to grow.

One of the Abbeyites, Dr. Dan, was a seminary professor who designed a Christian earthkeeping concentration and was leading his students in understanding how the gospel intersected with taking care of the earth.[4] He helped the little abbey keep sustainable practices in mind as they formed. How much space did they each need for themselves? When could they share cars and use transit? How did their ordinary choices express their value for justice? What was the relationship between earthkeeping, global systems, and issues such as racism, sexism, and poverty, and where did they need to make changes individually and as a community? How did their chosen lifestyle impact their neighborhood and even the world? How could Urban Abbey become a school of praxis to apprentice young seminarians and other developing leaders for the church?

---

4. Christian earthkeeping concentration: http://www.georgefox.edu/seminary/programs/christian-earthkeeping.

The Abbeyites were not super-saints. They were just ordinary "used-to-be" suburban Christians working hard to make one simple change after another. They were willing to open themselves to learn from their neighborhood and from one another. They knew they needed transformation and that being transformed was a process. They knew that making even simple changes against the grain of a culture would require plenty of challenging conversation, good supportive companionship, and some propping up at times. They were learning to live out a new narrative in a culture whose dominant script is consumerism and individualism.[5] Planting a community garden, sharing responsibility for meals, living in active reconciliation with earth and neighbor, preserving food for the winter, and reevaluating spending practices all became more feasible when tackled in community.

> Our practices do shape our view of the world. The old language of prescribing to a so-called Christian worldview no longer works for me. I've given that up for what you describe here, a relationship with our world that instructs our points of view. This teaches me repentance over and over, because intentional engagement with a dynamic local context requires flexibility and a secure-yet-humble sense of vocation. *Troy Bronsink*

Hybridity and Hospitality

As is often the case, where artists dwell there is room for difference and room for the other. Community members held friendships with people all over the world, with gay and lesbian friends, with priests and poets, with agnostics and addicts. All these relationships helped to shape the abbey and its members. Real friendship made it possible to honor the stories of "the other" by living fully into the story of Jesus.

Pluralism in Real Life

The Urban Abbey community was composed of a Lutheran, some ex-charismatics, some new charismatics, a Presbyterian, a Vineyard-ite, a member raised in the Roman Catholic Church, an Anglican-Anabaptist hybrid, a seminarian, a seminary professor, a therapist, an addictions counselor, two pastors, and an assortment of nondenominational friends. They were

---

5. Theologian Walter Brueggemann emphasizes that the dominant script in our society is a script of technological, therapeutic, consumer militarism that socializes us all, liberal and conservative. It is the work of the church to offer an alternative script rooted in the Bible and enacted in the tradition of the church. We are called to live out a counternarrative. See http://www.religion-online.org/showarticle.asp?title=3307.

intergenerational, with members in their thirties, forties, fifties, and sixties, along with one teen, two young children, and two babies. As one can imagine, this passel of traditions and perspectives led to some occasional conflict and lively conversations. It also brought a wealth of experience and goodness to the community.

Despite the denominational and theological hybridity, there was no denying it: in this ethnically diverse neighborhood the Abbeyites were all white, white as could be. The teenaged son of the dreamer attended a multicultural high school where as a white boy he was an ethnic minority. He enjoyed challenging the Abbeyites, reminding them that their stated values and ideals were somewhat disconnected from this reality.

Following the advice of the wise Dr. Perkins, the dreamer began to attend neighborhood gatherings and to learn from longtime neighbors. Her dear friend Donna helped by sharing her own experiences and perspective as a black woman in the predominately white Pacific Northwest. One relationship at a time, one story after another, is how the best transformation takes place. The little abbey was open to be taught.

> I'd be willing to bet that your openness is a direct benefit of your abbey's denominational diversity. Appreciation of many perspectives and teachings not only leaves room to reimagine, but it presupposes it. At Neighbors Abbey, after a three-year walk with the Presbyterians, we learned the hard way that denominations root momentum on eliminating such rethinking. *Troy Bronsink*

Creative Spirit

Urban Abbey was blessed with a plethora of artists: a potter, a painter, two graphic designers, and a multimedia artist. These community members imagined art as a gift to the neighborhood. They imagined public art installations and hands-on art in the neighborhood days—art to heal, art to provoke, art to unite. They also imagined shared workspaces not just for themselves but also for others in the neighborhood. They wondered if such workspaces could foster collaboration and inspire creative energy as artists with various mediums brought their studios together under one roof. Who knew what might come of this!

Spirit and Soul

The dreamer and the professor both had their eye on a smoky neighborhood bar where they imagined holding Sunday morning Taizé prayer services with espresso shots administered upon entry. The dreamer, who spent a good deal of time at her craft of writing and as a pastor-at-large, liked to hang out in the local coffee shop with her prayer book, her laptop, and a collection of small stones to dispense as blessings. She welcomed friends, talked with strangers, and held space for praying the hours.

She was curious to discover how, over time, integrating prayer, ritual, and tangible spiritual practice into the rhythm of day-to-day life right in the middle of bars and coffeehouses (in an unobtrusive manner) might shape the abbey and the neighborhood. In a culture that is attuned to and longs for a new spirituality, the Holy Spirit is already at work. Nonthreatening and easily accessible points of connection are invitations to come on in.

> Kelly's story paints, in a very real way, how the Word became flesh and moved into the neighborhood. Kelly shows how the process of becoming rooted into a context involves dirt and everyday change, neither of which are glamorous or easy. *Ruth Skree*

A Way Forward

The questions that simmered up between the dreamer and the mentor over coffee have begun to be lived out. Scheduling ahead and driving across town has been replaced by wandering across the street to sip tea on a front porch. Mowing single family lawns and trimming hedges has been replaced by digging in the dirt with a friend and making pesto from a community garden. Conflicts can be resolved by believing the best about the other and meeting face-to-face in short order. It is easier to imagine how to make more with less as Abbeyites stand together in the transformative process. Neighbors, be they the single mom down the street, the shop owner around the corner, the stripper who lives next door, or the pastor of the historic neighborhood church, are becoming friends and teachers. Worship and practice wind through the ordinary details of ordinary people making meals, gardening, problem solving, and making friends together.

> In my experience conflicts are the greatest points of growth. I wish you could unpack that some more. The space between "others" is the place of transformation. Often prejudice is only the beginning. Ideology must also soften in relationships, and that takes years of working side by side. And then pride must finally be melted away, which requires deep spiritual maturity along the lines of Rumi or Jean Vanier. All three of these—pride, ideology, and prejudice—are hidden tools that can fund larger projects and mega-ecclesiology. I think you are onto something with micro-ecclesiology when the Abbeyites are honest about these three hidden tools. *Troy Bronsink*

What if the small actions and ordinary gifts of many were joined together in small, nimble communities of faith? What if these micro-communities partnered with or were even birthed by neighborhood churches to incarnate the spirit of Jesus in neighborhoods all over this country and even around the world? These nimble little churches just might embody the very spirit of the Triune God who exists in community.

> Bean presented us with a beautiful story of a journey of obedience to serve God in urban Portland. While some churches in suburbia have mythologized the gentle-urban-other from a safe distance, Bean presented us with "the other" as "one of us." Stories like this replicate past and present stories of bold leaders responding to God's calling to abandon the lies of the world and seek God's kingdom above all things. This story shows us that missional activity takes place through incarnation; there are no recipes, and much discernment is required along the way! *Osías Segura-Guzmán*

This is the time for the Western church to truly embody the gospel, to be Jesus in neighborhoods, to reshape and reimagine economic and social dreams, and to cultivate practical, winsome, authentic, and redemptive community. The biggest problems present the biggest possibilities. And the biggest possibilities will be best achieved by living into the small ideas. Maybe the best way to start is to plant broccoli in the front yard.

Part 5

Traditions

26

Indigenous and Anglican

A Truly Native Church Emerges in the Anglican Church of Canada

Mark MacDonald

In this chapter, I hope to share some of the dimensions of a contemporary movement of spiritual renewal among the indigenous peoples of Turtle Island,[1] otherwise known as North America.[2] There are a number of angles from which the renewal may be identified. One, for example, is to note the growing ministry and influence of indigenous evangelicals. The leadership of Terry LeBlanc, Richard Twiss, Randy Woodley, and Ray Aldred are worthy of mention.[3]

1. Turtle Island is the often-used aboriginal term for the area now known as North America.
2. Though we limit much of our discussion to Canada, we note that, from an indigenous perspective, this is unnatural and, to some degree, an imposition. Much of what will be said, however, will either directly or indirectly cross the borders of colonial occupation.
3. See http://www.naiits.com/index.html for information on the North American Institute for Indigenous Theological Studies. Richard Twiss's webpage is found at http://www.wiconi .com/, and Randy Woodley's Eagle's Wings Ministry at http://www.eagleswingsministry.com /index.htm.

Tradition

Here we will trace some of the significant aspects of the emergence of a self-determining indigenous church within the Anglican Church of Canada. In that tracing, it is important to note that this is a part of a constellation of interrelated positive events among indigenous peoples, including the leadership mentioned above, the growth of a truth and reconciliation process among the churches and peoples of Canada, and a larger movement of indigenous self-determination within the Anglican Communion, beginning in New Zealand/Aotearoa.

> As an Australian, I feel we have a lot to learn from Canada and New Zealand, who are decades ahead of us in recognition of indigenous self-determination, at church and national political levels. Darren Cronshaw

It is important to remember that this story is told against the backdrop of the revelations about the Anglican Church's involvement in the abuses of the Canadian Residential School system.[4] An indigenous church emerging from the wreckage of such a disaster is a story of resurrection. Such a church has the potential to make a unique and significant contribution to an emerging global missiology.

A New Past Frames a New Future

The indigenous peoples of the Americas have an almost universal reputation for two things: the tragic dignity of their living relationship with the land and the misery that came in the wake of the occupation of their lands by the colonial powers of Europe. The Western churches' role in this narrative of misery is significant and culpable. The ideology supporting the colonial project included a prominent church-endorsed claim to a singularly privileged relationship to knowledge and truth. In addition, Western churches played a significant supporting role in many aspects of colonial occupation. The high profile of the Western churches in some of the worst aspects of this clash of civilizations is, for good reason, widely known and criticized, even by their own members.

There is, however, a quite different story to be told. Though it does not exonerate the Western churches, it describes something of vital Christian significance—the largely unrecognized achievement of indigenous survival. This is, at many levels, a story with miraculous meaning. A full account of

---

4. This story was chosen to be the case study for Edinburgh 2010's Theme Four: Mission and Power. Daryl Balia and Kirsteen Kim, eds., *Edinburgh 2010*, vol. 2, *Witnessing to Christ Today* (Oxford: Regnum, 2010), 86–115.

this amazing resilience also includes the emergence of a distinctly indigenous Christian faith and its post-Christendom flowering in our time.

This story is the foundation and frame of the spiritual renewal that is now spreading among indigenous peoples throughout North America, especially among indigenous Anglicans. They understand the renewal they are experiencing as a part of the saving trajectory of the Word of God among indigenous peoples throughout the ages.[5] This story includes both the development of indigenous faith in the midst of the severe oppression of the past and an account of the present-day adaptation of indigenous life to Christian faith—and Christian faith to indigenous life. In all these aspects it is, most of all, a story of the sovereign grace and power of God, of the primacy of the spiritual over the material.

> Is this a recovery of an older or deeper mystical appreciation of the Christian faith that can make deep connections with a premodern transrational experience form of faith, which rightly critiques a more "modernist" expression of Christianity found wanting in our now postsecular contexts? *Ian Mobsby*

The idea that there has been a viable and distinct indigenous expression of Christian faith is a contrast to almost all Western descriptions of indigenous religious development during the colonial period. The response of the indigenous peoples of Turtle Island to Christianity has always been judged to be a failure by virtually all Western observers, regardless of their theological or ideological orientation. Secular observers were often disappointed that Christian faith had adulterated indigenous religious traditions. Religious observers always defined success as the capacity to mimic Western institutions and religious practices. When indigenous communities didn't respond to Western-style worship or other patterns of Christian community, it was seen as either a lack of commitment to the essentials of Christian faith, a lack of capacity for civilized (Western) behaviour, or both at the same time. When indigenous forms of faith and worship developed and prospered, they were, when noticed, often seen as syncretistic or misguided—the product of religious mind-set that was fatally distorted by a connection to a primitive and false worldview. Though native people often showed great devotion in prayer and singing, they showed little corporate capacity or interest in the

---

5. Chief Donny Morris provides an example of sentiment in his message at the beginning of his people's history: "We acknowledge our ancestors and our God who guided them to this place. We believe we are here for a reason and we believe this community has the potential to advance." Dianne Hiebert and Marj Heinrichs, *We Are One with the Land: A History of Kitchenumaykoosib Inninuwug* (Kelowna, B.C.: Rosetta, 2007), 17.

formality and timing schemes of Western mainline worship. Nor were they able to embrace, in any way or form, the Enlightenment dichotomy of the spiritual and material.

> This is the shame of colonialism. Thankfully in our emerging postcolonial era the church is beginning to celebrate what people of all cultures know of God. *Darren Cronshaw*

Despite the considerable obstacles, an incarnational development of faith, what may be called an indigenous Christianity, emerged in multiple contexts across the Americas. The still viable Northwest Coast Shakers[6] blend different Christian traditions with their own indigenous practices in completely unique but authentically Christian ways. The Anglican nativism of the Gwich'in[7] offers resistance to industrial overdevelopment in the Arctic that is often seen, in our present context of ecological threat, as prophetic and courageous. The intense devotion of the circumpolar Inuit has inspired people around the world. Finally, the singing prayer meetings, found almost everywhere, show indigenous ingenuity and inspiration, adapting Christian faith and practice to serve indigenous need and Christian mission. These are just a few of the many examples that could be given.[8]

> In the Western world, we have so much to learn from indigenous theologies. Jacob Loewen suggests that God buried all sorts of treasure in Scripture insofar as no one culture can find it all until the interpretations and perspectives of different cultures of the world have been applied to them.[9] *Darren Cronshaw*

Though their own practices were outlawed, indigenous peoples used and adapted Christian forms of faith and worship to help carry their traditional worldview and values. At the same time, significant elements of Christian faith were integrated into indigenous life in a mutually transforming pattern. This faith was and is a sustaining element for many native elders.

The way these matters are viewed by nonaboriginal society is now beginning to change. A growing number of scholars are developing the capacity to describe some of the complex creativity of the spirituality of indigenous

6. For the Shakers and a much broader introduction to the diverse spirituality of the indigenous peoples of the Americas, see the excellent introduction by Peggy Beck and Anna Walters, *The Sacred* (Tsaile, AZ: Navajo Nation Community College Press, 1977).

7. Mark MacDonald, *The Chant of Life: Inculturation and the People of the Land* (New York: Church Publishing, 2003), xxii–xxiii.

8. Michael McNally, *Ojibwe Singers: Hymns, Grief, and a Culture in Motion* (New York: Oxford University Press, 2000).

9. Cited in Charles H. Kraft, *Anthropology for Christian Witness* (Maryknoll, NY: Orbis, 1996), 18.

Christians. Western models of understanding human culture have, until recently, been unable to perceive indigenous spirituality or track its continuing development in the colonial era. Now there are a number of significant voices calling for a reevaluation of customary Western assessments of indigenous culture and well-being.[10]

Some understanding of the dynamics of the past is critical to any presentation of recent developments among indigenous Anglicans. The recognition of a historic line of Christian development among their churches, much of it faithful and orthodox in its faith, has inspired and encouraged present-day indigenous Anglicans. They are beginning to see themselves as part of a creative trail of faith and practice that sustained their people through great hardship. The Christianized faith of the elders allowed indigenous peoples to offer creative resistance to Western colonization while, at the same time, allowing the useful incorporation of those aspects of the encounter that were welcome or helpful.[11]

The approach of the elders in times past also suggests patterns of faith practice that offer helpful guidance for the future. Nightly hymn singing was popular and important to earlier generations; it continues as a significant and regular part of life for many indigenous communities across Turtle Island today. The theologically creative translations of hymns and Scripture by the elders of earlier generations are often the work of theologically sophisticated and faithful Christians who were also deeply connected and faithful to their people and an indigenous worldview. These works of the past are ready to inform a faith for the future.

The Development of an Indigenous Anglican Church: Institutional Change and a Spiritual Movement

In the 1960s there was growing awareness of problems in the Indian Residential Schools (IRS) and in many other aspects of the church's overall policy and practice toward indigenous peoples. In 1967 the National Executive Council of the Anglican Church commissioned sociologist Charles Hendry to examine the present situation and make broad policy recommendations regarding the

---

10. Thomas R. Berger, *Village Journey: The Report of the Alaska Native Review Commission* (Vancouver: Douglas and McIntyre, 1985); Rupert Ross, *Dancing with a Ghost: Exploring Indian Reality* (Toronto: Penguin, 2006); John Ralston Saul, *A Fair Country: Telling Truths about Canada* (Toronto: Viking, 2008).

11. Steven C. Dinero, "The Lord Will Provide: The History and Role of Episcopalian Christianity in Nets'aii Gwich'in Social Development—Arctic Village, Alaska," *Indigenous Nations Studies Journal* 4, no. 1 (Spring 2003): 2–29.

Anglican Church's relationship with indigenous peoples. Thus began a period of proactive institutional change.

Delivered to General Synod in 1969, the Hendry Report, *Beyond Traplines*,[12] called for sweeping changes in the relationship of the church to indigenous peoples. Some changes began right away—hiring a consultant, greater awareness and commitment to issues of aboriginal rights and environmental justice—but other matters took some time to develop. In 1980 a committee of indigenous people was authorized to oversee the church's response to indigenous issues. This group became, over time, the Anglican Council of Indigenous Peoples. Through its leadership and the creative leadership of two successive national coordinators for indigenous ministries, Laverne Jacobs and Donna Bomberry, the voice of indigenous peoples began to express itself. Over time, it became clear that there was a need for parallel structures within the church to develop true self-determination.

Toward this end, a series of indigenous gatherings began in 1988, now known as Sacred Circles. These gatherings began to give indigenous Anglicans ways to address the great issues faced by their communities. The Sacred Circles gave shape to the growing movement toward self-determination and began to show, through prayer, consultation, and native-style celebration, the hopeful possibilities that could come from a truly indigenous church.

A critical point was reached at the Sacred Circle of August 1993 in Minaki, Ontario. Primate Michael Peers acknowledged the wrongs of the Indian Residential Schools and apologized to the gathering for the church's role in survivors' pain and trauma. His words had deep effect. In this one moment of honest recognition of guilt, a real hope was born that all parts of the church could find a new way of life in which indigenous peoples and their culture would be fully received and respected. To this day, many elders remember this as one of the great moments of their life.

> Apology, as we have been learning in Australia, is a critical step in the reconciliation process. Darren Cronshaw

The apology and the careful work of preparation by indigenous leaders and elders made the way for a number of critical actions over the next ten years. Leadership gatherings produced a number of key consensus documents, especially *Our Journey of Spiritual Renewal* and *The Covenant*.[13] These affirmed the commitment to self-determination but held out a "hand of partnership" to any who would help them reach their goal. Later, an implementation committee

12. Charles Hendry, *Beyond Traplines* (Toronto: Anglican Book Centre, 1998).
13. See http://www.anglican.ca/im/index.htm for background.

was able to present a series of proposals that would help them fulfill the covenant's commitments. Prominently, the group asked for the establishment of a National Indigenous Anglican Bishop (NIAB).

The 2006 Sacred Circle at Pinawa, Manitoba, reviewed the work of the implementation committee and responded with the request for the consecration of fifteen indigenous bishops across Canada, each with full authority and jurisdiction. Primate Andrew Hutchinson was unable to respond exactly as requested, given the governance structures of the church. He did, however, pledge to create a NIAB position within the year. In January 2007 he announced that he concurred with the selection of an indigenous search committee to ask Mark MacDonald, then the bishop of Alaska, to become the National Indigenous Anglican Bishop.

> MacDonald presented to us the struggles of the First Nation Peoples in Canada within the background of the abusive participation of the Anglican Church's Canadian Residential School system and the current emergence of a self-determining indigenous church within the Anglican Church of Canada. Reading this chapter, I wonder why the author did not discuss what the benefits might be for this indigenous movement to remain within the framework of the Anglican Church of Canada, rather than becoming independent and more free to be truly self-determining. *Osías Segura-Guzmán*

> Yes, many of our young people feel this way. Our elders, who suffered the most, have told us to seek peace in the church and seek God's way for us, if possible, by being true to the essence of Anglicanism and the Christian faith. This path, a path of the cross and reconciliation, is the preferred way. If we can become truly self-determining, much will be gained by all. If not, then we will seek other guidance, from Scripture and our elders. For now, it is a mixed bag, some good, some bad, but we feel secure in God's love, secure in the knowledge that God has a plan that will bring blessing, and secure that the indigenous peoples of North America have a vocation within the trajectory of God's plan for the nations. *Mark MacDonald*

The response among indigenous Anglicans and indigenous peoples was enthusiastic and supportive. It was seen by many, including First Nations political leaders, even those who are identified as traditional and non-Christian, as a bold statement of the Anglican Church's recognition of both the reality and authority of indigenous identity and the primal relationship of indigenous peoples with the land. Long accustomed to multiple loyalties in the construction of its own Canadian aboriginal identity, they were able to easily transition to the idea of having more than one bishop. The NIAB was seen as an extension of ministry of the primate, serving the special needs of indigenous peoples and conforming to the boundaries and borders of indigenous life, as opposed to those of colonial occupation.

The creation of a national indigenous bishop was not appreciated in the same way by most nonindigenous Anglicans. Though generally supported, it was largely seen as a special needs chaplaincy. The few who objected expressed concerns about jurisdiction and the wisdom of an ethnically based episcopacy. These were either unaware of or unconvinced by the assertion of aboriginal rights and consequent claims of a unique and primal relationship to both the land and Canadian society. Some were sympathetic, others not, but almost all saw the NIAB and other expressions of indigenous autonomy as political or social responses to the oppression of the past.

The work of the NIAB, as imagined by deliberations of the Sacred Circles,[14] was to provide four things:

1. a voice for indigenous peoples within the House of Bishops and the governance structures of the Anglican Church of Canada;
2. a person to act as a translator between the indigenous peoples and the rest of the church;
3. a voice for Mother Earth within the church, which included promoting an understanding of the unique and living relationship between indigenous peoples and the land; and,
4. to act as a kind of midwife to the creation of a self-determining indigenous church within the Anglican Church of Canada.

Soon after the NIAB was put in place, a series of consultations began, with issues of self-determination and church development being primary. The initial focus of self-determination was administrative, jurisdictional, and financial. Soon, however, the awareness that a movement of spiritual renewal was developing among Anglican indigenous peoples eclipsed the other aspects of self-determination. Though the emphasis changed, the institutional actions mentioned above were not seen as separate. The development of a spiritual movement was seen in concert with the other changes. The institutional change was the providential complement to the spiritual movement of God in human hearts.

14. See the video record of the Sacred Circles produced by Anglican Video for background on this. The leadership of indigenous ministries in the Anglican Church, along with ACIP, had directed Anglican Video to produce an "oral" rather than written record of their meetings. This has provided a useful summary and record of the important actions of the Sacred Circles. They are available through the Anglican Church of Canada at http://www.anglican.ca/im/indigenous-ministries/sacred-circle-videos.

The hopes of elders, spoken decades before, were remembered as people discerned God's presence in the flow of developments over time. The consultations, and the practices associated with them—singing, prayer, Gospel reading with group reflection—began to spread to other areas: Saskatchewan, Caledonia, Chisasibi First Nation, Winnipeg in the Diocese of Rupert's Land, and other scattered communities, mostly in the north. Soon, the consultation style and spirit was appearing in other gatherings related to Anglican indigenous peoples, including the meetings of the Anglican Council of Indigenous Peoples, committee work related to indigenous ministry, and, in 2009, the fifth Sacred Circle that gathered at Port Elgin, Ontario. People were often heard to say that they were a part of a spiritual movement "in the gospel."

The consultations practiced Gospel Based Discipleship (GBD), a practice of communal reading of a Gospel of the day.[15] In GBD, the group reads the Gospel three times. In the first reading, the group is asked: "What stands out for you?" After the second reading, "What do you hear God saying to us?" And the third, "What is God calling us to do?"

These discussions, sometimes held in one large group and sometimes in breakout smaller groups, are foundational to the work that follows in the consultation. During the parts of the discussion that are more easily identified as "business," the Gospel is often read again. At the end of the Gospel-based reflections, it is stated that anyone may call for the Gospel to be read at any time in the proceedings that follow. When the Gospel is called for, it is often quite helpful, setting the tone for all parts of the gathering and, more often than not, shaping and inspiring the work that is undertaken.

The key element was not the technique of GBD, but the sense of spiritual authority from the Word of God discerned in community. The authority of the circle, so critical to traditional governance, was recovered in a Christian context. Although the congruence of the style of deliberation with indigenous culture was welcome, the emphasis was on the presence and guidance of God in the ongoing life of indigenous churches, in all of its various aspects. This allowed the business sessions to avoid the dichotomies that were felt to plague more Westernized forms of deliberation and governance. The

> Some people who had given up on Bible reading, or who had been grinding on in a mechanical way, have come to appreciate afresh the rich spiritual treasure of Scripture by learning to meditate on the text.
>
> Eddie Gibbs (CN. 134)

---

15. The Gospel is usually taken from the lectionary for the daily celebration of the Eucharist, though some use the Daily Office Lectionary or some other device for selecting readings. A few people have chosen special Gospels for the day, based on the work at hand, and some have used portions from other parts of Scripture.

spiritual and the material were not separated; the voice of God was felt in the authority of the circle, inspired by Word and Spirit.

Almost all the consultations also included an evening program of singing, prayer, and testimony, often called a Gospel Jamboree. This form of gathering is a direct, but modernized, extension of some of the song and prayer styles mentioned above. Both as part of the consultations and standing alone as a form of gathering the faithful, Gospel Jams are growing in popularity. Well attended by young and old alike, found in the north but also in urban areas, and ecumenical in practice, these indigenous Christian gatherings are a vehicle of the spiritual movement. Gospel Jamboree is now brought to multiple communities on Aboriginal Radio and the internet. It has other names across the land—prayer meeting, revival, Singspiration—though the general pattern is similar. The deep resonance it has with the values and traditions of indigenous communities is part of its appeal.

> Biblically inspired meditation carries over into contemplation, which, drawing upon accumulated spiritual insight, opens up into a wider field of vision.
>
> Eddie Gibbs (CN, 134)

Forward Movement

In May 2010, Lydia Mamakwa was consecrated the bishop of the Northern Ontario region of the diocese of Keewatin, the first regional indigenous bishop over the first operational regional indigenous ministry. As this is written there are four other regions that are pursuing similar goals and strategies. Together, these developments will create one of the most comprehensive and significant changes in the history of the Anglican Church of Canada.

In June 2010, the General Synod of the Anglican Church of Canada met in Halifax and recognized the vitality and importance of the growing spiritual movement among indigenous Anglicans. The presentation by indigenous peoples was seen by many as a highlight of the event. The synod gave unprecedented endorsement of the movement by constitutionally recognizing the Anglican Council of Indigenous Peoples, the National Indigenous Anglican Bishop, and the Sacred Circle as a part of the church. This action allows indigenous people to craft the structure and life of their church communities with indigenous values and traditions. It effectively creates, in embryo, a self-determining indigenous church within the Anglican Church of Canada.

The spiritual movement that has inspired these events is developing in a way that is ecumenical, evangelical, and indigenous, all at the same time. Participants describe these events as the living Word of God becoming flesh, the Word "pitching its tent" among them. Christ is becoming embodied in indigenous life in ways that were unimaginable in the not-too-distant past.

The spontaneous outbreaks of this spiritual activity are found in indigenous communities all over Canada and certainly not confined to the members of the Anglican Church, spreading out among many communities and the different religious groups among them. The uncoordinated quality of these events is another aspect of what people mean when they say this is a spiritual movement. It is experienced as God directed and God inspired. Happening at a time when there is a great decline in the strength and viability of Western institutions, especially in indigenous communities, these developments echo the trajectory of faith in Global South communities over the past fifty years. In the Global South, the withdrawal of foreign missionary institutions was initially seen as a prelude to a certain catastrophe. Instead, local missions grew dramatically as the Western organizations pulled out. In hindsight, the withdrawal of Western institutions was seen as a necessary step toward growth and vitality with the local churches. This pattern appears to be repeating itself in North America.

The Way Ahead

It is impossible to provide comprehensive analysis in matters that are so complex historically, culturally, and spiritually. Within the limits of our space, we have tried to give enough background to suggest some avenues of reflection and investigation that will be fruitful to the work of God. At a minimum, we would like to suggest a reconsideration of the standard narratives of the relationship of the gospel to the indigenous peoples.

Taken in sum, tracing the trajectory of the Word of God in indigenous faith is an encouragement and inspiration. It is a trajectory that dramatically proclaims the power of the gospel, a power that can heal and prophetically inspire, regardless of the vivid contrast between its truth and the limitations of those who share it.

Many of my generation were raised in a pattern of thought that considered the trajectory of the Word of God in Western culture as normative. It was, in the training that many of us received, the only pattern of faith development that mattered, the necessary preliminary of any serious attempt at mission. Without trying to deny the importance of the Western tradition, we can now appreciate that the Word of God has a trajectory that is specific and often unique to each particular culture.[16]

16. Note, for example, the way the trajectory of the Word of God in Korean culture has departed from the standard histories of Christian development. This was dramatically evident

This calls us to a level of spiritual discernment in the relationship of mission to culture that is complex, dynamic, and dialogical in ways that echo what the early church encountered in its surrounding culture. On the one hand, they enthusiastically pointed to the seeds of the Word present in culture; on the other hand, they confronted those aspects of culture that denied or distorted the Word of God as a fundamental and ongoing discipline of the spiritual life.

The Western churches' approach to indigenous peoples and other groups who are not a part of the Western cultural framework has been seriously compromised by an idolatrous relationship to the artifacts of their own history and context. The churches of a Western cultural framework have seen both their spiritual capacity and horizon of mission hindered by the continuing presence of cultural chauvinism and xenophobia. Within the churches' own cultural context, this is damaging enough. Beyond their own context, as their history with indigenous peoples demonstrates, they risk their integrity, their essence.

God's mission to indigenous peoples in the Americas has a brilliant horizon. It shows real promise for the renewal of the people of the land. It also has the capacity to blaze a trail of renewal and influence into other communities, for the ridiculed and persecuted spirituality of indigenous peoples has a resonance, especially with young people in the larger culture and society. The striking combination of individuality within community, practiced within a family-based and ecologically connected Christian faith, is immediately attractive and, in our time, an urgent need.

The Western churches, for their own sake, must allow the embodiment of the living Word of God in the culture of their indigenous members and pray for its fulfillment within their own communities and contexts. There is here the capacity to develop new forms of worship, governance, and corporate spiritual discipline that will speak to a new generation of believers, indigenous and nonindigenous. There is in this trajectory a real promise of reconciliation, hope, and the power of resurrection. Less circumscribed by the capacity of the cultural institutions and prejudice that now constrain it, such a renewal could suggest ways to become a church that the poor can afford and a place where the outcast will hear the good news of Jesus, the Saviour and Ruler of creation.

---

in the Korean presentations to the Edinburgh 2010 Conference; see especially Balia and Kim, *Edinburgh 2010*, 2:238–39.

27

Turning the Ocean Liner

The Fresh Expressions Initiative

Graham Cray

The title of this chapter comes from a comment made about the "Fresh Expressions Initiative" by Brian McLaren, who said that we seemed to have found a way to turn around an ocean liner. He then remarked, wistfully, that it might be easier than turning around a flotilla of a thousand motorboats!

Tradition

A Brief History

In 1994 the House of Bishops of the Church of England published a report on church planting entitled *Breaking New Ground*.[1] It was important because it was the first official Church of England document to comment on the significance of networks, along with neighborhoods, as the basis of community, and therefore as relevant to church planting.

1. *Breaking New Ground: Church Planting in the Church of England* (London: Church House Publishing, 1994).

In 2002 I was asked to chair a new working party to review *Breaking New Ground*, to make an assessment of progress with church planting as a mission model and of the changing cultural and ecclesial contexts. What was the environment in which we are called to be and do church? We were also asked to look at issues of "emerging church" and "new church" and to comment on a number of forms of church new to the Church of England, such as youth churches, cell churches, multiple congregations, and network churches.

Our report was published in 2004 as *Mission-Shaped Church: Church Planting and Fresh Expressions of Church in a Changing Context.*[2] Its central recommendation was to supplement our geographically based parochial system with "fresh expressions of church": "In each diocese there should be a strategy for the encouragement and resourcing of church planting and fresh expressions of church, reflecting the network and neighborhood reality of society and of mission opportunity. This strategy should be developed with ecumenical collaboration."[3]

The report was unanimously commended to the dioceses and departments of the Church of England by the General Synod. The working party had coined the term "fresh expressions of church" as a coverall for the variety of new or recent forms of church plant or culturally focused congregations it had identified. In my speech to the General Synod I said, "This is primarily a report on what the Church of England is *already* doing in many dioceses, rather than a recommendation that it begin something novel. There is good news to tell, and our recommendations come from a review of actual practice."

> Two aspects of the report are particularly refreshing: first, its ecumenical spirit. It draws from the insights and experience of a wide variety of church planting endeavors from other historic denominations as well as from independent networks. Second, it reaches beyond Europe to gain from the insights of the growing churches in the Global South.
>
> Eddie Gibbs (CM, 68)

> The German reform publication *Kirche der Freiheit* (2006) argues vice versa by making recommendations for the future. *Markus Weimer*

The most important consequence of the synod vote was the decision by Archbishop Rowan Williams to create a team to act as a resource to the dioceses, as the recommendations were put into practice. The Methodist Church immediately asked to be a partner, and from the beginning the Fresh Expressions

2. *Mission-Shaped Church: Church Planting and Fresh Expressions of Church in a Changing Context* (London: Church House, 2004).
3. Ibid., 145.

Team and Initiative has been ecumenical. The United Reformed Church and the Congregational Federation are now partners, and there is close cooperation with the (Presbyterian) Church of Scotland. There are also mission agency partners: CMS (Church Mission Society), The Church Army, The Church Army Sheffield (research) Centre, Anglican Church Planting Initiatives, and the 24/7 Prayer Movement.

The Church of England has created a track within its ordained ministry called Ordained Pioneer Ministry, with 120 candidates in training or deployed to plant fresh expressions of church. A new legal provision, known as a Bishops' Mission Order,[4] has been created to give formal legitimacy to those network fresh expressions which are not developments of the work of a local parish.

We do not know precisely how many fresh expressions there are. The most accurate records are those kept by the Methodist Church, which has 1,200, amounting to one out of every five Methodist churches planting a fresh expression. A great deal has happened in a short time!

The current spectrum of fresh expressions of church ranges from:

- an existing local church reimagining itself for mission in the light of these developments, to
- churches where there has been a lay-led shift from a project to engage with the community to the development of a congregation around that project, to
- new communities planted whose reach is wider than that of a parish, often on a deanery or circuit basis, sometimes with some funding from diocese or district, to
- larger projects, involving a funded post, authorized in the Church of England through a Bishops' Mission Order.

It is clear to me that we have caught a wave of the Holy Spirit. The God who delights to surprise, the God who works in the least likely situations so that the glory is his alone—this God has worked in the last place anyone with a mind for mission would have expected: a historic, Christendom-shaped mainline denomination in Europe!

> The Church of England is the only mainline church in Western Europe that has successfully integrated new ways of being church into the existing parochial structure. *Markus Weimer*

---

4. See http://www.churchofengland.org/clergy-office-holders/pastoralandclosedchurches/pastoral/bmos.aspx.

There is a threefold ecology in which this movement has flourished.

- At the local level there is a new imagination about the forms of church for mission. Mainline Christians are imagining being church in ways they would not have considered before. Fundamentally this is a grassroots movement of the Spirit.
- At a senior leadership level there is a new era of permission for missional initiatives and experiments. Rather than thinking "the bishop would never allow it," parishes are discovering that the bishop would be very disappointed if they did not try. (This means that there are both bottom-up and top-down elements at work.)
- Finally, the national team provides resources to help parishes develop missional imagination and training to help them learn best practice.

This combination of imagination, permission, and resources allows fresh expressions of church to develop across substantial parts of the participating denominations.

> The unique momentum is that the grassroots level has been blessed by the church authorities and that visionary leaders in local initiatives are kept loyal to their church.
> *Markus Weimer*

Archbishop Rowan Williams championed fresh expressions from the beginning. He continued to give this work visible and generous support. His other important contribution was the idea of a "mixed-economy church"[5]—that there were two elements within the one economy of the church's mission: our long-term inherited approach and the newer development of fresh expressions of church. This is not a device to enable the two to operate in parallel, but as a partnership, where each is enriched by the other. Fresh expressions are not to replace more traditional approaches, but to complement them.

This commitment, to honor our tradition and to develop it respectfully, lies behind the choice of the term "fresh expressions of church." Here "fresh" has a dual meaning. From one perspective it is a coverall term for that which is new, fresh, to the Church of England. The term is also deliberately drawn from the Declaration of Assent, which every Church of England minister makes at their ordination and each time they are licensed to a new ministry.[6]

The bishop declares that "The Church of England is part of the One, Holy, Catholic and Apostolic Church, worshiping the one true God, Father, Son

5. See http://www.emergingchurch.info/reflection/rowanwilliams/index.htm.
6. *Mission-Shaped Church*, 34.

and Holy Spirit. It professes the faith uniquely revealed in the Holy Scriptures and set forth in the catholic creeds, which faith the Church is called upon to proclaim afresh in each generation." In response each minister affirms their "loyalty to this inheritance of faith" as their "inspiration and guidance under God in bringing the grace and truth of Christ to this generation."[7]

In other words, "bringing the grace and truth of Christ to this generation" requires a "proclaiming afresh" of the historic gospel and may now require an "embodying afresh" in new congregations. We wrote, "One of the central features of this report is the recognition that the changing nature of our missionary context requires a new inculturation of the gospel within our society."[8]

The Core Process

A Working Definition

In 2006, the Fresh Expressions Team drafted a provisional definition:

A fresh expression is a form of church for our changing culture, established primarily for the benefit of people who are not yet members of any church.

It will come into being through principles of listening, service, incarnational mission and making disciples.

It will have the potential to become a mature expression of church shaped by the gospel and the enduring marks of the church and for its cultural context.[9]

> In the established church in Germany, we call these experiments "projects" rather than churches. *Markus Weimer*

"Fresh expression" is always an abbreviation of "fresh expression of church." It always involves the development of a new congregation or the transitioning of an existing piece of work into a congregation. This is usually a new congregation of an existing local church, but it could also be a church plant. We do not apply the term to projects whose long-term aim is to transfer people to an existing congregation. Fresh expressions begin as fledgling churches, with the potential to become mature, but they are church. When they become mature

7. From *Common Worship: Services and Prayers for the Church of England* (London: Church House Publishing, 2000), xi.

8. *Mission-Shaped Church*, xi.

9. http://www.freshexpressions.org.uk/about/introduction.

they will not be like the church which planted them, because they are designed for a specific cultural context which was not being reached by the planting church.

Recently we have developed a complementary definition, using four theological terms. Fresh expressions are:

- missional—serving people outside church;
- contextual—listening to people and entering their culture;
- formational—making discipleship a priority;
- ecclesial—forming church.

Changing Culture

The context for this initiative is provided by the substantial cultural change undergone by Western societies, where postmodernity interfaces with post-Christendom. The culture of the West has grown further and further apart from the culture of the church. The most obvious evidence of this in England is in church attendance. Thirty-four percent of adults have never had any significant contact with any church of any denomination. Another 31 percent used to be involved, often as children, but are involved no longer. Seven percent belong to other world faiths. To two-thirds of British adults the church is an alien world. Were those under sixteen to be included this proportion would increase substantially. What we face is the need to reevangelize our nation.

Revitalized traditional ministry, while essential, is not enough. An Australian archbishop said to me, "More of the same means less of the same." Decline is not halted. In *Mission-Shaped Church* we wrote:

> The Anglican pattern of ministry, built around parish and neighborhood, can lead to a way of thinking that assumes that all people, whether attending or not attending, are basically "our people." All people are God's people, but it is an illusion to assume that somehow the population of England is simply waiting for the right invitation before they will come back and join us. The social and mission reality is that the majority of English society is not "our people," they haven't been in living memory, nor do they want to be. The reality is that for

> [The *Mission-Shaped Church* report] recognizes that Britain is now a post-Christian society that has bypassed the influence of the institutional church in redefining its core identity. Changing social mores reflect the progressive influence of secularization, pluralism, and relativism. The parochial system is crumbling, due to shrinking local pools of support, and its approach has become too static for a mobile and fragmented society. It therefore needs to be complemented by more innovative and experimental forms of Christian community.
>
> Eddie Gibbs (CM, 67)

most people across England the Church, as it is, is peripheral, obscure, confusing or irrelevant. . . . The task is to become church for them, among them and with them, and under the Spirit of God to lead them to become church in their own culture. The gap is as wide as any that is experienced by a cross-cultural missionary. It will require a reworking of language and approach, and it is here that both church planting and fresh expressions of church offer real possibilities.[10]

Discernment in Context

The move from a "they come to us" approach to mission to "we go to them" cannot be achieved by taking church as we know it and putting it somewhere else. Nor will it be adequate to clone something that works somewhere else. There are no packaged answers for the reevangelization of former Christendom nations. The key to planting a fresh expression is discernment in context. Two phrases have emerged to summarize our most important emphases: "Seeing what God is doing and joining in" and "Dying to live."[11] The first is based on the assumption that the Holy Spirit is the lead missionary and is at work ahead of us, when we "go to" a new group or context. The second is based on the assumption that cross-cultural missionaries do not impose their cultural preferences upon those they are trying to reach. Rather they cooperate with the Holy Spirit to create authentic church "for them," if necessary at the expense of the missionaries' comfort and preferences. We believe that this emphasis on "dying to live," drawn from John 12:24–26, is a distinctive contribution to church planting practice and theory. Otherwise planting is really cloning.

> The disappointing results of denominational church planting efforts in the preceding fifteen years have made it clear that church planting must not be construed as church cloning.
>
> Eddie Gibbs (CM, 67)

We are aware that this sort of cross-cultural planting cannot be reduced to a formula with one stage neatly following another. However, for beginners, we recommend the following sequence. First, *listen* to God, the local church, and the community; it is not just a starting point, but the ongoing foundation for all that develops. Second, *serve* by being the good news before sharing the good news; this provides the points of contact. Third, *build community* and create relationships; rather than ministering to disconnected individuals, build up relationships, because doing so is vital if the fresh expression is to be a community rather than a weekly event. Fourth, *make disciples* over the long term. Fifth, *create worship* which takes proper note both of the gospel and

10. *Mission-Shaped Church*, 39–41.
11. Ibid., 30.

its traditions *and* the specific people and context for whom it is intended. A frequent mistake is to start with an act of worship before relationships have been formed that would guide the design of that act of worship. This is an incarnational approach, not an attractional one. The sixth and final step is to *do it all again.*

The listening process—to God, the local church, and the community—is not just a starting point, but the ongoing foundation for all that develops. Serving—being good news before sharing good news—provides the points of contact. The essence of church is community. Building community and mutual relationships, rather than just ministering to unconnected individuals, is vital if the fresh expression is to be a community rather than a weekly event. From the beginning, the call is to long-term discipleship. A public gathering for worship can then be shaped which takes proper note both of the gospel and its traditions *and* the specific people and context for whom it is intended.

Is This "Emerging Church" without the Angst?

One of the most difficult questions I am asked is, "Is this part of the emerging church movement?" The answer has an element of both no and yes. On the one hand, no, because this is an initiative and a movement from within the Church of England, seeking to reconnect with a changed and changing culture. It is more about proclaiming afresh a gospel in which we have confidence than questioning our theological inheritance. The truths of Scripture and the creeds are precisely what our culture needs. On the other hand, yes, fresh expressions is part of the emerging church movement because it is impossible, in a networked world, to explore questions about the relationship between gospel, church, and culture without finding yourself part of an important global conversation, which is very varied and of uneven quality.

> **Many church authorities ignore the fact that the creeds have been developed in a time of vital church planting.** *Markus Weimer*

In *Mission-Shaped Church* we acknowledged the term "emerging church"[12] because it had been used in earlier helpful documents on contemporary mission, but we deliberately avoided using it, preferring to develop our own language. We wished to avoid an (often acrimonious) debate that operated primarily in the evangelical constituency. Our colleagues in the Church of Scotland have retained the emerging church vocabulary, but make this important distinction:

12. Ibid., 33ff.

Two distinct dynamics that can lend a very different character to Christian communities run through the emerging church conversation. Some people are particularly concerned for *mission* and they value the conversation, because it has helped them to think about how to reform the church in ways that will increase their capacity to see churches grow as they reach out to others in a post-Christendom society.

Other groups have found in the emerging conversation resources to enable them to reinvent church when they were on the verge of leaving. For them the key concern has been with *authenticity*, with creating a space in which they could express their spirituality honestly and practice their faith with integrity.[13]

The latter is an honorable motive and activity, but it is the missional developments which concern the Fresh Expressions Initiative. Fresh expressions of church come under the missional category. They express a confidence in the historic gospel, but also a need to reengage with much of the population by planting contextually appropriate churches and congregations.

What Shapes the Ecclesiology?

The effect of the cultural transitions of postmodernity and post-Christendom has been to raise questions about what is essential to church in every generation, and what is not. The Lausanne consultation "Contextualization Revisited" recognized that "There are many who still fuse the meaning and forms of the Gospel"[14]—meaning that the specific cultural forms, which the gospel and the church take in a particular era, can be wrongly identified with the gospel itself. Rather, "A faithful Church is continually shaped by its inner dynamic: the flow of Apostolic Tradition, with Scripture as its norm. The Church is, however, also shaped by the kind of world in which it finds itself. This must mean a constant receiving of the Gospel into our particular context."[15]

A theological conviction underlying our understanding of fresh expressions of church is that the fundamental form of church is a community of disciples around and on the move with Jesus. The Church of Scotland report "Church without Walls" understood church as "People with Jesus at the centre, traveling wherever Jesus takes us." In his forward to *Mission-Shaped Church*, Archbishop Rowan Williams states, "If 'church' is what happens when

13. "Report of the General Assembly of the Church of Scotland," 2009, 3.1/6.
14. *Mission-Shaped Church*, 91.
15. Ibid., quoting Michael Nazir-Ali, "Future Shapes of the Church," House of Bishops paper, 2001.

people encounter the Risen Jesus and commit themselves to sustaining and deepening that encounter in their encounter with each other, there is plenty of theological room for diversity of rhythm and style, so long as we have ways of identifying the same living Christ at the heart of every expression of Christian life in common."[16] For the archbishop, "church" is an event around the risen Jesus before it is an institution or anything else.

The further theological foundations upon which we then build are:

- That mission is *missio Dei*, the mission of God, that it is the Triune God's activity before it is an activity of the church, and that the church is both the fruit and the instrument of the divine mission, in which we participate in Christ. As a consequence mission is of the essence of the church, rather than an activity of some Christians. Mission becomes "seeing what God is doing and joining in."

- That the practice of mission is to be incarnational. We have been greatly helped by Roman Catholic, post–Vatican II missiology with its emphasis on "inculturation" based on the analogy with the incarnation. An incarnational approach takes seriously the way of the cross as the model of an incarnate life. It does not just emphasize that Christ took human form within a particular culture. The historic incarnation was a once-for-all divine act, but it then becomes the model for discipleship and cross-cultural mission. Christology shapes missiology which then shapes ecclesiology.

- That mission is pneumatological. Not only does the Spirit empower and direct the church's mission, but the Spirit brings the anticipation of the future into the present. The Spirit enables the church to live as an anticipation of God's future in the present day, and within each culture. The presence of the Spirit is the guarantee that a local church can develop missional imagination for its context.

The term "expressions of church" aims to hold together two truths: that Christ is fully present in each community of his people, and yet each community is incomplete without the others. "Only in Christ does completeness, fullness, dwell. None of us can reach Christ's completeness on our own. We need each other's vision to correct, enlarge and focus our own; only together are we complete in Christ."[17] Or, as the archbishop stated, "If Christ is the embodi-

---

16. *Mission-Shaped Church*, v.
17. Andrew Walls, *The Cross-Cultural Process in Christian History* (Edinburgh: T&T Clark, 2002), 79.

ment of God, and the Church is his body on earth, then no single expression of church can ever exhaust Christ."[18]

From Models to DNA

If fresh expressions of church should not be cloned, but require discernment and missional imagination in context, what characteristics ought they to have in common? If there can be great diversity, what provides the unity and coherence? We suggest that any missional congregation or community will be characterized by some specific values—a missional DNA.

In *Mission-Shaped Church*[19] we suggest that a missional church will be:

- focused on God the Holy Trinity
- incarnational
- transformational
- disciple making
- relational

We have learned that this whole DNA needs to be understood and intended from the beginning of the planting process. It is very difficult to bolt on key elements which have not been given due attention later in the process.

Discipleship

This is particularly important when it comes to disciple making. It is possible to make the environment and culture of a fresh expression so welcoming and comfortable that it gives no indication of the costliness of following Christ. We are still early on the learning

> To these five values, I would add two more: First, a missionary church is reproducible. By this I mean that new faith communities are produced, not simply carbon copies of the mother church. The genius of the early church arose from the fact that each faith community had within itself, in reliance on the equipping and guidance of the Holy Spirit, all the necessary resources to give birth to new faith communities. . . . The second value I would add is that a missionary church combines local engagement with global concerns and commitment. The Great Commission challenges every faith community to begin with its local context, and then to see beyond its immediate context to the peoples of the world, both near and far.
>
> Eddie Gibbs (CM, 66)

18. Rowan Williams, at a 2004 fresh expressions seminar question-and-answer session. This seminar led to the setting up of a fresh expressions team.

19. *Mission-Shaped Church*, 81ff.

curve when it comes to making Christian disciples in a culture that makes disciples for other values so effectively. Western consumer culture corrodes commitment, individualises, forms character, and counterfeits spirituality. It makes disciples better than most churches do!

It will be vital that fresh expressions of church develop patterns of community which major on the development of Christian character and which sustain public discipleship. The ultimate test of any church is what kind of disciples it makes!

Unity and Diversity

The mixed economy approach is an attempt to engage with the twin challenges of Christ's work of reconciliation. The purpose of Christ's life, death, and resurrection is the reconciliation of all things and all people to God.[20] The church is to demonstrate the reconciliation of those who are in Christ.[21] So we are presented with twin challenges: a church which has not reached the full breadth of its community, and the challenge of visible unity between all Christians in that community. The mixed economy attempts to address both the breadth of the mission field and the depth of Christian unity.

This work has only just begun. This is a young movement. It is not a quick fix to put right decades of increasing disconnection between church and culture. The challenge we face calls for long-term incarnational mission among the majority, the never churched.[22]

> It took several centuries to convert Britain to Christianity but it took only a few decades to get rid of it. The journey that the Church of England has started is adventurous and could serve as a model for the mainline churches in Western Europe. *Markus Weimer*

20. Eph. 1:10.
21. Eph. 2:15–16.
22. The work being done in the UK now is built on the foundation of the work of previous pioneers and teachers. It is a particular privilege to dedicate this chapter to Eddie Gibbs. Eddie's work as a trainer for the Bible Society in England was part of that foundation. His teaching and writing have continued to be a most special encouragement. In particular I want to honour his continual capacity to read the changing Western context and to identify the things that God is doing, particularly through young leaders. Thanks be to God.

28

On the Move

Toward Fresh Expressions of Church in Germany

Markus Weimer

Church is uniquely community-shaped; it is Spirit community, love community.[1]

The church is the church only when it exists for others.[2]

Tradition

The Evangelical Church in Germany (Evangelische Kirche in Deutschland, EKD) is an established church, rich in tradition and parochially organized. It is currently facing substantial challenges. If current trends continue, by 2030 membership will shrink from 26 million now to 17.6 million,[3] annual income

*This article—including all quotes—was translated into English by my friend Christoph Lindner (Gerrards Cross, UK). He is currently training for ordained pioneer ministry in the Church of England. I am very grateful to him for this accurate translation.

1. D. Bonhoeffer, *Sanctorum Communio. Eine dogmatische Untersuchung zur Soziologie der Kirche*, DBW 1 (Munich: Kaiser, 1986), 185.

2. D. Bonhoeffer, *Widerstand und Ergebung: Briefe und Aufzeichnungen aus der Haft*, ed. C. Von Gremmels (Gütersloh: Kaiser, 1998), 560. This quote is from the draft of a publication that Bonhoeffer was planning during his time in prison.

3. Kirchenamt der Evangelischen Kirche in Deutschland, ed., *Kirche der Freiheit: Perspektiven für die Evangelische Kirche im 21. Jahrhundert* (Hannover: Kirchenamt der EKD, 2006), 22.

from church taxes will be halved from 4 billion euros now to 2 billion,[4] and the number of ordained ministers will decrease from 20,400 now to 13,000.[5] This is the alarming forecast of the reform publication *Kirche der Freiheit* (Church of Freedom), which was published July 6, 2006. In December 2004 a "perspective committee" had already been given the task of developing action strategies until 2030. The committee clearly understood the necessity of change and was exploring innovative ways of securing the future of the EKD.

In 2007 the Evangelical Church entered a decade of reform, which will end with the anniversary of the Reformation in 2017. Retired Bishop Wolfgang Huber already expressed the task ahead at the end of the 1990s:

> The key question in our current crisis is how the church—as an "old institution"—will answer the questions of people today, how she will become a place where people of all generations find firm orientation in their search for meaning, how her message of faith will reach people through her practical actions and her contributions to formation and learning in society.[6]

In all this we should not forget that all our attempts at reform must never aim merely at the survival of an institution. A self-contained and self-sufficient church would be a contradiction in terms. How can the gospel of Jesus Christ be proclaimed in a way that is relevant to our culture and society, within the context of a rapidly changing and fragmenting postmodern society? Which steps are unavoidable, which strategies helpful, which networks necessary, to move forward with courage?

> This is the probing question for the Scandinavian church as well. Although not a sign of a trend change, the central role the church of Norway had in serving the people after the terror attacks of summer 2011 was a temporary glimpse of what this could look like. It shows that there is still potential for the church to be relevant on a societal level. *Ruth Skree*

Moving from Anxiety to Courage

The German church must change its perspective to enable us to leave behind our fear of change. The 2004 "perspective committee" of ten people was given the task to write a courageous discussion paper, a "conceptual long jump,"[7]

---

4. Ibid.
5. Ibid., 24ff.
6. W. Huber, *Kirche in der Zeitenwende. Gesellschaftlicher Wandel und Erneuerung der Kirche* (Gütersloh: Verl. Bertelsmann-Stiftung, 1999), 234.
7. T. Begrich and T. Gundlach, "Reaktionen und Stellungnahmen zum Impulspapier des Rates der Evangelischen Kirche in Deutschland" (Hannover 2006), 1.

which was deliberately not bound to existing structures. Hence the paper demands "a mentality change in the Protestant churches. Moaning and groaning will not shape the future. Rather, we need confidence and hope, courage and trust as key sources of strength for our journey."[8]

We are easily worried, though, that change might not be achievable. This was no different in Reformation times and can be retraced in the robust words of the reformer from Wittenberg to his comrade-in-arms Philipp Melanchthon. In a letter from June 27, 1530, Martin Luther wrote:

> I heartily hate your miserable worries, which—as you tell me—devour you. It is not owed to our great cause that they rule in your heart, but to our great lack of faith. . . . Why do you torture yourself without ceasing? . . . I truly pray with diligence for you and it pains me that you—an incorrigible worry leech—make my prayers futile. At least as far as our cause is concerned, I am not worried, but rather of better cheer than I was expecting to be. Whether this is due to my foolishness or to the Spirit is Christ's concern.[9]

Great fear of failure seems to be a "German phenomenon." We lack a culture that is "failure friendly," that is grounded in God's promises. The church in particular often lacks the courage to choose a new path, especially if that path is still shrouded in darkness. "It is obvious that we need many mistakes and attempts to find a truly visionary path."[10] We therefore need a spiritual change of mentality that allows the Lord of the church to show her a new direction. "We would do well to let our thinking about the future be guided by what we hope. Because hope belongs to faith as love does."[11]

> This applies to planting a new church in Denmark as well. Allowing ourselves to be an "experiment" (yet, accountable for those participating) was liberating. *Andreas Østerlund Nielsen*

Moving from Structural Hierarchy to Relational Interaction

Relationships between the church authorities and local churches in Germany are often marked by critical distance. Within the context of our established church we need to develop a new quality of relationships between overall

8. *Kirche der Freiheit*, 12.
9. WA Br. 5, 399ff., in *D. Martin Luthers Werke. Kritische Gesamtausgabe. Briefwechsel*, Bd. 1–15 (Weimar, 1930–78).
10. C. Hennecke, *Glänzende Aussichten: Wie Kirche über sich hinauswächst* (Münster: Aschendorff, 2010), 19.
11. W. Huber, "Evangelisch im 21. Jahrhundert," in Kirchenamt der Evangelischen Kirche in Deutschland, ed., *Zukunftskongress der Evangelischen Kirche in Deutschland*. Lutherstadt Wittenberg 25.-27. (January 2007), 29.

church leadership and the local church. In some cases, a certain ignorance will have to be overcome. Repeatedly, local parishes express the view that the church leadership is too far removed from the local realities; hence they feel justified in ignoring the church "hierarchy" in their own decision making. Retired bishop John Finney summarizes the issue with simplicity and humor: "Be nice to your bishops and archdeacons. Theirs is a lonely job and they need our prayer and praise. . . . I do not imply that you should flatter superiors, but relate to them as fellow-humans."[12]

Church authorities mistrust local churches by questioning their leadership competencies. This hardening on both sides is a key obstacle to transformation within the established church. These urgent changes can grow only in the soil of mutual trust and service (Mark 10:45). Only relational interaction will lay the foundations for lasting change. Bishop Stephen Cottrell (UK) describes two tasks of church leadership.[13] First, leadership needs to be permission giving and reflective, so that fresh expressions of church can grow. Second, "We need to foster a new type of church where innovators and pathfinders, who venture into new territory, are met with sympathy and encouragement, rather than distrust and resistance."

Church authorities must recognize the needs of local parishes, reflect on those, and engage in open, enabling conversation with initiators. "Church grows wherever these spontaneous new developments are received and given space."[14] The Archbishop of Canterbury, Rowan Williams, led the way in the Anglican Church in this respect: "It seems clear that a culture of permission-giving is Archbishop Rowan's intention."[15] This approach establishes an authority that is respected in local churches. Too many rules and a lack of trust prevent organic growth.

We need people at a grassroots level who rid themselves of a spirit of isolated local leadership,[16] and who include the church authorities from early on in their thinking and planning. There is no renewal of vision without a renewal of community. To achieve this, leaders who possess different convictions,

12. J. Finney, "Mission shaped ecclesiology—Impulse für eine 'Mission in der Region,'" in Kirchenamt der Evangelischen Kirche in Deutschland, ed., epd-Dokumentation 41/2010, mehr-wert: Mission in der Region. Dokumentation der Tagung zum Start des EKD-Zentrums "Mission in der Region" (Kloster Volkenroda, 8.–9. Juni 2010), 10.

13. Stephen Cottrell, interview with Markus Weimer, Reading, UK, September 2009.

14. Hennecke, *Glänzende Aussichten*, 16.

15. P. Bayes, *Mission-Shaped Church: Building Missionary Values*, Grove Evangelism Series 67 (Cambridge: Grove, 2004), 10.

16. See T. Latzel, Mission in der Region—ein weites Feld öffnet sich, in Kirchenamt der Evangelischen Kirche in Deutschland, ed., epd-Dokumentation 41/2010, mehr-wert: Mission in der Region. Dokumentation der Tagung zum Start des EKD-Zentrums "Mission in der Region" (Kloster Volkenroda, 8.–9. Juni 2010), 7.

competencies, and theological perspectives need to treat one another with respect. A lasting process of transformation and, flowing from it, the growth of fresh expressions of church will succeed only when the ugly trench between local churches and the regional or national leadership is bridged constructively, when both sides renew their attempts at listening to one another.

> Who is the church? Established, democratically organized, national churches tend to eliminate the congregation as ecclesial subject. *Andreas Østerlund Nielsen*

> Yes, but within the inherited church you cannot skip the reality of traditional structures and settings. These structures can be very helpful for the local congregation. *Markus Weimer*

Moving from Parochial Focus to Mixed Economy

Any process of transformation in the established church structure in Germany must address the parish system. "Since the days of Charlemagne our church structure has had a particular pattern. My place of residence determines my church membership. My church has a building and offers the services of an ordained minister. This is where I go to church, where I am baptized, confirmed, married and buried. . . . We call this principle parochial church."[17]

This area requires yet another courageous transformation. "We are not questioning the parish system per se. It would be foolish to demand that. What we do need is the courage to welcome a diversity of structures; we need to respond to the changing circumstances and develop creative new answers."[18] This simple insight may sound like common sense, yet it is highly contentious among traditionalist church members[19] who suspect a veiled attack on the unity of the church. The resistance is often expressed as a morphological fundamentalism[20] that denies any innovation the right to exist.

The Church of England with its similar structures and its successful process of reform (mission-shaped church) can be a helpful partner in dialogue here. This is how Rowan Williams describes the new path: "We used to, in Wales,

17. M. Herbst, *Wachsende Kirche: Wie Gemeinde den Weg zu postmodernen Menschen finden kann* (Gießen: Brunnen, 2008), 33ff.

18. M. Herbst, ed., *Mission bringt Gemeinde in Form: Gemeindepflanzungen und neue Ausdrucksformen gemeindlichen Lebens in einem sich wandelnden Kontext* (Neukirchen-Vluyn: Aussaat, 2008), 20.

19. On different milieus in Germany, see the highly recommended study of the Heidelberg institute Sinus Sociovision, ed., *Milieuhandbuch: Religiöse und kirchliche Orientierungen* (Heidelberg, 2005). A new edition including the "new milieus" is planned.

20. See Hans Schmidt, "Morphologischer Fundamentalismus," in *Mission als Strukturprinzip: Ein Arbeitsbuch zur Frage missionarischer Gemeinden*, ed. Hans Jochen Margull (Genf: Oekumenischer Rat der Kirchen, 1965), 127–30.

talk about the 'mixed economy' church—that is, one which is learning how to cope with diverse forms and rhythms of worshipping life."[21] We urgently need to complement the parish system[22] with fresh expressions of church that attempt "to reach into the manifold postmodern ways of life through diverse expressions of Christian life."[23] "The mixed economy seeks to give expression to this. It wants to avoid the hurt that would be caused by many in established churches if fresh expressions disowned their heritage, and the pain that many pioneers of fresh expressions would feel if existing denominations and traditions said there was no room for them."[24]

> It is noteworthy that a parochial church is defined by its obligation to its geographical context and thus, in principle, missional by definition. *Andreas Østerlund Nielsen*

Moving from Uniformity to Creativity

The established church in a highly diversified society cannot rely on uniform structures that reach only a subset of existing social environments (milieus). We can learn much from church history: Beginning in 1520, German church reformers attempted to complement the Latin Mass with a German form of Mass. They wanted to give people the opportunity to participate more directly in the service. A few years later Luther wrote a new liturgy, which was introduced by a visionary preface detailing his understanding of religious services. Luther noticed that people were "pressing for a German mass and liturgy."[25] The German order of service has a missionary function for Luther. With creativity and sensitivity toward the target milieu, he does not direct his reform attempts primarily at the highly cultured and educated social class, but opens the church up to people from other milieus. "For their sake we must read, sing, preach, write prose and poetry; and if it were helpful and necessary I would ring all the bells and play all the organ pipes and let everything ring that has the faculty to ring."[26]

21. R. Williams, "Presidential Address to the General Synod," July 2003, quoted in Bayes, *Mission-Shaped Church*, 10.

22. Cf. also the approach of Uta Pohl-Patalong, *Von der Ortskirche zu kirchlichen Orten: ein Zukunftsmodell* (Göttingen: Vandenhoeck & Ruprecht, 2006).

23. H. Hempelmann, *Nach der Zeit des Christentums: Warum Kirche von der Postmoderne profitieren kann und warum Konkurrenz das Geschäft belebt* (Gießen: Brunnen, 2009), 170.

24. M. Moynagh, "Do We Need a Mixed Economy?," in *Evaluating Fresh Expressions: Explorations in Emerging Church: Responses to the Changing Face of Ecclesiology in the Church of England*, ed. L. Nelstrop and M. Percy (Norwich, UK: Canterbury Press, 2008), 180.

25. M. Luther, Vorrede zu: Deutsche Messe und Ordnung Gottesdiensts (1526), in *Martin Luther. Ausgewählte Schriften*, band 5, *Martin Luther: Kirche, Gottesdienst, Schule*, ed. K. Bornkamm and G. Ebeling (Frankfurt/Leipzig: Insel, 1995), 74.

26. Ibid., 75ff.

> This is a rich legacy to draw from in the search for fresh expressions. It echoes the dream of Mary in the Magnificat, a liturgy attentive to the poor and ordinary. *Steve Taylor*

> The task becomes one of discerning what people are pressing for today, especially those people who have been beyond our vision. Dag Stang suggests that this was impossible for him while working in the Christian enclave; only by working in the marketplace was he able to hear what people were pressing for. *Ruth Skree*

This goal cannot be achieved through a palette of uniform attractional offers. It needs churches who find creative ways of living missionally; who will go where the people are and immerse themselves in their world (1 Cor. 9:22). "We need ministries that transcend milieus, that seek to reach people who have so far not been the focus of our mission goals at all, or only to a lesser degree."[27]

Moving from Maintenance to Mission

Our goal cannot be to save a particular church structure, institution, or liturgical tradition. In a postmodern age church is either mission-shaped or it will not be at all. "It's not the church of God that has a mission, but the God of mission who has a church."[28] At the EKD synod in 1999 Eberhard Jüngel already challenged the church in this way: "If church had a heart, a heart that is still beating, then evangelism and mission would determine the heartbeat of the church to a large degree. And deficits in the church's missionary activity, deficiencies in its *euaggelisasthai* [*preaching the gospel*] would immediately lead to serious cardiac arrhythmia."[29]

> Fresh Expressions recognizes that a changing social context, resulting in the increased marginalization of the church, has necessitated alternative forms of church. These will be distinct from the parochial model that has prevailed throughout England and in most of Europe.
>
> Eddie Gibbs (CM, 67)

If the church of God incarnate has a healthy heart, then it moves toward people; it is mobile and flexible and it does not stubbornly insist on familiar places and traditions. It will be permeated in all its ministries by the *missio Dei* (Matt. 28:16–20).

27. Hempelmann, *Nach der Zeit des Christentums*, 135.

28. T. Dearborn, *Beyond Duty: A Passion for Christ, a Heart for Mission* (Monrovia, CA: MARC, 1998).

29. E. Jüngel, "Mission und Evangelisation," Vortrag auf der Tagung der 9. Synode der EKD vom 7–12. November 1999, in Leipzig, http://www.ekd.de/print.php?file=/synode99/referate _juengel.html (accessed January 13, 2011).

Wolfgang Huber, the former chairman of the Council of the Protestant Church in Germany (EKD), puts it like this: "At the same time mission does not indoctrinate or overwhelm; it is wholly different and seeks an honest and fair dialogue about convictions and values, life philosophies and ethical stances. In this sense mission is an expression of the life and being of the church, who 'desires everyone to be saved and to come to the knowledge of the truth' [1 Tim. 2:4 NRSV]."[30]

Mission in this sense is understood as integrated mission, a dovetailing of proclamation and practical application, and as participation in God's life of love. In his presidential address to the General Synod in 2003, R. Williams said:

> Mission, it's been said, is finding out what God is doing and joining in. And at present there is actually an extraordinary amount going on in terms of creation of new styles of church life. We can call it church planting, "new ways of being church" or various other things; but the point is that more and more patterns of worship and shared life are appearing on the edge of our mainstream life that cry out for our support, understanding and nurture if they are not to get isolated and unaccountable. . . . All of these are church in the sense that they are what happens when the invitation of Jesus is received and people recognize it in each other. Can we live with this and make it work?[31]

> It is a challenge, for "fresh" entrepreneurs especially, to be patient enough to find out what God is doing before the creative process begins. *Andreas Østerlund Nielsen*

Models of Hope: Practical Insights

A look at the situation in England shows a variety of fresh expressions of church within and side-by-side with the parish system of the Church of England. In the established Protestant churches in Germany this development is still in its infancy. However, there have been a number of pioneering and courageous initiatives. In recent years, C. Hennecke writes, "experiments have been started in various places. They represent the exciting attempt of a process of inculturation."[32] It remains a core responsibility of the church to explain how her mission is shaped in the present and how she can engage in a practice of conspiracy and cooperation with the Spirit of God.

> The UK "fresh expressions of church" initiative has inspired several initiatives in Denmark, and it is being considered by several bishops of the national Lutheran Church. *Andreas Østerlund Nielsen*

---

30. Preface by Wolfgang Huber in Herbst, *Mission bringt Gemeinde in Form*, 9.
31. Williams, "Presidential Address," 9.
32. Hennecke, *Glänzende Aussichten*, 19.

Rudolf Bohren has described this intertwining of sovereign, divine action and the human exercise of Spirit-given charismata as theonomous reciprocity.[33] "When we speak of 'theonomous reciprocity' we mean a God-given interchange, a mutuality, an exchange, a partnership, which would be simply unthinkable in Christology."[34] In what follows, three very different initiatives are presented; all of them are helping to foster fresh expressions of church in our established church.

Practices

Worship and Formation in Fresh Expressions

In 2000, a small youth group of the Stiftsgemeinde Church in Stuttgart[35] started an alternative service (Jesustreff, "Jesus meeting") for young adults. No one would have foreseen that it would create such a gravitational pull that this service now attracts 400 young people and is led by a team of 150 volunteers.[36] Young adults began to use their talents and gifts to create a service that would connect with their peers. They experimented with the available resources. The evening service was first based in the church hall and characterized by modern worship music, relevant preaching, and engaging times of prayer. The joint postservice suppers helped newcomers to quickly become a part of the church.

In 2003, a new venue in St. Martin's Church (northern Stuttgart) was provided for the "youth church" project under the aegis of the Protestant Church in Württemberg. Many Jesustreff members struggled

> Fresh expressions are not simply shop windows or halfway houses, designed to provide an introductory experience of church for those alienated from traditional church life. They are not created with the intention of establishing temporary faith communities that will transfer later to the real thing. To the contrary, they are themselves authentic expressions of church that are indigenous to their cultural contexts, the contexts in which they exercise a missional calling. This entails a discerning cultural appreciation, as well as a willingness to submit to the critique of the gospel, both with a view to community transformation.
>
> Eddie Gibbs (CM, 68)

---

33. See R. Bohren, *Predigtlehre* (Munich: Kaiser, 1971), 76.

34. Christology is here understood in the narrower sense of soteriology: Christ's saving work, to which we can add nothing. M. Herbst, "Kirche wie eine Behörde verwalten oder wie ein Unternehmen führen? Zur Theologie des Spirituellen Gemeindemanagements," in *Spirituelles Gemeindemanagement: Chancen–Strategien—Beispiele*, ed. H.-J. Abromeit (Göttingen: Vandenhoeck & Ruprecht, 2001), 94.

35. See K. Büchle, R. Krebs, M. Nagel, eds., *Junge Gemeinden. Experiment oder Zukunftsmodell? Einsichten—Ansichten—Aussichten* (Stuttgart, 2009), 28–36.

36. In the German context these are very well-attended services.

with the change, as they had just gotten used to the familiar surroundings. However, in spite of initial resistance, this move into a larger venue proved to be important and helpful as the young church accelerated its growth. New bands emerged that created their own praise-and-worship culture. This resulted in a "song of the month" and a number of songwriting workshops.

Joint suppers were a core feature of Jesustreff. A new kitchen was specially designed to make sure that visitors could be catered for by volunteer teams. At present, young people between the ages of sixteen and thirty-five attend the services of Jesustreff on a Sunday evening. Members come from a variety of backgrounds; they find a space where they can explore and exercise their gifts. The church also developed a social ministry with the motto "blessing the city."

Since 2000, Jesustreff has moved on from its roots as a youth group; in its conception it is now a "young church," even if some aspects of church governance need to be clarified. Occasional offices such as baptisms and Holy Communion cannot be led by the local church team yet. They are in dialogue with church authorities to find a mode of existing as a fresh expression in a parochially structured church. "A focus on target groups, a diversification of ministries, an engagement with people's way of life and an open ear for them—all these developments should not be taboo topics as long as the message of the Bible is kept in view."[37]

> The relation between new forms of attractive, creative-event services and discipling community seems to be a general tension in the idea of fresh expressions inside established churches. *Andreas Østerlund Nielsen*

Mission in Fresh Expressions

In 2009 a group of Christians from ELIA Church[38] in Erlangen[39] decided to work toward the alleviation of poverty and more social justice in their region and the world. This idea for a new expression of faith was born during a course on poverty and justice run by the Micah initiative.[40] Fairlangen sensitized people from Erlangen and the region to issues of worldwide poverty; at the same time they encouraged them to become involved in creation care.

37. Büchle, Krebs, and Nagel, eds., *Junge Gemeinden*, 31.
38. ELIA Church is a young, independent local church in the Lutheran Church in Bavaria. More information is available at http://www.elia-erlangen.de (accessed January 18, 2011).
39. Fairlangen is a pun on the town of Erlangen, where the initiative is located, and the German word Verlangen (desire, longing). See http://www.fairlangen.org (accessed January 4, 2011).
40. See http://www.micha-initiative.de (accessed January 18, 2011). For more information about the international initiative, see http://www.micahchallenge.org (accessed January 18, 2011) and http://www.micahnetwork.org (accessed January 18, 2011).

The goal of an "integrated approach to mission" is described in practical ways. Fairlangen has three basic aims:[41]

1. To work toward more social justice in the world, especially for disadvantaged people in poor countries (but also in Germany).
2. To develop a more sustainable relationship with our environment.
3. To encourage everyone in the region to join in. Practical suggestions are provided for the development of a more sustainable and "fairer" lifestyle.

The initiative Fairlangen began as a local church ministry and now affects the lives of people in Erlangen, thus transforming the cultural context.[42] The group's website helps people to reflect on personal habits and challenges them to live an alternative lifestyle: How do I treat our natural resources? Where can I buy fair trade products? How can I lead a mobile lifestyle and yet reduce my carbon footprint significantly? Where in our town can I get involved?

This initiative operates on the backdrop of the Christian conviction that those to whom much is given must care about the poor (Matt. 25:35–40). The central theme from Micah 6:8 is a motivation for the local church to get involved in issues of poverty in their environment. Justice is the "protection or restoration of balanced, harmoniously ordered, life-affirming conditions: in human relations as well as in our relationship with God."[43] This approach encourages expressions of church that meet people where they are: "If the Church can focus on bearing witness to the kingdom of God in its own life and community, if it can discover and embody that kind of culture, the kind of culture that produces people of virtue, then it might, as a byproduct, make quite a difference to the cultures and societies in which it is placed."[44]

Leadership in Fresh Expressions

About fifteen people witnessed the start of the ChurchConvention[45] network in 2006. They all shared a passionate hope for the future of their church. With

41. See http://www.fairlangen.org/informieren/wer-sind-wir (accessed January 2, 2011).

42. See G. Tomlin, "Can We Develop Churches That Can Transform the Culture?," in *Mission-Shaped Questions: Defining Issues for Today's Church*, ed. S. Croft (London: Church House, 2008), 66–77.

43. D. Hufeisen, "Wer wir sind?," http://www.fairlangen.org/ueber-uns/biblisches-sicht (accessed January 2, 2011).

44. Tomlin, "Can We Develop Churches," 72.

45. See http://www.churchconvention.de (accessed January 18, 2011). The description of the network is here focused on development of competence in leadership.

the means available to them they wanted to be active in the transformation process toward a "mission-shaped church": a church that learns what it means to be a sent people (*missio*) in a postmodern context, to be sensitive to their milieus and relevant to society.

ChurchConvention sees itself as a professional support network for students of theology, curates in training, and ordained ministers within the EKD who want to be servant leaders in their sphere of influence and activity. Currently the network is composed of about a hundred people in Germany. They are guided by a vision that was jointly developed in 2007–2008:[46]

1. Connected in friendship ("Verbunden in Freundschaft")
2. Spiritually on the move ("Geistlich im Aufbruch"—working and praying for spiritual renewal)
3. Passionately involved in life ("Leidenschaftlich im Leben")

The network operates nationwide and has established three regional groups so far (Baden, Württemberg, and Hannover). The smallest and most important units are "couchconventions": members meet in their local context, support one another spiritually and practically, and develop visions for their region. The national and regional leadership invest in the leadership development of their members. A mentoring system has been developed to help them discover and employ their gifts and talents. The members of ChurchConvention regard themselves as "loyal radicals": they work with passion in their church as it is now, and at the same time they express and live out their vision of the future of the church.

> Networks of accountability and mentoring like ChurchConvention are paramount in areas where church planting is still rare and poorly supported by existing church structures. Bykirken could not have existed without it. *Andreas Østerlund Nielsen*

ChurchConvention offers a context for innovators in which their visionary thoughts are heard, debated, and developed. This happens not in opposition to existing church structures, but is designed to complement and enrich the parish system with fresh expressions of church in the spirit of a "mixed economy." Inspired by the "guidelines on ordained pioneer ministry" within the Church of England, ChurchConvention also explores how to prepare people to go beyond the existing church structures with the specific intention of planting a new church community. Regional leaders seek close contact

46. For a comprehensive vision document, see http://www.churchconvention.de/files/leitbild .pdf (accessed January 18, 2011).

with church authorities, invite them to their meetings, and aim to contribute constructively to current church developments. This process will receive a boost from a major conference "Gemeinde 2.0—Frische Formen für die Kirche von heute"[47] (Church 2.0—Fresh Forms for Today's Church), which is designed around crucial contributions from the Church of England. It aims to create an ecumenical community of learners, helping members to shape the necessary process of transformation in a reflected way. "We must use the open 'window of opportunity.'" Today we can still draw on resources (both people and finance) that will most certainly diminish in the future. Now is the chance to grasp the existing opportunities and to invest in a sustainable future for the Protestant church.[48]

47. More information at http://www.gemeindezweinull.org (accessed January 18, 2011).

48. H.-H. Pompe, Mehr-wert: Wie es weitergehen kann . . . , in Kirchenamt der Evangelischen Kirche in Deutschland, ed.: epd-Dokumentation 41/2010, mehr-wert: Mission in der Region. Dokumentation der Tagung zum Start des EKD-Zentrums "Mission in der Region" (Kloster Volkenroda, 8.–9. Juni 2010), 39.

Conclusion

Ryan K. Bolger

How might the church not only survive but also thrive in the midst of environmental crises, hybrid cultures, pluralism, cultures of creativity and art, consumerism, and new spiritualities? How might the church situate its practices of worship, community formation, mission, and leadership within these cultures while challenging them at the same time? Throughout these twenty-eight chapters, I hope that we began to answer those questions. At the risk of simplifying a complex reality, I will narrate some of the patterns identified throughout the volume.

Getting Started

Those who start new communities often express frustration and dissatisfaction with Christian life as they previously knew it. They could not bring their friends to church. They were burned out. They needed some time to rethink everything they thought they knew about church. If these leaders did go to seminary, their theological training offered little help in the practical knowledge required to create and sustain a new movement. These pioneers gained skills in leadership through actually leading the new initiative, from planning to implementation.

It may be a solo leader who gets things started, but soon that leader is surrounded by a team. Some members are students, and some, married with children. Through brainstorming they imagine something they had never thought of before. These communities begin with immense creativity. They start off small; they are not usually a plant from another church. If they do get some support from a parent church, they are certainly not a clone. Church is an experiment.

Immersed in Local Cultures

These communities are deeply connected to the people in their context. The leaders have many conversations with the unchurched. They locate themselves in a space, within the culture, be it a café, a pub, a public building, or a home, but rarely in a church building. The community is made up of people with whom they interact every day as part of their network of relationships. The new community is simple in its structure.

Many of these Christians are deeply rooted in the local, walking where they can and buying local products when possible. They understand that all their actions, even purchases, impact the earth in one way or another. Living simply and in community helps preserve the earth's resources. Planting community gardens helps the earth and the neighborhood. They help the community take action on social justice issues that affect the entire community.

There is no evangelism in the formal sense; these Christians live by an alternative story and offer an explanation when asked. Those outside the church need to know that Christians love them, and that they are not trying to convert them. The church's mission is to connect to people's everyday lives. They are actively engaged in their neighborhoods, taking on the life of Jesus. They seek to live near one another, so people see one another in everyday life.

New communities create a space where faith is not required for inclusion in the community. They offer many on-ramps to people wherever they may be on the spiritual trek. Many need a place where they can question things. These communities do not make an effort to decide who is in the community and who is not.

In urban contexts, these new communities encounter a diversity of faiths in their midst. Their task, as they understand it, is to listen with openness and to welcome the other. They remain honest about their commitment to Christ while sincerely making room for those from other traditions. Instead of belonging before believing as the mode for Christian faith development, in a pluralistic culture it might become *believing (another faith) before belonging before believing in Christ.*

Churches in post-Christendom search for what God is doing in another culture and find ways to dwell there. They may find that those of another culture, because of migration, are living multiple lives, connected to two places, two homes, two ways of life. The task of the Christian may also be to dwell in these hybrid, in-between spaces. This represents a new way of doing mission in the West.

Church resources are offered to the surrounding community as well as to the church community. There is no distinction. Marriage classes are not just for church people; they are for everyone. Mercy and service are for everyone. This might mean helping someone who moved into an apartment, performing various acts of justice, or serving in mercy ministries. Hosted parties are for everyone. Spirituality discussions are popular for people both inside and outside the church, especially among the de-churched.

These Christians share their insider rituals with outsiders. These rituals are publicly performed and remixed with forms of popular culture. They might host a Bible study in a pub or sing in a bar, or they might create art for and with the larger community. When these churches create public art, they seek to shock and wake people up; they let the residents themselves do the interpreting. For some, it might awaken a passion for justice. The Stations of the Cross, done publicly at Easter, remain popular in many contexts. Often these events are provocative and done only once. They present dilemmas to people. Much of what post-Christendom churches do is in public space, dwelling with those outside, creating worship in the context.

Deep Formation

A new church often starts as a small group, possibly in a home. If the group grows, they may form a network of small groups, and perhaps, at that time, they may consider creating a monthly gathering. In some cases, much less likely, the church might start out as a monthly meeting that eventually adds small groups. The current pattern among new churches seems to be networked small groups that may or may not create a main gathering.

Small groups are sites of hospitality. They meet in homes weekly, usually around a meal. These groups discuss the Bible, pray, take Communion, and serve in mission together. Discipleship occurs around the table, sometimes over coffee or wine. Often there is no teacher, and discernment of Scripture is communal. It is an active learning environment. There might be singing, but frequently there is not.

For those who pursue a whole-life spirituality, new monasticism satisfies this quest. Formation intensifies in monastic settings, and small groups may choose to move in this direction. These groups create spiritual disciplines to cultivate virtues. They practice the daily office, and they develop their own rule of life as they create a corporate rhythm as a learning community. They participate in meditation and prayer. They stress the mystical journey and their connection to all of creation. They care for the poor and live a life of simplicity. They are led through communal discernment. These communities may focus on historic monasticism or more directly on the life of Jesus, and the patterns are similar: living by a rule generated by the community in conversation with the tradition begun by Jesus. The goal is nothing less than living as apprentices in the Way of Jesus, participating fully in the reign of God.

People want to take responsibility for their own lives in post-Christendom. Leaders are not responsible for the choices others make. Leaders are to offer guidance, but nothing more. They function as spiritual guides, they bring the church into the spiritual life, and they must be spiritual themselves. They must have the skills to help people experience and grow in Jesus. They are rabbinic-style leaders.

Leadership in new expressions of faith is flat and egalitarian. Everyone gets a voice and can lead. In a sense, the whole body leads. Small communities are a "bottom-up fraternity." They may democratically elect their leader. Some communities make their big decisions by consensus. The church might be led by a board that is elected yearly. Although it is very challenging and chaotic to have shared leadership, it is how these communities make decisions and discern the future.

Participatory Worship

New communities do not want visionary or directive leadership. They are suspicious of the powerful pastor. But there is no such thing as a leader-less church. There is always leadership; it always emerges as people begin to respect the opinion of some over others. A leader can be anyone in the community. A leadership team will consist of lay leaders and trained leaders intermixed. Leaders are both male and female.

Leaders encourage participation. The church supports people who have a passion to start something, and they are encouraged to move forward with their ideas. The leaders' role is to hear what people are passionate about and help them lead. Some communities create a structure where anyone can lead a particular task; they have no official leader, simply a board that hosts or facilitates these various initiatives. In other communities, the leader is more of an aggregator who puts the puzzle together. He or she helps people move from brainstorming to action. This kind of leadership is moving beyond con- sensus or going it alone.

New communities create worship where participation is built in from the very start. The Holy Spirit leads the meeting. The members might create bleach kits for drug users. They might create an icon together. They might discuss a text. They might tell stories. They may be in a process of collective discovery, rather than listening to a preacher.

In post-Christendom churches, the worship leader may serve as a curator. These new churches refuse the up-front worship leader and the traditional role of clergy. They return the worship experience to the laity, enabling each one to participate in worship creation. The creation of art is a relational process. The entire event may occur outside a church building, in a pub, an art space, or café, and it may involve poetry, painting, sculpture, writing of songs, or digital media. Typically there is very little teaching, if at all. In a service like this, there are no spectators.

Regarding the arts, the goal in discipleship is to train all to be artists with the ability to remix theology and culture. They are to create works of beauty and be taught by beauty as well. Creating involves every part of one's being; it is not copying or reproducing. The goal for the Christian community is to themselves become God's artwork, and they are drawn closer together as they produce public displays.

Worship services are not evangelistic as much as they are formational for the members of the community. They might provide a time for monthly meal and prayer. The community may host a brunch and coffee, for example. Some might include jazz music, tablecloths, video clips, or a theme. The people in the church prepare the food and bring it to be served. It is likely they will have Communion as well. These venues seek to be friendly, yet combine and remix the sacred and the everyday. To connect with the spiritual search of seekers in post-Christendom, they might use Catholic and Protestant symbols and chant the psalms. There may be candles, crosses, and tasty food. They hope to create something completely new, not something slightly improved.

The Postmodern Spiritual Seeker

In post-Christendom, church attendance continues to shrink. The practice of spirituality does not follow the same trend, however. People no longer feel obligated to practice their religion, but if going to a church service fits into their larger project of creating a spiritual self, they will attend. To what extent the searcher views the church as a spiritual resource depends on the different perceptions of Christian faith in the culture.

In late modernity, people are forced to choose (they have no choice!). This is a consumptive faith, but not necessarily a consumeristic one. One may have a faith that is chosen without necessarily being consumeristic, by choosing the good, the true, the beautiful. When a consumer equates the purchase of material goods or experiences as ultimately fulfilling, he or she distorts the goodness of creation. Either way, seekers craft an entire spirituality from what they find. They mix and match practices from many traditions. They choose, within each tradition, how involved they want to be. It is bricolage.

Postmodern seekers pursue opportunities for spirituality and service. Mission fulfills the desire for spirituality through a community that lives the faith. For the seeker, volunteer work in the city is the most popular connection with the church; some new communities create service opportunities before they even establish a church. Mission events are identity forming, but lead to few disciples.

Some new communities create worship services designed for the larger community to attend. A service like this may feature a small amount of preaching, music, and creative expression—elements valued by the spiritual seeker who is not yet ready for community. As such, seekers prefer low-participation, high-anonymity church services. Creative leaders may design experiences for people that move them to deeper spirituality and inspire acts of justice. There will be no forced participation at any point in the service, however. These services may also serve as the public expression of a network church.

Worship, in an individualized culture, is seen as a restaurant. Seekers come for their spiritual meal. They come back if it satisfied them and they continue to hunger. But it probably won't be weekly. It might feel constricting to the customer to eat at the same restaurant that often. However, the customer does not determine everything in the restaurant. The restaurant chooses what items it will be putting on the menu, when they will be offered, and how it will be served. The guest must choose from what is listed. The customer does not get to change the menu, but neither does the restaurant get to make choices for the customer.

In Western modernity, seekers pursue wholeness because their lives are so fragmented. Seekers desire to make connections in their personal lives; they want an integrated spirituality that addresses the whole of life. When they pursue community it is often coherence they desire, not more commitments. The practice of community must serve their spiritual quest, and for many seekers they do not see the connection between community participation and personal growth. What is challenging for these seekers is a weekly communal activity to which they are bound. In post-Christendom spirituality, the weight falls to the client, not to the institution.

Post-Christendom people want to experience acts of spirituality and justice, but not communal commitment. However, community formation is inherent to the Christian life. Small groups or neomonastic communities are offered as gifts to seekers who desire a holistic way of life. Most seekers do desire this coherence, but they need to be convinced that all the elements they perceive as necessary to their spiritual quest may be found in a single community.

A Foretaste of the Kingdom of God

In post-Christendom, a diverse congregation serves as a prophetic sign. It creates space on the borderland, between two cultures, where difference is celebrated. In these communities, churches maintain the centrality of Christ, a trinitarian understanding of God, practices of prayer, baptism, the Eucharist, and Bible reading. These new communities are flexible on the forms these elements take and whether other practices ought to be done at all, such as sermons, music, vestments, and various historic rituals.

In post-Christendom churches, worship is connected to all of creation, including the local community. These new expressions of faith practice the idea that worship may take place anywhere in their environs. With the non-modernists, post-Christendom Christians connect worship to the yearly calendar, to the seasons, and to the daily rhythms of the community. Many types of nonmodern forms of worship—be they contemplative or meditative; featuring drums, Celtic, or Taizé music; with candles, food, or showing digital media—are embraced in post-Christendom churches. God created all of reality, and the task of the people of God, as God's agents, is to offer all of reality back to him in worship.

Old and New

We must celebrate the move toward a mixed-economy church where traditional churches partner with new expressions of church. The fresh expressions movement in the UK is an exemplary model from which all other state church or mainline churches might draw inspiration. The indigenous church in Canada, also within the Anglican Communion, adds new voices to the conversation, offering creative and diverse expressions of church. What these movements share is an incarnational approach to church and mission: following God into the culture and joining in. As we learned from Rowan Williams and Graham Cray, the church is an event around the risen Jesus before it is an institution.

How might the church live missionally and embody the gospel in the post-Christendom West at this time? If the stories in this volume offer any clues, it might be something like the following: Very creative leaders start experiments of faith with like-minded souls. They love their urban neighbors as they spend time together planting vegetables, sharing meals, discussing faith, working for justice, and creating art. In their homes, they form small communities where, through Scripture reading, discussions, meals, and perhaps some wine, they learn how to follow Jesus better. With minimal structure or designated leadership, they might develop a rhythm of life that includes prayer, compassion, simplicity, and care of creation. As a small group, they discern where God might be leading them. Leaning on the artistic inspiration of the community, they create a more public worship service, inspiring for them but also for their neighbors. The riches of the local community and the gospel are both present, as food and music, candles and statues, meet. The postmodern seeker might pick and choose at this time, fearful of what comes next. But that is no matter to the Christians, who, tasting joyful worship through local culture, experience the kingdom of heaven.

Praise be to God.

Afterword

Eddie Gibbs

The Gospel after Christendom provides an avalanche of information. I am deeply grateful to Ryan Bolger for his diligent research in contacting so many people engaged in such a wide variety of situations, as well as to the many authors who contributed chapters, providing examples of emerging missional churches. I was as struck by the wide variety of examples arising out of local contexts as by the common themes that emerged. My personal response is twofold. On the one hand, I experienced encouragement and exhilaration at the spiritual vitality revealed. On the other hand, I felt a considerable measure of personal discomfort with the radical nature of some of the experiments!

With regard to the former, it is reassuring to know that there is increasing evidence of the survival of the church after Christendom, and that this survival arises out of a rediscovery of the nature of the gospel and the reconnecting of ecclesiology and missiology, which had become separated under Christendom to their mutual impoverishment and debilitation. In other words, survival is dependent on spiritual renewal and a willingness to die to all that inhibits the church from embarking on its ongoing mission in a post-Christendom world. In the present pluralistic and relativistic context the church no longer has a privileged position, but is one voice among many. Adjusting to this ever-present reality requires humility, discernment, and grace coupled with boldness in witness.

My second reaction, of discomfort, arises from the realization that I would not feel personally comfortable in many of the situations described.

My role over the years has been more that of an observer and commentator rather than that of a participant. All my life as a Christian I have been both a member and pastor within one historic tradition—that of the Anglican Church. Now in my mid-seventies I feel even more secure, despite my frustrations, within that tradition! But when I look around the congregations in which I feel comfortable I begin to notice the people who are not there. Where are my children's and grandchildren's generations? Where are the poor? Where are the recent immigrants? And where are those who have become de-churched by disillusionment and whom we fail to win and welcome back? And where are those who have never previously darkened the doorway of a church? Then I begin to realize that I have to deal with my own discomfort in order to engage in the ongoing mission of the ascended Lord, so that each generation will have opportunity to both hear and encounter the good news as it is lived out among his people.

In dealing with discomfort I first give thanks for those who are prepared to follow the example of the apostle Paul in risk-taking ventures for the further-ance of the gospel. It so happens that I have spent the last eighteen months immersed in the letters of Paul to the churches in Galatia, Philippi, Thessa-lonica, Corinth, Ephesus, Colossae, and Rome in connection with another writing project. I have come to realize afresh that Paul faced the same question that many church leaders voice today, namely, Where do we go from here? He faced the challenge of transposing the message of Jesus announcing the reign of God within a Jewish context into the Greco-Roman urban world in which Caesar reigned as Lord. He had to affirm the position of both Jew and Gentile in the new creation community in which reconciliation was taking place, a community brought into being by the death and resurrection of Jesus Christ. And he had to establish a structure that conveyed that message as a dynamic movement rather than one confined within a stalled and static institution. Having finished that demanding study I have come to the conclusion that the issues Paul addressed in pre-Christendom times are remarkably similar to the ones presented in this volume by those endeavoring to reevangelize post-Christendom generations.

Both Pauline and contemporary models of church demonstrate ground-breaking apostolic leadership and highly relational faith communities, relating the gospel to the whole of life precisely because the church was the church in the world 24/7, and in which creative participation was the order of the day, in contrast to the consumerist mentality so prevalent in the majority of contemporary churches. Worship is central to both first- and twenty-first-century churches. Shared meals play a significant part, and each person comes to contribute and not merely to consume.

The emerging missional churches have, in my opinion, rightly focused renewed attention on the ministry and mission of Jesus as recorded in the Gospels. At the same time they must not overlook the important missional lessons to be derived from Acts and Paul's ongoing conversation with young churches. I feel some concern lest we lose the sense of apostolic urgency and that our identification is always with a view to transformation. The role of the Holy Spirit is central to both of these concerns.

The leaders who share their stories in this book have come to realize that the challenge facing them is not simply that of planting new churches that are clones of existing churches, but of reimagining communities of Christ-followers, birthed within diverse cultural contexts. May the Risen Lord bless and guide the endeavors of the contributors to this volume and may their tribe increase!

Index